Music Education

The future is a funny thing. Everyone would like to know it. But, no one can. We can only deal with the present based on our knowledge of the past and the projection of our vision of the future. We know that at this point in the first part of the 21st Century information and technology are driving the pace of change and discovery at an unprecedented rate. This knowledge should affect the way that we as humans interact with the world including how we engage with music, and more importantly the teaching and learning of it. *Music Education: Navigating the Future* is written by both (1) authors who were at the time of this publication ambitious early career professors trying to earn tenure and receive promotion, and (2) veteran scholars and researchers who have paved the way for the present generation of leaders in music education. Through their combined efforts the authors were able to well articulate what the profession now needs as it moves forward. The end result—the coming together of past, present, and future—is a work that will be held in high regard by the profession for years to come. *Music Education* features chapters on music and leisure, new forms of media in music teaching and learning, the role of technology in music learning, popular music tuition in the expansion of curricular offerings, and the assessment of music education research. As such, it is an excellent reference for scholars and teachers as well as a guide to the future of the discipline.

Clint Randles is Assistant Professor of Music Education at the University of South Florida, USA.

Routledge Studies in Music Education

1 **Music Education**
Navigating the Future
Edited by Clint Randles

Music Education

Navigating the Future

Edited by Clint Randles

Routledge
Taylor & Francis Group

NEW YORK AND LONDON

First published 2015
by Routledge
711 Third Avenue, New York, NY 10017

and by Routledge
2 Park Square, Milton Park, Abingdon, Oxon OX14 4RN

*Routledge is an imprint of the Taylor & Francis Group,
an informa business*

Library of Congress Cataloging-in-Publication Data
Music education : navigating the future / edited by Clint Randles.
    pages cm.—(Routledge studies in music education ; 1)
  Includes bibliographical references and index.
  1. Music—Instruction and study. I. Randles, Clint, 1978–
MT1.M982413 2014
  780.71—dc23
  2014017949

ISBN: 978-1-138-02258-4 (hbk)
ISBN: 978-1-315-77700-9 (ebk)

Typeset in Sabon
by Apex CoVantage, LLC

Printed and bound in the United States of America by Publishers Graphics,
LLC on sustainably sourced paper.

This book is dedicated to Bennett Reimer. Thank you, Professor Reimer, for enriching our lives with your work in music and words. Music education is better off as a result of your efforts.

Contents

Preface   xi
Acknowledgements   xiii

PART I
Working Within the Domain

History

1   **Music Education History and the Future**   3
    MICHAEL L. MARK

Perspective

2   **In Response to Michael Mark**   13
    BENNETT REIMER

Philosophy

3   **Difference and Music Education**   16
    LAUREN KAPALKA RICHERME

4   **A Proleptic Perspective of Music Education**   29
    BRENT C. TALBOT

Perspective

5   **The Virtues of Philosophical Practice in Music Education**   43
    WAYNE BOWMAN

Perspectives
are implications
New ideas

PART II
Making Sense of Our Tools

The New Media Era

6   The Shifting Locus of Musical Experience from
    Performance to Recording to New Media: Some
    Implications for Music Education   63
    MATTHEW THIBEAULT

7   Inter/Trans/Multi/Cross/New Media(ting):
    Navigating an Emerging Landscape of Digital Media
    for Music Education   91
    EVAN S. TOBIAS

8   Is It the Technology? Challenging Technological
    Determinism in Music Education   122
    ALEX S. RUTHMANN, EVAN S. TOBIAS, CLINT RANDLES,
    AND MATTHEW D. THIBEAULT

Perspective

9   The Technology-Music Dance: Reflections on
    Making Sense of Our Tools   139
    DAVID BRIAN WILLIAMS

10 Understanding the Tools: Technology as a Springboard
    for Reflective Musicking   155
    FRANK HEUSER

PART III
Visualizing Expansion

Music for Life

11 Liminal or Lifelong: Leisure, Recreation, and the
    Future of Music Education   167
    ROGER MANTIE

Popular Music

12 Seeking "Success" in Popular Music   183
    GARETH DYLAN SMITH

Early Childhood

13 "Pssst . . . Over Here!" Young Children Shaping the
Future of Music Education   201
ALISON M. REYNOLDS, KERRY B. RENZONI, PAMELA L. TUROWSKI,
AND HEATHER D. WATERS

Teacher Education

14 Identity and Transformation: (Re)Claiming
an Inner Musician   215
KAREN SALVADOR

PART IV
Guiding Researchers

Research Snapshot

15 Methodological Trends in Music Education Research   235
MICHAEL S. ZELENAK

Qualitative Approaches

16 Critical Ethnography as/for Praxis: A Pathway
for Music Education   253
MARISSA SILVERMAN

17 Application of Sound Studies to Qualitative Research
in Music Education   271
JOSEPH MICHAEL ABRAMO

Perspective

18 Commentary on *Research Snapshot*
and *Qualitative Approaches*   292
RICHARD COLWELL

Quantitative Approaches

19 Structural Equation Modeling and Multilevel Modeling
in Music Education: Advancing Quantitative Research
Data Analysis   299
NICHOLAS STEFANIC

Perspective

20   Reflecting on *Guiding Researchers*   314
     PETER R. WEBSTER

PART V
Plotting a Course of Action

Conceptualizing Change

21   A Theory of Change in Music Education   323
     CLINT RANDLES

Perspective

22   The Role of Subversion in Changing Music Education   340
     JOHN KRATUS

     Names and Addresses of Contributors   347
     Index   351

Preface

From my perspective, we can best prepare students for the future by enabling them to deal effectively with the present.

Elliot Eisner

It's the end of the world as we know it, and I feel fine.

REM

The future is a funny thing. Everyone would like to know it. But of course no one can. We can only, as Eisner states, deal with the present. We know that at this point in the first part of the 21st century, information and technology are driving the pace of change and discovery at an unprecedented rate. This knowledge should affect the way that we as humans interact with the world, including how we engage with music and music education. Technology is not in the driver's seat, though; we are. We choose how we will act based on our goals and values as human beings. Of course, we have a history of how we have behaved and performed in the past to guide our theory and practice. This book is about bringing together voices of experience with some of the voices who will play a role in steering the ship—*Music Education*—as it moves into the future.

Few things that are worth our considerable time are easy. This project was no exception. The Suncoast Music Education Research Symposium IX (which I chaired), with the title *Navigating the Future,* is where the idea for this book started. The event was held at the University of South Florida in February of 2013. It brought together many of the scholars that have written for this text. In fact, many of the chapters were first projects that were accepted for presentation at the symposium. That being said, this collection of chapters is not a conference proceedings. The work took on a much larger form when I invited many scholars and researchers from around North America to read, respond, critique, comment, and sometimes provide entirely new insights on the topics that surround the initial chapters.

RISING STARS

Many of the chapter writers were at the time of this publication ambitious assistant professors trying to earn tenure and receive promotion. However, all of them had spoken at many of the premier national and international conferences in music education. They were chosen to be a part of this project as I felt they represented some of the most promising newer voices in the profession. Of course no one can ever be sure of these things. Hopefully time has been kind to my earlier predictions.

EXPERIENCED VOICES

Figures like Richard Colwell and Bennett Reimer have been around in the field of music education for the better part of 50 years. They can speak well about what the profession needs as it moves forward. What better writers for their respective sections? There was not a template for what each of the experienced authors' *perspectives* were supposed to look like. I left the decision for what each section needed up to the writers. This ambiguity going into the writing stage has resulted in a very unique book, one that we hope will be useful to the profession as it represents the desires and intuition of not one younger voice or even many younger voices, but that of younger and more experienced voices working as one.

COMING TOGETHER

The most striking quality of this book is the juxtaposition of newer generation thinkers and older generation thinkers laboring side by side to conceptualize the future of the profession. It is no small feat to gather such a diverse group of writers. Throughout the project there was a common bond that united all—the belief that the very best manifestations of music and music education should and must survive and thrive in the lives of the citizens of the world. I am pleased with the resulting product. The work that we have accomplished here will benefit generations of music educators to come and will serve as a time capsule for this point in the history of the profession.

Clint Randles
Tampa, Florida, 2014

Acknowledgements

A warm thank you to my colleagues and members of the Center for Music Education Research at the University of South Florida for their support of this work. Most of all I would like to thank Jack Heller for fighting with me during this my first four years in higher education. You have made me stronger my friend. As long as I am living and working in music education I will remember our time together fondly. The world needs more scrappy old academics to hone the younger generation. (I'm smiling as I write this, Jack.) Together, we represent the DNA of this book—the coming together of groups of minds for the good of the whole. I hope that some day I can do for someone else what you have done for me.

I would also like to thank my graduate and undergraduate students here at USF for inspiring me to work diligently on projects that have the potential to make music and music education better for future generations of students. It makes all of this work worthwhile when I think that these ideas will be in the hands of such wonderful musicians and teachers who will help change the music education world for the better. You have made it a joy to get up every morning. I wish all the best for you in all of your future endeavors. Know that you will always have a special place in my heart.

Part I
Working Within the Domain

1 Music Education History and the Future

Michael L. Mark

INTRODUCTION

This chapter describes four historic rationales that supported music education during certain periods of American history and how they were made a real part of American life. Taken together, they describe a history of success for music education in a changing world. The four rationales illustrate how music education has adjusted to social, political, and economic change and how it became an integral part of those contexts. This brief review of the role of music education in American life shows that it has historically been tied closely to the greater society, and that music teachers have been valued since the early times of our nation.

As times changed, so did music education. But some things do not change because they are right and because they work. An instructive example of something that has not changed throughout Western history is the contribution that music education has always made to the society that sponsors it. Another example is the joy of learning and making music in school settings. Music has existed in schools throughout Western history, often for religious purposes, at other times for a variety of other cultural reasons.[1] These are historic truths that music educators might convey to administrators and other decision makers who influence the role of music in schools.

A simple, basic principle that is probably known to most music educators expresses what it is that has made music education so successful for so long: education follows society. Society establishes new needs and new goals and music education adjusts. We, the music educators, lead from the rear, not the front, and this is how it has to be. It is why certain important planning symposia have been held periodically. For example, the primary purpose of the influential 1967 Tanglewood Symposium was to identify the role of music education in a society already undergoing such rapid change that it was no longer possible to predict needs beyond the next few years. A character in the novel *Gone Girl* (Flynn, 2012, p. 9) said it well: "We had no clue that we were embarking on careers that would vanish within a decade." And the speed of societal change becomes faster and faster to this day.

FOUR RATIONALES FOR MUSIC EDUCATION

The four rationales are derived from the principle that education follows society. They serve as a backdrop for a look at the broad scope of American history during the last 175 years. These are the rationales:

>   *Cultural Elevation.* It was a common belief in the young United States that European culture was supreme. The other side of that coin, of course, was that American culture was immature and not yet ready to advance to a higher level. From Lowell Mason's time in the 1830s, American music education perpetuated an Americanized version of the elite European musical tradition. It was really only during the second half of the 20th century that we finally began to shed our inferiority complex about our own music. American conductors were expected to train in Europe until well into the 20th century, and the music education profession did not officially recognize jazz in the curriculum until the Tanglewood Symposium of 1967 sanctioned it.
>
>   *Cohesive Society and Immigration.* The music education profession played an important role in helping immigrants adjust to their new country while performing a valuable service to itself by sponsoring a songbook that appealed to the masses, both children and adults.
>
>   *Commercial Prosperity.* This rationale has to do with the prosperity of business and industry, a key component in the evolution of school bands. It illustrates how the music business analyzes the needs of the music education profession and finds ways to satisfy those needs.
>
>   *Social Justice and Multiculturalism.* This rationale briefly reviews the history of segregated schools and the effects of the civil rights revolution on them. Multicultural education began to influence the music education profession during this time.

The narratives that follow illustrate how music education has supported national goals and even helped further them at times. Each rationale had implications for classroom practices. They influenced the day-to-day work of music educators in one way or another. These four rationales—cultural elevation, cohesive society, commercial prosperity, social justice—are points of reference for a look at the broad scope of American history during the last 175 years. Each rationale had a place in American history and each had a role in shaping music education.

THE FOUR RATIONALES IN AMERICAN LIFE

Cultural Elevation: The Industrial Revolution and Music Education

Music was not taught in most public schools before the Industrial Revolution of the early 19th century. Instead, itinerant music teachers traveled to villages, towns, and cities to teach music reading and singing to adults and children. Their popularity was an indication that music instruction was valued early in American history. Many of the teachers composed the music that they taught, and some of their music still lives today in church hymnals. The best known of the composers/teachers was William Billings. The music of these New England composers was strong, robust, and enjoyable to sing, but their training was minimal and their music crude in comparison to that of European composers.

A profound occurrence took place in 1838, when the new American nation was only 62 years old. In that landmark year, the Boston School Committee [board of education] became the first school authority to approve music as a curricular subject, meaning that its status in schools was equal to reading, writing, and arithmetic. Although music had been taught in some schools before 1838, at that time it was an extra activity rather than a curricular subject. To put this in historical perspective, when music was first adopted as a curricular subject in 1838, European classical music creativity was thriving. Mendelssohn and Schumann were actively composing. Schubert had died only ten years earlier and Beethoven one year before that.

As the expanding Industrial Revolution began to replace hand labor with machine production, manufacturing increased, as did the size of the upper and the middle economic classes. The proliferation of new wealth made it possible to realistically envision a new American cultural life. Affluent Americans wanted their country to resemble Europe's more cultured nations. To do this, the old musical offerings of itinerant singing masters had to be replaced with music on par with European music. That transition would only be possible if the schools provided music education to the masses.

Returning to the year 1838—from the humble beginning of music education as a curricular subject in Boston, music education spread throughout the rest of the 19th century to other schools and to other cities. By the beginning of the 20th century, school music was well established. The Industrial Revolution was a catalyst for profound change in American society, and one of its side effects was the remarkable transformation of music education.

A Cohesive Society: Immigration and Community

From about 1880 to 1918, a huge wave of immigration brought millions of people seeking better lives to the New World from Eastern, Central, and Southern Europe. These new Americans—Hungarians, Czechs, Italians, Slovaks, Poles, Serbs, Croats, Slovenes, Russians, Ukrainians, Romanians,

Greeks, and others—changed the demographics of the United States and its schools dramatically. These immigrants took advantage of their New World opportunities and they were welcomed by the owners and managers of American mills and factories. As hard as they had to toil, their living and working conditions in their new country were generally better than what they had left behind in their homelands.

The well-known term, "the Melting Pot," was created in this milieu. The melting pot was a metaphor for the "Americanization" of the new arrivals. The term originated in a play of the same name that Israel Zangwill wrote in 1908. A line in the script read, "America is God's Crucible, the great Melting-Pot where all the races of Europe are melting and re-forming" (Zangwill, 1908). Ideally, immigrants would be expected to shed their old national identities and live as Americans. This indeed happened over the course of the next generations. Succeeding generations spoke English, they lived in communities with neighbors from many countries, they belonged to the same labor unions, they served together in the military, and their children attended schools with the children of immigrants from other countries.

There was an amusing example of this melting pot ideal in Henry Ford's automobile factory. Recognizing the value of an educated work force, Ford founded a school for immigrant workers in his factory. The students presented a play about the melting pot in which immigrants were disembarking from the ship that carried them from the Old World to the New. They were dressed in threadbare immigrant clothes and carrying their tattered immigrant luggage. They climbed into a huge melting pot, a crucible. Their teachers stirred the contents of the pot with long ladles and when it began to boil over, out came the immigrants, now dressed in their best American clothes and waving American flags. As trivial as this play might have been, it effectively demonstrated the ideal of the melting pot metaphor.

It so happened that music educators were organizing their professional association during the massive surge of immigrants. The creation of the Music Supervisors National Conference in 1907 provided a framework for music educators to actively participate in the immigration phenomenon. In 1913, only six years after MSNC's initial organizing activities, a committee of its members compiled a pamphlet of eighteen songs that all Americans should know. *18 Songs for Community Singing* was intended for both adults and children and it helped many new Americans become familiar with American culture. The eighteen songs provided music that all immigrants could share with each other and with already established Americans. The pamphlet also helped Americanize children when it was used as a school songbook. The booklet's introduction explained:

> This pamphlet represents a movement which will be encouraged by all interested in Education in the United States—that the whole country shall know by heart and unite in singing the words and music of some of the best of the Standard Songs.

But of a much deeper significance than the mere singing of these few songs is the animating idea back of such performance, which is the spread of community feeling voiced in a better understanding, good will, a real brotherhood.

The singing, in its larger significance, is extended as a means of stimulating a feeling of solidarity which should exist in a community between man and man. For when a country becomes one in lifting its voice in singing the same good songs, a note is struck for harmony of understanding, mutual good-will, and similar ideals.

(18 Songs, 1913, inside cover)

These are the 18 songs in the pamphlet:

- America
- Annie Laurie
- Auld Lang Syne
- Blow, Ye Winds, Heigh-Ho
- Dixie
- Drink to Me Only with Thine Eyes
- Flow Gently, Sweet Afton
- Home, Sweet Home
- How Can I Leave Thee
- Love's Old Sweet Song
- My Old Kentucky Home
- Nancy Lee
- Old Folks at Home
- Round: Row, Row, Row Your Boat
- Round: Lovely Evening
- Star Spangled Banner
- Sweet and Low
- The Minstrel Boy

18 Songs was so popular that it underwent numerous revisions during its first few years. It evolved into a collection called *55 Songs for Community Singing,* then *Twice 55 Songs.* It aided the nation's efforts in 1918 during World War I by providing songs for civilian and military community sings. There were thousands of military song leaders and *Twice 55 Songs* was the songbook of choice for many of them.

Americans recognized the need for music education partly because music was a normal participatory element of community life through the 1930s and even later in some fortunate places. Industries sponsored choruses, bands, and orchestras. Community singing was popular. Between double features, movie audiences followed "the bouncing ball" on the screen as it skipped from one syllable of a familiar song to the next. Communities employed paid music directors as late as the 1950s, even later in some cities.

They were often assigned to departments of parks and recreation, and many of them were also school music educators. Parents appreciated the value of preparing their children to be adults who would actively participate in the musical life of the community.

The End of an Era

This topic begins the transition from the end of an era to the beginning of a new one. The emergence from the Great Depression and World War II as the leader of the free world revealed new, unforeseen conditions for the United States. The emphasis on community singing gradually became less relevant in the emerging society. Clearly, technology was going to bring changes to society that would have implications for music education, but no one knew what those implications would be. Music education leaders were concerned that their profession did not have a credible philosophical foundation to meet the needs of the time. Visionary leaders like Allen Britton of the University of Michigan and Charles Leonhard of the University of Illinois helped lead music education into a new era. They steered the rationale toward the inherent properties of music itself and away from its ancillary outcomes. That was when we began to use the term "aesthetic education."

At the same time, psychologists were beginning to analyze how students learn and how teachers teach. Benjamin Bloom's *Taxonomy of Educational Objectives,* published in 1956, helped educators shape new curricula and teaching methods. In 1960, Jerome Bruner presented a new theory of cognitive development in his book, *The Process of Education.* Psychologists were advancing new education theories as philosophers were working to relate aesthetic philosophy to the music curriculum. Their synergy helped music educators build a strong justification for curricular acceptance.

Commercial Prosperity and School Bands

Business and industry were key factors in the growth of music education. The transportation industry is a good example because it played a central role in the evolution of school bands, which helped solidify the place of bands in schools throughout the country. Frederick Fennell, renowned director of the Eastman Wind Ensemble, describes the process by which it took place in his book, *Time and the Winds* (Fennell, 1954, pp. 37–9, 48). Fennell explains how a business-oriented economic interest aligned itself with music education to help establish school bands throughout the country.

America loved bands. At the turn of the 20th century, professional concert bands played under conductors like Sousa, Herbert, Gilmore, Pryor, Creatore, and Conway. These bands were the models for community and school bands. America also loved amusement parks, where the professional bands played concerts on weekends. The parks were always located outside of a city, and since people did not have cars yet, they relied on traction companies (streetcars) to get to amusement parks. Not having the means to go elsewhere, they were a captive audience. But when Henry Ford made it possible for the average American to own a car, this newfound mobility gave people the freedom to go anywhere they wished. People bought cars and sought recreation in new places. Of course, attendance at amusement parks declined.

The automobile was only the first nail in the coffin of the professional concert bands. Another was the changing taste of the public. A large part of the bands' income came from playing for dances. They played the gallop, waltz, polka, and the two-step, but by the 1920s those dances were no longer popular. The public had fallen in love with new dances—the lindy hop, the Charleston, the jitterbug, the black bottom. Small jazz bands played for these dances, not large concert bands. As if it weren't challenging enough to contend with the new dances, the concert bands also found themselves in competition with the new technology of the time—radio, talking movies, and recorded music. And the Great Depression of the 1930s might well have been the bands' kiss of death. By the early 1930s the professional concert bands were no more, victims of the changing times. The bands epitomized the past when people needed to look forward. This is an example of 19th century Social Darwinism—the survival of the fittest. The American professional concert band did not survive because it was no longer the most fit entertainment medium.

The music industry had a lot at stake where bands were concerned. It was accustomed to doing a thriving band business that became even stronger during World War I because the army created a great number of military bands that needed to be equipped. But most of them were disbanded at the end of the war. The military bands disappeared as the concert bands were dying. The music industry needed a new source of income. It turned to the schools by promoting the band contest movement, which proved to be one of the most significant events in the history of school music. The contests solidified the place of bands in American education and it guaranteed a thriving market for instruments, music, uniforms, accessories, and all the other paraphernalia needed to support band programs.

All over the country, communities equated high school band contests with athletic events. As bands became commonplace in schools, support from communities sometimes depended on how well students entertained their communities with concerts, football halftime shows, and parades. Contests often dominated the scene and students were expected to represent their communities well, especially in communities where success in music contests were judged as if they were athletic events. A winning band was a source of community pride, especially during the Great Depression years of the 1930s, when community spirits needed uplifting (Mark, 1980, p. 13).

School bands were permanently bonded to their communities during the contest movement. They exemplify the relationship between music education and the greater society. They are the legacy of the old professional bands and a product of American industry.

Social Justice and Multicultural Music Education

Music educators began to include multicultural music in the curriculum in the late 1960s after the Supreme Court and Congress created civil rights laws that led the schools to expand their curricula to include the minority populations of the United States. The story of multiculturalism in the schools goes back to the 1896 Supreme Court decision, *Plessy v. Ferguson*, which created the infamous doctrine of "separate but equal" (*Plessy*, 1896). "Separate but equal" made racial segregation the law of the land for almost six decades. The races were separated in schools, public facilities, and almost every other venue of American life. Equality did not exist for African Americans. They had little or no opportunity to advance economically or educationally in American society.

Finally, the Supreme Court handed down a momentous decision in 1954: *Brown v. Topeka* (*Brown v. Topeka*, 1954). This law mandated that school segregation was unconstitutional,[2] and twelve years later, Congress passed civil rights laws that ended legal segregation in all of the nation's public facilities. This led to the recognition of the rights, traditions, and values of every culture and to consequential changes in curricula throughout the country. One of those changes was the adoption of multicultural music education, which finally released music educators to explore an incredibly rich new vein of cultural studies and musical styles and practices. The many minorities of the United States finally achieved recognition and respect in the music education curriculum.

AN ERA OF REFORM

We deviate from our focus on music education to comment on the broader subject of education reform. This is necessary because reform created the environment in which music education has existed from the 1950s to the present. Every new reform effort that has come along since then has had implications for music education.

The 1950s saw the beginning of a radical overhaul of education. It was only in 1953 that the federal government became involved in curricular issues when it created the cabinet level Department of Health, Education, and Welfare. Notice that Education was bracketed by Health and Welfare. The creation of the federal Department of Education as a discrete governmental agency was still decades away.

It is discouraging to realize that the issues the government addressed in 1953 still challenge American education to this day—substandard student performance in reading, mathematics, and foreign languages, as well as urban education problems and juvenile crime. For sixty years we have sought ways to solve these problems and the search still continues. Think Race to the Top and the Common Core Curriculum. The education writer Irving Kristol articulated the reason for our lackluster reform efforts. His first law of education reform is this: "Any reform that is acceptable to the education establishment, and that can gain a majority in a legislature, federal or state, is bound to be worse than nothing" (Kristol, 1994).

WHAT IT ALL MEANS

Knowledge of the three critical periods in American history and the story of school bands could assist in the professional planning process and in advocacy efforts. Music educators involved in these activities might build a knowledge base of how music education has served the United States for almost two centuries. Realistically, however, one must ask, "Do planners really take long ago events into account?" Probably not, but, historical precedents do exist. They are an important part of American history and music educators should know their own professional history, just as all Americans should know American history. It helps us understand how things came to be as they are now, and it is a source of professional and national pride. Despite the many historic and current complications associated with declining budgets and ever-changing curricula, school music has contributed to American culture for close to two hundred years. Recognizing the profession's vibrancy, vision, and vitality, it would be unrealistic to deny its influence on American life beyond the walls of academia.

It is especially important for music educators to keep in mind that while their work is shaped by events beyond the schools, they themselves exert their own cultural influences outward to society. Cultural elevation, societal cohesiveness, commercial prosperity, social justice—these are all important aspects of a society that depends in substantial, meaningful ways on the music education profession. Because music education benefits the individual, the school, the community, and the nation, music educators have a wide range of opportunities to examine relationships between societal need and music education.

We hope that future generations of music educators will take the time to understand our era and its social, economic, and political contexts so that we will help them as they plan for their future. We hope that they will look back and affirm that we, the first new generation of music educators of the 21st century, advanced both our profession and American society in meaningful ways.

NOTES

1. See Mark, *Music education: Source readings from ancient Greece to today,* 2013.
2. Although the Court decided that school segregation was illegal, it did not require them to be integrated. This has been the cause of much confusion and dissension since that decision was handed down.

REFERENCES

Bloom, B. (1956). *Taxonomy of educational objectives.* Retrieved from http://hs.riverdale.k12.or.us/~dthompso/exhibition/blooms.htm.

Brown v. Topeka. (1954). Retrieved from http://caselaw.lp.findlaw.com/scripts/getcase.pl?court=us&vol=347&invol=483.

Bruner, J. (1960). *The process of education.* Retrieved from www.infed.org/thinkers/bruner.htm.

18 Songs for community singing. (1913). C. C. Birchard & Company: Boston, MA.

This pamphlet appears to have been regarded as a minor project of MSNC. It is not even mentioned in the minutes of the MSNC Board of Directors.

Fennell, F. (1954). *Time and the winds.* Kenosha, WI: Leblanc Publications.

Flynn, G. (2012). *Gone girl.* Crown Publishing: New York.

Kristol, I. (1994, April 18). The inevitable outcome of "outcomes." *The Wall Street Journal.*

Mark, M. L. (1980, Fall). William D. Revelli: Portrait of a distinguished career. *Journal of Band Research, 16*(1).

Mark, M. L. (2013). *Music education: Source readings from ancient Greece to today* (4th Ed.). New York, NY: Routledge.

Plessy v. Ferguson. (1896). Retrieved from http://plessyvsferguson.com.

Zangwill, I. Retrieved from http://en.wikipedia.org/wiii/Melting_pot/Zangwill.

It should be noted that the Melting Pot ideal did not include African Americans, whose struggle for assimilation and equality has continued for many decades.

2   In Response to Michael Mark

Bennett Reimer

Professor Mark's overview of four rationales for music education is a thoughtful and useful guide to important ways that music education has been engaged with the larger culture of America. Each of those ways reveals an initiative our profession has both responded to and offered contributions to. His treatment of them reminds us of how central to our existence these cultural contexts have been and will no doubt continue to be. "Education follows society" is a strong message he offers, one that requires us to examine, as times change, whether and to what degree we are attending to the culture as it exists at various times, and whether and to what degree we are succeeding or failing with the obligations the cultural milieu demands of us.

Mark is extremely positive about our accomplishments in these regards, claiming "a history of success for music education in a changing world." Given his expertise in our profession's history, I hesitate to offer an alternative or perhaps complementary view. But I do feel it necessary to temper, somewhat, the accolades he bestows, in particular for music education over the present quarter century or so.

As we dig deeper into what music in our society has become during this period in which we have lived, and compare it with what music education in the schools has been before our time, I am led to emphasize not that our status has been one of being tightly entwined with the great variety of musical beliefs, practices, and enthusiasms of our present culture, but more as being uncomfortably distanced from them. Also, music education has not provided leadership toward deepening and broadening the musics so vital in the lives of most people, especially school-age people in America, but rather has largely ignored them. The gap, in present times, between the flourishing musics of the people and the limited musics in schooling cannot be disregarded. I suspect that Mark's view of that gap and mine are only partially disjunct—if that. Whatever the size of that gap, it is useful to dwell a bit on it to give credence to the view that our relation to the larger musical culture in our times is, at the least, not optimal.

The out-of-school and in-school gap, at least recently if not longer, has been caused in large part by the swift, dramatic growth of music making and taking technologies that have burgeoned in our society. Those technologies enable musically creative activities and responding activities (also creative) of a variety of sorts to be immediately accessible to youngsters, with little if any reliance on formal teaching contexts. Adding to that freedom has been the growth of small group ensembles in which composing and improvising are the prerogative of the group members themselves, now both owning the creativity and presenting it to eager recipients. Being more and more crowded out is the formal teacher/student interdependence that schools have traditionally relied upon, thereby marginalizing the music educator's role as we have known it for centuries.

Not entirely, of course. There remain, in the musical world, many musics, classical being the most obvious, that still require a good deal of teacher/ learner interdependence if those musics are to be understood and implemented successfully. Whether band, orchestra, or chorus, these being the mainstays of past and present music programs in schools, teachers steeped in those traditions continue to be needed, much to the relief of those who have spent their careers preparing for and providing those programs. Some music education thinkers now seem to want to abandon those programs on the grounds that they are obsolete or fast becoming so. Others are devoted to saving those programs, not only as relics of music history but as vital, growing, changing, and necessary involvements if music in its broad rather than narrow sense is to be known and experienced genuinely in any and all musical lives.[1] Many music educators have intimated that "saving" classical musics from abandonment is the major, even sole, obligation of music education.

Which leads directly to Mark's delineation of four rationales for music in American life, an insightful and productive contribution. The first, cultural elevation, is the basis of the desire to keep the classical tradition alive and well, for, in this view, if any music can be deemed to "elevate," it is that of the masterworks of the eighteenth through twentieth centuries. Clearly, it is claimed, much or at least some of the musics now dominant among youngsters can in no sense be deemed as uplifting. Instead, we are told, gangsta rap and other genres of that sort are instead demeaning our children's morality and musical taste. It is difficult to argue, then, that all children should be led to study, relate to, and internalize that sort of counterculture music, as they "should" be doing with the claimed higher-order musics of the classics.[2]

Or, on the other hand, that sort of deeply grounded protest music can be understood as a necessary confrontation with the failings of our society to offer comparable quality of life, including comparably relevant musical education of any sort of music that has achieved substantial popularity. Issues related to the role of music as "moralizing," as "uplifting," and as "wholesome" for even younger children, and whether and how music education might deal with the tangled controversies that such ideas are certain to bring to attention, will no doubt remain important, even essential, in our profession for an extended time. Our world has been complexified far more deeply than in our earlier history. We are left with whole new meanings of "cultural elevation" and with conceptual and ethical challenges difficult enough to require our best thinking and acting if we are to represent honestly the existing plethora of musics, and construals of music, of our times. In short, the gap between the realities of music outside of school and inside of school has become wider than ever before. Not encouraging, I'd suggest.

The second rationale Mark offers has to do with the cohesive effects music has had on our earlier culture, a description of deep insight and interest. I was delighted to be reminded about the songs that the Music Supervisors National Conference put together in 1913 as, in essence, the content of the music curriculum in schools. One can only shake one's head in wonderment at the simplicity, naivety, sentimentality, and similarity of that repertoire, *happy* as different from today's popular musics as can possibly be imagined. Our work would surely be far easier if we could return to those halcyon days. But clearly that is not only impossible but also regressive. We should revel in the complexity of our present needs for musical diversification, which, however challenging, makes our work more, not less, necessary to the health of our musical culture. If we fulfill its promises, that is.

The business side of music, especially as it interfaces with the needs of school bands, adds another useful dimension to the story of our profession, as does the discussion of our burgeoning interests in joining the larger movements toward emphasis on social justice in education. We are helped immeasurably to see ourselves, in these aspects of our growth and change and need for continuing change, more clearly and more deeply in light of Mark's scholarship. Our history tends to fade into the background against the rich tapestry of present events. Mark reminds us forcefully that we cannot do full justice to our work without a basis in what led us to the present. History, especially as forthrightly as he deals with it and clarifies its power, is an essential element in a healthy music educator's diet.

NOTES

1. According to a consumer profile by the Recording Industry Association of America in 2012, encompassing data by gender, age, race, ethnicity, and "favorite genres," the three most preferred musics (the higher the number the higher the preference) are 3: Alt. Rock, Modern Rock, Indie Rock, and Classic Rock; 2: Pop, Top 40 Hits; 1: Rap, Hip-Hop. The population covers the total of Internet users; 13+ in age; music buyers; CD buyers; digital buyers; PnP downloaders; music streamers; and paid subscribers.
2. For a fascinating panoply of positions in regard to the life or death of classical music in our present musical culture, see, online, http://artsjournal.com:deathwatch: "Is Classical music really dying?" Also, Death of Classical Music archive (50+ stories) at www.artsjournal.com/artswatch/aw-deathofclassical.htm.

3   Difference and Music Education

Lauren Kapalka Richerme

Do you recall the worksheets for children that ask them to distinguish between similar and different objects? For example, one might include a row of three apples and one banana preceded by the question, "Which one is different?" Children learn early on to identify similarities and differences. In fact, for thousands of years, such distinctions have enabled humans to survive, doing everything from recognizing edible plants to finding their way back to shelter. At first glance, difference seems like a straightforward concept, and the statement "we need to think differently about music education" appears simplistic and obvious.

Yet, with the advent of supermarkets, GPS systems, and smart phones, humans may find themselves spending only minimal time and energy recognizing differences *between* items and places. In a world of replication, rapid growth, and ongoing change, perhaps there might exist alternative ways of understanding difference. For example, perhaps one could focus on how the apples on the worksheet differ from each other and from themselves over time.

In order to examine the concept of difference, I begin by analyzing how Western philosophers commonly understand difference. Next, I investigate how the twentieth-century French philosophers Gilles Deleuze and Félix Guattari posit an alternative conception of difference. Third, I show how Deleuze and Guattari's philosophical figuration of a body without organs adds nuance to Western philosophers' writings about difference. Lastly, I draw on Deleuze and Guattari's emphasis on continual difference rather than discrete differences to posit the possibilities of examining to the questions "When is music?" and "When is education?"

IMAGINING DIFFERENCE DIFFERENTLY

Before explaining how one might conceive of difference in a new way, I will first examine how humans have traditionally articulated the concept of difference. The concept of difference implicit in a children's similar/different worksheet actually dates back a couple of millennia. Exploring how humans conceive of difference involves investigating our explicit or implicit understandings about the nature of human perception. In *The Republic,* Plato (1973) conceives of worldly objects and qualities, such as love and goodness, mimicking what he termed Forms, or archetypes or essences, of those objects and qualities. In other words, people perceive a fellow human as "good" by comparing her to an ideal Form or archetype of "goodness." Using Socratic dialogue, Plato articulates the notion of absolute beauty, writing:

> Then those who see the many beautiful, and who yet neither see absolute beauty, nor can follow any guide who points the way thither; who see the many just, and not absolute justice, and the like,—such persons may be said to have opinion but not knowledge? . . . But those who see the absolute and eternal and immutable may be said to know, and not to have opinion only?
>
> (p. 173)

This conception results in a dualism between the world of Forms and the world of perception; beauty exists in the world of perception, but "absolute beauty" exists only in the world of Forms. Although apples exist in a seemingly endless number of variations, Plato asserted the existence of a single ideal Form of an apple that transcends time and space and that all apples mimic. These ideal Forms allow humans to distinguish between everything from apples and cookies to goodness and justice.

While Western philosophers such as Aristotle have critiqued Plato's division between perception and Forms,[1] a conception of existence based on similarity and stability continued to dominate Western philosophy for hundreds of years. For example, in *Critique of Pure Reason,* Kant (1781/2007) espouses a philosophy based on similarity and stability rather than difference and fluctuation. Describing his principle of the unity of apperception,[2] Kant states:

> It must be the case that each of my representations is such that I can attribute it to my self, a subject which is the same for all of my self-attributions, which is distinct from its representations, and which can be conscious of its representations.
>
> (pp. 131–2)

Kant defines humans as separate, stable, reasoning beings, focusing on how humans differ from their surroundings rather than how they differ from themselves over time.

Music education discourse and practice revolves largely around the conceptions of similarity and difference that have dominated Western philosophy from the time of the Greeks to the Enlightenment. For example, teachers often ask students to categorize orchestral instruments. Just as students completing a similar/different worksheet must distinguish between a bicycle and a pencil, so might music students distinguish between a flute and a trumpet. Likewise, music educators often write about difference between music genres and forms of musical engagement. For instance, the first two National Standards for Music Education are "singing, alone and with others, a varied repertoire of music" and "performing on instruments, alone and with others, a varied repertoire of music" (Consortium, 1994). In both of these standards, the phrase "a varied repertoire of music" centers upon a certain conception of difference. Teachers utilizing such standards might, for example, ask how a choral piece written in nineteenth-century Europe differs from one composed in twentieth-century America. The authors of these standards, like the creators of similar/different worksheets, emphasize differences *between* various musical selections.

Such categorization of musical pieces into genres relates to Plato's Forms as well as other philosophies emphasizing the stability of existence. For example, music educators might look for similarities between the elementary school band's performance of "Ode to Joy" and Beethoven's *Symphony No. 9 in D minor,* and the high school jazz band's rendition of "Sing, Sing, Sing" and Benny Goodman's iconic recording. Just as Plato might contemplate the ideal Form of an apple which all real apples mimic, so do music teachers maintain an idealized version of Holst's *2nd Suite in F,* "Little Sally Waters," or "C Jam Blues," which they attempt to help students attain.

The National Music Standards also enumerate different types of musical engagement that teachers might implement including singing, performing on instruments, improvising, composing, reading notation, listening, and evaluating (Consortium, 1994). Again, music education discourse defines difference in terms of distinct categories. Like those following the instructions on the similar/different worksheet, music educators focus on how these types of musical engagement differ from each other. How does composition differ from performance? How does performance differ from listening? While these musical endeavors do differ from each other, might they also differ in other ways?

The poststructuralist philosophers Gilles Deleuze and Félix Guattari offer an alternative way of conceiving of difference. Although Deleuze and Guattari (1980/1987) acknowledge the aforementioned types of "numerical," "discrete" differences, they emphasize a conception of difference as "qualitative," "fusional," and "continuous" (p. 484). In other words, they imply the question, "How does a person, place, object, or idea differ from itself over time?" While readers following Plato's (1973) philosophy might ask how an apple is like the ideal Form of an apple and different from other fruit, those drawing on Deleuze and Guattari's (1980/1987) writing might wonder how the apple differs from itself with each passing moment.

People and objects clearly change over time. For example, a look at a person's high school yearbook pictures or changing Facebook profile pictures usually evidences noticeable variations in his or her appearance. Yet,

Deleuze and Guattari (1980/1987) implore readers to look more closely at existence's continual fluctuation. For example, how have you changed since you began reading this chapter?

A musical example might further illuminate Deleuze and Guattari's (1980/1987) alternative conception of difference. I once asked music education scholar Elizabeth Gould how she speaks about Deleuze and Guattari's work with her undergraduate music education students. She replied that she places a tenor saxophone on a table at the front of the room and then asks the students how the saxophone has changed since they entered the classroom. Gould continued that the students would sit in silence for some time before one might offer, "Well, maybe it has a bit more rust on it." Subsequently, other students would add varied ideas about the changing status of the familiar instrument (personal communication, September 22, 2011). Such an examination of difference clearly contrasts the more typical practice of defining the tenor saxophone as different *from* the flute or piano. Instead, the viewer focuses on the continually altering status of an instrument.

The tenor saxophone does differ from other instruments while simultaneously differing from itself over time. Deleuze and Guattari (1980/1987) distinguish between two types of difference, the first numeric, discrete, and homogenous and the second qualitative, continual, and heterogeneous. They summarize this notion, writing:

> There are not, therefore, two kinds of languages but two possible treatments of the same language. Either the variables are treated in such a way as to extract from them constants and constant relations or in such a way as to place them in continuous variation.
>
> (p. 103)

Conceiving of difference as continual variation rather than constants diverges from long-standing Western philosophical beliefs, enabling an alternative conception not just of difference, but of the nature of the world. Deleuze and Guattari do not just assert the existence of this second type of difference; they posit an ontology of existence based upon it.

TIME AND DIFFERENCE

In order to detail Deleuze and Guattari's ontology of existence based on difference, it may be helpful to understand their conception of time, in particular, their explanation of the essence of the present moment in time. According to Deleuzian scholar Todd May (2003), Deleuze utilized Bergson's image of the past as a cone to envision variegated histories integrally linked to, and in turn enveloping, each ephemeral moment. May elaborates: "The cone's point is the present with the past enlarging itself behind it. At each cross-sectional slice of the cone—including its point in the present—the entirety of the past exists,

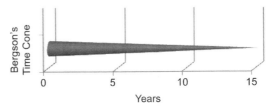

Figure 3.1   Visualization of Bergson's Time Cone

but in more or less 'contracted' state" (pp. 145–6). Figure 3.1 visualizes Bergson's cone for a fifteen-year-old person, with the cone's point representing the present. At each passing present moment, illustrated by the continually moving point of the cone, a person's entire past exists and grows as the cone's point moves forward in time. For example, when a person reaches fifteen years of age, she experiences each minute of her fifteenth birthday as both the present moment and as a compressed version of every moment from the past fifteen years. The present and the past exist concurrently.

According to Deleuze and Guattari (1991/1994), the past does not exist exactly like the present but rather as "virtual." They explain the "virtual" as the chaos "containing all particles and drawing out all possible forms, which spring up only to disappear immediately," elaborating that the "virtual" denotes not only the past but also the future that actualizes in the present (p. 118). Each passing moment consists of the present as well as the "virtual" past and future. Similarly, in his chapter, Talbot uses the cultural mechanism of *prolepsis* to offer a detailed explication of how music educators draw on their own pasts in order to project futures onto students.

We cannot choose what parts of our past and future influence our present thoughts and actions. A teacher's early exposure to everything from artistic activities to reading inevitably affects her current engagement with music education. Our entire history and future resides in every new moment. Such a conception of time contrasts the notion that time exists purely linearly and that each present moment relates little to others.

So how does this conception of time relate to difference? In short, May (2003) asserts that for Deleuze, difference comprises time's essence: "The content of time, since it cannot come in the form of identities or samenesses, must be difference" (p. 146). Since the past constitutes an integral part of the present, even repeated actions occur differently each time. For instance, my performance of a B flat scale is never the same; each time I repeat it, I actualize every prior experience of that scale, as well as the entirety of my past and future, in the present moment. I therefore experience the scale as a singularity with each repetition. Time not only enables difference, it demands it. Returning to the example of the saxophone, equating time with difference necessitates acknowledging that the saxophone changes with each passing moment. The saxophone differs not only from other instruments and objects, but also continually differs from itself. Likewise, the student perceiving the saxophone perpetually alters along with his or her evolving observations and experiences.

While philosophers such as Plato and Kant posit an ontology of existence based on sameness, Deleuze and Guattari (1980/1987) assert an ontology of existence based on difference. As May (2005) explains, Deleuze inverts the traditional relationship between identity and difference, writing, "It's not identity that captures what things are; it's difference that does it" (p. 81). Rather than centering the stability of people, objects, practices, and ideas over time, Deleuze and Guattari challenge readers to seek out the diverse chaos that constitutes existence.

Imagine if we approached the National Music Standards through Deleuze and Guattari's (1980/1987) ontology of existence. While Deleuze and Guattari's philosophy does not contradict the notion of exploring "a varied repertoire of music" (Consortium, 1994), teachers drawing on their writing might emphasize how each piece or musical endeavor changes from moment to moment and day to day. For example, within such a framework, music educators might exert less energy contemplating how "Ode to Joy" or "Sing, Sing, Sing" matched prior renditions of those pieces and instead focus on how they *differed* from previous articulations and from themselves over time. They would abandon aiming for "ideal" musical experiences, instead seeking out diverse ones. Rather than differentiating between categories of practices such as composing or listening, music educators seeking qualitative difference could ask how they and their students could engage in such endeavors differently. They would view standards and curricula as continually evolving and foreground the temporal *processes* of singing, performing on instruments, improvising, composing, reading notation, listening, and evaluating, emphasizing their integration and variability over time.

Understanding Deleuze and Guattari's conception of a world constitutive of difference means envisioning existence as ongoing motion rather than stability. As Colebrook (2002) writes, "Deleuze insists that we need to begin from a mobility, flux, becoming or change that has no underlying foundation" (p. 52). May (2005) echoes this notion, explaining that for Deleuze, "Difference is not a thing, it is a process. It unfolds—or better, it is an unfolding (and a folding, and a refolding). It is alive" (p. 24). Difference exists as constant movement, resisting all efforts to grasp, limit, or define it. Deleuze and Guattari (1980/1987) emphasize the temporal, changing nature of an existence composed of difference.

BODIES WITHOUT ORGANS

According to Deleuze and Guattari (1991/1994), artistic, scientific, and philosophic thinking constantly confront this underlying difference, temporarily organizing it in order to produce new concepts and products (p. 197).

One such concept is the body without organs, which Deleuze and Guattari (1980/1987) create to emphasize their ontology of existence based on difference and process. Deleuze and Guattari assert that the body without organs makes up the body; the body orders the body without organs in order to serve its needs (p. 159).

Perhaps the primordial soup that comprised the Earth shortly after its formation can serve as a useful metaphor for the body without organs. At that time, the Earth's oceans consisted of nutrient-rich molecules chaotically mixing together. Just as organisms organize the body without organs, so did early life occur as a result of the ordered combinations within the primordial stew. While disorder and ongoing processes constitute a body without organs, organization and stability compose a body or organism.

Deleuze and Guattari (1980/1987) spend less time explaining the body without organs than they do offering how one might move towards attaining a Body without organs. They explain that humans can begin becoming bodies without organs by thinking differently about their bodies: "The BwO [body without organs]: it is already under way the moment the body has had enough of organs and wants to slough them off, or loses them" (p. 150). Humans traditionally view organs or body parts as serving individual, predetermined functions—the mouth eats, the legs walk, the hands grasp, and so forth. For instance, using Socratic dialogue, Plato (1978) asserts, "Can you see, except with the eye? . . . Hear, except with the ear? . . . These then may be truly said to be the ends of these organs?" (p. 38). In short, Plato argues that each body part has a single, immutable function.

In contrast, Deleuze and Guattari (1980/1987) posit that humans attain a body without organs when they realize the restraints of perceiving each organ as only having the capacity for one action. They explain that bodies without organs occur when people "place elements or materials in a relation that uproots the organ from its specificity" (pp. 258–9). Offering an example, Deleuze and Guattari write:

> Is it really so sad and dangerous to be fed up with seeing with your eyes, breathing with your lungs, swallowing with your mouth, talking with your tongue, thinking with your brain, having an anus and larynx, head and legs? Why not walk on your head, sing with your sinuses, see through your skin, breathe with your belly.
>
> (pp. 150–1)

The body without organs contrasts concepts and principles, such as Kant's unity of apperception, that define humans as stable and stagnant beings. The images of walking on your head or singing with your sinuses challenges the notion that organs and bodies serve single purposes and prompt alternative thinking about default assumptions regarding our ways of being in the world.

It is important to note that the body without organs is a philosophical figuration and not a metaphor. St. Pierre (1997) distinguishes between philosophical figurations and metaphors, asserting:

> A figuration is not a graceful metaphor that provides coherency and unity to contradiction and disjunction. . . . A figuration is no protection from disorder, since its aim is to produce a most rigorous confusion as it jettisons clarity in favor of the unintelligible.
>
> (pp. 280–1)

The body without organs serves to complicate long-standing ideas about existence.

Although Deleuze and Guattari (1980/1987) offer the above suggestions for moving towards a Body without organs, they also explain that the body without organs is never completely realizable. Deleuze and Guattari argue, "You never reach the Body without Organs, you can't reach it, you are forever attaining it, it is a limit" (p. 150). Given the restrictions of the human condition, one can never completely return to the fluctuating chaos that composes existence. Yet, the process of attempting to become a Body without organs can alter thinking and action. Rather than asserting the body without organs as an achievable goal, Deleuze and Guattari use the notion to promote ongoing divergent thinking about bodies and life, emphasizing the difference and process that constitute existence.

Deleuze and Guattari (1980/1987) challenge us not just to acknowledge how objects, people, and ideas differ from themselves over time, but to question how we might look below patterns of organization to embrace the difference that constitutes life. They write, "How can we unhook ourselves from the points of subjectification that secure us, nail us down to a dominant reality?" (p. 160). Just as we can envision our bodies and their functions differently, we can imagine how music education experiences might occur in new ways. For example, Deleuze and Guattari ask, "What do you have to do in order to produce a new sound?" (p. 34). Moving towards a body without organs means transitioning from the organism to its constitutive difference. Likewise, we can move from the organized musical experiences with which we have familiarity to the difference that underlies them.

WHEN IS MUSIC? WHEN IS EDUCATION?

Deleuze and Guattari's ontology of existence based on difference inspires two questions relating to music education: "When is music?" and "When is education?" A brief story from my time as a middle school music teacher may elucidate the importance of the question "When is music?" When teaching my eighth grade general music students about John Cage, I would always begin by "performing" "4'33"" and then asking my students whether or not what they heard was music. Although I almost always received a resounding "no" along with confused and frustrated explanations, I found the process of having students define music engaging, educative, and enlightening for both them and me. Yet, as such an exercise demonstrates, any attempt to define music almost always leads to a definition too narrow to encompass the great wealth of human musical endeavors or too broad to be useful in anything other than a philosophical argument. Asking students to label "4'33"" as music or non-music reverts back to prior conceptions of difference. '4'33"" is either similar to or different from other music in preset categories. Instead, drawing on Deleuze and Guattari's (1980/1987) concept of continual difference, I might have asked how "4'33"" differs from itself over the course of its three movements and how one's experiences of it differ over time.

Changing the question from "What is music?" to "When is music?" yields drastically different results. Nelson Goodman's (1978) famous question, "When is art?" inspired my choice of the question "When is music?" Goodman asserts, "The real question is not 'What objects are (permanently) works of art?' but 'When is an object a work of art?'—or more briefly . . . 'When is art?'" (pp. 66–7). This emphasis on the ephemeral and variable functions of art aligns with Deleuze and Guattari's (1980/1987) key principles of time and difference.[3] Asking "When is music?" accentuates temporality and the idea of existence as continual processes, drawing attention to musical experiences rather than artistic works. Answers to "When is music?" tend to diverge into narratives shaped by our prior experiences, future aspirations, and current time and location.

As noted above, as a person's cone grows with the passage of time, Deleuze and Guattari (1991/1994) posit that the past and future actualize in each present moment. Humans' experiences with music in the present occur in integration with their past musical endeavors. As Dewey (1934) explains, "To see, to perceive, is more than to recognize. It does not identify something present in terms of a past disconnected from it. The past is carried into the present so as to expand and deepen the content of the latter" (p. 24). The question "When is music?" allows a student to *not* experience a performance of "4'33," Beethoven's *Symphony No. 9 in D minor,* or an Ewe drumming piece as music one day, only to find herself immersed in such performances or sections of such performances on another day.

Focusing on the temporal and fluctuating nature of music highlights students' continually evolving musical experiences. Similarly, in her chapter, Silverman articulates how critical ethnography can "create a space where teachers and students can conceptualize music class as a social act of becoming; where through music, teachers and students can go beyond what is to what can be." As renowned pianist Glenn Gould once stated, "I believe that the only excuse for being musicians, for making music in any fashion, is to make it differently, and to perform it differently, and to establish the music's difference vis-à-vis our own difference" (Hozer & Raymont, 2010). Such diversity exemplifies Deleuze and Guattari's (1980/1987) assertion that flux and change rather than stagnation underlie existence and centers the dynamic nature of musical experiences.

Asking "When is music?" is not enough; one can imagine a classroom with much music and little education. I posit that music educators also explore the question "When is education?" Think of a moment when you have had an educative experience. Of the many moments that come to my mind, all occurred as a result of prior experiences. As evidenced by May's (2003) aforementioned explication of Bergson's time cone, education does not occur absent the actualization of our entire past. For example, how has your conception of difference changed since the beginning of this chapter?

No formula exists for determining whether or not students have engaged in an educative experience. I have sat through numerous classes and at times whole courses without experiencing education only to have later educative experiences made possible by those classes and courses. The question "What is education?" like the question "What is music?" elicits singular answers either too specific to encompass all educative experiences or too broad to distinguish educative experiences from other experiences. In contrast, the question "When is education?" emphasizes a dynamic view of reality, in which developing individuals in changing places can engage in continually evolving educative experiences.

Deleuze (1990/1995) argues that educative materials and practices have value for a given person at a specific place and time. He asserts that when confronted with a book, "The only question is 'Does it work, and how does it work?' How does it work for you? If it doesn't work, if nothing comes through, you try another book" (p. 8). Educational experiences, like musical ones, continually develop, occurring differently for every person.

A SHORT ANECDOTE

A short anecdote about a student teacher I observed illustrates how emphasizing the questions "When is music?" and "When is education?" might play out in music teaching and learning. During our scheduled visit, I watched a student teacher try to maintain "order" in a large middle school band class as she taught the students tunes from a method book. Many students sat still as she corrected the rhythm of the flute players or went down the line of eight trombonists to make sure that they could play the written starting pitch, spending three minutes with a single student who never hit the correct note.

As I sat there observing, I made my usual list of things she could do differently. I, like a student circling the apples on the similar/different worksheet, saw her teaching in terms of similar to or different from my conception of effective teaching. I planned to begin our post-observation meeting as I always did and as my university supervisor had done when I student taught, by asking what she would have done differently. In my head, I had defined her entire lesson in terms of discrete differences. I do not doubt the value of such questions or concrete suggestions. Discussing discrete differences is a necessary part of reflecting upon and improving practice. Yet, as I sat there watching, I was struck by a different question.

After the lesson, I asked her, "When was music during that rehearsal?" She looked confused and responded that she wasn't sure there was any. I then asked her, "When was music for those students?" and she discussed sections of rehearsals in which she had musically engaged various students as well as posited how she might further facilitate such processes. She emphasized the temporal and variable nature of musical experiences, viewing them as continual and evolving. While I certainly do not attribute her later improvement solely to that conversation, our future dialog led me to believe that she had begun reflecting on continual differences in addition to discrete ones.

I, of course, have continually changed since that observation. Looking back on it now, I can think of the other questions that may have helped further emphasize ongoing differences: How did you (the teacher) differ over the course of that class? How did your lesson plan change as a result of your interactions with the students? How did students' cognition, emotions, bodies, and social interactions evolve in integration with their musical experiences? How did each of the students differ from themselves throughout the lesson? Similarly, in his chapter, Talbot posits the importance of engaging students in flexible, contextually situated learning processes that draw upon their current resources.

In order to facilitate the student teacher's understanding of education as an evolving process, I would have also focused on questions about the interrelationship of continual difference and education. For instance, I might have asked the following questions: When were those trombone players experiencing education? When was the rest of the band experiencing education? How was each of those students changing as a result of his or her educative experiences? How did these changes relate to students' past and future educative experiences?

Through the philosophical figuration of the body without organs, Deleuze and Guattari (1980/1987) challenge readers not just to acknowledge ongoing difference, but to ask how they might seek out existence's underlying difference. In other words, how might embracing continual difference enable unique, evolving reordering of that difference? As I sat there thinking of what suggestions I could offer the student teacher, I realized that at least half of them had come not from classes I took or observations I made, but rather my own experimentation and explorations. Through these endeavors, I complicated students, music, and education, seeking out difference rather than similarity. As a teacher, I observed that my students seemed most engaged in musical and educative experiences when I dropped everything I knew about music and education, moving away from my prepared lesson plans and curricula to embrace the chaotic unknown.

How might the concept of a body without organs encourage preservice teachers to move from their preconceived notions about music and education to the disorganized, fluctuating essence of life? Music teacher educators might consider how we can facilitate preservice teachers' explorations of and experimentations with difference. Starting from a place of complexity, teacher educators might assist preservice teachers in a continual reimagining of new possibilities for facilitating given curricula as well as for rethinking music education practices in general.

The body without organs may also help inspire changes in teacher education. For example, the music education profession might ponder questions such as: How can teacher educators develop dispositions towards continual difference and how can we assist preservice and practicing teachers in developing such dispositions? How can music educators move from our current forms of institutional organization to explore the underlying, fluctuating nature of music and education? How might the questions "When is music?" and "When is education?" help music teacher educators in reimagining our courses, content, and practices at the undergraduate and graduate levels? The music education profession might consider drawing on Deleuze and Guattari's (1980/1987) concepts of continual difference and the body without organs in order to challenge assumptions about boundaries, values, and actions.

I return to my opening statement: "We need to think differently about music education." Discrete, numeric, homogeneous differences still hold an important place in twenty-first century life. Humans still need to distinguish between the edible and inedible and the written starting note of a middle school band piece and a random note. Yet, in order to survive, companies such as Apple and Google must think not just about new products but about how existing ones, like smartphones and search engines, can evolve to meet the possibilities of changing people and societies. We live in a rapidly evolving world in which people must realize how we change through and adapt to technological innovations, multiplying global connections, and ever-increasing diversity.

In addition to utilizing discrete differences, the music education profession might consider emphasizing how continual difference might function in our classrooms and in the lives of teachers and students. Music educators might also embrace the difference underlying all music and education, diving into the disorder again and again to build new, temporary forms of organization. As we navigate our ever-evolving world, ongoing engagement with these questions and ideas may help bring about *continually different* music education theories and practices.

NOTES

1. See, for example, Aristotle's *Nicomachean Ethics*.
2. Pereboom (2009) defines apperception as "the apprehension of a mental state, a representation, as one's own."

3. Goodman's (1978) further explications of the question "When is art?" contrast Deleuze and Guattari's philosophy of difference in at least three ways. First, Goodman answers his question by offering five "tentative symptoms of the aesthetic," all of which assert the importance of symbols (pp. 67–8). In contrast, Deleuze and Guattari (1991/1994) emphasize the difference and uniqueness of art, arguing against symbols and definition. Second, while Goodman acknowledges that asking "When is art?" necessitates ongoing questioning about an object's function, he maintains the categories of art and non-art, writing, "The Rembrandt painting remains a work of art, as it remains a painting, while functioning only as a blanket; and the stone from the driveway may not strictly become art by functioning as art" (p. 69). Conversely, Deleuze and Guattari (1980/1987) argue against all stable identities, instead positing the constant fluctuation of all existence. Lastly, Goodman's elaborations revolve around artistic objects rather than processes. While his writing does not strictly contradict the notion that "When is art?" could apply to performers, composers, and listeners, he does not acknowledge such possibilities. In contrast, Deleuze and Guattari's (1980/1987) philosophy of art highlights composition and ongoing engagement with artworks and artistic processes.

REFERENCES

Colebrook, C. (2002). *Understanding Deleuze.* Crows Nest, NSW, Australia: Allen & Unwin.

Consortium of National Arts Education Associations. (1994). National standards for arts education. Reston, VA: Music Educators National Conference.

Deleuze, G. (1995). *Negotiations: 1972–1990.* (M. Joughlin, Trans.). New York, NY: Columbia University Press. (Original work published 1990)

Deleuze, G., & Guattari, F. (1987). *A thousand plateaus: Capitalism and schizophrenia.* (B. Massumi, Trans.). Minneapolis: University of Minnesota Press. (Original work published 1980)

Deleuze, G., & Guattari F. (1994). *What is philosophy?* (H. Tomlinson & G. Burchell, Trans.). New York, NY: Columbia University Press. (Original work published 1991)

Dewey, J. (1934). *Art as experience.* New York, NY: Minton, Balch & Company.

Goodman, N. (1978). *Ways of world making.* Indianapolis, IN: Hackett Publishing Company.

Hozer, M., & Raymont, P. (2010). Genius within: The inner life of Glenn Gould. In S. Lacy (Executive producer), *American masters.* Toronto, Canada: White Pine Pictures.

Kant, I. (1997). *Critique of pure reason* (2nd Ed.). (P. Guyer & A. Wood, Trans.). New York, NY: Cambridge University Press. (Original work published 1781)

May, T. (2003). When is Deleuzian becoming? *Continental Philosophy Review, 36,* 139–53.

May, T. (2005). *Gilles Deleuze: An introduction.* Cambridge, United Kingdom: Cambridge University Press.

Pereboom, D. (2009). Kant's transcendental arguments. In *Stanford encyclopedia of philosophy.* Retrieved from http://plato.stanford.edu/entries/kant-transcendental/

Plato. (1973). *The republic and other works.* (B. Jowett, Trans.). New York, NY: Anchor Books.

St. Pierre, E. A. (1997). An introduction to figurations: A poststructural practice of inquiry. *International Journal of Qualitative Studies in Education, 3*(10), 279–84.

4 A Proleptic Perspective of Music Education

Brent C. Talbot

INTRODUCTION

Cultural psychology and sociocultural approaches on identity formation offer great potential for music education and music teacher education—specifically a cultural mechanism known as *prolepsis* (Slattery, 2012; Cole, 1996; Stone, 1993; Stone and Wertsch, 1984). Prolepsis is "the representation of a future act or development as being presently existing" (Merriam-Webster). In this paper I argue that, like parents, we, as music educators, use information derived from our own cultural pasts to project a probable future on our students (often assuming that the world will be very much for our students as it has been for us). By explaining this cultural mechanism through examples of my own teaching, I posit that all too often educators' and teacher educators' (purely *ideal*) recall of our pasts and imagination of our students' futures become fundamentally materialized constraints on our students' life experiences in the present. This paper explores the following questions: How can understanding perspectives in cultural psychology reshape our communities of practice? What happens when projected futures are embraced, disrupted, and/or rejected? What barriers do we (un)consciously create for our students, ourselves, and our field? How can we use this knowledge to navigate the futures of our profession?

I draw upon my experience as an eighth grade general music teacher to illustrate how approaches in cultural psychology have transformed my own understanding of teaching and learning. I use a narrative form of representation (Clandinin & Connelly, 2000; Barrett & Stauffer, 2009, 2012) in order to allow the reader a more intimate lens from which to view these approaches. Narrative, according to Connelly and Clandinin (2006):

> . . . comes out of a view of human experience in which humans, individually and socially, lead storied lives. People shape their daily lives

by stories of who they and others are and as they interpret their past in terms of these stories. Story, in the current idiom, is a portal through which a person enters the world and by which their experience of the world is interpreted and made personally meaningful.

(p. 477)

NARRATIVE

In spring of 2007[1] I was hired to take over an eighth grade general music class in a suburban school in upstate New York in order to reduce the disciplinary conflicts a choir director had been experiencing with his large eighth grade all-boys choir. The school's administration, district music coordinator, and the middle school music teachers strategized that they could better manage the students' behavior by dividing the 70-member choir and using the eighth grade general music teacher as a second choir director. They hired me to cover the one section of eighth grade general music that met during the same period as the choir.

Coming into a classroom in mid-March posed three main challenges. First was establishing myself in a community of practice (Lave & Wenger, 1991) in which the participants had preestablished roles, identities, routines, rituals, and governing rules for teaching, learning, and behavior in the classroom setting. Students filled out worksheets and performed tasks on instruments *for* the teacher that were evaluated *by* the teacher and measured based on completion of the tasks assigned. Therefore, a second challenge for me was trying to introduce the class to a constructivist approach with which my philosophy of teaching was more closely aligned. Like Jerome Bruner (1990), I find constructivism in cultural psychology to be a profound expression of democratic culture:

> It demands that we be conscious of how we come to our knowledge and as conscious as we can be about the values that lead us to our perspectives. It asks that we be accountable for how and what we know. But it does not insist that there is only one way of constructing meaning, or one right way. It is based upon values that, I believe, fit it best to deal with the changes and disruptions that have become so much a feature of modern life.
>
> (Bruner, 1990, p. 30)

A third challenge was trying to help the students reconstruct their class narrative and identity (Bruner, 1990; Cronon, 1992; Middleton & Brown, 2005; Mishler, 2004; Vygotsky, 1987), which they had appropriated (Rogoff, 1998; Wertsch, 1998) from various students, teachers, and administrators, as being "bad" (McDermott, 1993; O'Connor, 2003).

The district curriculum I inherited mandated that I cover a musical theatre unit, explore the "Star-Spangled Banner," and continue with performance tasks on various instruments before the end of the year. I did not feel comfortable continuing with the previous teacher's agenda before having the opportunity to get to know the students with whom I would be working and decided—with permission from the district coordinator—to put the curriculum on hold for a few weeks to better understand the individuals in the class. After our initial introductions I asked the students to participate in a music identity project (Talbot, 2013), where we explored various genres of music and their relationships to the students' identities. I wanted to find out the students' musical preference(s), explore what role(s) music played in their lives and identities, and provide them an opportunity to articulate and perhaps reconstruct their class narrative away from one that was "bad." From this project we explored stereotypes, identities, and narratives, applying them to larger constructs like group, class, and nation. We extended this thinking through a world music unit that turned our focus to the music of the Caribbean and Latin America, looking specifically at how musical practices, including dance and musical styles and performance, in the Caribbean and Latin American countries are used to define whole nations (Austerlitz, 1997; Averill, 1997; Duany, 1994; Hobsbawm, 1990).

At the beginning of May, the eighth grade general music class and I had a significant transformative moment, in which myself, the participants, and the physical space dramatically changed as a result of a series of events. After six weeks of being off the curriculum, I decided a nice transition would be to take our discussion of group, national, and ethnic identity and show how these concepts were represented in musicals like *West Side Story*. Not only were the students able to draw upon the mambo and salsa stylistic features and dance steps from the Caribbean music unit, they also began to see musicals as a genre in which our nation tells its own narrative (Cronon, 1992). The next time we met, the class made an extensive list of all of the musicals we could recall, naming about forty ranging from *South Pacific* to *Wicked*. We then looked at this list and tried to identify various categories in which the titles could be placed. The students categorized them into five genres: religious oriented (*Jesus Christ Superstar*), gang related (*West Side Story*), rock musicals (*Hair*), period pieces (*Ragtime*), and movie musicals (*High School Musical*).

During our brainstorming session someone suggested that we make our own musical. To begin the process, we brainstormed what defined a musical (storyline, music, acting, dancing, singing, staging, etc.) and all of the various roles needed to develop and execute a musical production (script writer, lyricist, composer/arranger, choreographer, director, music director, set-designer, costumer, make-up specialist, lighting designer, sound engineer, actors, dancers, and musicians). Each one of us chose and encouraged each other into roles which we were most skilled in or interested in learning. In the end there were two screenplay writers, one composer/arranger, one pianist, one guitarist, two percussionists, a sound engineer, a lighting designer, a person to operate the camera, a director, a critic, a set and poster designer, and nine actors—one of whom requested adamantly that his character have a dramatic death scene. Many types of leaders emerged and I found myself most useful in facilitating equipment needs or mediating creative disputes among group members.

Once the roles had been established, we grouped ourselves in different areas of the room. The creative and organic nature of this lesson changed both the atmosphere and the physical space of the classroom. The screen-writers got together at a table in the back of the room. The actors moved a table to create more space for the nine members of that group. The composer went to the piano and started playing a familiar piece by Mozart; she then deconstructed the piece and began changing the meter and arpeggiating the chords to make it her own. The percussionists pulled out chairs and began playing along with congas and auxiliary percussion.

The director, who was encouraged into that role by the group because he was "the loudest," pulled me aside and said, "I think this is cool." The group in charge of lighting, sound, and video asked what they should be doing. I asked, "Who is in charge of the audio/visual equipment in the building?" They responded, "Mr. Jones." I replied, "Guess you need to go find Mr. Jones." One of the three said, "I think he's in room 120." They checked the directory on the wall and hurried out the door, returning ten minutes later with a boom poll, mics, headphones, and a video camera.

I went to check on the writers to see how they were doing with their plot. They said, "OK. All we've got so far is that there's a henchman who is paid by one mob family to take out the son of another mob family's boss. The cops are tipped off by someone close to the henchman, and it all goes down at a warehouse on the outskirts of town." "Good," I replied. "Now start writing for nine characters. We'll need at least one page by Monday." "Yeah," one of them said, "we can get together over the weekend and write a ton." One student, who had not spoken all term, was sketching a horse on some notepaper. The director came up and said, "Hey T-Bot, look at Amy's drawing. It's awesome." I suggested to Amy—who had initially not wanted any role—that she consider creating the poster for the show. She smiled and said, "OK." The bell rang and the students reluctantly gathered their belongings. A sense of disappointment was felt in the air.

INTERPRETATION

The beliefs and philosophies exposed in this music-learning environment reveal two approaches towards transmission in the field of music education. The first approach, which I label *direct teaching,* orientates individuals and the world as fundamentally separate, viewing the world as objective and knowable. Knowledge about music is acquired through learning an objectively knowable repertoire and taken to underlie and enable behavior in concrete contexts, which are assumed to have a determinate character apart from human activity and interpretation. In this view, learning is a matter of building up "standard knowledge" in the minds of individuals, which can then be transferred to other times and other contexts to be "applied." This view replaces learning with teaching, one where transmission of knowledge is paramount, where creativity and exploration are restricted, where identity is moved to the margins, and where hierarchical stratifications reign supreme.

The second approach, called *situated learning* (Lave & Wenger, 1991), orientates individuals in a fluctuating world. In this view, people flexibly and contingently contextualize their ongoing activity (Lave, 1993; Miller & Goodnow, 1995). "Activity is partially structured through the use of material and semiotic resources that have evolved within and are associated with particular practices" (O'Connor, 2003, p. 71). Meaning is therefore not determined by the use of objectively knowable resources associated with particular practices or methodologies, but instead is indeterminate, situated, and co-constructed, requiring an evaluative process of ongoing reflexive judgments in which all participants position themselves in the activity and the broader forms of social organization.

Lave and Wenger (1991) challenge us to rethink what it means to learn and understand. The common element they use is the premise that meaning, understanding, and learning are all defined relative to actional contexts, not to self-contained structures. William Hanks, in his forward for Lave and Wenger's *Situated Learning,* offers this interpretation:

> Learning for Lave and Wenger is a process that takes place in a participation framework, not in an individual mind. This means, among other things, that it is mediated by the differences of perspective among the co-participants. It is the community, or at least those participating in the learning context, who "learn" under this definition. Learning is, as it were, distributed among co-participants, not an action of one person. . . . [Similarly], understanding is not something a person does in his or her head, nor does it ultimately involve the mental representations of individuals. Understanding is not seen to arise out of the mental operations of a subject on objective structures. Instead, Lave and Wenger locate learning [and understanding] not in the acquisition of structure, but in the increased access of learners to participating roles in expert performances.
>
> (p. 15)

Learning and Teaching Curricula

With this understanding of learning and teaching, I want to return to the transformative experience in the general music class. As mentioned in my narrative, one of the challenges the class and I faced was orienting

our group to a learning curriculum from a teaching curriculum (Lave &
Wenger, 2002):

> A learning curriculum consists of situated opportunities (thus including
> exemplars of various sorts often thought of as "goals") for the impro-
> visational development of new practice. A learning curriculum is a field
> of learning resources in everyday practice *viewed from the perspective
> of learners* [italics in original]. A teaching curriculum, by contrast, is
> constructed for the instruction of newcomers. When a teaching cur-
> riculum supplies—and thereby limits—structuring resources for learn-
> ing, the meaning of what is learned (and control of access to it, both
> in its peripheral forms and its subsequently more complex and inten-
> sified, though possibly more fragmented, forms) is mediated through
> an instructor's participation, by an external view of what knowing is
> about. The learning curriculum in didactic situations, then, evolves out
> of participation in a specific community of practice engendered by ped-
> agogical relations and by a prescriptive view of the target practice as a
> subject matter, as well as out of the many and various relations that tie
> participants to their own and to other institutions.
>
> (pp. 114–5)

A learning curriculum, therefore, is one that acknowledges, values, and
finds use for the experiences, the histories, and the cultural, linguistic, and
musical tools and resources each participant brings to the classroom. A
learning curriculum uses the "funds of knowledge" each participant brings
from outside the classroom to develop a "participatory partnership" within
the classroom (Moll et al., 1992, p. 139).

Moving from one structure of understanding to another required the participants and myself to unlearn part of our previous socialization and to begin
recreating a new classroom culture and narrative. This required providing the
opportunity to explore identity so that the participants and I could reconstruct our personal and group narratives. Reconstruction involves the active
sequencing and appropriation of past events to recreate our past in order to
fit our current situation. As Middleton and Brown (2005) point out, memory
is a socially constructed experience and a key site where questions of personal
identity and social order are negotiated. Middleton and Brown draw upon
the work of William James (1890/1950), who suggests that memory:

> is to be approached in terms of the ability to connect together aspects
> of our experience as they appear in the ongoing flow of awareness. This
> implies some form of selectivity, we must exercise choice in relation to the
> nature of the connections to be made in order that our recollections can be
> best fitted to our current concerns and activities. Hence "in the practical
> use of our intellect, forgetting is as important a function as recollecting."
>
> (p. 679)

NARRATIVE PRODUCTION AND A NEW
CONCEPTUALIZATION FOR TEACHING

By exploring their musical identities, I had asked the participants of the class to produce their own narratives by drawing upon the cultural resources and tools they draw upon in and out of school. As other writers, anthropologists, philosophers, and psychologists have pointed out (Bakhtin, 1981; Bruner, 1990; Vygotsky, 1987), our cultural resources and tools invariably have a history of use by others; they are always half someone else's. This lead to questions about how our identities and narratives in and of the classroom are built into the very cultural resources and tools we employ as learners and teachers. I began to wonder how we could coordinate these resources and tools to help shape our learning environment.

In order for our class to shift from a teaching curriculum to a learning curriculum, I—as the teacher—had to first critically examine and reconstruct my own understanding of learning and teaching and (re)interpret what it means to be a teacher, a learner, and part of a classroom culture. I began by recalling what Bruner (1990) offers about participation in culture and our ability as humans to construct individual and group understanding:

> It is man's participation *in* culture and the realization of his mental powers *through* culture that make it impossible to construct a human psychology on the basis of the individual alone. . . . To treat the world as an indifferent flow of information to be processed by individuals each on his or her own terms is to lose sight of how individuals are formed and how they function. Or to quote Geertz, "there is no such thing as human nature independent of culture." . . . Given that psychology is so immersed in culture, it must be organized around those meaning-making and meaning-using processes that connect man to culture. This does *not* commit us to more subjectivity in psychology; it is just the reverse. By virtue of participation in culture, meaning is rendered *public* and *shared* [italics in original]. Our culturally adapted way of life depends upon shared meanings and shared concepts and depends as well upon shared modes of discourse for negotiating differences in meaning and interpretation.
>
> (pp. 12–13)

Drawing upon this view of culture, I attempted to conceptualize teaching in a way that could infuse Lave & Wenger's ideas on learning. This view makes room for both transmission and transformation (Heath, 2004) and bridges the dichotomous gap between teaching curricula and learning curricula to accommodate the need for teachers to adhere to curricular demands while at the same time providing opportunities for flexible, situated, and transformative moments of learning. This reflection process helped me expand my view of teaching as a relationship created through active partnership with a group of participants in a community of practice—in a sense it views each classroom as its own culture.

This view of classroom culture acknowledges that:

1. The appropriation and establishment of roles, routines, rituals, and rules for the individual and group shift over time, as members join or leave the group.
2. Participants place expectations upon themselves from both outside sources and internalized beliefs, and that these beliefs influence the potential one believes he or she possesses within and across various settings.
3. The ongoing (re)interpretation, (re)negotiation and action upon/reaction to these expectations informs behavior(s).
4. Future projections in terms of relationships and aspirations lend significance to past and current events and their interpretations; and
5. This complex intersection of past, present, and future plays a significant part in informing the ways in which both teachers and students simultaneously facilitate and limit potential pathways for themselves and others.

Prolepsis

I draw upon Michael Cole's (1996) cultural approach to viewing ontogeny and the idea of prolepsis to get at this idea of past, present, and future pathways.

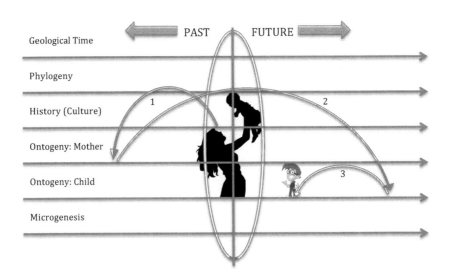

Cole (1996) explains:

> [That on this illustration,] the horizontal lines represent time scales corresponding to the history of the physical universe, the history of life on earth, (cultural-historical time), the life of the individual (ontogeny), and the history of moment-to-moment lived experience (microgenesis). The vertical ellipse represents the event of a child's birth. The distribution of cognition in time is traced sequentially into (1) the mother's memory of her past, (2) the mother's imagination of the future of the child, and (3) the mother's subsequent behavior.
>
> (p. 185)

Cole suggests in this sequence that the ideal aspect of culture is transformed into its material form as the mother and other adults structure the child's experience to be consistent with what they imagine to be the child's future identity.

This is easier to understand through an exercise I do with students in their first year on campus. At the beginning of each year, I ask them to close their eyes and ponder the following questions about themselves:

1. Who am I? How did I come to be in this particular place, in this particular time?
2. Was the decision entirely mine?
3. What factors, what individuals, what groups helped shape who I am and how I came to be in this particular place and time?
4. Is how I see myself the same as how others see me? Is this who I want to be?

To illustrate the point that our projected pathways may not be our own, I discuss my own experiences as an emerging adult (Arnett, 2000).

Throughout my childhood, my parents' future projection for me was to become a businessman and marry a woman. This was experienced through conversations, questions, and suggestions my relatives would make as to where I should attend college and about whom I should find sexually desirable. I discovered somewhere along my ontogeny/lifespan that I possessed a great interest in music and teaching and I also came to understand my sexuality differently. Because these projections of my identity conflicted with my parents', it was inevitable that a disruption of these projections would occur; and as such, I forged a new identity and a new narrative for myself and my family.

Cole (1996) argues that prolepsis is an important process of socialization/enculturation, and is based upon the mediation of cultural values and norms that are grounded in both the transmitter's past experiences and the expectations for the receiver's future roles. The assumption that the world will remain similar for future generations greatly informs the developmental experiences to which adults expose youth (Wyn, 2005). By being aware of prolepsis, music teachers can better understand the role we play in projecting and mapping our own past, present, and future onto our students.

The combination of the teacher's past personal experience(s) coupled with their future expectations set forth by adult role model(s) serves as possible catalysts for the constriction of the activities, knowledge, language, beliefs, and behavior(s) used in the classroom setting (Cole 1996; Erikson, 1968). For example, as Slattery (2012) points out:

> One of the most irritating comments that I often hear spoken at graduations . . . and other ceremonies of passage is "You are the future of the community" or "the future of the country." It should not be surprising that many young people refuse to engage in the social, cultural, religious, and political life of the community or to work for justice. The language of adults tells them to delay their participation until they are adults in the future. But we need the insights and energy of our young people now. It should also come as no surprise, then, that most students are bored in classrooms, and many drop out of school when subject matter is not meaningfully connected to current events, life experiences, and personal autobiographies.
>
> (p. 86)

Teachers diminish meaningful learning when they tell students to study aspects of music not because they are interesting or applicable at the present moment, but because they may need it for classes or work in the future. It is counterproductive to separate the future from the present. I posit we might be better off engaging our students in a learning process that (1) draws upon the cultural, musical, and linguistic resources of the participants in our classrooms, (2) is flexible and contingent, and (3) situated in the moment and context. In this way, every classroom construction can become an opportunity for all participants, both youth and adult, to create new learning and understanding of not only the academic content, but also one's self and group narrative and identity.

Narrative and Identity Shifts

To understand how Cole's idea of prolepsis can be applied to classroom contexts, let us return to the narrative of the eighth grade general music class and look at how the classroom narrative changed when a new teacher/adult model entered the group dynamic. Before I arrived at the middle school, the eighth grade boys' choir at the school had developed a reputation for being "bad." The students in the choir appropriated and internalized (Penuel & Wertsch, 1995) this label, drawing power from it as a result. For the choir to re-center and relocate power in the teacher, the adults in the community divided the group. This action sent clear messages to all the students of the eighth grade. First it acknowledged that students, especially adolescents, have power (Giroux, 2003), and second it indicated to students that when they resist, adults will do as much as possible to regain and maintain the power. Because such a large group of eighth graders were in the choir, the entire grade appeared to have appropriated and internalized this label, such that when I replaced the former eighth grade general music teacher, the class told me within the first few minutes that they were "bad" and that I was "not going to be able to manage" them. After our introductions, one of the students asked me to tell them more about the various contexts in which I participated outside of our class. At that time I was a PhD. student in music education and a teacher in the city school district. I explained that I performed in a community gamelan, conducted different generational community choirs, and taught music technology and production at a local community music school. The context that generated the most interest among the students was my city school teaching. When they learned I was a teacher for a different population of students their age, their perception of themselves dramatically changed. Because of my identity and participation in a different context that they saw as "really bad," their own identity and narrative shifted.

We can see in this example how learning implies becoming a different person with respect to the possibilities enabled by the systems of relations within a community of practice (Lave & Wenger, 1991; O'Connor, 2003); and that the introduction of one context into another can change perspective. As O'Connor (2003) suggests:

> Participants bring with them a history of participation in different contexts, and they will participate in still other contexts in the future. Actions performed and words spoken by a participant in the past, and identities adopted by or ascribed to them, can be made relevant in the present interaction, and the present interaction can in turn be made relevant in the future. It is important to note, furthermore, that these various contexts are not necessarily easily embedded within one another, and this introduces potentially destabilizing elements into social practice. This makes close attention to the dynamics of contextualization and identification important.
>
> (p. 71)

The revelation that I taught in different school environments was a catalyst that enabled us to explore our identities and narratives in relation to each other. It was through this moment that I became hyper-aware of the importance each persons' identity—enabled through their historical, cultural, linguistic, and musical resources—plays in all the learning processes of each music classroom. All too often our identities as musicians, improvisers, composers, performers, listeners, learners, and teachers are pushed to the side due to an emphasis on objectively knowable material and methods of efficient content delivery in our music classrooms. Instead, we may want to share and promote our identities and draw upon the cultural, linguistic, and musical resources and tools we all bring to the table. Perhaps then our classrooms can become sites of transformation as we share and co-construct knowledge and engage in participatory practice tied to our current contexts.

CONCLUSION

In conclusion, I suggest through this paper that we draw from approaches and tools in cultural psychology (Barab & Duffy, 2000; Cole, 1996; Keith, 2011; Kirshner & Whitson, 1998) and identity research (Arnett, 2000; Erikson, 1968; Mishler, 2004; Penuel & Wertsch, 1995; Rymes, 2001; Vygotsky 1987) to help examine how we learn and teach music in order to shape a new future for music education. By providing space for identity formation and narrative reconstruction in our music classrooms and music teacher education programs, stakeholders have agency and opportunity to create new narratives of ourselves and our musicking practices as individuals, as groups, and as a profession. When we acknowledge that power, knowledge, identity, and narratives are not objects bestowed on others, but are shared, shaped, and distributed through activity with each other and with our world, we are given agency to disrupt the projections that may not fit how we want to see ourselves, and instead we open ourselves and our profession up to projecting new futures and sharing new narratives. In this way, music education can become creative, collaborative, and responsive to our identities, to our communities, and to our current contexts.

NOTE

1. During this time, I was also employed in the Rochester (NY) City School District and found teaching in both settings to be significantly different in terms of demographics as well as approaches to curriculum and teaching. To help understand the changes in my teaching and in my own identity, I journaled regularly and kept video and audio of my classrooms.

REFERENCES

Arnett, J. (2000). Emerging adulthood: A theory of development from the late teens through the twenties. *American Psychologist, 55*(5), 469–80.
Austerlitz, P. (1997). *Merengue: Dominican music and Dominican identity.* Philadelphia, PA: Temple University Press.

Austerlitz, P. (1997). Merengue: *Dominican music and Dominican identity.* Philadelphia:Temple University Press.

Averill, G. (1997). *A day for the hunter, a day for the prey: Popular music and power in Haiti.* Chicago, IL: Chicago University Press.

Barab, S. A., & Duffy, T. M. (2000). From practice fields to communities of practice. In D. H. Jonassen & S. M. Land (Eds.), *Theoretical foundations of learning* (pp. 25–55). Mahwah, NJ: Lawrence Erlbaum.

Barrett, M. S., & Stauffer, S. L. (2009). *Narrative inquiry in music education: Troubling certainty.* New York: Springer.

Barrett, M. S., & Stauffer, S. L. (Eds.) (2012). *Narrative soundings: An anthology of narrative inquiry in music education.* New York, NY: Springer.

Bruner, J. (1990). *Acts of meaning.* Cambridge, MA: Harvard University Press.

Clandinin, D. J., & Connelly, F. M. (2000). *Narrative inquiry: Experience and story in qualitative research.* San Francisco, CA: Jossey-Bass.

Cole, M. (1996). *Cultural psychology: A once and future discipline.* Cambridge, MA: Harvard University Press.

Connelly, F. M., & Clandinin, D. J. (2006). Narrative inquiry. In J. L. Green, G. Camilli, & P. Elmore (Eds.), *Handbook of complementary methods in education research* (pp. 477–87). Mahwah, NJ: Erlbaum.

Cronon, W. (1992). A place for stories: Nature, history, and narrative. *Journal of American History, 78*(4), 1347–76.

Duany, J. (1994). Ethnicity, identity, and music: An anthropological analysis of Dominican merengue. In G. H. Béhague (Ed.), *Music and black ethnicity: The Caribbean and South America* (pp. 65–90). New Brunswick, NJ: Transaction Publishers.

Erikson, E. (1968). *Identity: Youth and crisis.* New York, NY: Norton & Co.

Giroux, H. (2003). Neoliberalism and the disappearance social in *Ghost World. Third Text, 17*(2), 151–61.

Heath, S. (2004). Risks, rules, and roles: Youth perspectives on the work of learning for community development. In A. Perret-Clermont, C. Pontecorvo, L. Resnick, T. Ziittoun, & B. Burge (Eds.), *Joining society: Social interaction and learning in adolescence and youth* (pp. 41–70). Cambridge, MA: Cambridge University Press.

Hobsbawm, E. (1990). *Nations and nationalism since 1780: Programme, myth, reality.* New York, NY: Cambridge University Press.

James, W. (1890/1950). *The principles of psychology.* Mineola, NY: Dover Publications.

Keith, K. D. (Ed.) (2011). *Cross-cultural psychology: Contemporary themes and perspectives.* Malden, MA: Wiley-Blackwell.

Kirshner, D. & Whitson, J. A. (1998). Obstacles to understanding cognition as situated. *Educational Researcher, 27*(8), 22–8.

Lave, J., & Wenger, E. (1991). *Situated learning: Legitimate peripheral participation.* New York, NY: Cambridge University Press.

Lave, J., & Wenger, E. (2002). Legitimate peripheral participation in communities of practice. In H. Roger, F. Reeve, A. Hanson, & J. Clarke (Eds.), *Supporting lifelong learning: Vol. 1. Perspectives on learning.* New York, NY: Routledge.

McDermott, R. P. (1993). The acquisition of a child by a learning disability. In S. Chaiklin and J. Lave (Eds.), *Understanding practice* (pp. 269–305). New York, NY: Cambridge University Press.

Middleton, D., & Brown, S. D. (2005). *The social psychology of experience: Studies in remembering and forgetting.* Thousand Oaks, CA: Sage.

Miller, P. J., & Goodnow, J. J. (1995). Cultural practices: Toward an integration of culture and development. In J. J. Goodnow, P. J. Miller, & F. Kessel (Eds.),

Cultural practices as contexts for development (pp. 5–16). San Francisco, CA: Jossey-Bass.

Mishler, E. (2004). Historians of the self: Restorying lives, revising identities. *Research In Human Development, 1*(1&2), 101–21.

Moll, L. C., Amanti, C., Neff, D., & Gonzalez, N. (1992). Funds of knowledge for teaching: Using a qualitative approach to connect homes and classrooms. *Theory Into Practice, 31*(2), 132–41.

O'Connor, K. (2003). Communicative practice, cultural production and situated learning: Constructing and contesting identities of expertise in a heterogeneous learning context. In S. Wortam & B. Ryhmes (Eds.), *Linguistic anthropology of education* (pp. 61–92). Westport, CT: Praeger.

Penuel, W., & Wertsch, J. (1995). Vygotsky and identity formation: A sociocultural approach. *Educational Psychologist, 30*(2), 83–92.

Prolepsis. (2012). In *Merriam-Webster.com*. Retrieved January 22, 2013, from www.merriam-webster.com/dictionary/prolepsis

Rogoff, B. (1998). Cognition as a collaborative practice. In D. Kuhn & R. S. Siegler (Eds.), *Handbook of child psychology: Vol. 2. Cognition, perception, and language*. New York, NY: Wiley.

Rymes, B. (2001). *Conversational borderlands: Language and identity in an alternative urban high school*. New York, NY: Teachers College Press.

Slattery, P. (2012). *Curriculum development in the postmodern era*. New York, NY: Garland Publishers.

Stone, A., & Wertsch, J. V. (1984). A social interactional analysis of learning disabilities. *Journal of Learning Disabilities, 17*, 194–9.

Stone, C. A. (1993). What is missing in the metaphor of scaffolding? In E. A. Forman, N. Minnick, & C. A. Stone (Eds.), *Contexts for learning: Sociocultural dynamics in children's development*. New York, NY: Oxford University Press.

Talbot, B. C. (2013). The music identity project. *Action, Criticism, and Theory for Music Education, 12*(2): 60–74.

Vygotsky, L. (1987). *The collected works of L. S. Vygotsky. Vol. 1. Problems of general psychology*. (N. Minick, Ed.). New York, NY: Plenum.

Wertsch, J. V. (1998). *Mind as action*. New York, NY: Oxford University Press.

Wyn, A. (2005). What is happening to "adolescence"? Growing up in changing times. In J. Vadeboncoeur & L. Stevens (Eds.), *Re/Constructing "the adolescent": Sign, symbol, and body*. New York, NY: Peter Lang.

5 The Virtues of Philosophical Practice in Music Education

Wayne Bowman

> A philosophical problem has the form: "I don't know my way about."
>
> —Ludwig Wittgenstein

> I should not like my writing to spare other people the trouble of thinking. But, if possible, to stimulate [them] to thoughts of [their] own.
>
> —Ludwig Wittgenstein

Despite its centrality to informed professional practice, music education philosophy has long been treated as a collection of esoteric ideas, prepared by a select few for consumption by the rank and file. Its primary purposes, we appear to believe, are rationalizing and securing support for the things music educators take pleasure in doing: philosophy is inspirational rhetoric devoted to the justification of customary activity. Philosophy may be interesting, then, or even professionally useful, but "practical" (how-to) skills and knowledge are what music educators most need.[1] And philosophical skills, conceived as they have been, are decidedly *im*practical. Accordingly, we expose[2] prospective music educators to philosophy primarily to make them aware of available options, so they can choose one when (or if) needed. Philosophy is a special (albeit peculiar) commodity to which we can turn if the going gets tough. It consists of truth claims to be deployed in defense of our actions when public support wanes. Ready-made answers are its stock in trade.

Understood this way, philosophy's importance stems from its capacity to make us feel good and its political utility. It exists to inspire us and to keep the dogs at bay; and if the dogs appear to be sleeping, there is little need for it. Because our reasons for studying music education philosophy are primarily to familiarize consumers with available options (should a need unfortunately arise), a brief introductory survey is all that is required. Fortunately (from a perspective I do not embrace), this requires little in the way of curricular time or resources. Nor is developing philosophical expertise particularly important for most music educators: its study and practice are rarely prominent components of postsecondary music education programs, even at the PhD level. Most music education philosophers are autodidacts.

The neglect of philosophical inquiry in the professional preparation of music educators has yet another disturbing consequence: the separation of philosophical proficiency from musicianship and "educatorship." This is hardly an auspicious state of affairs for a field devoted to educating musically.[3]

In short, music education has expected rather little of philosophical inquiry, and that is pretty much what we have gotten in return. Our teacher education curricula are bloated with how-to courses, largely without consideration of such crucial issues as whether-to, under-what-circumstances-to, when-not-to, and why—to say nothing of foundational issues like the nature and value of music or education. Our disregard for philosophical inquiry amounts, I submit, to professional negligence, and stems from serious misapprehensions about what philosophy is, what differences it should make, and how or by whom it should be done.

Philosophy is not advocacy, nor is it particularly well suited to advocacy's purposes; nor is it a commodity for consumption, a set of ready-made answers to questions no one is asking. What I will propose here is that philosophy is, like music, a *practice*. Like all practices, its health depends on its continued service to the goods it exists to serve. And yet, also like all practices, those goods are multiple, fluid, and variable. They change over time and from place to place. Philosophy's precise nature and value, then— the actions appropriate or inimical to it—are subject to ongoing dialogue, dispute, and refinement by its practitioners. Its purpose and worth are "created, contested, modified, and recreated amid human social interaction" (Bowman & Frega, 2012a, p. 25). Vital philosophical practice (as distinct from its occasional residues—its "products") is a dynamic process. Its most characteristic results are not answers but better questions.[4] It does not seek so much to eliminate problems as to clarify and transform them into other, better problems: problems more compelling, more relevant to practice, richer in implications for action.

What are the *goods* of philosophical practice? What are the ends it exists to serve? And what are its rivals—activities that resemble but weaken it by threatening to sever the nerve at its heart? Upon what kinds of actions, habits, attitudes, and dispositions is philosophical practice reliant? These are this brief chapter's primary concerns. My intent, however, is not so much to answer these questions definitively as to urge their centrality to professional practice in music education: the importance of approaching them in ways that maximize their practical benefits.

I will begin by extending what I have already begun to do: deliberating about what philosophy is and is not, about what distinguishes philosophical inquiry from endeavors that are often mistaken for it. I hope to do this in a way that respects the importance of debate, dispute, and dialogue to philosophical practice, characteristics often wrongly regarded as weaknesses.

I will argue that *practices* take their guidance from *ethical* dispositions,[5] guided by thoughtful engagement and critical reflection, without which their practical nature is rendered merely technical. And finally, I will undertake a cursory and preliminary survey of the *virtues* upon which it appears to me philosophical practice is reliant: the habits, dispositions, and values demanded of those who engage in it with the intent of assuring its advancement and maximizing its benefits.

WHAT PHILOSOPHY IS NOT[6]

I have already made some fairly strong assertions about what philosophy is not. But what interests me here are not the numerous things-not-philosophy that make no claim to philosophical status. My concern is, rather, the things commonly mistaken for philosophy: endeavors that resemble certain of its features while compromising its most promising potentials. I believe that inspirational rhetoric and advocacy are prominent among the endeavors most commonly mistaken for philosophy. But what others might we identify? What are the rivals of responsible philosophical practice in music education?

One notable rival is discourse that is deliberately inscrutable, that uses linguistic complexity to impress or obfuscate rather than to clarify or illuminate issues.[7] In music education's particular case we should probably add discourse that is devoid of discernable implications for practice. To be sure, philosophy often wrestles with issues that are complex, abstract, and theoretical. But as has been aptly observed, "For every complex problem there is an answer that is clear, simple, and wrong."[8] Those who criticize philosophical inquiry for its failure to provide catchy aphorisms that fit on bumper stickers, then, are looking for the wrong thing in the wrong place. Complex questions require deep answers that draw careful distinctions, seek precision, and respect the complexity of reality. However, complexity, accuracy, and precision do not mean opacity or indifference to the practical concerns at the heart of music education. Responsible philosophical practice steers clear of language and ideas that are gratuitously complex; it shuns distinctions that do not make differences. Philosophy is not needlessly dense or impenetrable, nor does it dispense simplistic slogans. Nor is it merely theoretical: indeed, good theory is probably among our most practical professional assets.

Second, philosophy is not a merely personal theory of this or that: philosophy is not the assertion of personal beliefs. It does not consist of deeply held conviction. Although everyone has beliefs and opinions, and usually in abundance, few of these amount to philosophy in a disciplined sense. The notion that everyone is somehow entitled to his or her own "philosophy" is deeply misguided, then: a symptom of the devaluation of philosophical knowledge. Unexamined opinion and unsubstantiated belief may be things to which everyone is entitled in some way or other, but they are not philosophical. "My philosophy is that the best musicians make the best music educators"; "My philosophy is that music makes people aesthetically sensitive"; "My philosophy is that children have to be taught what to think before they can think for themselves": claims like these operate on roughly the same level as "My philosophy is that a woman's place is in the home," which is to say they are better considered prejudice than philosophy. Philosophy involves systems of warranted belief: accounts developed with care, in light of competing alternatives, and subjected to rigorous critical scrutiny. At its best, its claims tend to take the form of hypotheses: of positions presumed valid yet open to ongoing analysis and, when warranted, revision. Unlike mere opinion, philosophy carefully incorporates mutually accepted ways of testing the merits of competing views. Without these, belief systems become ideological turf wars in which victory is more important than truth and the victors are those who shout louder or are better able to harness institutional channels to disseminate their views. Responsible philosophical practice submits to analytical and discursive standards. The notion that all such standards are purely arbitrary and that, therefore, all philosophical perspectives are equally valid—that anyone is entitled to his or her own "philosophy"—is not unlike the silly claim that everything is beautiful in its own way. This kind of anything-goes relativism is anathema to philosophical inquiry.

Third, philosophy is not synonymous with logic and reason. While many of its accomplishments stem from adherence to rational principles, it should not be equated with strict adherence to logical argument or positivistic proofs. Philosophy is not a knock-them-dead affair with logical tools and rational strategies capable of conferring upon its practitioners insights that magically transcend all perspective or point of view. While committing to the pursuit of truths through reason—and while embracing things like clarity, precision, and accuracy—philosophy does not consist in technically adept applications of logic. Nor does responsible philosophy presume itself capable of revealing "the" truth, of attaining ultimate insights into the innermost essences of the things upon which it is brought to bear. It seeks to enhance understanding without presuming itself a purveyor of absolute truths. In other words, good philosophy is fallibilistic: it acknowledges its potential shortcomings, and advances its positions as working hypotheses. It is a perspectival affair, always situated and invariably partial in its purview; and yet it embraces principles of rational discourse, rejecting things like obfuscation and deceit. Philosophy respects reason and seeks to be reasonable, but logic and consistency are not the sole measures of its worth.

Fourth, philosophy is not purely intellectual or theoretical, an introspective undertaking isolated from the "real world" and devoid of practical significance. As I said earlier, it does not pursue distinctions that do not make practical differences. Because music education is defined by its achievement of right results—musically and educationally—music education philosophy is necessarily and especially concerned with the connections between beliefs and actions. It is not unique in this regard: the ancient Greeks conceived of philosophy not just as the pursuit of "wisdom" in the abstract or for its own sake, but rather as the pursuit of answers to questions about how best to act, how best to live, what kind of person to be. Philosophy in its original sense was not a highly specialized, introspective affair, but an undertaking with broad practical significance, and essential to living well. The trajectories of music education philosophy have too often run in quite different directions, consisting of "mind trips" by and for philosophers—not unlike Babbitt's (1958) infamous notion of musical composition as a practice by and for composers.[9] Philosophical practice that ignores its connections to what Dewey called ends-in-view quickly becomes marginal, failing to deliver the goods it exists most fundamentally to serve.

Fifth, philosophy is not fashion.[10] By this I mean that philosophy does not consist in trends embraced for their novelty, popularity, or "currency" (viewpoints-du-jour), only to be tossed aside in pursuit of the next new thing. While it seeks to acknowledge and accommodate shifts in musical and educational practice, responsible philosophy is not notable for abrupt lurches this way or that. It does not casually discard previous findings in pursuit of mere novelty. Its history is progressive, and does not consist of arbitrary successions of unrelated interests and agendas. In other words, noteworthy philosophical innovations draw their nourishment from roots that extend into previous efforts and ways of thinking—things that delineate what kinds of future contributions count as genuinely philosophical. For this and other reasons, genuinely philosophical expertise is, like musical and instructional expertise, acquired through extensive periods of practical immersion devoted to learning and refining appropriate habits, attitudes, and inclinations. Good philosophy does not emerge *ab initio* or change with the seasons, in no small part because what constitutes responsible practice is determined by relationships with others who are similarly engaged and whose engagement is importantly shaped by the achievements of predecessors.

The last misconception I will mention here is the assumption that philosophical inquiry is a mere "research methodology"[11]—one set of research techniques and procedures among many; simply an alternative way of organizing and analyzing "data." Philosophy's purview is far more extensive, comprehensive, and foundational than that, and its fabric much more intricate. Whatever its similarity—as a mode of inquiry—to research techniques in general, engaging in philosophy differs in important ways from conducting case studies, developing multiple regression formulas, or testing hypotheses by isolating and manipulating independent variables. Philosophical practice typically deals in abstract, rational reflection, and is concerned with what can be known through different kinds of inquiry. And because it is, as suggested earlier, devoted to the identification, formulation, and analysis of problems—which are fundamental to all research—it is not so much a method or technique as a foundational practice.[12] It contributes in crucial ways to how any and all research is conceptualized, executed, evaluated, and applied to practice. Construing it as a mere research methodology significantly underestimates philosophy's aims, purposes, range, and utility.

WHAT PHILOSOPHY IS

I have identified a number of misconceptions that compromise philosophical inquiry's contributions to music education, leading us to neglect of a tremendously valuable professional resource. Characterizing these misconceptions as I have shows clearly that I have strong convictions about what philosophy is or should be: what distinguishes good philosophy from the not-so-good, or the just plain bad. It might reasonably be expected, then, that I would devote the remainder of this essay to explaining how best to separate philosophical wheat from chaff. However, that is not exactly what I propose to do here. Instead, I want to propose a way of thinking about philosophical inquiry that accommodates the striking diversity actually found in the field and helps correct some of the misconceptions I have just described—as well as others that space does not allow me to address here.

There are many different ways to approach the question of what distinguishes good from bad philosophy, each (my own included) with its advantages and disadvantages and each grounded in different beliefs about what philosophy is and should do. These differences often lead to disputes that non-philosophers mistakenly regard as pointless and professionally embarrassing. The why-can't-we-all-just-get-along criticism of philosophical argumentation involves at least two deeply troubling assumptions: first, that the ways we conceptualize things like music and education are not really all that important (they are not really worth arguing about); and second, that unity is more professionally important than truth. In the first place, what concepts mean are matters of the utmost professional importance; and in the second (and for that very reason), disputes and differences are not liabilities but potentially valuable professional resources, affording opportunities to revise, refine, and extend both our ideas and their attendant actions. To capitalize on these opportunities, however, requires that we think carefully about the nature of philosophical argumentation, the ends it serves when done well, and how best to distinguish its successes from its failures. Because there are no simple answers to these questions, we need different understandings of philosophy than those to which we have grown accustomed: understandings that accommodate difference and debate, and view philosophy as a usefully contested process. Philosophy, I want to argue, is—precisely like music—a *practice*. Or, more accurately, a *diverse human practice*.[13]

Does the idea of philosophy as an open and contested process mean that no one's claims are better than anyone else's? Does that mean in turn that music education philosophy is anything anyone wants it to be, so long as he or she can drum up enough support from like-minded others? I do not believe this is the case, any more than the existence of musical differences renders pointless any discussion of quality. However, it does point us toward issues that warrant our very careful consideration: What *are* human practices? How do they differ, say, from mere activities? What makes and keeps them vital or enables them to thrive, and what threatens their vitality or sustainability? And how might the idea that philosophy is a practice alter how we understand, engage in, and criticize it (what we expect of it)?

THE DISTINCTIVE NATURE OF HUMAN PRACTICES[14]

On a basic level, practices consist in human actions: they are *things people do*. However, people do *many* things, and most of these do not warrant being considered practices.[15] This section will seek, therefore, to identify what I mean when I assert that practices—like philosophy, I am suggesting, but also like music—differ in important ways from mere activities; why practices are not reducible without significant loss to techniques; and why distinctions among practices, technical endeavors, and mere activities are worth drawing carefully.

How do practices differ from other modes of human activity? In the first place, practices involve *actions* not mere *activity*: practical activity is intentional, devoted to the pursuit of ends-in-view. Authentically engaged practitioners embrace means that are intimately related to the practice's proper ends—ends acknowledged by fellow practitioners as the reasons their actions, and embraced by them as the proper way of carrying them out. There is an intimate and dialectical relationship between the ends a practice serves and the ways true practitioners may be expected to pursue them. This relationship is not rule governed, but a consensual, intersubjective affair where what constitutes right or authentic action (action that pursues the right ends, in the right way, to the right extent, and so forth) is subject to interpretation, critique, and continual modification. Accordingly, which of a practice's numerous ends distinguish and define it (which are the ones without which it could no longer exist) and what kinds of action (or whose) most faithfully represent the practice are open questions.

Practices are habitual modes of collective action guided by *ethical*, as distinct from *technical*, considerations.[16] They are intentional, cooperative modes of activity devoted to the attainment of ends whose priority and means of attainment are not set in stone. What constitutes the nerve of a given practice is thus necessarily subject to critical scrutiny and debate; and the resultant dynamic tensions are crucial to a practice's vitality *as a practice*. A practice, Higgins (2012) explains, is a

> socially rooted, complex, coherent, and cooperative activity that grows over time into its own ethical world. . . . What distinguishes a practice

from other activities is the way it becomes home to a distinctive set of answers to the basic ethical questions: What is it excellent to achieve or become? Through participating in a practice, we learn how to appreciate and realize the "internal goods" of the practice, internal because their value can only be articulated in the terms of the practice, can only be appreciated by those who have apprenticed themselves to it, and cannot be cashed out in instrumental terms.

(p. 224)

Dunne's (2005) account focuses on the intricate relationship between the integrity of a practice and its distinctive "ecological" needs—needs according to which it succeeds or fails in "being true or false to its own proper purpose." A practice, he explains, is

a coherent, complex set of activities that has evolved cooperatively and cumulatively over time, that is alive in the community who are its practitioners, and that remains alive only so long as they remain committed to sustaining—and creatively developing and extending—its internal goods and its proper standards of excellence.

(p. 368)[17]

Which goods are internal to a practice, and which are external—which are essential to its integrity as a practice, and which serve ends that, despite their importance, are primarily personal or institutional—are pivotal concerns here. For a practice to remain viable *as a practice,* its external goods—those *not* constitutive of the practice—must not be permitted to eclipse those that *are.* The protection and preservation of a practice's internal goods are thus crucial if it is to continue faithfully serving its characteristic ends. Technical skills, competencies, or proficiencies are clearly important. However, whether these are put to use in service of the practice's characteristic ends or are devoted instead to the pursuit of external goods like money and status depends on practitioners' *virtues of character.* Character virtues, Dunne (2005) observes, are "qualities acquired and exercised by practitioners through their apprenticeship into the practice, their answerability to its standards of excellence, and their submission to the demands of achieving its characteristic ends" (p. 368).

A musical example may help clarify these admittedly abstract claims: disputes as to what constitutes "proper" or "authentic" jazz practice. Among its ardent devotees are many who believe that real jazz practice earns its claim to authenticity through its continuity with its "classic" forbears. To them, tradition has established what all jazz deserving of the name must do and be, and players not steeped in or deferential to tradition are poseurs: engaged in something jazz-like yet not jazz. Others, however, contend that the nerve of all authentic jazz practice consists of novelty, innovation, or creativity—things that necessarily entail departure from norms and conventions. To them, practice rooted in classics is derivative: again, activity resembling jazz, but not the "real" thing. The ends jazz practice exists to serve and the proper ways to act in their service (the nerve of jazz practice and how best to remain true to it) are open and sometimes contentious issues, with opposing sides concerned to protect what they regard as authentic practice from each other's influence. The dialectical push and pull between and between adherents of these rival perspectives is an important part of what keeps jazz practice living, growing, extending itself, while at the same time resisting the notion that anything and everything counts as jazz.

Traditions in which tensions like these have been definitively resolved—in which ends are universally accepted and in which the sole concerns involve the most efficient technical means of achieving them—are practices that are either dying or dead. They are modes of human activity in which specifically *practical* know-how has been reduced to *technical* know-how. To be an authentic *practitioner*, then, is to engage in appropriate actions, intelligently, responsibly, and in light of desired or anticipated consequences. However, in practices—as distinct from technical activities—what "propriety" and "responsibility" involve (by what proper ends they are gauged) are questions whose answers are not set for all times. To become a practitioner is to enter into particular kinds of relationships with contemporary and past practitioners, relationships rooted in shared ethical commitments to sustaining, creatively developing, and extending the practice's proper ends—while what constitutes its proper ends remains an open question.

There are obvious tensions at play here. Practitioners can resist the corrosive and erosive influences of things that threaten to subvert a practice only where there is clarity about its nature. And yet, precisely because practices are complex, and cooperative modes of action whose ends and means require constant adjustment (precisely because practices are dynamic affairs), clarity of purpose cannot be prescriptive or doctrinaire. Practices are not fixed but moving, toward futures that, if they are to be, will emerge from their pasts (and from pasts that will be redefined by their futures). When a practice is healthy, then, it is always and necessarily constituted in part by arguments about (a) the ends it exists properly and fundamentally to serve; about (b) which means do so most effectively; and about (c) the kind of person a practitioner must be in order to contribute to the continued health of the practice. A living practice, writes MacIntyre (1984), is "an historically extended, socially embodied argument precisely about the goods which constitute [it]." Vital practices "embody continuities of conflict" (p. 222).

A thorough explanation of this understanding of practices would require considerably more space than I have here,[18] so this sketch will have to suffice for now. Let me speak, however, to some of the reasons I think it a potentially useful refinement of what we understand music education philosophy to be. First, our infatuation with technical rationality (our shortsighted assumption that technical knowledge is the gold standard of professional know-how) has led us to technicize philosophical practice. To technicize a practice, Dunne explains, is "to make it over in such a way that control over its key operations is maximally assured by a method whose successful implementation can be monitored systematically and unambiguously" (2005, pp. 374–5). The technicization of philosophical practice reduces something properly regarded as a complex, coherent, cumulative, and cooperative mode of ethically guided action to a mere set of techniques and proficiencies, answerable neatly to determinate criteria and nicely amenable to dispensation in brief instructional units. Where practices are reduced to techniques, concerns about ends are set aside in the interest of perfecting means. The result is an undertaking in which the character and practical judgment of the practitioner are replaced by *method*, creating in effect a practitioner-proof mode of knowing and action. Music education philosophy is not a set of technical skills, but a practice: it cannot be rendered technical without compromising many of its most important potentials.

Second, acknowledging philosophy's practical nature helps establish that its characteristic debates and disputes need not be signs of professional weakness or sources of professional embarrassment. They are utterly crucial to its vitality, integrity, and utility as a practice. Nor do philosophy's answers need to be unequivocal, absolute, or final to be useful: the ability to ask better questions is a more characteristic and often more useful outcome of philosophical practice.

Third, since the distinctions between a practice's internal and external goods (between what it truly means to excel as a practitioner and the accrual of benefits that are merely personal or institutional) can easily elude those who have not been inducted into the distinctive ways of being that constitute a given practice,[19] it is imperative that initiation into philosophical practice involve sustained apprenticeship. The habits, dispositions, and abilities crucial to practical know-how are more caught than taught. They are not so much sets of skills to be deployed as manifestations of the kind of person one has become through sustained immersion in the practice and relationships with others who are similarly immersed. Where casual exposure and technical acquaintance are presumed adequate to initiation, the result is ersatz philosophical activity: inspirational rhetoric mistaken for philosophical sophistication; big words and complex sentences mistaken for important philosophical insights; rhetorical flourishes mistaken for practical discernment; activity that benefits the careers of philosophers more than music education. Where the expression of personal opinion is the presumed basis of philosophical inquiry, the results are equally meager. One finds one's philosophical voice not by mastering techniques or through personal introspection but by reading and engaging with philosophers and the philosophical traditions of which they are a part.

Fourth, the viability of philosophical practice in music education (its achievement of the ends on which its existence is predicated; inquiry into how what we know can be used to more fully achieve the future musical and educational needs of society; the creation of a place welcoming and rewarding to those with philosophical propensities) is threatened by anti-rational tendencies within the field and society more broadly. Skepticism toward logic, reason, analysis, and our ability to render rival views commensurable; the reduction of truth to political power; the willful fragmentation of a field fundamentally reliant upon coherence and continuity: each of these undermines the integrity of philosophical practice, diminishing its potential to make discernable and durable differences not just to music education but human flourishing.

Fifth, and in what might wrongly be taken to contradict what I have said about the centrality of debate to vital practices, it is essential that argumentation be undertaken in ways that serve goods internal to philosophical practice. Since, as I have suggested, practices are built around relationships and concerns about the kinds of action that enhance relationships of the right kind, creating and maintaining a culture that welcomes new voices and treats differences in ways that assure they support rather than undermine the sustainability of the practice are crucial concerns. It is imperative that we distinguish between disputes that advance the practice and those that undermine it. In philosophy's case, "being right" and attaining "truth" are not ends that justify any and all means. Debates are not battles in which prevailing over others is the primary objective; indeed, philosophical "victories" achieved in service to a practice's internal goods are by their nature successes that benefit all practitioners by enriching philosophical practice as a whole.

In short, the viability, integrity, and sustainability of practices depend fundamentally upon the habits, attitudes, dispositions, and ultimately the *character* of its practitioners. Practices take their guidance not from rules or codes of conduct, but from ethical concerns about what kind of actions serve their internal goods, and how—and, in turn, about what kind of person it is important to be within the context of the practice at hand. The vitality, relevance, and sustainability of philosophical practice (delivery on its claim to basic status among the kinds of knowledge and action that render music education professional) depend upon the quality of practitioners' contributions. The actions of practitioners, after all, construct practices. And yet, as Dunne (2005) asserts, there is an even greater sense in which practices construct their practitioners (p. 382). To enter into a practice is to enter into particular *kinds of relationships* with fellow-practitioners, and the goods by which we define those relationships (that are, in turn, constitutive of that practice) are *virtues*.

PRACTICE, RIGHT ACTION, AND VIRTUES

Williams (1985) defines virtues as "excellences of character": internalized dispositions of action, desire, and feeling that are "central to the life of practical reason"(p. 35). This relationship between virtues and practices is made even more explicit by MacIntyre (1984), who defines virtue as "an acquired human quality the possession and exercise of which tends to enable us to achieve those goods which are internal to practices and the lack of which effectively prevents us from achieving any such goods" (p. 191). Thus, *virtues are central to practices,* and where they are not valued not only do practices fail to flourish, they become corrupted: their internal goods become confused with and displaced by external ones. Institutions created to serve internal goods become ends in themselves. As we have said, practices rest upon the acceptance by individuals of certain features of particular kinds of social life, and through them the creation of distinctive relationships to other practitioners who are similarly engaged. It is these ways of relating that assure the continued integrity of a practice *as practice* (as distinct from an institution, a set of techniques, or mere imitative activity). Practices thus require that practitioners remain attuned to ethical questions about what kind of person the relationships definitive of the practice necessitate that they be: what kind of action habits they must cultivate and which they must avoid.

What kind of person must a philosophical practitioner be in order to contribute authentically to the ends philosophy exists to serve? What are these ends? And why do they matter? What kinds of habits, dispositions, and (excellences of) character are required of those who practice philosophy, and how may they best be cultivated? What are the virtues of philosophical practice in music education? Daunting though these questions are, and elusive though their answers undoubtedly may be, they are central. The question how to do philosophy well cannot be adequately addressed with lists of criteria, in no small part because the actions it involves are situation-specific. "Right" and "wrong" here take their guidance from the kind of person one is, or, more accurately, from the kind of person one must be to engage in actions that are genuinely philosophical—and, in the case at hand here, educational and musical. Techniques and criteria are unacceptably blunt instruments by comparison.

My earlier claims about things philosophy "is not" may have sounded black and white. I think, though, that closer scrutiny will show that most of the misunderstandings I criticize tend to lie at opposing ends of spectra ranging from too much of a given tendency to too little. Saying what good philosophical work "is" is considerably easier than doing it in precisely the right way—to the right extent, with the right ends in mind, and so on. Identifying unacceptable extremes and deciding upon an apt verbal description for the desired alternative is one thing; but action is another matter. Because we cannot identify the best path between unacceptable extremes in any but a general way, such generalizations are not terribly useful or reliable for choosing the right *course of action* in particular circumstances. Unlike the temperature of the three bears' porridge (too hot, too cool, or just right), what counts as "just right" in practical human realms like philosophy (or music, or education) is seldom neatly determined.

My criticisms of misguided philosophical activity gravitated toward what might be described as vices of excess and deficiency; but I was deliberately evasive about what the "real thing" might be. Good philosophy is, for instance, neither inscrutable (too much complexity) nor simplistic (too little); it is neither purely novel (too little engagement with the insights of others) nor merely derivative (too much reliance upon them); it is neither a slave to logic (too dependent) nor indifferent to rational considerations (too independent); it is neither purely theoretical nor wholly practical; it is neither purely personal nor does is it splash along with the current of common knowledge. But what, in each of these instances, constitutes the optimum solution: the one that most successfully avoids the ways of going wrong? Determining the best course of action in specific situations requires something more reliable and closer at hand than rules and generalizations. That "something," I am suggesting, is character-based ethical judgment.

I make no claim to originality in this claim. Aristotle considered virtues "means" between vices of deficiency and excess.[20] The virtue of courage, for instance, is situated somewhere between vices of cowardice and recklessness. Yet, what constitutes the most courageous course of action in a particular situation cannot be decided in advance, by abstract deliberation: courageous actions are much more easily labeled than done. Similarly, the virtue of generosity lies somewhere between the vices of wastefulness and stinginess; magnanimity lies somewhere between vanity and pusillanimity; temperance lies somewhere between overindulgence and self-abnegation; and so on. What I am suggesting here is that practitioners develop virtues of this kind through their engagement in practices—and more particularly, that practices are the *primary* places where such development occurs. It is through conscientious engagement in practices that we develop the kind of character that enables us to determine right courses of action on the fly. And with specific regard to the practice of philosophical inquiry my point is that what constitutes right action is always a pressing concern, even—perhaps particularly—for those who are most proficient.

To pursue the right thing, in the right way, with the right intent, to the right extent (etc.) requires making highly sensitive action decisions in domains without set tolerances. And yet this is precisely what expert practitioners do, often with remarkable precision and consistency. They do so, I submit, not because of supernatural endowments or adherence to codes of conduct, but because of who they are: because of their intimate acquaintance, through the practice and through relationships with other practitioners, with virtuous courses of action.

With all this as background let me propose a very tentative list of what might be considered philosophical virtues, each followed by the vices of excess and deficiency between which it seems to me the actions of philosophical practitioners must often navigate.

Philosophical Virtue	Vice of Deficiency	Vice of Excess
Rigor (precision, accuracy)	Carelessness, sloppiness	Pedantry
Clarity (careful definition, argumentation)	Obscurity, equivocation, enigma	Gratuitous complexity
Practicality (means guided by ends-in-view, ends related to means)	Merely "theoretical" or academic (preoccupation with ends at expense of means)	Preoccupation with perfecting means (without regard for ends)
Adequate sense of relevant tradition, historically informed	Arbitrary, radically novel, willful, amnesic	Slavish adherence to past, merely derivative
Fairness, justice	Deceit, distortion, dishonesty, misrepresentation	Mindless tolerance, abject relativism, indiscriminate acceptance
Courage, bravery	Cowardice	Rashness, recklessness
Humility, recognition of one's limitations or ignorance	Arrogance, bombast, pretentiousness	Diffidence
Respect	Contempt	Unwarranted veneration, obsequiousness
Responsiveness	Obduracy, aloofness	Tractability, selflessness, submissiveness
Reasonableness	Logocentrism	Irrationality, intemperateness
Consistency	Lability, incoherence	Rigidity, dogmatism
Cooperation, interdependence, dialogue	Isolation, recalcitrance, monologue, solipsism	Blind conformity
Autonomy, self-reliance	Manipulability, dependence	Insularity, alienation

Acting rightly amid concerns like these bears no relationship to painting by numbers. Nor is it purely a matter of rational deliberation: of identifying, refining, and following technical rules. Choosing and maintaining the right or virtuous course among these vices in a particular action situation involves the kind of person one has, as an ethical practitioner, become—and aspires to be. Exactly what kind of philosophical actions are implicated by commitment to any of these virtues singly, in a particular situation, involves complex ethical questions whose answers rely upon: (a) one's understanding of the practice's internal goods; (b) the kind of person the practice requires authentic, responsible practitioners to be; and (c) the extent to which one has become, through one's engagement in the practice, that kind of person. If acting rightly in light and of any single virtue is complex, interactions among various virtues complicate it exponentially.[21] My reasons for stressing this complexity have been, first, that we not reduce philosophical practice (or, for that matter, musical or educational practice) to techniques or sets of skills, or confuse them with institutions created in their service; second, that we ask more critically what conscientious philosophical practice in music education demands of those who engage in it; and third, that we acknowledge richness and breadth of philosophical inquiry's potential benefits for the music education profession.

In what ways has music education philosophy fallen short of these ethical challenges? That is a question well worth debating but one I will not presume to answer conclusively. Let us examine it briefly, however, through the lenses of two characteristics central to practices: cooperation and coherence. Actions that are cooperative involve dispositions like sharing, empathy, and reflexivity. Whether music education philosophy has adequately embraced these is a question I will dodge for now in the interest of posing a few others that show how enormously challenging philosophical practice can be: Cooperation with whom? To what extent? And to what ends? What does music education philosophy share, for instance, with music philosophy (and philosophers)? With educational philosophy (and philosophers)? With feminist theory (and theoreticians)? With philosophy of "art"? With philosophical practice in general? In other words, what is the proper range and purview of music education philosophy? What internal goods do related philosophical practices share with music education philosophy? To what extent and in what way, then, might music education philosophers rightly be expected to engage cooperatively with these others? What, if anything, does music education philosophy bring to the table that these others do not? How diffuse can music education philosophy become, how interconnected with these others, without compromising its own essential coherence as a practice? How does cooperation clarify, and when might it obfuscate or even sever the nerve of the practice of music education philosophy—the awareness essential to preserving its own internal goods?

While these are not inconsequential questions, my primary reason for posing them here is to illustrate their intricate connection to others that are even more basic: What kind of person should a music education philosopher be?[22] Of what is he or she most fundamentally a practitioner and what virtues do one's answers to that question implicate? Whom, or what kind of person, does the practice, as currently constituted, interest or attract or deter? With what professional consequences?

It may be objected—in fact I will be surprised if it is not—that my claim to practical status for music education philosophy is much ado about nothing, and that this is altogether too "thin" a definition to be very useful. I suppose that depends in part on what one expects definitions to accomplish. I have not sought to offer a definition that satisfies technicist predilections, explaining step-by-step and in practitioner-proof terms what philosophy must do and how it must be done. What I have tried to do, rather, is to show that a technical accounting of philosophical inquiry is inadequate. As a practice it involves not just persuasive skill; not just the ability to avoid inferential fallacies; not just the ability to say what one means and to mean what one says—crucial though these undoubtedly are. It involves fundamental considerations about what kind of person one needs, as a philosophical practitioner, to be, and how one's practice of philosophy contributes to those ends.

Doing philosophy well is not just a matter of successfully engaging in logical argument, but is inextricably linked to the one's character. This realization confers additional benefits, not least awareness that philosophical practice is an ethical and ethically guided affair. As such, disagreements are not necessarily or invariably obstacles to be overcome: they may be important features of who we are and of our relationships to others. Approached rightly, disagreements can, as Williams (1985) has observed, shape both our attitudes toward others and our understandings of ourselves: "In relation to other people, we need a view of what is to be opposed, rejected, and so forth, and in what spirit; for ourselves, disagreement can raise a warning that we may be wrong, and if truth or correctness is what we are after, we may need to reform our strategies" (p. 133). Understood this way, philosophical practice in music education is no mere technique, nor is it the spectator sport or blood sport for which we have too often mistaken it. It is, rather, an extraordinarily valuable professional process in whose success all music educators have a stake.

NOTES

1. Please note the use of quotation marks here. I use them because "practical" is commonly, but inappropriately, used in this way. "Technical" would be a more fitting term, for reasons that will become clear in due course.
2. Exposure is often all we seek to accomplish: a strategy that resembles conventional and largely unsuccessful approaches to "music appreciation."
3. Among its many consequences: our casual substitution of philosophies of "art" and "the arts" for philosophy of music education.
4. See Bowman (2005). It might be countered that "better questions" are themselves "products" in a manner of thinking. My point is that philosophical action consists more fundamentally in framing and posing questions than in answering them so as to bring an end to the process.
5. By "ethical" I do *not* mean "moral." Although the differences between these terms are both substantial and important, space does not permit me to explore them here. See Higgins (2011, 2012) and Williams (1985) for illuminating accounts of the distinction.
6. Clearly the claims I will advance here are normative in nature. Because philosophical work clearly exists that contradicts these claims, some might prefer to read these as assertions about philosophy done well, or responsibly. I have written more extensively about some of these issues in Bowman & Frega (2012a, 2012b).
7. This is the "baffle-them-with-BS" strategy.
8. Attributed to H. L. Mencken.
9. This title was not Babbitt's, but that need not concern us here.

10. It might also be argued that it is not particularly fashionable, but if it's not fashion that seems to beg the point.

11. Of course, it can be and has been widely represented as such. My point is not so much that it lacks a specific technique or "method"—although that might well be argued—but that it is not properly understood as one kind or species of research among many. Its roots penetrate deeply into all areas of research, and the shortcomings of many a research project can be traced to neglect of philosophical issues.

12. A claim by Wittgenstein (1958, §133) may warrant consideration here: "There is not *a* philosophical method, though there are indeed methods, like different therapies."

13. Or, perhaps more precisely still, a constellation of diverse human practices, without a single unifying core.

14. The particular understanding of "practice" I advance here is neo-Aristotelian in nature, with intimate connections to virtue ethics. Space constraints prevent extensive elaboration here, but MacIntyre (1984), Dunne (2005), Higgins (2011, 2012), and Bowman & Frega (2012a, 2012b) offer more detailed accounts.

15. Misinformed criticisms of David Elliott's claim that music is fundamentally "something people do" (Elliott, 1995, p. 14) generally fail to grasp that his broader concern lies with the distinctive *kinds* of doings musical *practices* involve. That music involves human activity is but the beginning of an argument pursuing a much more significant point.

16. This is not to say that practices cannot draw upon technical considerations, only that the latter are not constitutive. Please note once again my concern that "ethical" not be equated with "moral." See note 5.

17. That practices are cumulative pertains in important ways to my claim that philosophy is not fashion. The claim to creative extension reminds us that what constitutes right action differs between practices, changes over time, and is necessarily open to criticism.

18. Fortunately, excellent explanations can be found elsewhere. See especially MacIntyre (1984), Dunne (1997, 2005), and Higgins (2011, 2012).

19. These can also easily elude would-be practitioners whose engagement is technical rather than practical.

20. Although I will draw on this Aristotelian view in what follows, I do not embrace the idea that virtues are "means" in any but a broad, metaphorical sense. The right course of action in practical situations cannot be specified without careful context-specific considerations, and the notion that right action consists invariably in moderation is a depressing one.

21. Indeed, a three dimensional representation of these interrelationships and tensions would better exemplify their ethical nature than my two dimensional chart.

22. Note that this question is less about how one should write than how one should live; more, it might be said, about being than knowing.

REFERENCES

Babbitt, M. (1958, February). Who cares if you listen? *High Fidelity.*

Bowman, W. (2005). More inquiring minds, more cogent questions, more provisional answers: The need to theorize music education—and its research. *Music Education Research, 7*(2), 153–68.

Bowman, W., & Frega, A. L. (2012a). What should the music education profession expect of philosophy? In W. Bowman & A. L. Frega (Eds.), *The Oxford handbook of philosophy in music education* (pp. 17–36). New York, NY: Oxford University Press.

Bowman, W., & Frega, A. L. (2012b). But is it philosophy? In W. Bowman & A.L. Frega (Eds.), *The Oxford handbook of philosophy in music education* (pp. 495–507). New York, NY: Oxford University Press.

Dunne, J. (1997). *Back to the rough ground: Practical judgment and the lure of technique.* Notre Dame, IN: University of Notre Dame Press.

Dunne, J. (2005). An intricate fabric: Understanding the rationality of practice. *Pedagogy, Culture and Society, 13*(3), 367–89.

Elliott, D. (1995). *Music matters.* New York, NY: Oxford University Press.

Higgins, C. (2011). *The good life of teaching: An ethics of professional practice.* Oxford, UK: Wiley-Blackwell.

Higgins, C. (2012). The impossible profession. In W. Bowman & A.L. Frega (Eds.), *The Oxford handbook of philosophy in music education* (pp. 213–230). New York, NY: Oxford University Press.

MacIntyre, A. (1984). *After virtue.* Notre Dame, IN: University of Notre Dame Press.

Williams, B. (1985). *Ethics and the limits of philosophy.* Cambridge, MA: Harvard University Press.

Wittgenstein, L. (1958). *Philosophical investigations* (G. E. M. Anscombe, Trans.). New York, NY: Macmillan.

Part II

Making Sense of Our Tools

6 The Shifting Locus of Musical Experience from Performance to Recording to New Media

Some Implications for Music Education

Matthew Thibeault

When stories of music in the 20th Century are told, the importance of sound recordings will be central to their plots. Certain concerts will, of course, also be remembered, such as the 1913 Paris premiere of the *Rite of Spring*, Marian Anderson's 1939 recital on the steps of the Lincoln Memorial, and the Woodstock Music and Art Fair of 1969. But it is impossible to think about music of the past hundred years without an essential place for recordings: Enrico Caruso's 78s, Louis Armstrong's Hot Five and Hot Seven recordings, the ten thousand recordings made by Duke Ellington, and the Beatles and the British Invasion. Recordings also afforded musical realms built from recordings, such as hip-hop sampling and techno music. The more recent extension of recordings into new media represents the latest extension of the possibilities of circulation and creation via sound recording. One cannot credibly tell the story of our century's music without sound recordings, the emergence of which is the central concern of the present article.

Recordings are not merely a way to store music and make it more accessible; they are a catalyst for profound changes in music, musician, and audience. In this sense, *sound recording* is a blanket term meant to invoke both media and the networks that constitute them—media such as the gramophone, radio, and MP3; and the networks of each medium, assemblages of people, practices, institutions, and technologies. This understanding of sound media as contingent networks of recurring relations builds on work in sound studies, especially Sterne (2003, 2012a). This particular approach also resonates with educational efforts to study technological change from a pragmatic philosophical perspective, a Deweyan approach with a strong contemporary literature (Hickman, 2001; Waddington, 2010).

Before moving forward with an account of the shifting locus, it is important to acknowledge the many other writers who have considered technological shifts and their relationship to art, a rich intellectual heritage that informs the present account. Benjamin (1935/1968) provided a Marxist accounting of art in the rising age of technological reproduction, finding a withering of works with aura and a rise in a doctrine of art for art's sake. McLuhan (1962/2008; 1964/2003) theorized that each era was dominated by a particular sense, such as the dominance of the visual sense in the print age, or our current audile-tactile "field of electronic all-at-onceness" (1962/2008, p. 63). Heidegger (1954/1977) presented technology as a framework for being, within which humans were reduced to standing resources, with art as an antidote to this reduction of being. Borgmann (1984), following Heidegger, developed the *device paradigm* to convey the process by which technology reduces once-rich focal practices such as playing the piano, to always-available commodities—recordings provided by devices such as speakers. Attali (1977/1985) provides a sweeping account of shifting networks in the political economy of music, from the ritual and sacrificial origins through a network of representation made possible by sheet music, then to the repeating network of recordings, finally heralding a coming network of composition that he relates to free jazz.

While many writers explore change as a progression wherein technological changes and advances contribute to shifting practices, others, notably ethnomusicologists, have discussed these innovations without such directionality. Nettl (2005) discusses modes of musical transmission: from aural, to written, to printed, to recorded, noting, "These could even represent a chronological order, valid for Western civilization, but it is also a continuum of relationships, from close to distant, among composer, performer, and listener" (p. 292). Turino (2008) presents a four-field framework based on Peirce's semiotics: participatory and presentational musical fields within live music practices, and high fidelity and studio audio art musical fields for recorded music. Like Nettl, Turino stresses the possibility for all fields to be present and active, to ebb and flow, while noting a progression in places such as the United States and Zimbabwe, where the pressures of a capitalist system for commodification favor the easily commodified presentational and high fidelity fields.

While each of the previous accounts provide tools and conceptions for making sense of the profound changes in music over the past hundred years, central to educators are the experiences of young people in their daily lives, which are explored here through the gradual but profound shifting locus of musical experience. Figure 6.1 provides a visual overview of the basic argument. The ways that music was most commonly experienced in the Western world shifted over one hundred years; from face-to-face live performance, to recordings (which we might refer to today as analog media), and currently to new media—perhaps most memorable when shortened to a shift from performance to recording to data. Whereas nearly all musical experience was once had in the physical presence of live performers, today nearly all musical experience comes through sound recordings experienced via new media. The Kaiser Family Foundation (Rideout, Foerh, & Roberts, 2010) estimates that school-age children in the United States spend nearly eight hours of each day engaging with media, and a recent survey by Neilsen Media (2012) found that "more teens listen to music through YouTube than through any other source (64%)" (p. 1).

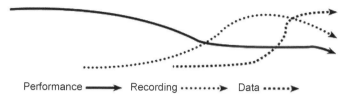

Figure 6.1 A conceptual visualization of the shift in the locus of musical experience over the 20th century from performance to recording to data. Former loci of experience persist, but it is argued that musical habits are heavily influenced by the dominant locus, an influence that changes the context and meaning of older loci.

What makes the shifting locus compelling for educators is the relation of experience to habit formation in the educational process. Habit has been a central concern for pragmatic philosophers and psychologists discussing education, including James (1899) and Dewey (1938/1963). Turino uses habit to discuss learning, proposing "a unitary framework for thinking about the concepts of *self, identity,* and *culture* in relation to each other—a framework based on the focal concept of *habits*" (p. 94). Habits both flow from and are shaped by our experiences, and as Turino notes, habits are central for the richer notions of self, identity, and culture.

As the locus of musical experience has shifted from performance to recording to data, there has been a change in the ways in which musical experiences were had and the subjective meanings of musical experience. Attention to the locus brings attention not to the moment a technology emerges, but to when that technology has become a widespread component of experience. While sound recording can be dated back to the 1857 invention of the phonautograph, this paper focuses on the early 20th century as the period when sound recording flourished, rapidly becoming more ubiquitous over several decades through innovations in the gramophone, phonograph, film, and broadcast radio. Technologies gain importance for consideration by educators as they become a part of everyday life, as they become a likely part of the experiences that beget habits.

The locus also reminds us not to focus on the technology in isolation, but as part of a larger network of people, practices, institutions, and technologies. Just as Benjamin (1935/1968) wrote of an *age* of mechanical reproduction, thereby indicating changes that would reach perhaps all aspects of art and not only the works that were reproduced, so we can find implications for the locus in areas that appear less technological. Even a concert choir should be understood as deeply enmeshed with the shifting locus: from new competition for audience time outside and inside the concert hall; to audiences who expect more of performers, having heard so much edited, perfected, and now Auto-Tuned music; and to the social significance of that concert as the world around it changes. This kind of attention to the shifting locus invites us to explore the implications of Marx's famous words, "The forming of the five senses is a labor of the entire history of the world down to the present" (Marx & Engels, 1844/1988, p. 108).

The shifting locus provides a fit for music educators who need to come to terms with technology without losing the social and educational dimensions, and who require richer causal accounts of technology that go beyond technological determinism (Ruthmann et al., 2015; Smith & Marx, 1994). While there are many possible approaches to understanding the enmeshment of music, technology, and education, the particular needs of educators are here foregrounded by focusing on the enmeshment of people, practices, institutions, and technologies as they become ubiquitous enough to form the basis of habits. Whether one wishes to resist or embrace this shifting locus, the conceptualization presented in this article can help music educators organize action and begin to make sense of the fact that to perform in the world now involves different values and practices than to have done so when performance was the locus of musical experience.

The view of the shifting locus is derived here from two short stories where music plays a central but contrasting role, and the exploration of the careers of three musicians whose work is both held in high regard and emblematic, perhaps even a prototype, of each locus. The view of the performance locus comes through James Joyce's (1914/1969) story "The Dead." The skeptical resistance to recording is captured through an examination of John Philip Sousa's (1906) essay, "The Menace of Mechanical Music." Glenn Gould's writings and interviews allow a shift to the evangelistic adoption of the possibilities of recording, and the full extent of the data locus of today is achieved through an examination of Richard Powers's (2008) story "Modulation." Fiction provides not only rich accounts, but the opportunity to take into consideration the cultural and subjective side of sound from the perspective of those who lived within those cultures. As noted by Bijsterveld (2008), introducing her study of the problem of public noise, "Our challenge, then, is to historicize the sensory experience of sound and to listen to the sounds of technology through the ears of those people who complained about these sounds" (p. 26). This follows also the spirit of work by Schafer (1977/1994), whose World Soundscape Project created a database of thousands of accounts and mentions of sound in literature. The article closes with a recapitulation of the ways that music educators might begin to take more seriously the reality of teaching and making music within the new media era.

THE PERFORMANCE LOCUS AS DEPICTED
IN JAMES JOYCE'S "THE DEAD"

James Joyce's (1914/1969) "The Dead," the final story in his collection *Dubliners*, offers a glimpse of the world just before sound recording became a ubiquitous part of everyday life. Published in 1914, Joyce wrote "The

Dead" in 1907, and set the story during a dinner held on Epiphany in 1904. To read Joyce's story is to be immersed in a time when music was nearly always experienced through face-to-face live performance.

In "The Dead," Gabriel Conroy and his wife Gretta attend the annual dance given by his Aunts Kate and Julia Morkin. Both sisters are singers and music teachers. The story is built around musical moments such as this one, where Joyce describes pianist Mary Jane's accompaniment of Aunt Julia [all quotes retain Joyce's unique spelling and punctuation]:

> A murmur in the room attracted his attention. Mr Browne was advancing from the door, gallantly escorting Aunt Julia, who leaned upon his arm, smiling and hanging her head. An irregular musketry of applause escorted her also as far as the piano and then, as Mary Jane seated herself on the stool, and Aunt Julia, no longer smiling, half turned so as to pitch her voice fairly into the room, gradually ceased. Gabriel recognised the prelude. It was that of an old song of Aunt Julia's—*Arrayed for the Bridal.* Her voice, strong and clear in tone, attacked with great spirit the runs which embellish the air and though she sang very rapidly she did not miss even the smallest of the grace notes. To follow the voice, without looking at the singer's face, was to feel and share the excitement of swift and secure flight. Gabriel applauded loudly with all the others at the close of the song and loud applause was borne in from the invisible supper-table. It sounded so genuine that a little colour struggled into Aunt Julia's face as she bent to replace in the music-stand the old leather-bound song-book that had her initials on the cover. Freddy Malins, who had listened with his head perched sideways to hear her better, was still applauding when everyone else had ceased and talking animatedly to his mother who nodded her head gravely and slowly in acquiescence. At last, when he could clap no more, he stood up suddenly and hurried across the room to Aunt Julia whose hand he seized and held in both his hands, shaking it when words failed him or the catch in his voice proved too much for him.
>
> (1914/1969, pp. 244–5)

In "The Dead," this performance is at the foreground of the party. The moment captures three key aspects of the performance era: house-music culture, the skills of performers who only knew music through performance, and the skills of listeners to appreciate performances. These aspects, emanating from the physical presence of the performers, draw the attention of the partygoers from even the supper-table in the next room.

House-music culture thrived throughout Europe until the rise of recording, a culture where amateur music making formed a central part of an evening's entertainment (Philip, 2004). Now largely forgotten, the need and desire to make music in the home was filled through performances of a mix of professionals and amateurs. Philip details how even the most accomplished composers arranged their music for amateurs:

> Brahms himself understood the importance of this market as a way of enabling his public to get to know his works. He wrote more than twenty piano-duet arrangements of orchestral and chamber works, and also arranged the third and fourth symphonies for two pianos.
>
> (2004, p. 7)

Rather than today's occasional performances, performers regularly made music. From the turn of Aunt Julia toward the audience, to her old songbook, Joyce portrays her comfort as a regular performer. She *connects* with her audience. She feels their appreciation, blushing at their applause. The bond between performer and audience, their unity in space and time, connects them in the way music was then experienced. The songbook's appearance is a testament to heavy use, reinforced by Gabriel's recognition of the tune from his aunt's previous performances.

The ephemeral nature of live performance encouraged attentive listening. Joyce details for the reader Gabriel's attention to tone quality and "the smallest of grace notes" which allow him to "share the excitement of swift and sure flight." The performance ends with Freddy's compliments to Aunt Julia. The audience connects with the singer through listening but also socially and even physically. Julia's performance is, for this particular audience, with them, and comes and goes in a moment, echoing Karl Marx's (1861/1975) statement:

> The service a singer performs for me satisfies my aesthetic needs, but what I enjoy exists only in an action inseparable from the singer himself [sic], and once his work, singing, has come to an end, my enjoyment is also at an end; I enjoy the activity itself—its reverberation in my ear.
>
> (pp. XXI)

Given the unique and ephemeral realities of music in the performance age, memory is all-important for musical experiences to live on. In "The Dead," talk around the table turns to voices remembered and those now gone:

> —O, well, said Mr Bartell D'Arcy, I presume there are as good singers to-day as there were then.
> —Where are they? asked Mr Browne defiantly.
> —In London, Paris, Milan, said Mr Bartell D'Arcy warmly. I suppose Caruso, for example, is quite as good, if not better than any of the men you have mentioned.
> —Maybe so, said Mr Browne. But I may tell you I doubt it strongly.
> —O, I'd give anything to hear Caruso sing, said Mary Jane.

—For me, said Aunt Kate, who had been picking a bone, there was only one tenor. To please me, I mean. But I suppose none of you ever heard of him.

—Who was he, Miss Morkan? asked Mr Bartell D'Arcy politely.

—His name, said Aunt Kate, was Parkinson. I heard him when he was in his prime and I think he had then the purest tenor voice that was ever put into a man's throat.

—Strange, said Mr Bartell D'Arcy. I never even heard of him.

—Yes, yes, Miss Morkan is right, said Mr Browne. I remember hearing of old Parkinson but he's too far back for me.

(p. 254)

Unlike Mr. Browne, it hardly makes sense to ask *where* good singers are today. Today, musical voices are always everywhere, digitally available at all times. For Joyce's characters, the best singers were most commonly heard in centers of power and commerce. Ironically, Mary Jane longs to hear Caruso, who in 1904 was just beginning to record under his first contract, soon to become the most famous recorded voice. Unlike the disappeared voice of Parkinson, and while not as Mary Jane hoped, everyone today and forevermore can hear Caruso.

Joyce's story evokes how performers and their efforts continued to exist within the memories of the living. This aspect of music, the emotional memories that persist, is key to the central epiphany of "The Dead." As Gabriel and his wife are preparing to leave, he sees her at the top of the staircase, transfixed by a singer he cannot hear over the din of the rest of the party. She is listening as someone sings *The Lass of Aughrim*. Back at their hotel, Gretta reveals that the song had been sung to her by Michael Furey, a past love who died when young. The final words of the story capture Gabriel's thoughts as he looks at the snow falling outside his window:

It was falling, too, upon every part of the lonely churchyard on the hill where Michael Furey lay buried. It lay thickly drifted on the crooked crosses and headstones, on the spears of the little gate, on the barren thorns. His soul swooned slowly as he heard the snow falling faintly through the universe and faintly falling, like the descent of their last end, upon all the living and the dead.

(p. 286)

The ephemeral nature of music in Joyce's time provided an ideal metaphor for the ephemeral nature of life, something all his readers would intimately know. Every musician and every performance of that era became a shade, at best a memory in the minds of those who also must pass. For Gretta, the experience of hearing *The Lass of Aughrim* reconnected her to Michael Furey and the loving friendship they shared, his singing gone but for her memory. The experience of music was inseparable from the ephemeral nature of life. Performance was unique, live, in person, and unamplified in a way that encouraged close listening and connection. The work of learning and making music required teachers whose students apprenticed and worked together, and the party at Aunt Kate and Julia's home in "The Dead" captures the friendship and pleasure that accompany this work, the social and physical connections that were inseparable from every experience with music. As Philip notes about music and audiences before the rise of recordings, "It did not come to them with the press of a button. Music was therefore not just an aural experience, as it has largely become. It was also a matter of physical presence, social interaction, and direct communication between musicians and audience" (2004, p. 5).

"The Dead" brings us closer to a time today's readers cannot know, a time when the experience of music was fundamentally different from ours, and a time when musical sensibility must also have been profoundly different. Although we still have recordings of performances from that time, the network of music and social relationships that flourished when only live performance existed, it can be argued, is so changed as to be dead to us save for the collective memory and echoes of its existence. We can have Caruso's voice, but not the experience of sitting around the table recalling voices forever gone save in our memories, nor can we listen with ears that know each performance is ephemeral. In place of the ephemeral nature of music in "The Dead" we have what Stanyck and Piekut (2010) refer to as *deadness*, a quality of music today that flows from recordings that allow a perpetual reengagement of the living and the dead exemplified through duets such as between Natalie Cole and her father after his death, about which the authors write, "We might even say that this is the only guarantee that sound recording offers: being recorded means being enrolled in futures (and pasts) that one cannot wholly predict nor control" (p. 18).

Music in "The Dead" required a physical communion, the presence of performers and an audience united within a moment that will never come again. Much of the poignancy in Joyce's tale—the blushing cheek, the holding of hands, and the remembrance of past moments—derives from the uniqueness of the performance moment. Performance required constant social organization to learn, make, and share music. The scale was limited to the distance by which the music could be reasonably enjoyed, seldom more than an amphitheater for voices skilled at projection. Audiences always knew that each performance was a unique opportunity, and that to neglect it was to miss it forever. And audiences were limited to local performances, wishing to "give anything" to hear the voice of Caruso. While it is possible to regard this solely with nostalgia, it is also a reminder of how scarce music was, and how it was often available to the powerful and wealthy.

For musicians whose wants, needs, values, and practices were shaped by the performance locus, the rise of recordings could be seen as a threat to central aspects of music as they knew it. No one wrote more passionately about what might be lost than John Philip Sousa.

SOUSA AS SKEPTIC OF THE RECORDING ERA

A year before Joyce began writing "The Dead," John Philip Sousa wrote his infamous critique of recording technology and the potential threats to live performance, "The Menace of Mechanical Music" (1906). As Katz (2012) notes, "Given Sousa's prominence in early twentieth-century American culture and the widespread discussion that his article generated, it is fair to say that he, more than anyone else, set the terms of the debate about the value and influence of sound-reproducing technologies" (p. 462). Just as reading Joyce helps tell the story of the performance era, Sousa's views allow us to better understand the apprehension and sense of imposition felt as recordings worked their way into the world and interacted with people to change the wants, needs, values and practices around music. Sousa also clearly articulates versions of several key positions that live on in many music educators' philosophies today.

Sousa dealt with *mechanical music*—player pianos as well as phonographs and cylinder players. Throughout his essay, he draws a sharp distinction between live music and recorded music. For Sousa, machine music could never convey the essential human component. From the opening sentence, machines are portrayed as displacing human thinking, interpreting, and performing:

> Sweeping across the country with the speed of a transient fashion in slang or Panama hats, political war cries or popular novels, comes now the mechanical device to sing for us a song or play for us a piano, in substitute for human skill, intelligence, and soul.
>
> (1906, p. 278)

Sousa is at his most poetic when proclaiming the connection between live performance and musical value, championing experiences like those captured by Joyce:

> Music teaches all that is beautiful in this world. Let us not hamper it with a machine that tells the story day by day, without variation, without soul, barren of the joy, the passion, the ardor that is the inheritance of man alone.
>
> (1906, p. 282)

For Sousa, soul, humanity, and intelligence can exist in music when made live, but not when bleached out by machines that present music without any variation. He also located humanity in variations that naturally occur in each unique presentation of music. To estrange music from live performance separates it not only from human performers, but results in music devoid of all humanity, exchanging soul for the same story day by day.

Sousa predicted that musical taste would suffer should machine music proliferate its emaciated conception of music. He wrote, "I forsee a marked deterioration in American music and musical taste . . . by virtue—or rather by vice—of the multiplication of music-reproducing machines" (p. 278). He saw the history of music in terms of the enhanced expression of the human soul, worrying that people's experiences would be limited to machines, "which are as like real art as the marble statue of Eve is like her beautiful, living, breathing daughters" (p. 279). Seen from Sousa's rich notion of musical connection, mechanical music, and the ersatz experience it provided would naturally cramp and deaden living musicians. His examples evoke displacement and replacement across the range of musicians: infants put to sleep by machinery, love songs caroled by gramophone, soldiers rallied to battle by "a huge phonograph, mounted on a 100 H.P. automobile" (p. 282).

The envisioned decline in taste and the gradual displacement of human musicians led Sousa to predict problems for music education. These problems existed both through the damage machine music would inflict upon taste, as well as the continued displacement of amateur musicians in the face of the effortlessness with which music was recreated by machines; essentially, the decline of house-music culture. Sousa located a love of music among the working classes, evidenced by their purchase and study of instruments like the guitar, mandolin, and banjo. He goes on to declare:

> The cheaper of these instruments of the home are no longer being purchased as formerly, and all because the automatic devices are usurping their places. . . . And what is the result? The child becomes indifferent to practice, for when music can be heard in the homes without the labor of study and close application, and without the slow process of acquiring a technic [sic], it will be simply a question of time when the amateur disappears entirely, and with him a host of vocal and instrumental teachers, who will be without field or calling.
>
> (p. 280)

Sousa worried that those who might continue to play would experience mechanical music to such an extent to cause irreparable harm. Sousa warned that real music would cease to exist, or that those attempting to make it would see their efforts hampered by exposure to music without humanity:

> Children are naturally imitative, and if, in their infancy, they hear only phonographs, will they not sing, if they sing at all, in imitation and finally become simply human phonographs—without soul or expression?
>
> (p. 281)

Sousa's sense of music grew from the ritual and spectacle of live performance, and Warfield (2011) argues that his approach to performance was heavily shaped by his work in the theaters of Washington, D.C. Sousa so disdained recordings that he famously refused to conduct his band for any recording dates or broadcasts until 1929, three years before his death. He articulated strong beliefs and a coherent view of the ways recorded music might negatively impact the musical world he knew and loved. Today, as we begin to imagine how different music was for Sousa and Joyce, their writings allow us to imagine how strange our world would have sounded to them.

Anecdotally, when working with preservice teachers and graduate students, most agree with Sousa. Their values emanate from habits of performance, and they continue to privilege their work within a network of practices built on performances with sheet music. I frequently hear comments about how one can't judge a performer or know a work until heard live, and that recordings often allow edits they consider a form of cheating. But few go quite as far as Sousa did. Most are thrilled and honored to participate in the recording sessions their ensemble directors have arranged. And though students may still favor live over recorded music, few would deny humanity and soul to recordings such as Louis Armstrong's "What a Wonderful World."

The first half of this paper presented views from those who lived through the rise of sound recording technology. Joyce and Sousa's ideas about music were born out of the performance locus, and they lived on through the emergence of recordings. Although recordings were immediately popular, it was not until the 1960s that musicians, born and raised in the recording era, did come to appreciate and understand the artistic and aesthetic possibilities of the recording era. Many began to appreciate and sing the praises of that which Sousa had feared so much, though none more eloquently than Glenn Gould.

GLENN GOULD AS EVANGELIST OF THE RECORDING ERA

One can't find a more emphatic rejection of performance than by Glenn Gould, who in an interview in 1981 declared:

> The concert has been *replaced,* you know. . . . Technology has the capability to create a climate of anonymity and to allow the artist the time and the freedom to prepare his conception of a work to the best of his ability, to perfect a statement without having to worry about trivia like nerves and finger slips. It has the capability of replacing those awful and degrading and humanly damaging uncertainties which the concert brings with it; it takes the specific personal performance information out of the musical experience. Whether the performer is going to climb the musical Everest on this particular occasion no longer matters. And it's for that reason that the word "immoral" comes into the picture. It's a difficult area—one where aesthetics touch upon theology, really—but I think that to have technology's capability and not to take advantage of it and create a contemplative climate if you can—*that* is immoral!
>
> (Gould, 1984a, p. 452)

Recordings completely replaced the concert for Gould in his work—he famously retreated from the stage forever in 1964, both as a performer and as an audience member. He spent the rest of his life making music in the studio. Fifty years after Sousa fought to keep performance alive in the emerging networks of recording, Gould completely rejected live music. Sousa, then, is the Cassandra of the early recording age, and Gould, with his complete embrace of recording, is a herald of a world where music can exist completely outside face-to-face performance. Their respective orientations toward recording expose fundamentally changed conceptions of music, musician, and audience as the locus of experience and habit shifted from performance to recorded networks.

Of course, attitudes toward recording changed in part due to advances in recording technology. Sousa's band had to arrange itself around a single microphone; Gould used multiple microphones for even a single piano. Sousa's band recorded using a mechanical process; Gould used the more sensitive electronic recording techniques that became available after 1925. Bands in Sousa's time could not splice together takes, while Gould artfully spliced. Stereo recordings replaced the monaural soundscape with a three-dimensional panorama for the listener. Finally, Gould had access to long-play records, allowing for much longer works to be captured and shared. As recordings became more prevalent, and as technical advantages expanded, wants, needs, values, and practices also evolved. Gould, perhaps better than anyone, understood and articulated a far-reaching new conception radically different from any that could have emerged through live performance alone.

Whereas Aunt Julia was in the room and intimately connected to Gabriel and Freddy as she sang *Arrayed for the Bridal,* had she made a recording she would have been separated from her audience. Recordings gained permanence while losing the traditional connection. As Benjamin (1935/1968) noted, this is analogous to the difference between an actor on stage and one in a film. On stage, an ephemeral connection exists between audience and performer, and the performer can respond to the audience. By contrast, a film actor may be filmed in multiple takes, perhaps from multiple angles, and often out of sequence from the final film. For Benjamin, with regard to the final product of the film, "During the shooting [the actor] has as little contact with it as any article made in a factory" (p. 231).

Just as films found advantage in estrangement, Gould envisioned benefits Sousa did not. Two years before he stopped performing, Gould published the essay "Let's Ban Applause," wherein he stated, "I have come to the conclusion, most seriously, that the most efficacious step which could be taken in our culture today would be the gradual but total elimination of audience response" (1962/1984b, p. 246). Given the estrangement of recordings, it would seem that Gould supposed concerts and recordings could be brought into harmony by trying to import the estrangement of recordings into the concert hall via what he called GPAADAK, or the Gould Plan for the Abolition of Applause and Demonstrations of All Kinds (p. 248). Furthermore,

Gould explicitly invokes the example of listening to a recording as a template for concert etiquette in countering the claim that applause is a natural response to a performance:

> I reply that one may listen to a recording of a Beethoven symphony alone or in the company of friends and, though deeply moved at its conclusion, experience no more urgent need than a quick trip to the icebox for a soda water.
>
> (p. 247)

Gould's embrace of estrangement between audience and performer would have shocked Sousa, and this shift is a central ground for my claim that it is worthwhile to distinguish the performance locus from that of recording. To embrace estrangement in exchange for repeatability is not merely to create a new space for music; live, face-to-face performance is also consequently changed. Audience and performer come into a live situation with habits of estranged listening acquired through experience with recordings, and one may both speculate that they may be better prepared by knowing pieces, but also perhaps less attentive than those who knew each listening would be ephemeral and music scarce. Perhaps they want a similar experience to recordings, or perhaps they have never developed the habits of connection that were natural to Sousa and Joyce. The habits that shaped musical ideas were formed in experience with music that was live or recorded in consequential ways.

Isolated sound and the appreciation of a purely sonic object fill the void left by the estrangement of recordings. Without a connection between audience and performer or even the visual element of music in recordings, music increasingly became associated with the idea of a sonic object. Sousa's disdain for a story told the same way day by day naturally resulted in a focus upon the story's telling, the sound. Philip (2004) captures how musicians, left only with sound and their audible mistakes etched forever for all to hear, increasingly valued flawless and repeatable performances over spontaneity and surprise. As with estrangement, the new aesthetic worked its way into the live setting. Live performances increasingly aspired to match the perfection that recordings made possible.

What makes Gould valuable here is his ability to understand the positive potential within these changes. What were horrible problems for Sousa became amazing possibilities for Gould. In Gould's opinion, recordings allowed for the realization of a new aesthetic. By fully embracing the changed conception of music, recording became the locus of musical achievement, with performance a distant second, as he said in an interview:

> From the moment I began broadcasting, *that* medium seemed like another world, as indeed it is. The moment I began to experience the studio environment, my whole reaction to what I could do with music

under the proper circumstances changed totally. From then on, concerts were less than second best—they were merely something to be gotten through. They were a very poor substitute for a real artistic experience.

(Mach, 1991, p. 90)

As Gould's prominence rose, he made real the opportunity to live life as a musician who never performed, focusing instead on the creation of edited and engineered recordings which are among the most celebrated in the history of the medium, with one of his recordings receiving intergalactic distribution on the Voyager space probe's Golden Record. He achieved a complete de-coupling of music from live performance, championing such aspects of recording as the tape splice and the deeper exploration of sonic spaces made possible by multiple microphones.

While Gould wished to ban applause, he had an expanded view of opportunities for the listener of recordings. Gould was attuned to the fact that, even through manipulation of the humble volume knob, listeners were able to interact with music as never before. He foresaw the techniques of the recording studio engineer eventually becoming available to the listener:

At the center of the technological debate, then, is a new kind of listener— a listener more participant in the musical experience. The emergence of this mid-twentieth-century phenomenon is the greatest achievement of the record industry.

(1966/1984c, p. 347)

Participant listeners, Gould foresaw, could be granted the same options that allowed engineers to mix multiple takes, to speed up or slow down a take, to add effects such as reverb, etc. This was a gradual evolution that began with the binary ability to turn a recording on or off, followed by the ability to adjust playback volume, then to apply equalization. In the end, "There is, in fact, nothing to prevent a dedicated connoisseur from acting as his own tape editor and, with these devices, exercising such interpretive predilections as will permit him to create his own ideal performance" (p. 348). In fact, Gould's prediction became a reality perhaps most famously through the work of Joyce Hatto, a pianist who, it was revealed, had released dozens of recordings that were lightly remixed and edited versions of other pianists' recordings (Singer, 2007). Again, of course, the ideal performance consists of a sonic object, but Gould radically locates its genesis in the recompiling and manipulation of recordings by listeners who would participate in a new way. Out of the estrangement of the listener come new abilities to participate.

Gould was familiar enough with the musical world to know that the idea of a participant listener represented a substantial shift in power: "[The listener] is also, of course, a threat, a potential usurper of power, an uninvited guest at the banquet of the arts, one whose presence threatens the familiar hierarchical setting of the musical establishment" (1966/1984c, p. 347).

The consideration of Gould's views provided up to this point reveals the changes in music, musician, and audience made possible by the emergence of the recording era. The recording audience lost the connection of the performance era, but gained the ability to be a participant in a new way through participation with recordings. The estrangement of recordings that separated performer from audience helped to usher in the notion of music as sonic object, leading to a conception of music more sonic than social. This change in the status of music accompanied changes in musicians akin to actors on the stage and in film. Sousa and Joyce exemplify the values of music in the performance locus, while Gould sees the new conception of music and new relationships between performers and audiences made possible by recordings.

Gould also went beyond the recording era with his vision for music. The kinds of experiences he foresaw that listeners would be able to construct did not become widespread until the rise of music and computers. Happening gradually over the past 30 years or so, this rise represents the emergence of a new media era of music. Lev Manovich (2002) defines the term "new media" as the convergence of computing and media technology. In his words, this represents "the translation of all existing media into numerical data accessible through computers—the result is new media—graphics, moving images, sounds, shapes, spaces, and texts that have become computable; that is, they comprise simply another set of computer data" (p. 20).

The rise of new media connected music to computers in ways that amplified and transformed aspects of music that originated in the recording era. Computers made the tools and experiences that had been limited to corporations and studios affordable and available to a greater audience, with a few thousand dollars enough to set up a good quality home recording studio. The Internet also provides an inexpensive distribution network by which artists can quickly connect to audiences without a record contract. But just as Sousa couldn't foresee the ramifications of the recording era, it is likely that Gould would be surprised with the locus around new media that was only beginning to emerge when he died in 1982.

THE NEW MEDIA ERA AS DEPICTED IN RICHARD POWERS'S "MODULATION"

Just as James Joyce evoked the performance locus, Richard Powers's short story "Modulation," written one hundred years after "The Dead," richly represents the dense network of music via the Internet and new media:

> A Korean kid covering a Taiwanese kid whose arrangement imitated the video game *Pump it Up* whose soundtrack mimicked an old Brian Eno performance uploads an electrifying guitar video of Pachelbel's Canon in D, already the most hacked-at piece of the last three hundred years,

and immediately, people from Panama to Turkmenistan post hundreds
of shot-perfect recreations, faithful down to every detail of tempo and
ornament.

(2008, p. 98)

This quote captures much about the new media world: a drastic rate
of change as connections are made across the globe, mixing and mash-
ing of music drawn from hundreds of years of history, and the rise of an
amateur culture of creativity that blurs the line between their work and
that of professionals, remaking the idea of house-music culture. The hundreds of re-creations posted by others point to participant audiences whose
contribution rises to a level that blurs the distinction between creator and
audience.

Powers, formidable when writing about music as well as science and
technology, presents, through "Modulation," an extreme view of music in
the new media era. The plot centers on the global dissemination and eventual synchronized activation of a musical computer virus. These events
tie together four separate characters whose musical lives capture much
about music in today's world: Toshi Yukawa, a former music pirate, works
with record companies to find other pirates; journalist Marta Mota writes
about the uses of music by the American military in Iraq; ethnomusicologist Jan Steiner looks back on his life's research through recordings; and
DJ Mitchell Payne presents a set of "chiptune" 8-bit audio that satisfies
his audience's "nostalgia for the blips and bleeps of their Atari childhood"
(p. 91). Music is nearly always experienced via mobile phones, iPods, laptops, and other computers. Echoing Sousa's worries, Steiner notes that all
of these are "an instrument that everyone could learn to play without any
effort" (p. 91).

Nearly all the music and audio experienced in "Modulation" is recorded
and shared digitally. For example, Marta is embedded as a journalist to
write about troops preparing for battle, and Toshi's work focuses on investigating endless networks of pirates trafficking in downloaded music files.
If one holds an expanded notion of what can constitute a performance, two
examples are found in the story. One evokes a present day Aunt Julia, as
Marta connects to her boyfriend via Skype to help rid her of an earworm:

And into his tinny laptop computer microphone in Bahrain, in a frail
but pretty baritone she hadn't heard for way too long, he sang a few
notes that re-materialized in her Frankfurt hotel as the theme song from
Mission Impossible.

(p. 95)

A song sung, the repertoire itself from broadcast media, filtered and mediated by tinny microphone and tiny speaker, virtually re-presented nearly three
thousand miles away. The second instance of performance is DJ Payne's set
for the Chiptune Blowout:

But as soon as he got the backing tracks looping, the MSX emulator bumping, and his Amiga kicking out the MIDI jambs to the principal theme from the old blockbuster game *Alternate Reality,* he remembered just what Face-to-Face was all about, and why nothing would ever replace live performance.

(p. 98)

DJ Payne's live work consists of triggering loops and working with digital information via MIDI. He plays a role closer to conductor and composer, more invoker and gatekeeper, than performer. However, for Payne, getting background tracks looping to a video game soundtrack *is* performance.

Joyce and Sousa's vision of music exists for Powers as only a distant echo. There is irony in Power's description of Payne's work, Sousa's machine music, as live performance. It is also likely that Sousa would have been not fully comfortable calling the singing of Marta's boyfriend a performance. Gould as evangelist would have welcomed the world DJ Payne presents, but Gould never predicted just how far the culture would change. In Gould's terms, Payne represents the rise of the participant listener come full circle, a participant listener as performer, and the triggering and playing of prerecorded and synthesized music as performance.

In place of traditional performance, music is presented throughout "Modulation" in a variety of modern roles: as a virus, as a means for exploitation, as a pharmaceutical, and constantly as a commodity. Toshi reflects on the corporate nature of the relationship between music and consumer:

There was pay what you want and genetic taste matching and music by statistical referral. Customers who liked Radiohead also listened to Slipknot. If you like Slipknot, you may also like the Bulgarian Women's chorus. The vendors had your demographic, and would feed it to you in unlimited ninety-nine cent doses or even free squirts that vanished after three listens. He owed his job to saltwater syndrome. Drinking made you thirsty. Buffets bred hunger.

(p. 93)

Music is more commodity than experience; and in place of musicians performing, "Modulation" presents musicians via roles such as vendor, pirate, and trafficker. Instead of the organic connection between performer and audience, music fits more into the mold of producer and consumer, a role that recalls the economic analysis of Jacques Attali (1977/1985) in his book *Noise*, one that situates recordings as part of the overall rise of repetition in society:

Mass production, a final form, signifies the repetition of all consumption, individual or collective, the replacement of the restaurant by precooked meals, of custom-made clothes by ready-wear, of the individual house built from personal designs by tract houses based on stereotyped designs, of the politician by the anonymous bureaucrat, of skilled labor by standardized tasks, of the spectacle by recordings of it.

(p. 128)

The climactic event of "Modulation" is the activation of a musical computer virus. The piece spreads across networks into every device capable of playing music. The virus synchronizes the playback of a single piece of music that is at once an unforgettable experience while simultaneously impossible to remember:

> And here it was again, after an eternity away: a tune that sold nothing, that had no agenda, that required no identity or allegiance, that was not disposable background product, that came and went for no reason, brief as thunder on a summer night.
>
> (p. 102)

One reading of the role of the virus in "Modulation" is that it serves to show the profound shift in music. Whereas music was always ephemeral in "The Dead," by the time of "Modulation" an ephemeral experience with music exists only as science fiction. Every sound worth hearing today is captured, recorded, shared, and sold. Like Powers, only with a feat of imagination or a leap of faith can we admit the possibility of a sound that will never be sold. It is this situation that "Modulation" helps us to mark, the distance between Aunt Julia and DJ Payne, from Michael Furey's remembered song for Gretta to an ephemeral event made available through an anonymous computer virus.

The story presented thus far captures the shift in music, musician, and audience: the exchange of the ephemeral for a reproducibility that also estranges performer from audience, the rise of the concept of music as sonic object that favors unblemished recordings which feed back to put pressure on live musicians to create flawless performances. "Modulation" gives us, however tentatively, the ability to begin to understand how our habits of music, musician, and audience evolve as the Internet and new media become the locus for musical experience.

The recording era was dominated by production and distribution systems owned by corporations that regulated what was released. For example, Gould worked with Columbia and the Canadian Broadcasting Corporation, among others. By contrast, corporate sites like YouTube allow musicians to decide what work to share. In fact, Powers's story channels real events, as in his depiction of a Korean kid's homemade guitar video, a real version of which was covered in the *New York Times*:

> Last year Jerry Chang, a Taiwanese guitarist who turns 25 on Thursday, set out to create a rock version of the song, which he had been listening to since childhood. It took him two weeks. Others, like Brian Eno, had

done so before him, and some listeners say his arrangement is derivative of one composed for the video game "Pump It Up." But one way or another, his version, "Canon Rock," rocked.

(Heffernan, 2006, p. 10)

A search of YouTube in September 2010 found over seven thousand videos in homage or response to "guitar." These participant-listeners-turned-performers capture another aspect of the new media era, that is, the incredible rise in the availability and promotion of publicly available creative works. The Internet has served not only as a place for individuals to post their content; it has helped to spur or reveal creativity that was unacknowledged during the recording era. The Pew Research Center's Internet and American Life Project states that 38% of teens reported in the affirmative when asked if they "share something online that you created yourself, such as your own artwork, photos, stories or videos" (Pew Research Center, 2009). This development was something not understood in the earlier days of the Internet, as described by Virtual Reality pioneer Lanier (2011):

Many of the lectures I gave in the 1980s would end with a skeptic in the audience pointing out loudly and confidently that only a tiny minority of people would ever write anything online for others to read. They didn't believe a world with millions of active voices was remotely possible—but this is the world that has come to be.

(p. 101)

The consolidation of power in the recording era, then, gave way to what appears to be a democratization of access to the means of creation and distribution. The inexpensive home studio, the personal website, and the ease with which art in digital form can be shared and enjoyed is perhaps the most fundamental change of the new media era, changes that closely align with the notion of convergence culture put forward by Jenkins (2006).

Another consequence flows from the ease of distribution as we transition from a recording era, namely, the rise of an overabundance of content. Recordings that were tangible were limited to the estimated commercial audience; but in the digital world, copies are created on demand. Reviewing a recent biography of Keith Richards that locates access to then-scarce blues records as critical for the creation of the Rolling Stones, Dan Chiasson (2011) captures this transition:

The experience of making and taking in culture is now, for the first time in human history, a condition of almost paralyzing overabundance. For millennia it was a condition of scarcity. . . . Nobody will ever again experience what Keith Richards and Mick Jagger experienced in Dartford, scrounging for blues records. The Rolling Stones do not happen in any other context: they were a band based on craving, impersonation, tribute: white guys from England who worshiped black blues and later, to a lesser extent, country, reggae, disco, and rap.

(p. 19)

As with the rise of music as commodity, this overabundance is part of a broader trend that extends to other areas including academic scholarship (Jensen, 2007). Chiasson captures the sense of both something gained and something changed, in his formulation, something lost. In the context of Chiasson's review, the Stones emerged, in part, due to recordings. However, it was not enough that they lived in a time when recordings existed; they lived in the recording era when scarcity created a yearning that does not exist in a new media era replete with content. We might agree, or begin to imagine that as Gould foresaw new vistas of possibility we can also imagine new ways that young people will find opportunities to distinguish themselves to create new music that resonates.

The new media locus can therefore be distinguished from the recording locus in increasing the availability of the means of production and distribution. The locus is also characterized by the further rise of the participant listener to roles that could be considered, in an earlier era, only within the realm of producers, creators, and performers. More members of society are taking advantage of the means to make and share their ideas globally via the Internet (whether poems, stories, or songs), and this has combined with the digital availability of historic and corporate content, with a resultant overabundance of creative content available. Although a more nuanced understanding of this era will certainly emerge, it is not too early to begin to make sense of the possibilities and opportunities for music education in a new media era.

MADLIB AS NEW MEDIA ARTIST

To better understand some of the values and practices of the new media era, this article now considers as an emblematic example Otis Jackson Jr., who performs under many monikers but is best known as Madlib. His name aptly recalls Mad Libs, the fill-in-the-blank games that originated in the 1950s, an approach Jackson uses in his music and even in his fictional biography, which samples heavily from that of Redd Foxx (Stones Throw Records, n.d.a.). His work illuminates many of the avenues by which musicians are expanding their horizons, creating in new ways, and using samples of music to connect with audiences beyond performance.

Madlib, like many musicians today, does much of his recording and music making from a home studio, profiled in the book *Behind the Beat: Hip Hop Home Studios* (Raph, 2005, pp. 99–105). His home studio is emblematic of new media music production: it is filled with tens of thousands of records from which he draws samples, beats, and ideas. Also visible are many traditional instruments: drum set, double bass, various percussion, and piano keyboard. Additionally, one can see a host of production tools such as mixers, microphones, turntables, and sample trigger hardware.

The rise of the home studio can certainly be seen as part of the larger trend of the democratization of tools and means of distribution previously limited to corporations. Previously, most distributed music came about through studios such as Abbey Road or Motown, what Cogan and Clark (2003) capture with the title of their book *Temples of Sound*. The rise of the home studio is made possible by the lowered cost of computing and recording equipment. As a consequence, this equipment has become a central part of the creative process. Whereas Gould would go to a studio to record, Madlib's and others' work relies on constant access to studio tools that supplement or replace more traditional instruments as the vehicle for musical creativity. In short, a studio *is* his primary instrument. Frere-Jones (2008) notes how the studio-based musician has become the emblematic musician of the new media locus, writing of producer Flying Lotus, "His setup is typical of the twenty-first-century musician: a collection of laptops, keyboards, and processing units, none of them large and most of them portable" (p. 2).

Madlib's voice is extended using technologies, for instance through his work under the alter ego Quasimoto. As Quasimoto, he raps with a voice pitched higher than Madlib's voice. This is achieved by first making a beat, then rapping atop a slowed-down version, then returning the combined recording back to the original speed. This higher voice is mixed into the final recordings alongside Madlib's voice at the original pitch, allowing for contrasts and conversations.

In another creative approach, Madlib began releasing recordings in 2001 under the name Yesterday's New Quintet, which consisted solely of Jackson recording all the instruments while listing fictitious collaborators with colorful names like Malik Flavors, Monk Hughes, and Joe McDuphrey. In some instances, he samples previous recordings of himself, and subsequent recordings made through the same process were released under a further list of new group names like The Jazzistics, The Young Jazz Rebels, Suntouch, The Last Electro-Acoustic Space Jazz & Percussion Ensemble, and The Yesterdays Universe All-Stars. The use of real instruments but a host of pseudonyms creates a link to the obscurity hip-hop producers prize, the delight in finding recordings of forgotten and failed musicians who might have left behind a few seconds that can be looped or recombined to be given new life.

Similar to a jazz musician who intentionally inserts quotes of other songs into their solos, today's producers weave webs of significance that combine a knowledge of songs and how they have been used by producers. Joseph Schloss (2004) presents an example from Madlib that must be quoted at length due to the richness of connections:

> An unusually overt example of this philosophy can be found in a cover version of the song "Daylight" that appears on the 2001 album *Angles*

without Edges by Yesterday's New Quintet (a pseudonym of the producer Madlib). The original version of the song was recorded in 1977 by RAMP on their album *Come into My Knowledge*. It is best known among producers because a two-bar sample of its melody provided the basis for the classic hip-hop song "Bonita Applebaum" by A Tribe Called Quest on their 1990 album *People's Instinctive Travels and the Paths of Rhythm*.

As a result of being sampled, the previously obscure RAMP album became highly prized by hip-hop producers, sometimes selling for hundreds of dollars, until it was reissued on vinyl in the late 1990s. On the Yesterday's New Quintet album, Madlib constructs a cover version of "Daylight" from samples of *other* songs (augmented by his own keyboard work). Moreover, the rhythm of Madlib's drum track is not based on the rhythm of the original version of "Daylight," but on the drum loop that A Tribe Called Quest combined it with to make "Bonita Applebaum," taken from the blues-rock band Little Feat. In short, Madlib's version of "Daylight" is a virtuoso demonstration of production technique and knowledge, referencing the social and economic history of a commodity (the RAMP album), its use in the hip-hop community ("Bonita Applebaum"), and Madlib's relationship to both.

(pp. 158–9)

Madlib completes a cycle: the 1977 album has a short portion sampled, numerous producers use it in combination with other samples for their own work, and Madlib comes along and incorporates samples of their songs, along with his own instrument playing, to produce a cover of the original song that is aware of the numerous other uses. For a listener steeped in hip-hop, Madlib creates a work that acknowledges the recording as only the beginning of a creative process of reinterpretation. This process has even been welcomed by record labels, with Madlib invited by Blue Note records to remix their catalog, released as *Shades of Blue*, another album that seamlessly mixes samples and remixes with overdubbed instruments.

Madlib has plundered from and reworked his own releases, notably his work with MF DOOM as the group Madvillain. Their 2004 album *Madvillainy* was a critical success, with Madlib's production captured by *New Yorker* critic Frere-Jones (2004): "Madlib, especially, seems able to hide music inside other music. His samples lie on each other like double exposures, or like a cassette tape that allows the previous recording to bleed through the new one." Four years later, Madlib released a new album, *Madvillainy 2—The Madlib Remix*, consisting of the original rhymes by MF DOOM atop all new beats, giving the same recordings of the rap an entirely new sonic context.

When recordings largely replace performing, it is possible to release more recordings, and Madlib's official discography on the Stones Throw record label's website (Stones Throw Records, n.d.b), accessed in July of 2011, quantifies and categorizes his releases as follows: 113 entries for "Artist/ Group Recordings," 6 entries under "MC (not producer)," 79 entries for "Producer," 22 entries for "Remixes," and 18 entries for "Mixtapes, Video, Promo, Misc." In other words, in the 15 years Madlib has been commercially releasing recordings, he has released on average 14.7 recordings each year, for a total of 220 releases (and this figure omits works distributed on the Internet but not commercially released). In 2010 alone, he put out a series called "Madlib Medicine Show," which was described in the press release as:

> a once-a-month, twelve-CD, six-LP series through the year of 2010 on his own imprint, Madlib Invazion. Odd numbers, beginning with #1 in Jan. 2010, will be original hip-hop, remix, beat tape and jazz productions; even numbers will be mixtapes of funk, soul, Brazilian, psych, jazz and other undefined forms of music from the Beat Konducta's 4-ton stack of vinyl.
>
> (Stones Throw Records, 2009)

The even-numbered releases are mixtapes, Madlib works due to the kinds of changes Gould foresaw for the participant listener: Madlib's shortening or lengthening or excerpting of a recording; the change of pitch or tempo; the juxtaposition of tunes on the particular mix; and the layering and mixing in of other material. Madlib often includes spoken word text of old "party records," explicit comedy from African American performers like Redd Fox or Moms Mabley. Several of these mixes are released under another name, Beat Konducta, one that playfully joins the classical notion of a conductor with one who works with previously recorded beats.

Madlib exemplifies some of the possibilities of music in the new media era: the ability to build new creations from existing recordings from across history and around the world, the ability to play traditional instruments in new and old contexts, the home studio as a central creative tool, and the use of recordings and the Internet as primary venues for sharing music. While much room for greater understanding and consideration of Madlib's ways of making music exist, music educators are increasingly addressing these kinds of creativity (Burnard, 2012; Randles, 2012; Tobias, 2015).

HEARING A NEW MUSIC EDUCATION STORY

The story of music in the 20th century presented here foregrounds the increasing importance of sound recording, and the narrative draws a distinction between musical experiences had through performance, recording, and new media. An aim of this story is to complicate our notions of performance in a new media era. One hundred years ago, *performance* could viably be said to account for nearly all musical experience; today, performance is an increasingly diminished portion of our overall experiences with music, and in the case of some types of music, an impossibility.

To illustrate the changes of the shifting locus, this article focused on subjective musical experience as presented in "The Dead" and "Modulation," and also by tracking practices of musicians who are emblematic of each locus—Sousa, Gould, and Madlib. Through the work of these writers and musicians, large shifts are apparent. These shifts are consequential for educators because, as the locus of experience shifted, differing musical habits were formed. Marx, quoted previously, argued for recognition of the role played by modernity in the formation of the senses. Adorno (2009) wrote in the late 1930s of the problem of a "new type of human being" (p. 461), arguing against the notion that human nature is unchanging and that, "in certain situations, this culture becomes such a contrast to real living conditions that it can no longer carry out the task imposed on it. . . . The fiction is maintained that inducing people to listen to Beethoven symphonies, read Milton, and gaze upon Raphael madonnas [sic] is equally 'progressive' and humanistic at all times" (pp. 461–2). Adorno, like Marx, saw radical changes in the social conditions and productive forces brought about in concert with modernization and technologization, writing, "Regardless of how educators might assess such issues as drive structure, sublimation or culture, their work is only of use if their reflections take the real changes that have gone on, both in people and in the power of culture, into account without any illusions" (p. 462).

It may be the case that little, if anything, of the new media locus as evoked by Powers can meaningfully be taught through performance. This musical world of data is largely foreign to music education practices characterized by competitions and festivals, emulation of military bands, and makers of traditional band and orchestra instruments. As Cavicchi (2009) notes about what I describe as the recording locus:

> The recording industry has been in existence since the 1910s, urban blues and rock 'n' roll have been around since the 1940s, and MTV's codification of music and fashion is over twenty years old now. Yet only rarely do the behaviors associated with modern, commercial, and popular music—from DJing and dance to power chords and social protest—make it onto the radar of school musicality, except as phenomena to ignore or even oppose.
>
> (p. 103)

In "The Dead," Mary Jane says that she'd give anything to hear Caruso. Some music educators may believe that we did give up everything special about music, gaining the ability to hear Caruso's wonderful voice for eternity in exchange for the humanity and soul estranged by the preservation process. For those music educators who remain wedded to the performance locus and the values that flow from it, they will continue to hold similar beliefs, perhaps to notice only what is lost, and to cling to the idea that only live performance can provide worthwhile musical experiences. This paper makes clear that this is far from the only option, and that other ways to understand and appreciate differing mediated networks of music exist—ways that educators can both enjoy and understand, including how these practices change the context and meaning of performance approaches.

Mediated networks are consequential for educators, above all, because these networks are the locus of musical experience from which habits emerge, the networks within which the majority of musical experience occurs today. People today have experiences predominantly through new media, which afford a different set of possibilities and different kinds of experience than when music was primarily experienced through physical recordings and radio broadcasts, or had via performances. From an educational standpoint, habits connected with these shifting loci are constitutive of notions of self, identity, and culture. Even when making music in the traditional context, such as a church choir, it can be argued that the singers and audience bring with them habits formed in the new media locus of music as data, habits with different expectations and aspirations than those in Joyce's time.

It is beyond the scope of this paper to settle these issues. My goal instead has been merely to raise them to the attention of the field—to provide a sense, a story, of some of the ways that technological innovation resonates with changes in educational ideas. Hearing these resonances might lead to alternate histories of some of the central movements within music education. We might hear music appreciation as a technological practice, or reconsider the introduction of recordings into pedagogy through the Suzuki approach. We might notice how SmartMusic is an example of the rising importance of algorithms for music education (Thibeault, 2014). These kinds of efforts might better connect music education with the field of sound studies, and build upon not only the work of current scholars (Pinch & Bijsterveld, 2012; Sterne, 2012b), but the music educators whose work has inspired those in sound studies, most notably Schafer (1977/1994) and Small (1977, 1998). It would be a welcome development for music educators once again to engage in the kinds of ideas once popular in our field, one where we surely still have valued contributions to make.

My hope is that this paper, while at times speculative, nevertheless articulates a way of thinking about the mediated networks involving sound, education, and technology that resonate in a meaningful way for educators. We can hear the world anew, we can hear our practices as educators anew, and we can shift our dreams for the future based on a different understanding of the past. It is a project both pleasurable and rewarding, one that invites not only the social sciences but the humanities to help enhance the conduct of educational practice as it relates to all aspects of music in the world today.

88   *Matthew Thibeault*

REFERENCES

Adorno, T. W. (2009). The problem of a new type of human being. In R. Hullot-Kentor (Ed.), *Current of music: Elements of a radio theory* (pp. 461–9). Malden, MA: Polity.

Attali, J. (1985). *Noise: The political economy of music*. (B. Massumi, Trans.). Minneapolis: University of Minnesota Press. (Original work published 1977)

Benjamin, W. (1968). The work of art in the age of mechanical reproduction. In H. Arendt (Ed.), *Illuminations* (pp. 217–52). New York, NY: Schocken Books. (Original work published 1935)

Bijsterveld, K. (2008). *Mechanical sound: Technology, culture, and public problems of noise in the twentieth century*. Cambridge, MA: MIT Press.

Borgmann, A. (1984). *Technology and the character of contemporary life: A philosophical inquiry*. Chicago, IL: University of Chicago Press.

Burnard, P. (2012). *Musical creativities in practice*. Oxford, UK: Oxford University Press.

Cavicchi, D. (2009). My music, their music, and the irrelevance of music education. In T. A. Regelski & J. T. Gates (Eds.), *Music education for changing times: Guiding visions for practice* (pp. 97–107). New York, NY: Springer.

Chiasson, D. (2011, March 10). High on the Stones. Retrieved from *The New York Review of Books*, www.nybooks.com/articles/archives/2011/mar/10/high-stones/?pagination=false

Cogan, J., & Clark, W. (2003). *Temples of sound: Inside the great recording studios*. San Francisco, CA: Chronicle Books.

Dewey, J. (1963). *Experience and education*. New York, NY: Collier Books. (Original work published 1938)

Frere-Jones, S. (2004, April 12). Doom's day. *The New Yorker*. Retrieved from www.newyorker.com/archive/2004/04/12/040412crmu_music

Frere-Jones, S. (2008, December 1). Heavy Water. *The New Yorker*. Retrieved from www.newyorker.com/arts/critics/musical/2008/12/01/081201crmu_music

Gould, G. (1984a). Glenn Gould in conversation with Tim Page. In T. Page (Ed.), *The Glenn Gould reader* (pp. 451–61). New York, NY: Alfred A. Knopf.

Gould, G. (1984b). Let's ban applause. In T. Page (Ed.), *The Glenn Gould reader* (pp. 245–50). New York, NY: Alfred A. Knopf. (Original work published 1962)

Gould, G. (1984c). The prospects of recording. In T. Page (Ed.), *The Glenn Gould reader* (pp. 331–53). New York, NY: Alfred A. Knopf. (Original work published 1966)

Heffernan, V. (2006, August 27). Web guitar wizard revealed at last. *The New York Times*. Retrieved from www.nytimes.com/2006/08/27/arts/television/27heff.html

Heidegger, M. (1977). *The question concerning technology, and other essays*. New York, NY: Harper & Row. (Original work published 1954)

Hickman, L. A. (2001). *Philosophical tools for technological culture: Putting pragmatism to work*. Bloomington: Indiana University Press.

James, W. (1899). *Talks to teachers on psychology: And to students on some of life's ideals*. New York, NY: H. Holt and Company.

Jenkins, H. (2006). *Convergence culture: Where old and new media collide*. New York: New York University Press.

Jensen, M. (2007, June 15). The new metrics of scholarly authority. *The Chronicle of Higher Education*. Retrieved from http://chronicle.com/article/The-New-Metrics-of-Scholarly/5449

Joyce, J. (1969). *Dubliners*. New York, NY: Modern Library. (Original work published 1914)

Katz, M. (2012). The amateur in the age of mechanical music. In K. Bijsterveld & T. J. Pinch (Eds.), *The Oxford handbook of sound studies* (pp. 459–79). New York, NY: Oxford University Press.

Lanier, J. (2011). *You are not a gadget: A manifesto.* New York, NY: Random House.

Mach, E. (1991). *Great contemporary pianists speak for themselves.* Mineola, NY: Dover.

Manovich, L. (2002). *The language of new media.* Cambridge, MA: MIT Press.

Marx, K. (1975). The productivity of capital: Productive and unproductive labour (B. Fowkes, Trans.). In *Karl Marx Frederick Engels collected works 1861–1863* (B. Fowkes, Trans.) (Vol. 34, pp. 121–46). London, United Kingdom: Lawrence & Wishart. Retrieved from www.marxists.org/archive/marx/works/1861/economic/ch38.htm. (Original work published 1861)

Marx, K., & Engels, F. (1844/1988). *Economic and philosophic manuscripts of 1844.* Amherst, NY: Prometheus Books.

McLuhan, M. (1962/2008). *The Gutenberg galaxy: The making of typographical man.* Toronto, Canada: University of Toronto Press.

McLuhan, M. (2003). *Understanding media: The extensions of man* (W. T. Gordon, Ed.) (Critical Edition). Corte Madera, CA: Gingko Press. (Original work published 1964)

Neilson Media. (2012). Music discovery still dominated by radio, says Nielsen Music 360 Report. Retrieved from www.nielsen.com/us/en/insights/press-room/2012/music-discovery-still-dominated-by-radio—says-nielsen-music-360.html

Nettl, B. (2005). *The study of ethnomusicology: Thirty-one issues and concepts* (New Ed.). Urbana: University of Illinois Press.

Pew Research Center. (2009). Online activities: What teens do online. *Pew Research Center's Internet & American Life Project.* Retrieved from www.pewinternet.org/Trend-Data-for-Teens/Online-Activites-Total.aspx

Philip, R. (2004). *Performing music in the age of recording.* New Haven, CT: Yale University Press.

Pinch, T. J., & Bijsterveld, K. (Eds.). (2012). *The Oxford handbook of sound studies.* New York: Oxford University Press.

Powers, R. (2008). Modulation. *Conjunctions, 50,* 87–103.

Raph. (2005). *Behind the beat: Hip hop home studios.* Berkeley, CA: Gingko Press.

Randles, C. (2012). Music teacher as writer and producer. *The Journal of Aesthetic Education, 46*(3), 36–52.

Rideout, V. J., Foerh, U. G., & Roberts, D. F. (2010). Generation M2: Media in the lives of 8- to 18-year olds (p. 85). Henry J. Kaiser Family Foundation. Retrieved from www.kff.org/entmedia/upload/8010.pdf

Ruthmann, A., Tobias, E., Randles, C., & Thibeault, M. (2015). Is it the technology? Challenging technological determinism in music education. In C. Randles (Ed.), *Music education: Navigating the future* (pp. 122–138). New York: Routledge.

Schafer, R. M. (1994). *The soundscape: Our sonic environment and the tuning of the world.* Rochester, VT: Destiny Books. (Original work published 1977)

Schloss, J. G. (2004). *Making beats: The art of sample-based hip-hop.* Middletown, CT: Wesleyan.

Singer, M. (2007, September 17). Fantasia for piano: Joyce Hatto's incredible career. *The New Yorker.* Retrieved from www.newyorker.com/reporting/2007/09/17/070917fa_fact_singer

Small, C. (1977). *Music, Society, Education: A radical examination of the prophetic function of music in Western, Eastern and African cultures with its impact on society and its use in education.* London, United Kingdom: Calder.

Small, C. (1998). *Musicking: The meanings of performing and listening.* Middletown, CT: Wesleyan University Press.

Smith, M. R., & Marx, L. (1994). *Does technology drive history? The dilemma of technological determinism.* Cambridge, MA: MIT Press.

Sousa, J. P. (1906, September). The menace of mechanical music. *Appleton's Magazine, 8,* 278–84.

Stanyek, J., & Piekut, B. (2010). Deadness: Technologies of the intermundane. *TDR: The Drama Review, 54*(1), 14–38.

Sterne, J. (2003). *The audible past: Cultural origins of sound reproduction.* Durham, NC: Duke University Press.

Sterne, J. (2012a). *MP3: The meaning of a format.* Durham, NC: Duke University Press.

Sterne, J. (Ed.). (2012b). *The sound studies reader.* New York, NY: Routledge.

Stones Throw Records. (n.d.a). *Madlib.* Retrieved from www.stonesthrow.com/madlib

Stones Throw Records. (n.d.b). *Madlib discography.* Retrieved from www.stonesthrow.com/madlib/discography

Stones Throw Records. (2009, November 10). *Madlib medicine show.* [Press release]. Retrieved from www.stonesthrow.com/news/2009/11/madlib-medicine-show

Thibeault, M. D. (2014). Algorithms and the Future of Music Education: A Response to Shuler. *Arts Education Policy Review, 115*(1), 19–25. doi:10.1080/10632913.2014.847355.

Tobias, E. S. (2015). Inter/trans/multi/cross/new media(ting): Navigating an emerging landscape of digital media for music education. In C. Randles (Ed.), *Music education: Navigating the future* (pp. 91–121). New York, NY: Routledge.

Turino, T. (2008). *Music as social life: The politics of participation.* Chicago, IL: University of Chicago Press.

Waddington, D. I. (2010). Scientific self-defense: Transforming Dewey's idea of technological transparency. *Educational Theory, 60*(5), 621–38. doi:10.1111/j.1741-5446.2010.00380.x

Warfield, P. (2011). The march as musical drama and the spectacle of John Philip Sousa. *Journal of the American Musicological Society, 64*(2), 289–318.

7 Inter/Trans/Multi/Cross/ New Media(ting)

Navigating an Emerging Landscape of Digital Media for Music Education

Evan S. Tobias

On a September evening in 2008, I sat in Gammage auditorium at Arizona State University with my laptop on as a concert began. Normally, in such formal concert settings, my typing and glowing screen in the darkness might be considered rude. In this case, conference organizers encouraged audience members to make use of a dedicated online chat room throughout the concert. Several audience members discussed the music, composers, sound of the performers, and other related or unrelated issues online while located in a specified area in the hall. I was captivated by this experiential layer juxtaposed with the physicality of being in the concert hall and the music to which I was listening, a convergence of physical and virtual presence afforded by digital media while attending a concert. I was able to interact with the music and others in the physical place of the concert hall in ways that would not have occurred without digital media.

This is but one example of how digital media are playing an increasing role in how people experience and engage with the arts in general (Burnard, 2011; Partti, 2012; Partti & Karlsen, 2010; Väkevä, 2009; Webster, 2007). The rate at which technology advances and the varied ways digital media intersect with musical engagement present ongoing challenges to music educators interested in addressing such developments. Developing understanding of the landscape of digital media in relation to the arts and artistic practices can assist music educators in making sense of a confounding array of media content, constructs, characteristics, and technological tools or techniques (Jenkins, 2006a, 2006b; Lister, Dovey, Giddings, Grant, & Kelly, 2009; Manovich, 2002; Miller, 2011).

In line with this book's theme of navigating the future of music education, this chapter serves as a starting point to orient ourselves amidst such a landscape and inform how music educators might negotiate complex relationships between digital media, music, and musicking. After a brief introduction to intersections of media and musicking and describing the notion of new or digital media, I outline two types of cultural contexts in which people engage with media. I then highlight three frameworks with potential to assist music educators in making sense of digital media, envisioning related pedagogy and curriculum, and developing critical perspectives that balance possibilities with potential negative aspects of integrating digital media in music programs (Ruthmann et al., 2015; Ferneding, 2007).

While some might consider how digital media and the frameworks outlined throughout this chapter might be addressed in the context of particular pedagogies or in existing curricular structures such as bands, orchestras, choruses, or general music classes, this chapter emphasizes new possibilities for musicking and music education. As music educators continue to reconcile the types and rate of evolution or transformation of music teaching and learning most appropriate for students in the 21st century (Jorgensen, 2003; Kratus, 2007; Miksza, 2013; Regelski, 2013; Tobias, 2013; Williams, 2007, 2011), this chapter challenges the maintenance of the status quo while encouraging music education to at minimum acknowledge the possibilities, challenges, and problematic aspects of digital media while making space for a broader range of creative musical engagement.

INTERSECTIONS OF DIGITAL MEDIA, MUSIC, AND MUSICKING

The pervasiveness of digital media in contemporary society extends to spaces such as concert halls that have traditionally encouraged people to put away technologies that could distract from what occurs on stage. Cultural organizations such as symphony orchestras are leveraging digital media to engage the public in new ways, ranging from encouraging people to tweet about concerts in Tweet Seats (Berger, 2011; Hondl, 2012; Wise, 2011), to inviting submissions of melodies via web-based notation applications such as Noteflight to inspire an improvisation streamed live online (Detroit Symphony Orchestra, 2012). During popular music and many outdoor concerts it is standard for people to take photos, record video, text friends, update Facebook, or Tweet about their experiences with mobile devices.

Contemporary musical engagement is often saturated and intertwined with digital media. Web-based services such as Spotify and Pandora mediate listening while interfaces and controllers can mediate how one creates and performs music. Whether MIDI controllers used to perform recorded audio and video,[1] or tactile controllers such as mobile tablets with applications such as Samplr that allow one to manipulate sound,[2] digital media opens a range of musical possibilities and challenges in terms of musical engagement and the relationships between people and technology. Music educators are gradually incorporating such media and technology into their teaching. While related discourse can often focus on particular technologies or applications, a growing number of music educators who address technology and digital media in their research and practice are signaling a turn from a focus on technology to a broader and more nuanced perspective that includes media and new media to inform pedagogy and curriculum.

In discussing the relationship between media and music, Thibeault (2012) emphasizes that "the ideas that come from media are inextricably linked with technology, but they organize a set of concerns in a different way . . . [including] questions about the uses, indications, and new aggregations of society that emerge in interplay with technologies" (p. 519). Gee (2010) discusses growing interest in digital media and learning and suggests that educators look beyond digital tools to consider "new forms of convergent media, production, and participation as well as powerful forms of social organization and complexity in popular culture" to think more broadly about learning in and out of school (p. 14). If music education is to fully address the complexities of digital media and its relationship with music, musicking, learning, and teaching, it is critical to expand beyond a focus on tools and techniques and to consider the larger contexts and systems in which media, musicking, and education exist.

Researchers are addressing how new media and music-focused social networks can support musicianship and foster communities of practice related to musical engagement (Partti & Karlsen, 2010; Salavuo, 2006; Waldron, 2009, 2011) and teaching (Bauer, 2010; Ruthmann, 2007; Ruthmann & Hebert, 2012). The recently published second volume of the *Oxford Handbook of Music Education* (McPherson & Welch, 2012) contains separate sections on Music Learning and Teaching through Technology and Media, Music, and Education. The media section addresses themes such as sound recording and post-performance (Thibeault, 2012), new literacies and interactive media such as videogames (Tobias, 2012a), performing with digital and multimedia systems (Brown & Dillon, 2012), and virtual and hybrid learning environments (Ruthmann & Hebert, 2012).

Those interested in addressing contemporary media can quickly become overwhelmed in an endless array of content. Without conceptual frameworks to make sense of the multitude of media, music educators might focus on particular technologies, techniques, or media examples and miss larger contexts or ideas that inform musical engagement, pedagogy, and curriculum. Furthermore, Ferneding (2005, 2007) cautions arts educators to be wary of adopting a technocentric perspective in which technology is celebrated uncritically and related social, cultural, or political systems are ignored. Ferneding (2005) thus stresses the importance of addressing the nature and ethics of technology and science in arts curricula. Ferneding (2007) urges arts educators to critique technology from a philosophical perspective and address the relationship between values and technology.

DIGITAL MEDIA

Medium 2: a means of effecting or conveying something: as
   a (1): a substance regarded as the means of transmission of a force or effect (2): a surrounding or enveloping substance.

b plural usually media (1): a channel or system of communication, information, or entertainment—compare mass medium (3): a mode of artistic expression or communication.

(Merriam-Webster, n.d.)

Digital media are media in digital form and are often referred to as new media (Gee, 2010; Jackson, 2001; Lister et al., 2009; Manovich, 2002). Lister, Dovey, Giddings, Grant, and Kelly (2009) highlight how the term new media avoids reducing such media to technical or formal definitions, stressing single aspects of the media, or particular technologies or practices (p. 12). Given that the term new media can be problematic in terms of its multiplicities, fluidity, and temporal or cultural issues regarding what is or is not considered "new," it is sometimes used interchangeably with digital media.

The types of media to which the terms new media and digital media refer, along with related aspects of engagement, interaction, and participation they foster or limit, pose challenges to music educators. For the purpose of this chapter I will refer primarily to *digital media* rather than *new media*. More specifically I will address *multimedia, intermedia,* and *transmedia* as ways of framing digital media and its potential integration in music programs.

To situate how people engage with music in relation to digital media, I offer the conceptual frameworks of convergence culture and participatory culture (Jenkins, 2006a, 2006b). Rather than thinking of these frameworks as the only ways to conceptualize digital media and music, I encourage readers to see convergence and participatory cultures as helpful for considering how digital media might be integrated in music programs in ways that account for more than specific tools or techniques. While digital media content such as sound recordings, music videos, graphic user interfaces for controlling sound, or even code can all be valuable when contextualized for music teaching and learning, this chapter focuses on content that includes multiple media and how media can mediate musical engagement and learning. It is critical that music educators view such aspects of digital media in connection with specific media, media practices, particular contexts, and people's artistic engagement to avoid reducing related dialogue to discrete characteristics or technologies. For this reason, this chapter focuses primarily on cultural contexts and overarching frameworks of which digital media are a part.

CULTURAL CONTEXTS OF MEDIA ENGAGEMENT

Helibroner's (1967) question "What is the mediating role played by technology within modern Western society?" (p. 344) might be reframed in the context of music education to think deeply about how media mediate people's musical experience. However, while media can mediate one's experience and engagement with music, educators ought to be cautious of framing media or technology as determining one's musical engagement, experience, or learning (see Ruthmann et al. in this book pp. 122–138). By situating digital media within social and cultural contexts, music educators might develop nuanced and sophisticated ways of integrating media in music programs while attending to the ways that media can mediate students' engagement and learning. Similarly, music educators ought to acknowledge how digital media are socially constructed. This means that media and the ways people conceptualize or engage with media are informed by particular traditions, values, experiences, and worldviews. The following two frameworks of convergence culture and participatory culture may be useful for music educators interested in thinking about aspects of digital media in larger contexts and considering how digital media might be integrated in music programs.

Convergence Culture(s) and Participatory Culture(s)

Jenkins (2006a) uses the term convergence to articulate the flow of content across multiple media platforms, the cooperation between multiple media industries, and the migratory behavior of media audiences who will go almost anywhere in search of the kinds of entertainment experiences they want (p. 2). He suggests that convergence should be viewed as a cultural shift rather than a purely technical process given altered relationships "between existing technologies, industries, markets, genres, and audiences" and changes in how media are produced and consumed (pp. 15–16). Music educators might consider how convergence culture is occurring in the arts as well as the potential for convergence in music programs.

What does convergence culture mean for musicians? The musician Beck Hansen (n.d.) exemplified how an artist might reconcile newer and older media when he released an album in the form of a song reader with his music notated on sheet music for people to engage with. While composers and songwriters regularly create music to be performed by others, Beck deviated from the role of artists in popular culture providing fans with definitive versions of their songs and instead encouraged the public to share their own versions of his notated music. These older media forms and ways of engaging with music converged with newer media and ways of sharing music when people uploaded videos of themselves performing the music to YouTube, which were featured on Songreader.net. In this case Beck engaged in what might be considered a traditional process of distributing composed music via standard notation while embracing the ethic of people posting videos of themselves performing their interpretations of music to share with others.

Music educators might consider how integrating new media along with related principles and practices in music programs could occur in the context of convergence culture. This means addressing how people engage with intersections of older and newer media as well as how digital media might mediate musical engagement and learning in the context of music programs.

In other words, new media and contemporary musical practices can coexist with acoustic music and musicking or other *older* ways of engaging with music (Tobias, 2013). Jenkins (2006a) argues that in convergence culture, "old media are not being displaced. Rather, their functions and status are shifted by the introduction of new technologies" (p. 14).

This has significant implications for both the types of music and media we include in music programs along with the opportunities we afford young people in terms of musical engagement. A perspective of convergence allows for creative ways of integrating digital and analog media and music in virtual or physical spaces and places. In such scenarios one might find students musicking in variegated combinations of instruments and equipment, such as a group of young people creating and performing music together with trumpets, saxophones, electric guitars, mobile devices, MIDI controllers, and laptops, while located in different physical places.

Rather than simply integrating a particular technology, tool, technique, or type of media, music educators ought to consider questions such as: How might music be experienced in terms of digital media? What aspects of digital media are beneficial or problematic in terms of engaging with or developing understanding of music? What cultural shifts or convergence might take place if new media texts, processes, practices, and aesthetics are included in music programs? Reconciling such questions can assist music educators in avoiding a deterministic approach to integrating new media (see Ruthmann et al. in this book, pp. 122–138).

Closely related to convergence culture is a *participatory culture* characterized by:

> Relatively low barriers to artistic expression and civic engagement, strong support for creating and sharing creations with others, some type of informal mentorship whereby what is known by the most experienced is passed along to novices, members who believe that their contributions matter, and members who feel some degree of social connection with one another (at the least they care what other people think about what they have created).
>
> (Jenkins, Purushotma, Weigel, Clinton, & Robison, 2009, p. 5–6)

Jenkins, Purushotma, Weigel, Clinton, and Robison (2009) outline a range of participatory cultural forms such as (1) affiliations: formal and informal memberships in online communities centered around various forms of media such as The Online Academy of Irish Music (Waldron, 2011), YouTube, or the music education Twitter group #musedchat that meets online on Monday evenings; (2) expressions: producing new creative forms, such as remixes, mash-ups, sample-based productions, or interactive music videos; (3) collaborative problem solving: working together in formal or informal teams to complete tasks and develop new knowledge such as a recent public effort to determine if the show *Glee* used Jonathan Coulton's

(2013) acoustic arrangement of Sir Mix A Lot's "Baby Got Back"; and (4) circulations: shaping the flow of media such as blogging, tweeting, or creating media-based narratives such as on Storify.com (p. 9).

That people engage with one another and media in these ways is not specific to a digital context, although digital media support such practices (Ito, 2006, 2007; Jenkins, 2006b; Löwgren, 2010). Participatory cultures in which people engage and interact with media prior to the prevalence of digital technology range from performing in community music groups to creating and distributing comic books and zines. Jenkins (2006a, 2006b), for instance, discusses how fans engaged with texts prior to web-based media by creating additional or alternative narratives known as fan fiction that are connected to plotlines or characters. Acknowledging older media practices that did not rely on technology for participation, Ito (2006) argues that "the new technologies of internet communication and exchange are produced by old fan activity as much as they are productive of new forms of social and cultural practice" (p. 52).

Addressing the role that contemporary technology and media play in how people engage with cultural texts, Jenkins et al. (2009) describe how "participatory culture is emerging as the culture absorbs and responds to the explosion of new media technologies that make it possible for average consumers to archive, annotate, appropriate, and recirculate media content in powerful new ways" (p. 8). As Deuze (2006) emphasizes, "People not only have come to expect participation from the media, they increasingly have found ways to enact this participation in the multiple ways they use and make media" (p. 68). The type of participatory culture that Jenkins et al. (2009) describe is not specific to digital media but is characteristic of how many people engage with digital media in contemporary society.

Before delving into digital media and how it supports participatory culture, it might be helpful to frame participatory practices in music that are less focused on digital mediation. In highlighting diverse examples of participatory musicking that occur in more acoustic settings throughout society, Regelski (2013) suggests that music educators acknowledge and include a broader range of performing experiences that better reflect how people engage in music outside of school music programs. Thibeault and Evoy (2011) provide a rich sense of how participatory music practices might occur in a school setting in the context of a Homebrew Ukulele Union (HUU) that incorporates resources such as YouTube videos but focuses on the social participatory musicking through building ukuleles; sharing, learning, creating, and performing music on ukuleles; and connecting with the local community. Citing musical traditions such as Sacred Harp singing and the punk do-it-yourself (DIY) ethic and describing the HUU, Thibeault discusses how this approach to doing and learning music is representative of what Turino (2008) refers to as participatory music.

In making a strong case for considering multiple fields of musical practice, Turino (2008) describes participatory performance as "a special type of artistic practice in which there are no artist-audience distinctions, only participants and potential participants performing in different roles, and the primary goal is to involve the maximum number of people in some performance role" (p. 26). Turino differs participatory performance with presentational performance, which "refers to situations where one group of people, the artists, prepare and provide music for another group, the audience, who do not participate in making the music or dancing" (p. 26). Turino also discusses how high fidelity recordings and studio audio art constitute two additional fields that differ from participatory music and are more connected to presentational music through the creation of recordings that are intended to be listened to.

Jenkins et al.'s (2009) framework of participatory culture is helpful for addressing musical practices that involve affiliations, expressions, collaborative problem solving, and circulations of original and existing music and media, whether live or recorded. This framework is particularly helpful in making sense of such musical engagement that is participatory but not necessarily in the context of participatory performance practices as framed by Turino (2008). For instance, one can find countless examples of people engaging with popular music or other musics they find meaningful by creating cover versions, arrangements, parodies, satires, multitrack-produced versions, remixes, sample-based productions, mash-ups, tutorials, remediations into other types of content and practices such as movement or visual media, or commenting on and discussing the media through social media and websites (Tobias, 2013).

Turino (2008) accounts for additional ways that people can engage in participatory musicking, suggesting that the four fields he outlines (participatory live performance, presentational live performance, high fidelity recording music, and studio audio art recording music) ought to be seen as a continuum and in terms of potential combinations rather than "airtight rubrics for neatly categorizing styles of music" (p. 88). While the videos and music people create and share may be considered presentational, the practices and ways that others engage with these various versions of music can be viewed as existing within participatory cultures that extend beyond performing and where the social aspect is more distributed across time and space via digital mediation.

Löwgren (2010) suggests considering new media as a type of participatory media, arguing that "the culture of the participatory media are marked strongly by creative appropriation . . . [and] that people's engagement in the participatory media is fundamentally social in nature" (p. 22). In addition to Turino's (2008) framework for understanding fields of practice and specifically participatory music through performance, music educators might benefit from frameworks such as Jenkins's (2006b) notion of participatory culture to make sense of how people engage with music in the context of participatory practices outside the realm of participatory live performance. By acknowledging such cultural contexts, educators might better understand new media practices, media art works, and ways that people engage with music in the context of media. This in turn can inform the development of appropriate pedagogy and curricula.

AN EMERGING LANDSCAPE OF DIGITAL MEDIA: THREE FRAMEWORKS

When situated in social and cultural contexts, a closer look at types of media can expand our thinking further in terms of musical and media engagement that might be included in contemporary music programs. This section outlines multimedia, intermedia, and transmedia as overarching frameworks for navigating the landscape of new and digital media and developing pathways forward to address media with potential for musical engagement, teaching, and learning. Any borders between these frameworks ought to be seen as fluid and overlapping. While labels sometimes have the tendency to encourage categorization or organization, this section invites ways of thinking about and engaging with digital media and music to catalyze possibilities in music education. This section also contributes a small part of larger efforts needed to develop a critical lens from which to make sense of the existing, emerging, and evolving digital media landscape.

Multimedia[3]

The very term multimedia forefronts the idea that multiple types of media can and do coexist or work together as a medium or form of content. Music educators have long included relationships between music and film, art works, or written texts (Barrett, McCoy, & Veblen, 1997; Jenkins, 2008; Lum, 2009; McConnell, 1947). From a pedagogical perspective, music educators often include visualizations of music such as listening maps (Blair, 2008; Dunn, 2006; Kerchner, 2009). The digital nature of digital media supports compelling ways to interact with or visualize music unavailable with static or standard notation. For instance, Thibeault (2011) makes a case for analyzing music with multimedia spectrograms as a way for students to look at sound and notice aspects of music that are not communicated with standard notation. Digital media support a spectrum of music visualization and notation systems that can be animated and synchronized with sound. Multimedia such as the vertical scrolling icons synced with sound in the application Synthesia,[4] highlighted standard notation synced with YouTube videos in MuseScore,[5] videos of select components of scores with accompanying music,[6] and close up views of one performing music combined with information such as chords in music tutorials posted online,[7] all demonstrate how people leverage multimedia to mediate musical engagement in contemporary culture.

Deemer (2013) discusses how composers are creating and sharing video scores that focus on or animate notation with accompanying music to generate interest in their work. He draws attention to how viewing video scores can bring certain aspects of the music into focus. While such media are not yet used as notation for performers, media could be used to communicate music to performers or listeners. As access to and understanding of digital media increases among musicians, the notion of standard notation will need to evolve along with how people leverage technology to communicate and visualize music.

The ability to emphasize relationships between visual image and music through digital media also allows for interpretive, artistic, and multimedia analyses of music. For instance, one can combine a digital music recording with imagery and text providing information about the music as YouTube user Steve Macready did to create video analyses of art music.[8] Visual and sonic arrangements of music that leverage multitracking are also pervasive online such as those created by YouTube users Arronicstuff[9] and Mike Tompkins.[10] Given the interactive potential of digital media and the desire of many to engage with music in participatory culture, platforms such as Soundcloud.com, Hooktheory.com, and YouTab.me support multimedia musical analyses via the Internet. The ability to embed comments directly in the context of music, as with Soundcloud, or synchronize music and video with animated melodic, harmonic, and rhythmic information, as with Hooktheory and YouTab, exemplifies how new media, multimedia, and multimodality can afford engaging ways for people to interact with and develop musical understanding.

Webb's (2010) notion of cross-modal listening clips, or CLCs, provides a helpful heuristic for understanding similar types of media and engagement. Webb (2010) explains that:

> The image content of CLCs is inextricably linked to, derived from and/ or strongly responsive to the properties (rhythmic, melodic, textural, structural, and so on) of the musical "script" it is aligned with. As a result, a reciprocal relationship occurs between how one interprets the image content and how one listens to the music of a CLC.
>
> (p. 315)

In other words, CLCs serve as an overarching category encompassing digital media where the visual imagery closely align with and relate to specific aspects of music. CLC's can range from direct correlations between sound and imagery, such as in Stephen Malinowski's animated graphical score of Stravinsky's *Rite of Spring*,[11] to visual interpretations of music, such as in Michal Levy's digital animation of musician Jason Lindner's jazz composition, *One*.[12] Students' engagement with and creation of such types of multimedia can open spaces to explore music in deep and meaningful ways. Given the relationships between the media and music, CLCs and similar media can mediate musical experience and understanding. Furthermore, providing students opportunities to engage with CLCs and similar multimodal multimedia might provide a foundation for related lifelong musicking beyond school contexts.

Webb's (2010) work with CLCs is helpful in providing a concrete framework for leveraging new media for pedagogical and artistic purposes and means. We might for instance consider a convergence between paper listening maps as older media and newer digital media to develop multimedia and even interactive visualizations of music. Similarly, the intersection of aural and analytical skills, theoretical knowledge, and digital media in the context of CLCs is representative of convergence culture. Such work involves aural, analytical, and technical skills, musical understanding, and musical decision making. Given the broad range and sheer multitude of media that visualize music in varied ways online, it seems that many people enjoy musicking in this way. This type of musical and media engagement is reflective of participatory culture.

To summarize, the combination of multiple media forms such as sound and imagery can be considered multimedia. As with other media forms, people can create and interact with multimedia art. In the context of this chapter, multimedia can be digital in nature, and therefore a form of digital media. By allowing for the combination of visual imagery and sound, multimedia support expansive ways to present musical information ranging from animated scores using standard notation to animated iconic representations of sound. In some cases, applications, software, and interactive media take advantage of multimedia to help people learn or engage with music by emphasizing connections between sound and imagery. Multimedia can also be interpretive of music. On the other hand, music can be but one component of multimedia in response to visual media. People of varied skill levels can create multimedia that highlight or connect with aspects of music. Members of the public can also share, discuss, and circulate multimedia online through social media (Jenkins et al., 2009). When emphasizing music, educators might benefit from considering the engagement with and creation of multimedia as a form of musicking.

Intermedia

Though not exclusive to digital media, the characteristics and principles of new media allow for content that blurs lines between existing forms, categories, or labels. Fluid in nature, *intermedia* can be seen as both an in between state between media (Higgins, 2001) as well as a "fusion of several media into a new medium—the intermedium—that supposedly is more than the sum of its parts (Schröter, 2012, p. 16). Rajewsky (2005) describes a process of media combination which is "the result or the very process of combining at least two conventionally distinct media or medial forms of articulation" (p. 52). Rajewsky (2005) explains that "these two media or medial forms of articulation are each present in their own materiality and contribute to the constitution and signification of the entire product in their own specific way" (p. 52). What differentiates intermedia from multimedia is the degree to which the combined media are interconnected, though this is a fine line that in many cases could be debated.

Schröter (2012) suggests that some instances and perspectives of intermedia are similar to Wagner's notion of *Gesamtkunstwerk* in favoring interconnected media over monomedia. Drawing on the work of Higgins (2001), Schröter (2012) explains how:

> In mixed media the mediated forms meeting there can at any time be regarded by the viewer as separate while in intermedia or in intermedial forms a conceptual fusion occurs, making it impossible to view only one of its origins. Rather, it forces the viewer into perceiving them as simultaneous and inseparable.
>
> (p. 19)

Media such as Booktrack,[13] which embeds sounds and music into an electronic text, could be considered intermedia, mixed media, or multimedia depending on one's perspective, the relationship between the media, how they are integrated in the end product, and how one engages with the media. Thinking through such issues may be helpful to students interested in creating music for inclusion in intermedia or those who wish to create intermedia works. From a critical perspective educators and students might consider how such media and types of engagement factor in one's experience with texts and media that may typically be engaged with as monomedia. This means considering the experience and implications of engaging with intermedial works from a range of lenses and perspectives. Students and educators might collaboratively address questions such as: What does the convergence of texts such as books, digital media, and audio mean in terms of how one experiences stories or music?

Such questions become more complicated when one considers who determines what audio or music connects with other media. For instance, representatives of the companies Booktrack and Indabamusic.com hosted a contest and invited people to create or record original music, sound effects, and ambient audio corresponding with specific aspects of H. G. Wells's story *The Time Machine* in the Booktrack format.[14] Along with being representative of participatory culture, the contest and resulting audio files draw attention to varied interpretations of how *The Time Machine* might sound. Similar projects would provide opportunities for students to wrestle with issues ranging from how to express a particular aspect of a story in sound to how specific audio impacts one's experience of *reading* a book. Whether those creating the distinct media that come together in an intermedia project are doing so collaboratively, simultaneously, or separately also factors into such engagement. These and related issues are important to consider and address in the context of contemporary musicking and media making. Allowing students opportunities to engage with intermedia in general might inform or broaden ways of engaging with music, media, and other art forms in music and arts programs.

Further complicating an intermedia framework is how it can help "define works which fall conceptually between media that are already known" (Rajewsky, 2005, p. 52). Rajewsky (2005) forwards the notion of intermedia's boundary blurring the potential and ability to offer:

> New ways of solving problems, new possibilities for presenting and thinking about them, and to new, or at least to different views on medial border-crossings and hybridization; in particular, they point to a heightened awareness of the materiality and mediality of artistic practices and of cultural practices in general.
>
> (p. 44)

Thus, an intermedial perspective is helpful for making sense of media works or musicking that defy compartmentalization (Higgins, 2001). While films could be considered intermedia in the way that included media are interrelated, the term tends to be used in cases that do not fit into preexisting categories. Media works that straddle between multiple forms of media, such as the interactive documentary *Bear 71* (Mendes & Allison, 2012), can be considered intermedia works. Similar intermedia that combine text, narrative, sound, music, video footage, visual imagery, and elements of interactivity are possible through affordances of digital media. Such intermedia works can include preexisting music or music created specifically for the work. Music created as monomedia and originally intended to be experienced as such can thus be shared or experienced as intermedia. The release of the album *Glass Rework* as an iPad app that features remixes of Philip Glass's music with interactive imagery and the ability to create music idiomatic of Glass's oeuvre,[15] or Bang on a Can's performance of Michael Gordon's piece "Yo Shakespeare" within the game *Rock Band*,[16] exemplify how musicians might participate in the convergence of music and new media through intermedia.

By leveraging augmented reality, where virtual spaces are layered on top of physical spaces (Azuma, 1997), one could transform a particular medium such as a book into intermedia, a process of intermediality. By placing QR codes,[17] which link to musical recordings, in paper books, one can provide opportunities similar to that of Booktrack in which people could experience the book along with coinciding music. Music educators and students might thus consider the potential intermediality of any given medium or media content. Students might transform music, other art works, or media into intermedia works of which music is an integral part. Students might also be encouraged to create works that are designed as intermedia from their inception. This raises interesting questions about artistic processes, collaboration, and the boundaries of what ought to occur in music programs. To what extent and how might students think musically and intermedially in music programs?

Intermedia as a boundary-blurring framework can also refer to performing and creating that combine physical embodied performing and creating with new or digital media. Mike Tompkins's combination of performing live vocals, recorded video, and audio to perform dubstep could be seen as a form of intermedial musicking.[18] Depending on the context, intermedial performing is described with terms such as controllerism, live production, digital djing, or vjing. While these musical practices may not be typical in school music programs, music educators might foster spaces for students to engage in related intermedial musicianship.

Intermedia works that include music can also be categorized as digital opera or intermedial dance, theatre, and installations (Crossley, 2012; Macpherson, 2012; Ryan, 2012). The intermedial nature of these works blurs boundaries between disciplines, art forms, and media. For instance, the group Iduun describes their work *Kadambini*[19] as follows:

> Kadambini is an audio-video show, a meeting between the art of the stage and the digital technologies. The show combines upstream video and animations, edited and sound designed on-stage. The stage play-manipulation of frames, objects or sounds, but also mapping, video FX and shooting—interacts with the movie projected on the screen, so that one can not exist without the other and vice-versa. We forget the computer and acting finds an important place on stage and on the screen.
>
> (Iduun, n.d.)

Similarly, the intermedial work *SuperEverything**,[20] an example of a "live cinema event," combined recorded and live audio along with multiple projections of documentary footage, text, and motion graphics to "explor[e] the relationship between identity, ritual and place in relation to Malaysia's past, present and future." The work addresses the question of "who [are we] and what we might become as both individuals and as a society" (SuperEverything, n.d.a). According to the creators of *SuperEverything**:

> A live cinema performance allows artists the freedom to experiment and improvise within a selection of different material, prepared video clips, audio visual samples . . . allow[ing] the artist to present their work as a fully live and interactive performance, adding different audio and visual effects to their material on-the-fly.
>
> (SuperEverything, n.d.b)

*SuperEverything** also included opportunities for audience interaction and participation by allowing people "to interact . . . by responding to different assignments" via social media prior to the performances. The live cinema also featured live Twitter feeds as a visual aspect of the performance by displaying live updates of the #supereverything hashtag related to the performance itself along with dialogue regarding the issues addressed in the performance (SuperEverything, n.b.c).

The fluidity and porous nature of intermedia makes it difficult to pin down as an organizing category for types of media or media engagement. It might be considered in terms of "a possibility wherever the desire to fuse two or more existing media exists" (Higgins, 2001, p. 53). Music educators might benefit from using the concept of intermedia as a catalyst to expand thinking and engagement related to media rather than as a label to identify particular examples of media. Higgins (2001) alluded to this in suggesting that:

> The term [intermedia] is not prescriptive; it does not praise itself or present a model for doing either new or great works. It says only that intermedial works exist. Failure to understand this would lead to the kind of error of thinking that intermedia are necessarily dated in time by their nature, something rooted in the 1960s, like an art movement of the period.
>
> (p. 52)

Higgins further suggests that intermediality "allows for an ingress to a work which otherwise seems opaque and impenetrable, but once that ingress has been made it is no longer useful to harp upon the intermediality of a work" (p. 53). Thus, the notion of intermedia is useful to music educators in that it allows space for envisioning and making sense of media that do not fit into prescribed categories typically addressed in K-12 music programs. In other words, music educators might focus less on trying to determine if a particular phenomenon or example of media is intermedia or multimedia and instead consider how intermediality might allow for new possibilities in music teaching and learning.

Intermedia and intermedial works raise interesting issues and questions to consider and address in music programs. Music educators and their students who engage with intermedial paradigms will need to make sense of the multiple layers of live and digital media or performing. This may also include issues ranging from developing understanding of the relationships between media and aspects of live intermedial performances, to determining what aspects of intermedia, if any, are perceived as dominant (Fenton, 2007; Macpherson, 2012). Rutherford-Johnson (n.d.) raises similar issues in the following excerpt of a write-up on composer Michel Van Der Aa's cello concerto *Up-close,* which is for a solo cello, string ensemble, and film:

> Are the elderly woman and the cellist playing out the same role? The film is seen in excerpts "inserted" into the music, so is the music driving the film, or the film the music? The music never "narrates" the

film, but somehow the two layers seem to extend one another around a common subject. Furthermore, the live instruments are augmented with an electronic soundtrack, which at some times seems closely related to their music and at others appears to derive from the "concrete" sounds of the action on screen. Are these plural realities or versions of a single experience?

(para. 3)

The types of issues and questions raised by intermedia and intermedial engagement call for music educators to consider curriculum and pedagogy in ways that might differ from or expand upon a monomedia focus on music. For instance, those who tend to focus mostly on rehearsing music for performances or on varied activities that focus on particular music concepts or elements may consider other ways to organize curricula and teaching. Students' inquiry and engagement might address the relationships between music and media in ways that are not currently addressed in typical K-12 programs. Students might explore similar questions as those raised by Rutherford-Jones (n.d.) for intermedia works and types of musicking. From a pedagogical and curricular perspective music educators might need to determine the degree to which they can address the varied aspects of these types of works and practices and identify when they may need to draw upon the expertise of knowledgeable others. Collaboration may be critical in this type of teaching and learning.

Addressing intermedia is further complicated by telematic intermedial performance, where performers and those engaging with the performance may be located in several different physical or virtual spaces and places, as in Deal and Burtner's (2011) telematic opera *Auksalaq*. The opera, designed to be performed over five remote sites via the Internet, includes:

> Staged musicians, actors and dancers, music, video projections of image and text including scientific data, prepared commentary from experts in the fields of science, anthropology, sociology, political science, journalism, and literature; video feeds of the staged musicians, actors, and dancers, and a projected feed of a chatroom in which audience members can contribute and interact.
>
> (p. 511)

While the complexity involved in creating, producing, and performing intermedia works such as *Kadambini, SuperEverything**, and *Auksalaq* might be difficult to accomplish in typical school arts programs, music educators might consider including opportunities for students to create, produce, and perform similar types of intermedia at an appropriate level. Incorporating intermedial musical engagement and combinations of new media and older media within music programs allows for hybrid forms and ways of being musical that may otherwise be excluded from students' in-school musical experience and learning. Student collaboration with peers and experts within music and across other arts disciplines and opportunities to engage with music would be critical aspects of such work and play.

While intermedial works can be presentational in nature (Turino, 2008), both the process of collaborating to create intermedial works and support of audience engagement with the work and related ideas can forefront participation. For instance, students and community members could be encouraged to generate media content, music, text, and other material to be integrated in a work based on their lived experience or perspectives on an issue. Such an approach might blur boundaries between what is considered presentational, participatory, recorded, or live (Turino, 2008). A convergence of newer and older media and ways of engaging with music, media, other art forms, and practices offers compelling possibilities for young people and music programs.

To summarize, the concept of intermedia and intermediality describe media and media engagement that are interconnected and combine or straddle between multiple media or media forms. An intermedia framework provides educators with ways of considering and making sense of new types of media forms that blend aspects of existing or emerging media in ways that are atypical or do not fit into existing categories. Music programs might broaden beyond a focus on music as monomedia and include intermedia and related engagement. This might range from interacting with or creating live audio visual works in the vein of *SuperEverything**, to supporting students' exploration of interactive media in connection with music. Music educators might also consider how music and musical engagement can be intermedial through blurring boundaries between types of musicking, art forms, disciplines, and media. This might require broadening the types of performing, creating, analyzing, and interacting with music and media beyond what is typically included in music programs. This may also entail creating alternatives to compartmentalized approaches to curriculum and types of curricular structures available to students.

Transmedia

Whereas intermedia addresses multiple media in the context of a single work, a framework of *transmedia* addresses multiple media dispersed across platforms such as websites, novels, films, video games, comic books, or physical locations (Dena, 2009; Jenkins et al., 2009). Sometimes referred to as "cross media," "multiple platform," "networked entertainment," or "integrated media" (Dena, 2009; Miller, 2008; Scolari, 2009), transmedia projects are characterized as "exist[ing] over more than a single medium . . . at least partially interactive," and "[consisting of] different components that are closely integrated and used to expand the core material" (Miller, 2008, p. 151).

Jenkins (2006a) focuses primarily on transmedia storytelling projects, typically as part of media franchises. Such projects can include the creation of additional plotlines and stories across media platforms such as blogs, websites, and other media; inclusion of fan-generated content, Twitter accounts of characters, spinoff novels, and detailed wikis such as the Lostpedia, a community generated wiki that detailed all aspects of the series *Lost*. According to Jenkins (2006a):

> In the ideal form of transmedia storytelling, each medium does what it does best—so that a story might be introduced in a film, expanded through television, novels, and comics, and its world might be explored and experienced through game play.
>
> (p. 96)

According to Jenkins et al. (2009), following the flow of a storyline across media and media platforms is a process of transmedia navigation.

Dena (2009) frames transmedia more broadly. She explains that "transmedia involves creating projects that exist across distinct media or artforms, with each one of these elements contributing to the meaning-making process" (Dena in Kopp, 2011, para. 2). Dena (2011) explains how transmedia can connect with or be a part of performance-event based arts and artworks. Providing concrete examples of transmedia in the arts, she describes how Jason Grote's play *1001* incorporated a fake blog that people could read before or after attending the performance. Dena also describes how the theatre work, *Fatebook* involved characters with social network identities who interacted with each other and audience members; and how the "transmedia theatrical event" *Feeder: A love story* included characters blogging, giving video updates, and tweeting prior to the physical event as a "problog" and an "epiblog" following the event." According to Dena, the writer of *Feeder: A love story,* considered all elements across media as part of the total work" (para. 9). Given that transmedia can be "another artform that an artist chooses to do" (Dena in Kopp, 2011, "What is the number one reason," para. 1), Dena's (2009) framework of transmedia practice can be helpful to music educators interested in aspects of transmedia that do not fit within a specific storytelling or narrative paradigm.

Just as with multimedia and intermedia, transmedia can be understood as a cultural form, artistic engagement, and in terms of teaching and learning music. To consider transmedia in the context of music teaching and learning, I offer a "worked example" (Gee, 2010) of a project that students and I engaged in during the Spring 2012 semester of my *Digital and Participatory Culture in Music* course.[21]

The John Cage Project, also known as #Whenismusic, was situated both as a way to synthesize concepts, principles, and practices related to digital culture and participatory culture that we had addressed throughout the semester and as an experiment in developing a transmedia project related to a John Cage festival on our campus. Along with addressing and leveraging characteristics of digital media, we looked at how we might apply concepts such as hypermedia, interactivity, collective intelligence, and collaborative curation of web-based media to create transmedia that could generate interest in the festival among the local community, engage people in interactive opportunities related to the ideas and music of John Cage, and encourage concert attendees to participate in aspects of the project. I share this example as a kernel of an idea of what might eventually be developed and to show the potential of transmedia and associated practices (Dena, 2009) in music teaching and learning.

Planning, discussions, and development were core to our project and the educational aims of its integration in the course. To facilitate this process we used a Google document as a central location to record and organize our ideas and developed a website as a hub to connect the transmedia components we created (Tobias, 2012b). Both new media and older media played a role in our development, ranging from using Soundcloud.com to store and share potential audio files that might be contributed by the public, to poster boards for people to write on in the concert hall's lobby, to paper with QR codes for people to scan to interact with our website. Rather than engaging in transmedia storytelling (Jenkins, 2006a), we developed a transmedia musical engagement project consisting of media and opportunities for people to engage with the music and ideas of John Cage. In this context, our transmedia practice (Dena, 2009) focused on learning and musical experience rather than franchising or extending a narrative.

We began by generating essential questions (Wiggins & McTighe, 2005) to serve as the foci of each transmedia component with an overarching question of: When is music? The following three questions framed the transmedia project: (1) Can existing music become new music? (2) Is music happening now? and (3) When is an instrument? With input from a music theory colleague, we collaboratively determined several of Cage's key ideas and specific works such as *Child of a Tree, 4'33"*, and *Imaginary Landscape #5* that had potential for the project in connection with the festival. To provide entry points into the transmedia project I placed posters around the school of music with an image of John Cage and the #whenismusic hashtag.[22] We also leveraged social media such as Facebook and Twitter and #whenismusic to generate interest in the project.

The interactive media project designed around the question "Can existing music become new music?"[23] invited people to create and share their own imaginary landscape. It included software tutorials, directions for creating music in this style, and related lesson plans for educators. The project centering on the question "Is music happening now?"[24] highlighted *4'33"*, provided related information, and encouraged people to share their thoughts on various topics in the comment section. The project addressing the question "When is an instrument?"[25] was connected to the piece *Child of a Tree* and invited people to create their own instruments or to prepare existing instruments and upload sounds and music on these instruments to a dedicated Soundcloud page and to submit a video recording or photo of them playing their instrument. Each of these components could be engaged prior to or after attending the festival, though they functioned as independent projects regardless of one's concert attendance.

We also encouraged concert attendees to engage with the transmedia project. For one concert, we projected our website and a twitter feed with the #whenismusic on a lobby wall and featured posters titled with each of the essential questions and markers for people to record their answers or whatever they wished to share. Additional ideas that we did not implement ranged from designing and coordinating a scavenger hunt connecting web-based media related to John Cage's music and ideas with physical spaces across campus and the Phoenix Metro area, to inviting people to create imaginary landscapes in a computer lab during the festival. With more time we would have integrated additional entry points into the project across the campus and local community. Our experiment in creating a transmedia project was situated in a developing understanding of participatory cultures and convergence cultures while we considered aspects of digital media ranging from the nonlinear ways people might experience the project to the ways that participation with the music and ideas of John Cage could be facilitated and fostered.

Though we were limited by time, logistics, and minor constraints related to the festival, the project demonstrated the potential of digital media and transmedia in the context of music teaching and learning. Perhaps most powerful were the discussions about the project and related issues that flowed throughout and across our class, dedicated blog, Google document, and students' Facebook accounts. Furthermore, the focus of the project could have shifted to emphasize learning about the music and ideas of John Cage through the process of creating the transmedia project in a different course. Thus, creating transmedia might be seen as a form of applied musicology, co-created curricular development, and musicking.

Developing transmedia in the context of music teaching and learning necessitates an understanding of digital media, principles of participatory cultures, and the convergence of newer and older media in terms of technology, media, and culture. This calls for interdisciplinary and relational thinking (Barrett, 2007; Barrett & Veblen, 2012). Barrett and Veblen (2012) explain that "meaningful connections arise through juxtaposition, which is exercised when teachers place key ideas, works, and disciplines in close proximity to one another to invite relational thinking" (p. 366). They further explicate that "the artistry of teachers is revealed in the way disciplines, works, or themes are arranged within the curriculum, inviting creative interplay, investigation, and invention" (p. 366). This type of relational thinking is critical for creating and navigating transmedia projects that rely on complex interwoven relationships that emphasize meaningful connections between media, music, art works, ideas, themes, and aspects of the human experience.

For instance, students designing a transmedia project in relation to the life and music of John Cage can develop deep understanding of this topic when identifying relationships between the composition *Child of a Tree,* Cage's use of prepared instruments, the idea of inviting members of the public to prepare found objects in nature to perform their own version of *Child of a Tree,* and the overarching question "When is an instrument?" Identifying and connecting between these varied ideas and aspects of music, and forms of relational thinking, can be considered artistic processes in and of themselves.

Transmedia navigation (Jenkins et al., 2009) and the development of transmedia (Dena, 2009, 2011) may provide students opportunities to think in these ways and develop similar types of artistry. Such work invites students to think in terms of ongoing, nonlinear, and rhizomatic connections (Barrett, 2007; Barrett & Veblen, 2012; Deleuze & Guattari, 1987; Miller, 2011) between music, musicking, the arts, and other disciplines, along with interacting with others. Barrett and Veblen (2012) highlight the richness of students "employ[ing] musical understanding as a way of making sense of new concepts and ideas in other fields" (p. 369). Furthermore, they suggest that:

> When [students] bring insights from other studies that in turn enrich their expressive responses to music, the curriculum becomes integrated into their ways of thinking, feeling, creating, judging, and valuing music as a site for knowing themselves and their worlds.
>
> (p. 369)

Leveraging new media in the context of transmedia has potential for students to engage in music in such ways.

To summarize, transmedia constitutes a connected set of multiple media across a range of platforms. Some transmedia projects are narrative in nature. Transmedia projects can also be organized to allow for any particular element to be experienced on its own, while engaging with multiple elements can contribute to meaning making and a deeper experience or investigation of a particular phenomenon, idea, or art work. Transmedia can connect to existing art works or serve as an art form or artwork. Engaging with transmedia often includes playing a participatory role with the media. Thus, transmedia works and projects can include content submitted by those who choose to engage. Creating and engaging with transmedia can foster relational thinking and emphasize connections between media, ideas, artworks, and other aspects of the human experience that might not otherwise have been apparent.

PATHWAYS FORWARD

When considered in conjunction with characteristics and principles of media and cultural contexts such as participatory culture and convergence culture, frameworks of multimedia, intermedia, and transmedia offer music education compelling ways for students to know and do music. Addressing relationships between music and media does not mean removing opportunities for students to focus on music and musicking as an independent artistic form or discipline. Nor does addressing digital media equate to abandoning acoustic music and musicking. As stressed throughout the chapter, music educators ought to consider the implications of digital media for musical engagement, teaching, and learning through critical lenses while envisioning their potential to broaden and deepen students' musical engagement and understanding.

Including Digital Media in Music Programs

Music educators might encourage students to consider how music can relate to other media, arts, disciplines, and modalities and then create and engage with multimedia. Students might also be provided with opportunities to contribute their musicianship to intermedia and transmedia works in the context of music programs and in collaboration with peers and experts across a range of disciplines. Given the complexities involved when engaging with digital media, music educators ought to provide students with opportunities to wrestle with issues ranging from how media mediate their experiences to how digitally mediated engagement factors into one's embodiment and relationships with others (Ferneding, 2005, 2007).

When including digital media in programs, however, music educators ought to be cautious of doing so in a technocentric manner (Ferneding, 2005, 2007). This involves identifying potential values and biases that are part of technology and digital media, given that they are socially constructed and designed by people. Technocentricism occurs when educators adopt particular technologies or digital media uncritically (Ferneding, 2007). Music educators must be deliberate in analyzing the potential impact of digital media on artistic thinking and doing as well as learning. While digital media are not necessarily inherently positive or negative, their use in music programs can both support and constrain creative possibilities, learning, and musical engagement. The ways music educators and students use and interact with digital media in music programs ought to be informed by strong foundations in curriculum, pedagogy, learning theory, philosophy, socio-cultural contexts, and related research.

Addressing issues of embodiment is particularly important as music educators incorporate digital media in music programs. It is critical that music educators consider how students' physical and sense of selves relate to or are impacted by the types of media engagement discussed throughout this chapter. Armstrong (2001) cautions educators of the potential for integrating technology in ways that do not account for musicking that relies on one's body such as singing or performing instruments. Music educators ought to be cognizant of how particular ways of integrating or engaging with digital media may stifle or suppress students' bodily engagement with music (Armstrong, 2001). Similarly, music educators ought to consider the types of communication, engagement, and relationships involved in social media and musicking in virtual settings where those participating are not necessarily located in the same physical place. It is thus important to provide students opportunities to reflect on and articulate their experiences and how they feel when engaging with digital media. Creating and facilitating hybrid structures that embrace multiple ways to engage with music where digital media coexist with other media and ways of musicking can assist in this regard.

Including Opportunities for Intermediality

Along with including intermedia in music programs, music educators might envision intermedial aspects of music programs. Given how digital media allow for blurred boundaries between musical roles such as performing, creating, listening, and analyzing, among others, music educators might draw upon an intermedial paradigm to blur compartmentalized aspects of the music or arts program. This could mean blurring boundaries between ensembles and courses by creating hybrid types of programs that allow for multiple ways of being musical (Tobias, 2012c) or allowing for intermedial aspects of existing curricular structures. Considerations of how intermedia might be integrated in music programs ought to include determining the balance between digitally mediated and other ways of being musical in a program. In other words, music educators might think of integrating digital media in terms of convergence rather than replacing aspects of music programs that are not digitally mediated.

Providing students with opportunities to create and perform intermedial projects that address questions such as those posed by *SuperEverything** could encompass research, learning, meaning making, and musicking. Furthermore, such projects can promote dialogue among students, their peers, families, and communities in connection with the issues and musical engagement involved in such work. The development and facilitation of transmedia projects by collaborative teams of students, educators, and experts in other disciplines might also be included in music programs as ways for students to engage with music and society in new ways. Intermedia or transmedia works and practices have potential to foster participatory and convergence cultures that broaden the types of participatory musicking, artistic engagement, and issues that young people and their communities find meaningful.

Considering Benefits and Problematic Aspects of Digital Media Frameworks and Labels

When trying to make sense of a constantly expanding and unwieldy array of media, art forms, and artistic practices, the ability to name a phenomenon or example can be helpful. Similarly, naming or acknowledging the existence of particular types of media and media engagement can broaden the ways we think about and engage with music and media. The overarching frameworks of multimedia, intermedia, and transmedia ought to be considered as heuristics to assist music educators in navigating the landscape of digital media and broadening the opportunities for students to engage with music in these new and emerging ways. However, frameworks and labels can also be used in ways that are more static in nature and that reify ideas. Music educators must be careful to acknowledge that media and media practices are socially constructed, fluid in nature, and evolve.

Rather than solely focusing on particular frameworks as specific definitions of what *is* and then working to replicate particular examples, music educators might think in terms of what *could be* and provide time and space for themselves and their students to explore the possibilities of engaging with music and digital media. Similarly, music educators and their students might expand beyond focusing on how particular media and media practices fit into categories. They might critique existing frameworks and examples of how digital media and music intersect or recontextualize these phenomena for music teaching and learning. Furthermore, music educators and their students ought to be imaginative about the possibilities of digital media and music, possibly creating their own examples and frameworks that do not fit neatly into existing categories. In other words, music educators should avoid a restrictive or deterministic reading of the frameworks in this chapter and instead consider them springboards for thinking and musicking expansively.

Reimagining Concerts and Arts Events

This chapter began with a description of a concert experience that involved a blend of the formality of sitting silently in a concert hall and the everyday engagement of chatting with others through digital media. This slight modification of the concert opens possibilities to think about what concerts and arts events could be. What happens when presentational musics (Turino, 2008) are experienced in ways that are more participatory in nature than in the tradition of formal Western-classical concerts? How might concerts and arts events be transformed and reimagined when a participatory ethic is applied in conjunction with digital media?

Music educators might collaborate with students, colleagues, and other experts to transform the paradigm of concerts to allow for interactive intermedia or transmedia events. Such an approach recasts the concert as solely framed in terms of presentational performance (Turino, 2008). Concerts might also be reimagined as unfolding from a single culminating event to multiple transmedia experiences and interactive opportunities for musical engagement leading up to, during, and after a concert (Dena, 2011). The #whenismusic project is an example of a small step in this direction. In these ways students, educators, and community members might explore the potential for digital media in terms of providing additional avenues for participatory musical practices in addition to participatory and presentational performance (Turino, 2008).

Increasing possibilities for concerts and arts events that involve aspects of participatory culture and digital media is not equivalent to abandoning traditional formal concert experiences that exclude technology. Music educators might think in terms of multiple types of concert and arts event formats that provide a broad range of experiences, some mediated through digital media and some that opt for a minimalist approach where those in the audience sit and listen to music performed by others in the same physical setting without engaging in other ways. In a society that is increasingly digitally mediated, music educators ought to acknowledge people's desire for and in some cases lack of experience with musical engagement that does not involve technology.

Adjusting for Change

While some may consider digital media and the frameworks outlined throughout this chapter in terms of their potential for broadening and deepening music teaching and learning, others may see a threat to the status quo and traditions of K-12 music education. Regardless of whether music educators choose to conserve the types of curricular structures and content typical in music programs throughout the 20th century, society will continue to evolve. Dialogue and tension regarding such change is to be expected (Jorgensen, 2003; Kratus, 2007; Miksza, 2013; Regelski, 2013; Tobias, 2013; Williams, 2007, 2011). If music education is to evolve along with society, it must look both outward and inward to determine how it may need to adapt, modify, and transform.

One aspect of this evolution is the presence of and people's interaction with a range of digital media. Philosophical, curricular, pedagogical, and cultural changes may be necessary for music programs to support the integration of digital media in ways that connect to contemporary society. When acknowledging and addressing the presence of new media forms, artworks, and practices, music educators will need to reconcile the extent to which existing curricular structures are able to support and foster related musicking and learning. While some may try to fit multimedia, intermedia, and transmedia with related practices into existing structures such as band, chorus, and orchestra, music educators might consider other ways of organizing music teaching and learning.

For instance, compartmentalized course sequences and strands that focus on particular ways of knowing and doing music are antithetical to the notion of intermediality. Ensembles designed for a focus on performing existing notated acoustic music as monomedia may need to be modified to account for an expanding array of multimedia, intermedia, and transmedia. Approaches to teaching general music that focus on short-term activities that emphasize particular music concepts or elements might need to be transformed to accommodate the ways of knowing and doing music indicative in contemporary musicking. How might music education adjust for change?

Educators might restructure music and arts programs to allow for collaboration, and multimedial, intermedial, and transmedial engagement within and across their programs and other disciplines. Music educators might also consider how the histories, contexts, and hegemony of terms such as performing, listening, composing, creating, and analyzing as they are applied in music education relate to musical engagement in the context of digital media. In navigating the future of music education, music educators ought to consider the broad array of existing and emerging multimedia, intermedia, and transmedia along with the varied ways that young people might engage with music and media throughout their lives.

This is more complex then simply incorporating a new software program or adding digital instruments to an ensemble or music class. Music educators ought to think deeply in terms of how media mediate students' musical experience and learning and what the ramifications are of incorporating digital media, multimedia, intermedia, or transmedia in their programs. Music educators ought to consider an array of hybrid curricular structures that embrace the spirit of intermediality and account for music in the context of other media forms and practices. While navigating the landscape of digital media, music educators might address new media purposefully, artistically, and pedagogically, providing students with rich opportunities to engage with music and media and reflect on what this means in their lives.

NOTES

1. For an example see www.youtube.com/watch?v=VRuLi8geo7Q.
2. For an example see http://samplr.net/.
3. Throughout this section specific media references that provide concrete examples of what is discussed in the text are included as footnotes rather than cited references to assist with reading flow.
4. www.synthesiagame.com/.
5. http://musescore.com/videoscores.
6. www.youtube.com/watch?v=8PJm5A9nYGQ&.
7. www.youtube.com/watch?v=vhT16DZ5_Tk.
8. www.youtube.com/watch?v=l7chHNocFAc.
9. www.youtube.com/watch?v=11Y6Tqw17BM.
10. www.youtube.com/watch?v=dV0F8PNiBhE.

11. www.youtube.com/watch?v=02tkp6eeh40.
12. www.youtube.com/watch?v=qypqwcrO3YE.
13. http://booktrack.com.
14. https://beta.indabamusic.com/opportunities/booktrack-the-time-machine-soundtrack/details.
15. www.snibbestudio.com/rework/.
16. www.youtube.com/watch?v=f6TqadAVk40.
17. QR codes are visual representations of links to content online. Devices with applications that recognize QR codes can scan and then access the related content online.
18. www.youtube.com/watch?v=VRuLi8geo7Q.
19. www.iduun.com/kadambini/.
20. http://supereverything.net/.
21. Gee (2010) calls for scholars working in the area of digital media and learning to offer "worked examples" by imagining and discussing proposed exemplars in new and emerging areas of scholarship. I offer the following description of the John Cage Project in this spirit.
22. http://cdppcme.asu.edu/whenismusic/spread-the-word/.
23. http://cdppcme.asu.edu/whenismusic/can-existing-music-become-new-music/.
24. http://cdppcme.asu.edu/whenismusic/is-music-happening-now/.
25. http://cdppcme.asu.edu/whenismusic/when-is-an-instrument/.

REFERENCES

Armstrong, V. (2001). Theorizing gender and musical composition in the computerized classroom. *Women: A Cultural Review, 12*(1), 35–43.

Azuma, R. (1997). A survey of augmented reality. *Presence: Teleoperators and Virtual Environments, 6*(4), 355–85.

Barrett, J. R. (2007). Music teachers' lateral knowledge. *Bulletin of the Council for Research in Music Education, 174,* 7–23.

Barrett, J. R., McCoy, C. W., & Veblen, K. K. (1997). *Sound ways of knowing: Music in the interdisciplinary curriculum.* New York, NY: Schirmer Books.

Barrett, J. R., & Veblen, K. K. (2012). Meaningful connections in a comprehensive approach to the music curriculum. In G. E. McPherson & G. F. Welch (Eds.), *The Oxford handbook of music education* (Vol. 1, pp. 361–80). New York, NY: Oxford University Press.

Bauer, W. I. (2010). Your personal learning network: Professional development on demand. *Music Educators Journal, 97*(2), 37–42.

Berger, K. (2011). Classical music waltzes with digital media. *Los Angeles Times.* Retrieved from http://articles.latimes.com/2011/aug/07/entertainment/la-ca-classical-technology-20110807

Blair, D. V. (2008). Do you hear what I hear? Musical maps and felt pathways of musical understanding. *Visions of Research in Music Education, 11,* 1–23.

Brown, A. R., & Dillon, S. C. (2012). Collaborative digital media performance with generative music systems. In G. E. McPherson & G. F. Welch (Eds.), *The Oxford handbook of music education* (Vol. 2, pp. 549–66). New York, NY: Oxford University Press.

Burnard, P. (2011). Educational leadership, musical creativities and digital technology in education. *Journal of Music, Technology, and Education, 4*(2 & 3), 157–71.

Coulton, J. (2013). Baby got back and glee. Retrieved from www.jonathancoulton.com/2013/01/18/baby-got-back-and-glee/

Crossley, M. (2012). From LeCompte to Lepage: Student performer engagement with intermedial practice. *International Journal of Performance Arts and Digital Media, 8*(2), 171–88.

Deal, S., & Burtner, M. (2011). *Auksalaq, a telematic opera.* Paper presented at the International Computer Music Conference, Huddersfield, UK.

Deemer, R. (2013, June 28). Visual enhancements. Retrieved from www.newmusicbox. org/articles/visual-enhancements/

Deleuze, G., & Guattari, F. (1987). *A thousand plateaus: Capitalism and schizophrenia.* Minneapolis: University of Minnesota Press.

Dena, C. (2009). *Transmedia practice: Theorising the practice of expressing a fictional world across distinct media and environments* (Doctoral dissertation). University of Sydney, Sydney, Australia.

Dena, C. (2011). Transmedia for event-based arts. *Connecting: Arts audiences online.* Retrieved from http://connectarts.australiacouncil.gov.au/transmedia-for-event-based-arts/

Detroit Symphony Orchestra. (2012). DSO taps Noteflight to enable global audience to compose during live performance. Retrieved from http://blog.dso.org/2012/04/dso-taps-noteflight-to-enable-global-audience-to-compose-during-live-performance/

Deuze, M. (2006). Participation, remediation, bricolage: Considering principal components of a digital culture. *The Information Society, 22*(2), 63–75.

Dunn, R. E. (2006). Teaching for lifelong, intuitive listening. *Arts Education Policy Review, 107*(3), 33–8.

Fenton, D. (2007). Hotel Pro Forma's *The Algebra of Place*: Destabilising the original and the copy in intermedial contemporary performance. *International Journal of Performance Arts and Digital Media, 3*(2 & 3), 169–81.

Ferneding, K. (2005). Embracing the telematic: A techno-utopian vision of art and pedagogy for the post-human age of control. *Journal for the American Association for the Advancement of Curriculum Studies, 1,* 1–17.

Ferneding, K. (2007). Understanding the message of the medium: Media technologies as an aesthetic. In L. Bresler (Ed.), *International handbook of research in arts education* (pp. 1331–52). Dordrecht, Netherlands: Springer.

Gee, J. P. (2010). *New digital media and learning as an emerging area and "worked examples" as one way forward.* Cambridge, MA: MIT Press.

Hansen, B. (n.d.). Song reader. Retrieved from http://songreader.net

Helibroner, R. L. (1967). Do machines make history? *Technology and Culture, 8*(3), 335–45.

Higgins, D. (2001). Intermedia. *Leonardo, 34*(1), 49–54.

Hondl, B. (2012). To tweet or not to tweet—A changing relationship with the audience. Retrieved from http://symphonyforum.org/?p=1395

Iduun. (n.d.). Kadambini, an audiovisual and cinema show by Iduun. Retrieved from www.iduun.com/kadambini/

Ito, M. (2006). Japanese media mixes and amateur cultural exchange. In D. Buckingham (Ed.), *Rebekah Willett* (pp. 49–66). Mahwah, NJ: Lawrence Erlbaum.

Ito, M. (2007). Technologies of the childhood imagination: Yugioh, media mixes, and everyday cultural production. In J. Karaganis & N. Jeremijenko (Eds.), *Structures of participation in digital culture* (pp. 88–110). Durham, NC: Duke University Press.

Jackson, T. A. (2001). Towards a new media aesthetic. In D. Trend (Ed.), *Reading digital culture* (pp. 347–53). Malden, MA: Blackwell.

Jenkins, H. (2006a). *Convergence culture: Where old and new media collide.* New York: New York University Press.

Jenkins, H. (2006b). *Fans, bloggers, and gamers: Exploring participatory culture.* New York: New York University Press.

Jenkins, H., Purushotma, R., Weigel, M., Clinton, K., & Robison, A.J. (2009). *Confronting the challenges of participatory culture: Media education for the 21st Century*. Cambridge, MA: MIT Press.

Jenkins, J. (2008). A kaleidoscopic view of the Harlem Renaissance. *Music Educators Journal, 94*(5), 42–9.

Jorgensen, E.R. (2003). *Transforming music education*. Bloomington: Indiana University Press.

Kerchner, J.L. (2009). Drawing middle-schoolers' attention to music. In J.L. Kerchner & C.R. Abril (Eds.), *Musical experience in our lives: Things we learn and meanings we make* (pp. 183–98). New York, NY: Rowman & Littlefield Education.

Kopp, I. (2011). Christy Dena on the creative potential of cross-platform. Retrieved from www.tribecafilminstitute.org/filmmakers/newmedia/116654949.html

Kratus, J. (2007). Music education at the tipping point. *Music Educators Journal, 94*(2), 42–8.

Lister, M., Dovey, J., Giddings, S., Grant, I., & Kelly, K. (2009). *New media: A critical introduction* (2nd Ed.). New York, NY: Routledge.

Löwgren, J. (2010). Designing for collaborative crossmedia creation. In K. Drotner & K.C. Schroder (Eds.), *Digital content creation: Perceptions, practices, and perspectives* (pp. 15–36). New York, NY: Peter Lang.

Lum, C.-H. (2009). Teaching world music through feature films. *Music Educators Journal, 95*(3), 71–5.

Macpherson, B. (2012). Embodying the virtual: "Digital Opera" as a new Gesamtkunstwerk? *International Journal of Performance Arts and Digital Media, 8*(1), 49–60.

Manovich, L. (2002). *The language of new media*. Cambridge, MA: MIT Press.

McConnell, S. (1947). Can film music be used educationally? *Music Educators Journal, 33*(4), 30–1.

McPherson, G.E., & Welch, G.F. (Eds.). (2012). *The Oxford handbook of music education* (Vol. 2). New York, NY: Oxford University Press.

Medium. (n.d.) In *Merriam-Webster dictionary*. Retrieved from www.merriam-webster.com/dictionary/medium?show=0&t=1361227321

Mendes, J., & Allison, L. (2012). Bear 71. Retrieved from http://bear71.nfb.ca/

Miksza, P. (2013). The future of music education: Continuing the dialogue about curricular reform. *Music Educators Journal, 99*(4), 45–50.

Miller, C.H. (2008). *Digital storytelling: A creator's guide to interactive entertainment* (2nd Ed.). Burlington, MA: Focal Press.

Miller, V. (2011). *Understanding digital culture*. Thousand Oaks, CA: Sage.

Partti, H. (2012). Cosmopolitan musicianship under construction: Digital musicians illuminating emerging values in music education. *International Journal of Music Education, Online*, 1–16.

Partti, H., & Karlsen, S. (2010). Reconceptualising musical learning: New media, identity and community in music education. *Music Education Research, 12*(4), 369–82.

Rajewsky, I.O. (2005). Intermediality, intertextuality, and remediation: A literary perspective on intermediality. *Intermédialités: Histoire et théorie des arts, des lettres et des techniques,* (6), 43–64.

Regelski, T.A. (2013). Another perspective: A response to "Toward Convergence." *Music Educators Journal, 99*(4), 37–42.

Rutherford-Johnson, T. (n.d.). *Up-close*: Description. Retrieved from www.vanderaa.net/up-close

Ruthmann, S.A. (2007). Strategies for supporting music learning through online collaborative technologies. In J. Finney & P. Burnard (Eds.), *Music education with digital technology* (pp. 131–41). New York, NY: Continuum International Publishing Group.

Ruthmann, S. A., & Hebert, D. G. (2012). Music learning and new media in virtual and online environments. In G. E. McPherson & G. F. Welch (Eds.), *The Oxford handbook of music education* (Vol. 2, pp. 567–84). New York: Oxford University Press.

Ruthmann, S.A., Tobias, E., Randles, C., & Thibeault, M. (2015). Is it the technology?: Challenging technological determinism in music education. In C. Randles (Ed.), *Music Education: Navigating the Future* (pp. 122–138). New York: Routledge.

Ryan, D. (2012). Opera outside of itself. *International Journal of Performance Arts and Digital Media, 8*(1), 11–30.

Salavuo, M. (2006). Open and informal online communities as forums of collaborative musical activities and learning. *British Journal of Music Education, 23*(3), 253–71.

Schröter, J. (2012). Four models of intermediality. In B. Herzogenrath (Ed.), *Travels in intermedia[lity]: Reblurring the boundaries* (pp. 15–36). Lebanon, NH: Dartmouth College Press.

Scolari, C. A. (2009). Transmedia storytelling: Implicit consumers, narrative worlds, and branding in contemporary media production. *International Journal of Communication, 3*, 586–606.

SuperEverything. (n.d.a). What is SuperEverything? Retrieved from http://supereverything.net/what-is-supereverything/

SuperEverything. (n.d.b). What is live cinema? Retrieved from http://supereverything.net/what-is-live-cinema/

SuperEverything. (n.d.c). How can I get involved? Retrieved from http://supereverything.net/how-can-i-get-involved/

Thibeault, M. D. (2011). Learning from looking at sound: Using multimedia spectrograms to explore world music. *General Music Today, 25*(1), 50–5.

Thibeault, M. D. (2012). Music education in the postperformance world. In G. E. McPherson & G. F. Welch (Eds.), *The Oxford handbook of music education* (Vol. 2, pp. 517–30). New York, NY: Oxford University Press.

Thibeault, M. D., & Evoy, J. (2011). Building your own musical community: How YouTube, Miley Cyrus, and the ukulele can create a new kind of ensemble. *General Music Today, 24*(3), 44–52.

Tobias, E. S. (2012a). Let's play! Learning music through video games and virtual worlds. In G. McPherson & G. Welch (Eds.), *The Oxford handbook of music education* (Vol. 2, pp. 531–48). Oxford, United Kingdom: Oxford University Press.

Tobias, E. S. (2012b). When is music? Retrieved from http://cdppcme.asu.edu/whenismusic/

Tobias, E. S. (2012c). Hybrid spaces and hyphenated musicians: Secondary students' musical engagement in a songwriting and technology course. *Music Education Research, 14*(3), 329–46.

Tobias, E. S. (2013). Toward convergence: Adapting music education to contemporary society and participatory culture. *Music Educators Journal, 99*(4), 29–36.

Turino, T. (2008). *Music as social life: The politics of participation.* Chicago, IL: University of Chicago Press.

Väkevä, L. (2009). The world well lost, found: Reality and authenticity in Green's "new classroom pedagogy." *Action, Criticism & Theory for Music Education, 8*(2), 1–28.

Waldron, J. (2009). Exploring a virtual music "community of practice": Informal music learning on the Internet. *Journal of Music, Technology, and Education, 2*(2 & 3), 97–112.

Waldron, J. (2011). Conceptual frameworks, theoretical models and the role of YouTube: Investigating informal music learning and teaching in online music community. *Journal of Music, Technology, and Education, 4*(2 & 3), 189–200.

Webb, M. (2010). Re viewing listening: "Clip culture" and cross-modal learning in the music classroom. *International Journal of Music Education, 28*(4), 313–40.

Webster, P. R. (2007). Computer-based technology and music teaching and learning: 2000–2005. In L. Bresler (Ed.), *International handbook of research in arts education* (pp. 1311–28). Dordrecht, Netherlands: Springer.

Wiggins, G. P., & McTighe, J. (2005). *Understanding by design.* Alexandria, VA: Association for Supervision and Curriculum Development.

Williams, D. A. (2007). What are music educators doing and how well are we doing it? *Music Educators Journal, 94*(1), 18–23.

Williams, D. A. (2011). The elephant in the room. *Music Educators Journal, 98*(1), 51–7.

Wise, B. (2011). Symphony goers, start your smart phones. Retrieved from www.wqxr.org/#!/blogs/wqxr-blog/2011/nov/28/symphony-goers-start-your-smart-phones/

8 Is It the Technology? Challenging Technological Determinism in Music Education

Alex S. Ruthmann, Evan S. Tobias,
Clint Randles, and Matthew D. Thibeault

In preparation for the 2012 annual joint meeting of the Association for Technology in Music Instruction[1] (ATMI) and the College Music Society[2] (CMS), I invited three of my colleagues—Clint Randles, Matthew Thibeault, and Evan Tobias—to join in a panel discussion of technological determinism and music education. By *technological determinism* we are referring to the common societal *habit* (Sterne, 2003) to anthropomorphize technology by assigning *it* human characteristics such as agency (Smith, 1994), and the ability to have "causal influence on social practice" (Bimber, 1994, p. 83) in and of itself.

Technological determinism has its roots in music education in writings beginning in the early 20th century (see Thibeault's section later in this chapter), continuing through the advent of computer-based music education in the late 1960s where computer technologies were seen as a potential proxy for the music teacher framed around "its potential" for providing individualized instruction, audio-visual enhancement, and personalized feedback (Allvin, 1971; Kuhn & Allvin, 1967). In the 1980s, Jack Taylor (1983) presented a model of a music computer-based instruction (CBI) system using line drawings of instructional music technologies of the time (Figure 8.1). Taylor's "music CBI system" presents only physical representations of the various pieces of technology that, when taken alone, privilege and focus the reader on the technology itself rather than the students. However, in the body of the article Taylor proposes a set of fictional dialogues between a student and a computer illustrating how computers might be used to support and guide musical learning. Taylor's (1983) view is what Smith (1994) would refer to as *soft determinism,* because he cautions that it would be a "mistake . . . to regard computers and humans as separate, competitive entities" (p. 45). Taylor argues that computers and related music technologies are *extensions* of human practice in that "computers can become human-like in their teaching characteristics" (p. 43).

While many proponents of technology in music education argue that technologies are human constructions, best used when contextualized as part of a broader "system" (Taylor, 1983), experiential context (Williams & Webster, 1996/2008), or "relational pedagogy" (Ruthmann & Dillon, 2012),

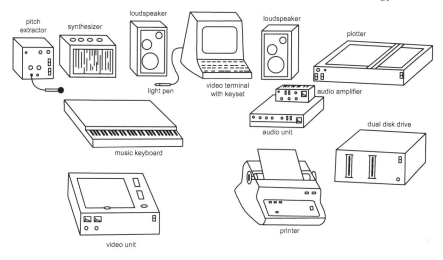

Figure 8.1   Jack Taylor's (1983) model of a music computer-based instruction system.

industry advertisements, researcher accounts, and informal descriptions of practice often make reference to the technologies themselves as agents of change or action. A current case-in-point could be the trend to share lists of favorite iPad apps shared across today's social media site in support of music making, learning, and teaching. It is a cultural habit (Sterne, 2000, 2006) to communicate technologies like the iPad as *the agent* that will bene-fit or positively effect music education practice. In reality, there is a complex set of relationships and practices at play where the effectiveness, usefulness, and experiential meanings of technologies-in-context are determined.

The purpose of this chapter is to invite you as the reader to think criti-cally about how you speak about technology. What do you omit? What do you include? Where are students and teachers in your discussion? Where is the broader community? Where are parents and administrators? How do you frame the purposes, possibilities, and pitfalls of technologies? Where is agency and action attributed? What might determinist language conceal and reveal (Dillon, 2007) about music education practices? To help assist in answering these questions, consider the following visions of "*technology as*," each of which appear in this chapter:

Technology as mediator of experience
Technology as having agency
Technology as a human creation, and reflective of human processes and
   needs
Technology as culturally situated in "human practice, habitat, and
   habit" (Sterne, 2003, p. 8).
Technology as . . . [insert your own thoughts here].

My personal perspective is to document and share detailed descriptions of how teachers and students interact, make music, and learn through the use of music technologies in specific contexts. By acknowledging the *contexts* within which we experience technologies and the *relationships* among students, teachers, music making, and technologies within and across contexts, we have the potential to re-center our discussions around children and teachers as agents of change, rather than the technology itself. This perspective resonates with that of Seymour Papert (1980, 1993) who in his writings on technology centrally framed his discussions around children and their experiences with the technology.

Each of my coauthors will now present their own critical perspectives on technological determinism within music education. Tobias discusses the distinctions between *hard* and *soft* determinism, problematizing the view that technology has a "causal influence on social practice" (Bimber, 1994, p. 83). Tobias advocates for a critical examination of and engagement with technology, investigating how people meaningfully use music technologies in their daily lives. Randles puts forward the archetypal example of Steve Jobs, arguing that the seemingly opposite beliefs of *free will* and *technological determinism* provide the dialectical tension needed to cultivate cultural creativity. Thibeault takes a societal perspective contextualizing why technologically determinist language and perspectives "make sense," while cautioning that these views are not necessarily "sensible." He argues that educators should explore an interactive understanding of technologies that takes into account Sterne's (2003) "institutions, technologies, people, and practices" (p. 182).

FROM THE PRESCRIPTIVE TO THE POSSIBLE

Evan S. Tobias

When thinking about Dvořák's music, one might not envision computers as part of the musical experience. However, for many people technology mediates musical experiences even in the context of Western art music. Consider for instance how one might use a computer and music application to remix Dvořák in the style of the dance music genre dubstep (FetOo, n.d.) or create a multimedia analysis of Dvořák's music (Corksmusic1, 2010). These examples demonstrate just two ways that people integrate technology in their musical engagement. Music educators interested in the potential of engaging with music in similar ways, however, ought to be cautious when integrating technology in their programs. Addressing the possibilities or transformative potential of technology for music teaching, learning, or musicianship can be enmeshed in perspectives characteristic of technological determinism.

Situating Technological Determinism

The aspect of technological determinism I will be focusing on in this section is "the claim . . . that technology itself exercises causal influence on social practice" (Bimber, 1994, p. 83). Technological determinism rears its head with claims of technology having beneficial or negative effects on music teaching and learning. Statements such as "this app will completely transform the classroom and help students learn how to play better in tune, understand functional harmony, or develop as composers" or "this technology will dehumanize the musical experience and destroy the tradition of performing music as we know it" are indicative of a technological deterministic stance. Though these are extreme examples, similar perspectives can surface when one considers relationships between technology and music teaching and learning.

Ferneding (2007) argues that:

> The manifestation of technology can thus be an expressive or artistic endeavor that enables creative possibility. It can also be used in an instrumental sense to control and dehumanize human reality. Thus, technology is far more complex than being "simply a tool" and it does not exist as neutral or value free—an assumption typical of common-sense perceptions about technology.
>
> (p. 1332)

While considering the possibilities of technology for music education and musical engagement, it is critical that music educators remain cautious about the role of technology in music teaching and learning and move forward with both a critical lens and the ability to consider how technology might facilitate teaching, learning, and musicianship and/or control and dehumanize (Ferneding, 2007).

Key to avoiding deterministic perspectives is consideration of the social context in which technology might be integrated and how it might be used along with a focus on musical practices and pedagogy (Folkestad, 2012; Grint & Woolgar, 1997; Oliver, 2011; Selwyn, 2012). For the purpose of this chapter I situate the issue of technological determinism and possibilities of technology in terms of the musical and learning goal of developing aural skills.

Technology played a key role in supporting the creation of the aforementioned dubstep remix and multimedia analysis of Dvořák's music. While those who create remixes or multimedia music analyses may not have the development of aural skills as the intent of their musical engagement, their processes and engagement may draw upon and develop such skills. Similarly, music educators might frame these types of engagement pedagogically in ways that might help students develop aural skills. Situating aural skills within a pedagogical framework and context of musical practices can assist music educators in considering the potential role of technology in students' development of aural skills without resorting to a deterministic perspective.

We might compare and contrast the types of aural skills applied and processes by which they are developed in remixing music or creating multimedia analyses with those applied and developed through the types of skill and drill approach often associated with Computer Assisted Instruction (CAI). Identifying which technologies, if any, are most beneficial to students' development of aural skills may not be as clear as choosing the software that is most often connected to this aspect of music teaching and learning or products that are marketed as such. To develop a more nuanced perspective of how technology might intersect with musical engagement, in this case the development of aural skills, one might move beyond a perspective of what technology might cause to a perspective of how technology might mediate one's musical engagement and learning.

Technology Mediates

By framing the integration of technology from a perspective of mediation one acknowledges the interaction between technology and context. Jones and Hafner (2012) speak to "the process through which people appropriate [technology] to accomplish particular social practices" (p. 13). They suggest how focusing on mediation might call attention to the tension between affordances (or possibilities for action) and constraints (limitations of action) of digital media. However, while a particular software program might mediate one's development of aural skills, we can problematize the notion that a software program inherently affords or constrains the development of aural skills. Furthermore, we ought to consider what values are being embraced when one asserts that a particular technology is most appropriate for a form of musicianship or pedagogy.

For instance, whereas one educator might value efficiency and the ability to gather quantitative data from a CAI program, another educator might value the thinking and musical context involved when one remixes music through using sequencing or DJ software. We might also consider the types of aural skills developed through the use of particular technologies and how they are integrated in practice. Decisions of whether technology should be used, what technology to use, or how it might be used are often made in relation to affordances and constraints of technology. These types of decisions can become mired in a technological deterministic perspective.

Affordances and Constraints

To understand how technology might be considered in terms of affordances, one might draw upon Gibson's (1986) broader explanation of the concept. Gibson suggests that:

> The affordances of the environment are what it offers the animal, what it provides or furnishes for good or ill. The verb afford is found in a

dictionary; but the noun affordance is not. I have made it up. I mean by it something that refers to both the environment and the animal in a way that no existing term does. It implies the complementarity of the animal and the environment.

(p. 127)

Without reducing people to animals, affordances might thus be thought of in terms of the possibilities they offer for action. For example, Hutchby (2001) explains how a rock may have the affordance for a reptile of being a shelter from the heat of the sun, or, for an insect, of concealment from a hunter (p. 447). Music creation software might thus have the affordance for one to create original music or to develop aural skills.

While one might perceive particular affordances in relation to technology, there is danger in conceptualizing affordances as inherent or embedded in the technology itself. Gibson (1986) explains that "an affordance is neither an objective property nor a subjective property" but rather is "both physical and psychical, yet neither" in that "an affordance points both ways, to the environment and to the observer (p. 129). Affordances exist in a contextual relationship between people and technologies.

Oliver (2011) warns that even when seeing affordances as possibilities it is misleading to view affordances outside of a context, stating that:

The idea of affordance has been argued to give insufficient recognition to the importance of social practice, meaning, and knowledge in this context, focusing unduly on the appearance of devices and underplaying the role of meaning and learning in the way that technology is taken up (Derry 2007).

(p. 375)

In other words, technologies are often ascribed affordances outside of particular contexts such as classrooms, ensembles, stages, or studios. Statements such as "this particular technology can improve students' development of aural skills" ought to be put into context.

While some technologies might enable one to analyze intervallic relationships or chord qualities in an efficient manner, statements that these technologies afford the development of aural skills can reify notions of aural skills as related to decontextualized exercises removed from musical practice. Music educators thus ought to be cognizant of how particular technologies are framed and marketed in education discourse. Pfaffenberger (1992) cautions people to consider how discourse can play a role in the multiple ways one might interpret technology. Music educators might consider how particular conceptions of technology can be limited, prescriptive, or reify specific practices.

While one can be inspired by conference presentations, workshops, information exchanged via social media, conversations, advertisements, and other ways technology is framed in contemporary society or music teaching and learning; music educators ought to view technology critically and in terms of other possibilities that are not necessarily forwarded in related discourse. Kritt and Winegar (2007) argue that "educators must have the will to question in a deep way rather than simply weighing competing sales pitches, reflecting upon how the new technologies are changing education, literacy, and human understanding" (p. 24). Educators might ask why certain technologies are marketed in terms of aural skills development or what values underpin discourse related to technology and skill development.

Key to avoiding technological determinism is considering the interaction between technology and context. Understanding the technology, its properties, and how it might be used in practice can inform pedagogy. Savage (2005) discusses how musicians can use technologies in their musicking but also draw upon their musical experience and understanding to avoid "being dictated to" by technology (Section 1, para. 2). By developing understanding of how technologies work, music educators can apply critical lenses from which to view potential affordances or constraints. We might then frame affordances and constraints of technology in terms of how they are perceived in relation to social, cultural, pedagogical, and musical contexts; and possibilities for musicianship, teaching, and learning (Grint & Woolgar, 1997; Savage, 2005; Selwyn, 2012).

While educators might identify potential affordances of technology in particular contexts, Orlikowski (2000) argues that:

> Saying that use is situated and not confined to predefined options does not mean that it is totally open to any and all possibilities. The physical properties of artifacts ensure that there are always boundary conditions on how we use them.
>
> (p. 409)

For instance, a particular music application might be designed to work only with MIDI data and therefore be incapable of recording or making use of digital audio; however, this boundary condition does not close off one's ability to develop aural skills or create music. In this way constraints are also perceived rather than inherent within technologies. Understanding the physical or computing limitations of technologies does not equate to what they may or may not be able to afford given that people can be quite creative in their engagement with technology. In other words, an aspect of a technology that one person sees as a limitation may not be a limitation for a peer. Again, a technology does not determine one's musical engagement or learning.

Critical Engagement with Technology

Jones and Hafner (2012) suggest that "the best way to become more competent users of technologies is to become more critical and reflective about how we use them in our everyday lives, the kinds of things that they allow us to do, and the kinds of things they don't allow us to do" (p. 1). Particularly, in music teaching and learning we ought to consider the role of technology in how practices or contexts are reified as well as how technology might become reified through particular practices and contexts. This includes identifying and examining values promoted by particular technologies (Ferneding, 2007). We might ask why particular technologies are used to help students develop aural skills, and how pedagogy and curriculum reify the use of these technologies or how these technologies contribute to the reification of aural skills. We might then consider additional possibilities of aural skills and technology in the same or new contexts.

In considering contexts, viewing technology through a critical lens, identifying multiple possibilities of technology, and envisioning how it might be used in ways that it was not originally intended, music educators can avoid deterministic analyses of the role that technologies play in music teaching and learning. Orlikowski (2000) echoes this perspective, arguing that:

> Awareness of alternative ways of using technology may motivate people to make changes in their technology and/or their use of it. It may also prompt them to make changes in the other structures that they constitute in their work practices.
>
> (p. 412)

As music educators look to the potential and possibilities of technology, it is critical that we situate its use through musical, social, cultural contexts, practices, goals, and pedagogy, whether technology is used in the context of creating analytical multimedia or Dvořák as dubstep.

THINKING DIFFERENT: STEVE JOBS, FREE WILL, AND CULTURAL CREATIVITY

Clint Randles

While preparing to be a part of the group of scholars that would address the notion of technological determinism in music education for the ATMI conference, I was reading Walter Isaacson's (2011) biography *Steve Jobs*. Jobs believed in a certain kind of technological determinism, perhaps the "soft determinism" that Smith (1994) refers to in his work, the idea that "technological change drives social change but at the same time responds discriminatingly to social pressures" (p. 2). Jobs harnessed these beliefs along with a strong sense of both the human desire to organize activity and the desire to engage with media, to fuel a *cultural creative process* through the development of a number of his products. Jobs seemed to understand the kind of personal fulfillment that could be experienced when individuals exercised their free will to manage their own worlds by way of the agency that technology helped to facilitate. Jobs believed that technology should not be "instruments used by Orwellian governments and giant corporations to sap individuality" (Isaacson, 2012, p. 162), what Smith (1994) referred to as "hard determinism," where "technological development" is "an autonomous force, completely independent of social constraints" (p. 2). Rather, technology—products and systems built by human hands—should be viewed as "tools for personal empowerment" (p. 162), which was his vision of what the Macintosh could be leading to the product launch in 1984.

Personal Empowerment

Personal empowerment in this case is what an individual achieves through the agency that technology mediates. It is a state of being where one is the director of one's own media-rich information world. What role did Steve Jobs play in the development of personal computing empowerment? I recognize, like Sawyer (2012), that there was a sociocultural component to the success of Apple computers that stretched beyond the individual contributions of Steve Jobs (p. 251). However, I would like to suggest here that Jobs served as the brilliant leader, or "superstar" to use Sawyer's terminology (p. 234), of a personal computing revolution that took shape most dramatically with the release of the Macintosh in 1984. Jobs believed that technology was a mechanism to assist individuals in developing their own capacities for self-expression.

Determinism, an extreme form of determinism, or "hard determinism" (Smith, 1994, p. 2), is the belief that because something exists a certain way—technology, or the activities that technology affords—society must therefore act a certain way or react a certain way, based on the overwhelming power of that something over what we do. Jobs understood determinism well. He probably in some way believed it. However, more importantly, Jobs understood that human aesthetic—expressed in and through music, movies, and art, among a host of other manifestations of media as some of the highest expressions of human achievement—brings meaning to the human experience. I would like to propose here that the way that Steve Jobs balanced *free will* with *deterministic beliefs*, or "soft determinism" (Smith, 1994, p. 2), might be a healthy way for music education to approach the idea of technological determinism in music education.

Free Will

While working at Atari during his young adult life, Steve Jobs shared his beliefs regarding the relationship between determinism and free will with a colleague: "We used to discuss free will vs. determinism. I tended to believe that things were much more determined, that we were programmed. If we had perfect information, we could predict people's actions. Steve felt the opposite" (Isaacson, 2011, p. 43). Perhaps Jobs recognized the potential

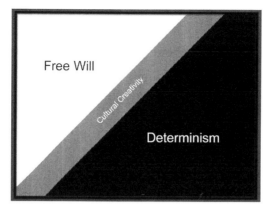

Figure 8.2 Free will vs. determinism.

liberating power that technology could have in the hands of humans who themselves possessed a desire to experience beauty. One might argue that Jobs—and his team of entrepreneurial thinkers, engineers, and designers—possessed the vision to see what the world might look like when a computer served as the hub for creative personal activity. Growing up, Jobs was a subscriber to the *Whole Earth Catalog,* which sold tools and educational materials. On the first page of the first issue in 1968, a slogan read: "a realm of infinite, personal power is developing—power of the individual to conduct his own education, find his own inspiration, shape his own environment, and share his adventure with whoever is interested" (Isaacson, 2011, p. 58). Here, deterministic overtones are charged by the power of human beings to control their own fate, to organize their own worlds. In the end, free will wins out over determinism. It is the balance, the tension if you will, between free will and "hard determinism" that allows for "soft determinism" and the ability for human beings to order their media-rich worlds (see Figure 8.2).

Cultural Creativity

Technological determinism can be framed a few different ways. As stated previously, Smith (1994) makes the distinction between (1) "soft determinism," where technology is in a reflexive relationship with societal pressures, and (2) "hard determinism," where technology forces society to change, independent from societal desires or constraints (p. 2). The first statement in a way places society in the driver's seat, while the second places technology there. Human beings invent technologies that transform their experience. The daily interaction of those technologies with human experience causes humans to engage in cultural creative processes where those technologies are concerned. Sawyer (2012) asserts:

> Cultural change always involves creativity. But this kind of creativity is very different than fine art painting or musical performance because it's the creativity of everyday life. In cultural creativity, novelty is a transformation of cultural practices and appropriateness is the value to a community.
>
> (p. 266)

Sawyer (2012) claims, as do other scholars in the study of creativity (Amabile, 1996; Csikszentmihalyi, 1999), that both novelty and appropriateness are signposts of creative processes and products. Who decides when something is both novel and appropriate? At the *Big C* creativity level, Csikszentmihalyi (1999) claims that the *Field*, those experts who have distinguished themselves in a given *Domain,* are the ones who collectively determine when something is creative (p. 315). On a basic level, though, *humans* decide when something—technology—is both novel and appropriate. So *humans* necessarily must be in the drivers seat, again mediated by the balanced constructs of *free will* and *determinism.*

Steve Jobs, as the visionary leader of Apple Computers, initiated a number of cultural creative processes during his tenure as CEO. Isaacson (2012) quotes Bill Gates, in describing the Macintosh: "To create a new standard takes not just making something that's a little different, it takes something that's really new and captures people's imagination. And the Macintosh, of all the machines I've ever seen, is the only one that meets that standard" (p. 160). It was Steve Job's understanding the human desire for *free will* and the agency that technologies afford, the first example of *determinism* mentioned previously, that fueled the development of not only the Macintosh but many of the groundbreaking new products that Apple has developed—iTunes, the iPod, the iPhone, and the iPad, to name a few. When balanced with a good understanding of the basic human need for *free will, deterministic beliefs* (of the first variety that I mentioned) are more fruitfully channeled.

A Way Forward

Isaacson (2012) described Jobs as possessing "the creativity that can occur when a feel for both the humanities and the sciences combine in one strong personality . . . " (p. xix). I would like to suggest here that music education might gain from enacting cultural creative processes that acknowledge both *free will* and *determinism.* These two constructs, like the humanities and the sciences, at face value might seem at odds with one another. However, they can also be viewed as complimentary. Similar to the ideas of *freedom* and *constraint* in the creativity literature (Barrett, 2003), when rubbed together or placed in close proximity, free will and determinism often produce action of some kind.

Put in practical terms, the music education profession would do well to embrace a "soft determinism" stance on the role of technology in the transformation of local music making practices. Reflexivity between technology and human beings should be one of our goals. Local music teachers then would be in the driver's seat of the incorporation of new technologies into expanded, culturally relevant music curricula. When in proper balance, deterministic beliefs really are not that bad, when formed and transformed by human beings who value truth, beauty, and goodness.

THE SENSE OF TECHNOLOGICAL DETERMINISM

Matthew Thibeault

I have a memory from *Cracked* magazine in the late 1970s. The back cover presented an advertising parody, with a headline that read, "Four out of five dentists recommend sugarless gum for their patients who chew gum. I'm the one who didn't."[3] A black and white photograph depicted a dentist, brown bag over his head, dumping a bag of sugar into his patient's mouth via a funnel.

Belief in technological determinism can seem akin to this ad. When defined as technology driving change with an inevitable trajectory unalterable by human effort,[4] believing that technological determinism describes how our world works is akin to the dentist who pours sugar into his patient's mouth. It is absurd.

In this portion of this chapter, I would like to offer an alternate view, a brief attempt to present four ways that technological determinism makes sense. My current view is that technological determinism, rather than an ideology simply to be rejected, is closer to a problem like racism, one baked into our culture in a way that produces what Eduardo Bonilla-Silva (2009) refers to as "racism without racists." We have determinism without determinists. Of course, the problem of technological determinism is not in any way as devastating as racism in America, but they similarly present as ubiquitous ideologies publicly claimed by few, but which nevertheless run rampant within our society. Both are supported in subtle and persistent ways that require explication and critique to lead to confrontation and change.

A first way that deterministic arguments make sense is that they are familiar. Deterministic accounts have been and continue to be prevalent. As far back as one hundred years ago, John Philip Sousa (1906) worried that machine music would end music education, sales of instruments, and leave those who made music simply imitators of phonographs.[5] In the 1960s, Glenn Gould (1966/1984) wrote, "We must be prepared to accept the fact that, for better or worse, recording will forever alter our notions about what is appropriate to the performance of music" (p. 337), and famously predicted technology would cause the concert to become "dormant in the 21st century" (p. 332). Today, most of us are familiar with the belief that Napster changed music in profound ways, or have heard that Jon Bon Jovi held Steve Jobs, through Jobs's technological innovations, personally responsible for killing the music business (Staskiewicz, 2011). We have heard that Google is "making us stupid" (Carr, 2008). And Victoria Armstrong's (2011) work on the gendered nature of technology in music education presents examples and a critique of deterministic hope, namely, that computers will automatically make creativity and composition flourish in the classroom. These accounts are all too familiar.[6]

A second way that technological determinism makes sense is our individualistic vantage point within society. It is rational to believe that I, personally, haven't done much to change the Internet, or contributed to the design of the iPod. But I certainly do believe that I am a member of a society that has profoundly contributed to the shaping of these technologies. It is only when we see ourselves as part of a movement, such as the civil rights movement or today's efforts on behalf of the LGBT community, that we clearly see ourselves as constituting a social force for change. The individualistic paradigm so commonly found in Western societies, as compared with collectivist notions popular elsewhere, likely makes us much more vulnerable to deterministic arguments.

A third way in which determinism makes sense is that it legitimately helps us begin looking for causes. At first glance, it does seem that the iPod and MP3 have had effects on music. It is hard to disagree with the notion that the Internet and computer music software are changing music, musicians, and audiences in fundamental ways. These arguments also help to motivate us to explore how technology is a part of change. Deterministic beliefs are a sensible place to begin, as long as we move beyond them, and we should be thankful for Marshall McLuhan's (1964/2003) expansive vision, Jacques Ellul's (1964) dystopian vision, and the philosophical critique of technology in contemporary life by Albert Borgmann (1984).

A fourth and last source of the sense of technological determinism is its promotion by technological industries. Merritt Roe Smith (1994), writes that:

> Advertising agencies, in short, not only sold the products of industrial capitalism but also promoted ways of thinking about industrial technology. . . . Such technocratic pitches constituted a form of technological determinism that embedded itself deeply in popular culture.
>
> (p. 13)

In other words, Apple sells not only iPods, but an ideology of technological determinism wherein so many of the great improvements of modern life originate in the creative mind of Jonathan Ive and Phil Schiller.[7] A web of legal and intellectual property concerns also depend upon a deterministic account of technological change, and dissuade us from discussing, for instance, the environmental degradation and obscene waste that often accompany technological innovation.[8]

I have shared four ways that technological determinism makes sense: namely, that these arguments are familiar, that they resonate with our individualistic vantage point, that they are a logical place to begin inquiry, and that they are advanced by commercial interests. But to claim that technological determinism makes sense is not to accept it as sensible, and the charge of today's panel is to challenge technological determinism. Perhaps the most potent critique of technological determinism comes from Jonathan Sterne (2003), who writes that these arguments "spring from an impoverished notion of causality" (p. 8). In their place, he suggests:

> To study technologies in any meaningful sense requires a rich sense of their connection with human practice, habitat, and habit. It requires attention to the fields of combined cultural, social, and physical activity—what other authors have called networks or assemblages— from which technologies emerge and of which they are a part.
>
> (p. 8)

Following Sterne's words, talk of the MP3 becomes meaningful when we embed that technology within an understanding of the medium that includes the interactions between "institutions, technologies, people, and practices" (Sterne, 2003, p. 182), something Sterne (2012a) provides in his exemplary book on format theory and the MP3. Thankfully, we increasingly have enriched accounts of technology and change, frequently from the field of sound studies (Pinch & Bijsterveld, 2012; Jonathan Sterne, 2012b). We have Karin Bijsterveld's (2008) wrestling with the "general public's acceptance of technological determinism" (p. 20) in the context of the public problem of mechanical noise. Rather than fear machine music as Sousa did, we have Mark Katz's (2012) account of amateur music making enmeshed with machine music, a celebration of play-along recordings, karaoke, and musical video games. And Emily Thompson (2002) locates a sense of technological progress in the very concert halls in which we perform, spaces that reflect the evolving understanding of acoustics, building materials, and aesthetic ideas. In these examples we begin to grasp an enriched notion of the networks or assemblages leading to deeper understanding, better questions, and a richer sense of how we might better our efforts in music education.

NOTES

1. http://atmimusic.org/.
2. http://music.org/.
3. I use quote marks, but I'm constructing this from memory, so I'm likely a bit off. But I maintain that the photo looked as I describe it. And memory of 1970s hair on the dentist's arms leads to the gendered pronoun.

4. It is important to note that many differentiate between "hard" and "soft" determinism. Soft determinism is much more reasonable, having more to do with the ways that technology exerts pressures on change. A classic exploration comes from Williams (1973), who in discussing Marx writes, "We have to revalue 'determination' towards the setting of limits and the exertion of pressure, and away from a predicted, prefigured and controlled content" (p. 6).

5. Take, for instance, this poetic quote:

> When a mother can turn on the phonograph with the same ease that she applies to the electric light, will she croon her baby to slumber with sweet lullabies, or will the infant be put to sleep by machinery? (Sousa 1906, p. 281)

6. I've also presented a critique of John Kratus's recent work as having an implicitly deterministic structure (Thibeault, 2011), a piece where I also presented a richer version of the pragmatic conception of technology that is only implicit in this paper.

7. Sterne (2003) refers to this as the "male birth model" of technological innovation (p. 181).

8. For example, Sue Halpern (2012) closes her review of Walter Isaacson's (2012) biography of Steve Jobs thusly:

> Next year will bring the iPhone 5, and a new MacBook, and more iPods and iMacs. What this means is that somewhere in the third world, poor people are picking through heaps of electronic waste in an effort to recover bits of gold and other metals and maybe make a dollar or two. Piled high and toxic, it is leaking poisons and carcinogens like lead, cadmium, and mercury that leach into their skin, the ground, the air, the water. Such may be the longest-lasting legacy of Steve Jobs's art.

REFERENCES

Allvin, R. (1971). Computer-assisted music instruction: A look at the potential. *Journal of Research in Music Education, 19*(2), 131–143.

Amabile, T. M. (1996). *Creativity in context: Update to "The Sociology of Creativity."* Boulder, CO: Westview Press.

Armstrong, V. (2011). *Technology and the gendering of music education.* Burlington VT: Ashgate.

Barrett, M. (2003). Freedoms and constraints: Constructing musical worlds through the dialogue of composition. In M. Hickey (Ed.), *Why and how to teach music composition: A new horizon for music education* (pp. 3–27). Reston, VA: MENC Publishing.

Bijsterveld, K. (2008). *Mechanical sound: Technology, culture, and public problems of noise in the twentieth century.* Cambridge, MA: MIT Press.

Bimber, B. (1994). Three faces of technological determinism. In M. R. Smith & L. Marx (Eds.), *Does technology drive history: The dilemma of technological determinism* (pp. 79–100). Cambridge, MA: MIT Press.

Bonilla-Silva, E. (2009). *Racism without racists: Color-blind racism and the persistence of racial inequality in America* (Third ed.). Rowman & Littlefield Publishers.

Borgmann, A. (1984). *Technology and the character of contemporary life: A philosophical inquiry.* Chicago: University of Chicago Press.

Carr, N. (2008, August). Is Google Making Us Stupid? *The Atlantic.* Retrieved from www.theatlantic.com/magazine/archive/2008/07/is-google-making-us-stupid/306868/

Corksmusic1. (2010). Dvorak – Symphony No. 9 in E minor, Op. 95 From the New World mov. . . [video file]. From www.youtube.com/watch?v=zyF1cLA2Izw

Csikszentmihalyi, M. (1999). Implications of a systems perspective of creativity. In R. J. Sternberg (Ed.), *Handbook of Creativity* (pp. 313–335). Cambridge: Cambridge University Press.

Dillon, S. (2007). *Music, meaning and transformation: Meaningful music making for life*. Newcastle-upon-Tyne, UK: Cambridge Scholars Press.

Ellul, J. (1964). *The technological society* (1st American ed.). New York: Knopf.

Ferneding, K. (2007). Understanding the messgae of the medium: Media technologies as an aesthetic. In L. Bresler (Ed.), *International handbook of research in arts education* (pp. 1331–1352). Dordrecht, The Netherlands: Springer.

FetOo. (n.d.). Anton Dvorak – Symphonie du Nouveau Monde Num9 4ème Mouvement (FetOo Remix), from https://soundcloud.com/fetoo/symphonieduno uveaumondefetooremix

Folkestad, G. (2012). Digital tools and discourse in music: The ecology of composition. In D. J. Hargreaves, D. Miell & R. A. R. MacDonald (Eds.), *Musical imaginations: Multidisciplinary perspectives on creativity, performance, and perception* (pp. 193–205). New York, NY: Oxford University Press.

Gardner, H. (2000). *The disciplined mind: Beyond facts, standardized tests, the K-12 education that every child deserves*. New York: Penguin Books.

Gibson, J. J. (1986). *The ecological approach to visual perception*. Hillsdale, NJ: Lawrence Erlbaum Associates.

Gould, G. (1984). The prospects of recording. In T. Page (Ed.), *The Glenn Gould reader* (pp. 331–353). New York: Alfred A. Knopf. (Original work published 1966)

Grint, K., & Woolgar, S. (1997). *The machine at work: Technology, work, and organization*. Malden, MA: Blackwell.

Halpern, S. (2012, January 12). Who was Steve Jobs? [Review of the book *Steve Jobs* by Walter Isaacson]. *New York Review of Books*. Retrieved from www.nybooks.com/articles/archives/2012/jan/12/who-was-steve-jobs/?pagination=false

Hutchby, I. (2001). Technologies, texts and affordances. *Sociology, 35*(2), 441–456.

Isaacson, W. (2011). *Steve Jobs*. New York: Simon & Schuster.

Jones, R. H., & Hafner, C. A. (2012). *Understanding digital literacies: A practical introduction*. London: Routledge.

Katz, M. (2012). The amateur in the age of mechanical music. In K. Bijsterveld & T. J. Pinch (Eds.), *The Oxford handbook of sound studies* (pp. 459–479). New York: Oxford University Press.

Kritt, D. W., & Winegar, L. T. (2007). Technological determinism and human agency. In D. W. Kritt & L. T. Winegar (Eds.), *Education and technology: Critical perspectives, possible futures* (pp. 3–30). Lanham, MD: Lexington Books.

Kuhn, W. E. & Allvin, R. (1967). Computer-assisted teaching: A new approach to research in music. *Journal of Research in Music Education, 15*(4), 305–315.

McLuhan, M. (2003). *Understanding Media: The extensions of man.* (W. T. Gordon, Ed.) (Critical ed.). Corte Madera, CA: Gingko Press. (Original work published 1964)

Oliver, M. (2011). Technological determinism in educational technology research: Some alternative ways of thinking about the relationship between learning and technology. *Journal of Computer Assisted Learning, 27*, 373–384.

Orlikowski, W. J. (2000). Using technology and constituting structures: A practice lens for studying technology in organizations. *Organizational Science, 11*(4), 404–428.

Papert, S. (1980). *Mindstorms: Children, computers, and powerful ideas*. New York: Basic Books.

Papert, S. (1993). *The children's machine: Rethinking school in the age of the computer*. New York: Basic Books.

Pfaffenberger, B. (1992). Technological dramas. *Science, Technology, and Human Values, 17*(3), 282–312.

Pinch, T. J., & Bijsterveld, K. (Eds.). (2012). *The Oxford handbook of sound studies*. New York: Oxford University Press.

Ruthmann, S. A., & Dillon, S. C. (2012). Technology in the lives and schools of adolescents. In G. McPherson & G. Welch (Eds.), *The Oxford handbook of music education, Volume 1* (pp. 529–547). New York: Oxford University Press.

Savage, J. (2005). Information communication technologies as a tool for re-imagining music education in the 21st century. *International Journal of Education and the Arts, 6*(2).

Sawyer, K. (2012). *Explaining creativity: The science of human innovation*. New York: Oxford University Press.

Selwyn, N. (2012). Making sense of young people, education and digital technology: The role of sociological theory. *Oxford Review of Education, 38*(1), 81–96. doi: 10.1080/03054985.2011.577949

Smith, M. R. (1994). Technological determinism in American culture. In M. R. Smith & L. Marx (Eds.), *Does technology drive history?: The dilemma of technological determinism* (pp. 1–35). Cambridge, MA: MIT Press.

Smith, M. R., & Marx, L. (1994). *Does technology drive history?: The dilemma of technological determinism*. Cambridge, MA: MIT Press.

Sousa, J. P. (1906). The Menace of Mechanical Music. *Appleton's Magazine, 8* (September), 278–284.

Staskiewicz, K. (2011, March 15). Jon Bon Jovi accuses Steve Jobs of being "personally responsible for killing the music business" | EW.com. *ew.com*. Retrieved November 13, 2012, from http://music-mix.ew.com/2011/03/15/jon-bon-jovi-steve-jobs-killing-the-music-business/

Sterne, J. (2003). *The audible past: Cultural origins of sound reproduction*. Durham, NC: Duke University Press.

Sterne, J. (2006). Communication as techné. In G. Shepherd & J. St. John (Eds.), *Communication as. . .: Perspectives on theory* (pp. 91–98).

Sterne, J. (2012a). *MP3: the meaning of a format*. Durham: Duke University Press.

Sterne, J. (Ed.). (2012b). *The sound studies reader*. New York: Routledge.

Taylor, J. (1983). Computers as music teachers. *Music Educators Journal, 69*(5), 43–45.

Thibeault, M. D. (2011, October). Response to John Kratus' "Transitioning to Music Education 3.0" [CIC paper]. *Matthew Thibeault*. Retrieved November 14, 2012, from http://matthewthibeault.com/2011/10/06/cic-paper-response-to-john-kratus/

Thompson, E. A. (2002). *The soundscape of modernity: Architectural acoustics and the culture of listening in America, 1900-1933*. Cambridge, MA: MIT Press.

Williams, D. B., & Webster, P. R. (1996/2008). *Experiencing music technology* (3rd edition). Boston, MA: Schirmer/Cengage.

Williams, R. (1973). Base and Superstructure in Marxist Cultural Theory. *New Left Review, I*(89), 3–16.

9 The Technology-Music Dance

Reflections on *Making Sense of Our Tools*

David Brian Williams

Music, like language and possibly religion, is a species specific trait of man.
—John Blacking, *How Musical Is Man?* 1973

We are the artists forming art, not the machines.
—David Brian Williams and Peter R. Webster,
Experiencing Music Technology, 2008

Technology is "technology" only for people who are born before it was invented.
—Alan Kay, Futurist, circa 1980

It is easier to move a cemetery than to effect a change in curriculum.
—Woodrow Wilson

The two chapters contributed by Tobias[1] and Thibeault, and the set of essays by Randles, Tobias, and Thibeault, provide material for philosophical thought, theoretical frameworks, and rich examples to contemplate as we address the topic: *Making sense of our tools.* Music and technology are inextricably intertwined. What an exciting dance we experience with technology, music practice, and music education.

I've been asked to comment on the writings and share my vision for the future of music education from the vantage point of some 50 years of working with, and evangelizing music technology in support of, music education. To facilitate references, I will refer to Evan Tobias's chapter as "Landscapes," Matthew Thibeault's chapter as "Shifting Locus," and the third set of essays as the "Determinism" chapter.

INVITATION TO THE DANCE

"Shifting Locus" provides rich stories from the 19th-century music life in the home of Aunts Kate and Julia, to Sousa who rebelled against the new recording technology, to Gould who embraced it to the extreme, to music dissemination and sharing through the Internet and handheld devices in the short story "Modulation," and finally to Madlib and his über-multimedia productions that grasp at anything analog or digital for music creativity. The stories help frame three themes I wish to develop:

> Theme 1. The evolving sophistication and complexity of music production, creation, and recording tools unfolding historically (the technology-music dance).
> Theme 2. The technology-music dance playing out in society, at large, and in the music classroom.
> Theme 3. The increased access to, and the greater flexibility available from, the variegated set of tools for music making—increasing democratization of music technology (more people invited to the dance).

Early in "Shifting Locus" the following is opined: "Whereas nearly all musical experience was once had in the physical presence of live performers, today nearly all musical experience comes through new media" (Thibeault, p. 64). The Kaiser Family Foundation 2010 study (ibid, p. 64) evidenced that children's time was dominated by media consumption. Upon my closer examination of the data, the largest contributing factor was TV viewing, viewing that was highly dependent on parental guidance. In support of live performance, a NAMM-commissioned Gallup survey (NAMM, 2003) showed that 54% of households have someone who plays a musical instrument and 48% play two or more. The longitudinal study, Monitoring the Future (Johnston, O'Malley, Bachman, & Schulenberg, 1976–2009), showed that over some 30 years, an average 57% of students in 8th, 10th, and 12th grades—not just those in music classes—reported that they play an instrument or sing outside of school (see Williams, 2012, for a full discussion of these data). Yes, perhaps there is less music making in the home like Aunts Kate and Julia, and our youth watch a good deal of passive TV, but these data suggest that live music performance is still doing well. The data also beg the need to assess the number of musicians that participate in such genres as old-time, bluegrass, and country music, as well as garage bands, church music, and more, in the presence of the easy access to recorded musical experiences through new media. If there is any entropy in live performance, it is in the classical music genre evidenced by the economic plight of such major institutions as the New York City Opera, Philadelphia Orchestra, and many others (see Farrell, 2013). I do sense an acknowledgement of live performance in Thibeault's thinking, particularly with participatory performance, when a hope is later expressed for an "open and more generous conception of music, musician, and audience . . . that will allow today's students to fully participate in today's music world" (Thibeault, p. 87).

"Shifting Locus" certainly acknowledges the power that new media provide toward democratizing music for all participants (Theme 3): the realization by the character Jay Steiner in "Modulation" that the music tools at their disposal provides "an instrument that everyone could learn to play without effort" (ibid, p. 87). And Thibeault's search of YouTube guitar videos revealed that "these participant-listeners-turned-performers capture another aspect of the new media era, that is, the incredible rise of creativity." Yes, listener-performers turned participant arrangers, mash-up artists, and composers. And yes, "the recording era, then, gave way to what appears to be a democratization of access to the means of creation and distribution" (ibid, p. 81) through home studio recording, looping software, websites, and access to social network tools like Facebook and SoundCloud.

FRAMEWORK FOR DANCES

The "Landscapes" chapter offers a framework for exploring, research-ing, codifying, and applying the evolving sophistication of music creativity tools to music activities and especially to music education practice. First, the concepts of convergence culture and participatory culture are examined and reflect on Themes 2 and 3. "Landscapes" draws heavily from Jenkins (2006a) and Jenkins, Purushotma, Weigel, Clinton, and Robinson (2009) for these concepts. Convergence culture is cast by Tobias as an opportunity where "new media and contemporary musical practices can co-exist with acoustic music and musicking[2] or other *older* ways of engaging with music" (Tobias, p. 96). Participatory culture as portrayed by Jenkins et al. (2009) embraces the "creating and sharing of performance and creation with oth-ers" with "relatively low barriers to artistic expression and civic engage-ment." Mentors freely pass their skills on to novices within the culture with "some degree of social connection" among members (Tobias, p. 96).

The convergence of acoustic and electronic music making, technology, and music practice old and new, and the culture which emanates from the milieu of music making, participatory musicking, and the engaged listener, comes through both in "Landscapes" and "Shifting Locus" from a theo-retical perspective as well as through the many examples shared. Again, the authors are portraying the exhilarating dance between technology and music.

I find Turino's (2008) continuum of participatory musicking (Thibeault, p. 97) especially useful in understanding the ways one might participate in the technology-music dance: participatory live performance, presentational live performance, high fidelity recording music, and studio audio art record-ing music. The beginning of the continuum might start with music from one of Thibeault's participatory ukulele sessions, then progress to Aunts Kate and Julia's home recital. The end of the continuum, the studio art music, is a perfect fit for Otis Jackson's (a.k.a. Madlib) studio: "A studio is his primary instrument," a home studio filled with records, traditional instru-ments, as well as computers, software, mixers, microphones, turntables and more (Thibeault, p. 83).

Convergence and participatory music cultures set the stage for the Tobias's framework of multimedia, intermedia, and transmedia. At the risk of being simplistic, one might offer the following observation: the advent of CD-ROM technology opened the opportunity for deploying digital media to create multimedia experiences (now moved to web-based and tablet-based apps); the advent of software like GarageBand, Abelton Live, and Max MSP opened the opportunity for creating intermedia art forms and experiences through both MIDI control and the ever expanding universe of digital samples and loops; and the advent of social networking and cloud computing tools (Twitter, Wikis, Facebook, SoundCloud, and more) provides the key elements needed for fully realizing experiences and art forms within the transmedia framework.

These are not mutually exclusive. The telematic opera *Auksalaq* that "Landscapes" notes could be considered transmedia as much as intermedia. The John Cage project that Tobias designed makes use of all media forms within the framework and the concomitant technology that makes this interplay possible. More recent examples in the news include the wireless opera, *Invisible Cities*, performed in Los Angeles Union Station where "attendees were equipped with wireless headphones and wandered the enormous main station hall—as well an adjacent waiting area and outdoor courtyard—following the similarly untethered performers as they emerged from all directions" (Shamoon, 2013). A recent exhibit at the New York Museum of Arts and Design was entitled "Out of Hand: Materializing the Postdigital," where artists referred to the "postdigital" as "bending digital techniques to their own expressive ends" (Sheets, 2013). Richard Dupont, a sculptor who creates "startling distortions of the human form," explains: "The forms I end up with couldn't have been done without using digital tools, but you have to disrespect them on some level." "It's much more interesting," he shares, "if you can disrupt the expectations of what the technology can do" (ibid).

To borrow from Tobias's summary point for the transmedia framework, "whether one works with or within multi-, inter-, or transmedia, an artist or a teacher can create an artistic and learning experience that emphasizes connections between media, ideas, artworks, and other aspects of the human experience that might not otherwise have been apparent" (Tobias, p. 111). The framework encourages us to expand our repertoire and explore either as a performer, composer, director, or teacher the phantasmagoria of media options: analog and digital, visual and sonic, static and movement.

The progression through the digital media frameworks adds further support to Theme 1, the continue evolution of the dance between technology and music. Extending this further to Theme 3, "Landscapes" reinforces the power of digital media to democratize artistic expression, quoting from Jenkins et al. (2009), "as the culture absorbs and responds to the explosion of new media technologies that make it possible for average consumers to archive, annotate, appropriate, and reticulate media content in powerful new ways" (Tobias, p. 97). An issue I will address more fully in a moment is the advice to music educators that hints at what transpires in the music classroom does not reflect on society in general (Theme 2).

WHO LEADS ON THE DANCE FLOOR?

The three essays in the "Determinism" chapter by Randles, Tobias, and Thibeault examine the philosophical position of technology determinism from various vantage points. Why is this important to a discussion of "making sense of our tools" and music education? The technology determinist would say that technology drives changes in how we experience and engage in music and how we, as educators, deliver instruction and design our strategies for student learning. The opposite of determinism, as the essays note, is free will. The question is thus, who leads on the dance floor, technology or music?

Randles develops the concept of "soft determinism" through the writings of Smith (1994) and the contributions to technology by Steve Jobs. "Technological change drives social change," he explains, "but at the same time responds discriminatingly to social pressures" (Randles, p. 129). He proposes "that the way that Steve Jobs balanced free will with deterministic beliefs, soft determinism, might be a healthy way for music education to approach the idea of technological determinism" (ibid, p. 129). Seeking a similar balance between determinism and free will, Tobias makes reference to Jones and Hafner (2012) and introduces "the tension between affordances (or possibilities for action) and constraints (limitation of action) of digital media" (Tobias, p. 126).

Thibeault's essay offers four ways that "deterministic arguments make sense" (Thibeault, p. 133): they are familiar to us; we believe we are part of technology initiatives by participating in them; it helps us look for causes; and they are promoted by corporate America. He is careful, on the other hand, to stress that "to claim that technological determinism makes sense is not to accept it as sensible." The common denominator through the three essays is the push-pull of technology with its "affordance and constraints" against free will set in the cultural context of "a rich sense of their connection with human practice, habitat, and habit" (Sterne, 2003, cited by Thibeault, p. 135).

TECHNOLOGY ADOPTION LIFECYCLE

The dance between technology and the people and ways (procedures) they make and experience music is a key thread throughout the three chapters. As we emphasized in *Experiencing Music Technology* (Williams & Webster, 2008, p. 12):

It is important to understand that *people using technology* is the most important component of a music system. Whatever great achievements flow from the process of using technology in music making, it is not the machines that should earn the credit. Rather, the human mind and creative spirit are responsible. . . . We are the artists forming art, not the machines.

Another perspective for considering "making use of our tools" is from the vantage point of people as "adopters" of technology, be they a consumer, musician, teacher, or student. Through several iterations, Rogers (2003) has expounded a model of the "diffusion of innovations" expressed as the technology adoption lifecycle. "Diffusion," he explains, "is the process in which an innovation is communicated through certain channels over time among the members of a social system" (ibid, p. 5). He divides technology adopters into the five categories shown in Figure 9.1: innovators, early adopters, early majority, late majority, and laggards. Plotted on a normal curve the mean lies between early and late majority. For Rogers, people decide to adopt a technology when the "innovation offers them a better way to do something, is compatible with their values, beliefs, and needs, is not

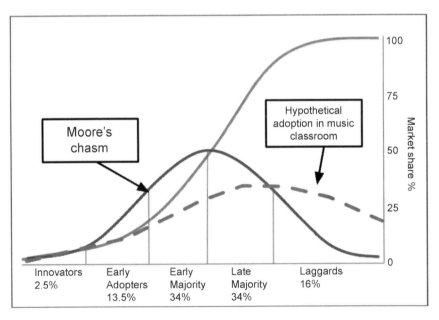

Figure 9.1   Rogers's (2003) diffusion of innovations curve as consumers adopt new technology. Shown with the addition of Moore's "chasm" between Early Adopter and Early Majority and a projected adoption curve for technology in the music classroom. Adapted from Rogers (2003) and Moore (2006).

too complex, can be tried out before adoption, and has observable benefits" (Surrey & Ely, 2007, para. 8).

Although Rogers's work is most often applied to consumer models, the concept also applies to technology's influence on music, music practice, and education. The three themes of my response, as well as the discussion of technological determinism, fit nicely within this model. Technology successfully evolves through Rogers's stages where innovators and early adopters challenge the new technology and their feedback brings about changes and advancements in the technology that permit advancement to the "early majority." Rogers (2003) casts "the early majority" as more conservative consumers, who are open to new ideas, and are active and influential in their respective community.

Geoffrey Moore in *Crossing the Chasm* (2006) expands on the model by focusing especially on the "chasm" between early adopters and the early majority, emphasizing that many technologies do not make it across to adoption by the early majority. LP stereo and CD recordings made it across and evolved to the point where the most conservative "late majority" and even a few die-hard "laggards" adopted the technology. CD-ROM music multimedia education discs, streaming web media, and GarageBand software have bridged the chasm at one time or another to the "early majority" but perhaps not to the "late majority"—they tend to be much more conservative and less open to trying new ideas and technologies.

Eventually the technology becomes ubiquitous as the adoption curve reaches saturation. At this point in its evolution, as Alan Kay (Tapscott, 1999, p. 38) suggests, it may no longer be viewed as technology. A new generation assumes it always existed; or, it has been replaced and the new generation never knew it existed. Our students of today do not view the CDs, MP3s, desktop computers, and the Internet as "technology."

EVERYONE IS INVITED TO DANCE

How the adoption cycle fits with our discussions of technological determinism is key to appreciating the technology-music dance and the *democratization* of music engagement through technology. Where technology determines application in music, I would suggest, is in the innovator and early adopter stages. It is typically those who are most curious and most technology proficient who are willing to hang out on the leading edge and experiment with ways to use technology in music making and music education. At this point in the cycle instructional quality may be overwhelmed by the demands or constraints of the innovative technology. A case in point is the considerable variability in the current quality of music education apps for Android and iOS devices—still in the innovator and early adopter stages—where the risk of technology undermining instructional quality is most likely. Where "soft determinism" comes into play is when the technology applications cross the "chasm" to the early and late majority and pedagogy hopefully dominates. For music in society at large, the cultural contexts of "human practice, habitat, and habit" (Thibeault, p. 135) determine whether the technology is useful and eventually becomes ubiquitous.

SOCIETY EMBRACES THE DANCE

Technology moving toward ubiquity in the adoption cycle is reflected in the evolution of music reproduction, performance, and creativity told through the stories in "Shifting Locus" and described through the framework for digital media in "Landscapes." Sousa was a laggard with the first vinyl records; Gould was an innovator with the first Sony digital recorders isolated in the studio; Madlib is an impresario among early adopters and the early majority employing analog and digital tools for massaging music and sound in myriad ways to prolifically create his albums.

We can begin with music reproduction, the desire to find ways to capture music performance and to be able to re-create it (preserve it) for future replaying. We can trace an analog evolution starting with music boxes and mechanical orchestras, to punch metal disc players, to player pianos, to wax cylinders, to vinyl recordings, and then to reel-to-reel and cassette tape recordings. One might consider that MIDI's introduction in the early 1980s picked up where player pianos left off to continue a mechanical way to capture and reproduce music performance.

With the advent of digital recording the evolution continues with digital CD discs, MP3 music files and players, Internet sharing of MP3 and more advanced compression formats like FLAC and AAC, and, now, streaming music delivery through apps like iTunes, Pandora, Spotify, and others. For each of these points in the evolution of music reproduction, technology helped *democratize* access to recorded music performance to a greater audience. With the digitization of images and video, the full repertoire of digital media in "Landscapes" is realized and multi-, inter-, and transmedia become possible—although not necessarily ubiquitous; more likely early majority in the adoption cycle.

Similar timelines can be drawn for performance, music training, publication, and creativity. By the 1990s, through the dance between technology and music, just about anyone who wanted to listen to music, play music, notate music, learn about music could do so through MP3 or CD recordings, acoustic instruments or MIDI instruments, software like Finale and Sibelius, and multimedia CD-ROMs on jazz, classical music, ethnic music, and more. The one music behavior missing from this mix was the capability for *anyone,* regardless of musical training, to create music by point-and-click manipulation of sonic events. Precursors to a major breakthrough to this need were software tools like Band-in-a-Box or ACID Music Studio. The introduction of GarageBand in 2004 provided essential software for creating music without the demands of reading traditional notation and playing a traditional music instrument. Just use your ear and point and click from voluminous libraries of loops and sound samples. The technology-music dance enabled people to express themselves musically in ways never before accessible: democratization of music creativity!

THE MUSIC CLASSROOM EMBRACES THE DANCE?

Tools that are adopted in society and bring freedom of musical expression, unfortunately, do not necessarily make it across the chasm to adoption in the music classroom. Someone shared an analogy a few years ago comparing a classroom teacher to a physician. A doctor of 50 years ago, if transported ahead to the present, would be lost using the medical technology of today. An educator or music educator transported ahead 50 years would be at home enough to function as a teacher. The music teacher would find comfort in the piano and chalkboard (or Smart Board essentially being used like a chalkboard).

Change in education, as the Woodrow Wilson quote cogently expressed, is very slow. Surveys by Reese (2003), Dorfman (2008), and Dammers (2012) have found that music teachers are more likely to be in the majority of adopters (early and late) only for technology that helps them personally: word processing, notation software, email and web browsing, and the like. Reese (2003) did a four-year follow-up of a 1998 survey of music teachers in Illinois. "Administrative and communication uses of computers," he reported, as well as "uses away from students to prepare teaching materials[,] continue to dominate the purposes for which teachers use computers most often" (p. 79). Confirming Reese, Dorfman (2008) found music teachers in Ohio "tend to use technology more for personal pursuits and for planning purposes than they do in pedagogical scenarios in which students are engaged with technology" (p. 33). And in the most recent study, Dammers (2012) concluded that "while previous surveys . . . have found that instructional use of technology in music classrooms lags behind teachers' productivity uses, . . . a relatively small number of music educators are moving beyond technology integration to teaching music in an environment where technology is a defining factor" (p. 81).

These studies emphasize that few technologies make it across the chasm to the early majority when it comes to integrating technology into the music curriculum. Such a push back from the classroom culture would seem to defy any notion of technological determinism. To use Tobias's terms, the non-technology constraints mask any consideration of affordances. Those constraints being teachers' time, energy, budget, lack of motivation, and lack of experience and training with the technology.

VISIONING FOR THE FUTURE: THE CHALLENGE

Let us center our focus now on the key issue that overrides all others. I return to the opening quote by John Blacking that music is a species-specific behavior of humans; everyone has a natural, inborn desire to engage with music in some form. When I try and make sense of the "tools" and what the future may hold, the evidence provided in the readings offers broad guidance for using the tools of music technology in society at large to enable anyone to engage in musical expression. The significant challenge, however, remains bridging the chasm to early and late majority adopters of music technology in the classroom (the teachers) and effectively using the technology in support of music teaching and learning. This is where music education needs to be the most diligent in finding clarity for "making sense of our tools."

What can we do to serve this long-standing need? Briefly, I offer two proposals among many we might consider: more inclusive training in technology at the undergraduate level of music and, secondly, as educators, embracing a model for curriculum development that ensures that technology supports instructional strategy and is not a determinant of instruction.

Training

Peter Webster and I (Williams & Webster, 2013) have attempted, over the past three years, to define a core set of technology competencies for which every undergraduate music student should be able to demonstrate proficiency before graduating. Our surveys of college music faculty have validated the critical need for competency in using notation software; understanding digital audio concepts, basic techniques for digital recording, and creating a CD or streaming audio file; building a basic music workstation; using presentation software; basic video editing; and understanding copyright and intellectual property rights related to music.

We also have gathered data on how these competencies are taught and the support and long-term planning schools have provided to ensure that technology skills are integral to music learning. Fifty-eight percent of the respondents in our most recent study indicated that "little is being done," or there is "little interest" in planning for delivery of music technology. Some 30% of respondents felt that students come to college with the necessary skills and understanding or they acquire them on their own without need for formal instruction. In contrast, Dammers and Phillips (2011), in examining the technology skills of high school students intending to major in music technology, reported that college instructors found them poorly prepared for more advanced music technology study.

What can we deduce from this evidence? Primarily that music technology competency is not a universal priority among undergraduate music programs in the United States, and how and where it is taught is not clearly defined or endorsed. The assumption that students learn these skills on their own may be unfounded and demands further study.

Return to the analogy of the physician and the classroom teacher. The physician's world of practice has radically changed over 50 years because technology is thoroughly embedded in required medical training and ongoing professional development. Until we take this same strategy in college music, not just for the music education curriculum, but throughout the music undergraduate curriculum, our music teachers will enter the school environment with minimal or no baseline skills for using technology in performance, arranging and composing, engaged listening, presentations, and instruction. Hence, when looking back across the chasm to the innovators and early adopters in our profession, they are overwhelmed with finding the time, motivation, and the skill sets to assimilate new technologies—all those wonderful tools that these three chapters so generously and richly present.

Models for Curriculum Design

Affordances, soft determinism, context: just three of the keywords that surface in the readings for "Making Sense of Our Tools" that stress the importance of developing technology as an integral component within the larger context. Just as developing a basic skill set of music technology competencies is critical, having an effective model for designing instruction and curricula is critical to bridging the technology adoption chasm.

In *Technology Based Music Instruction*, Dorfman (2013, p. 7) argues that "using technology as the major means for teaching music is a *learned skill*. Though teachers may demonstrate a proclivity toward using technology, it is unlikely that teachers will be able to do so naturally." Among the reasons he offers for this: technology pedagogy for music is a new skill, models to support music technology pedagogy are not readily available, and opportunities for improving skills "are rare, and difficult to find."

A model I have found effective is the TPACK model developed by Mishra and Koehler (2006) and graphically illustrated in Figure 9.2. Bauer (2014) uses the TPACK model extensively in his book, *Music Learning Today*, as does Dorfman (2013). Bauer provides background for the use of TPACK (p. 12):

> Many approaches to helping educators use technology have focused on the technological tools themselves. Inherent in these methods was the belief that teachers would be able to figure out how to apply the tools to curricular content. However, it is apparent that in many instances this has not been the case. Being able to use technology effectively requires not only an understanding of technology itself, but also of effective pedagogical approaches for utilizing that technology in a particular content area. In addition, the affordances and constraints of a technology for

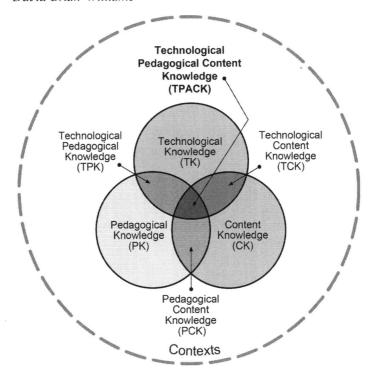

Figure 9.2   Mishra and Koehler's (2006) TPACK model showing the dynamic and transactional relationship between the three components and knowledge acquisition. (Reproduced by permission of the publisher, © 2012 by tpack.org)

use in a specific instructional context need to be considered. Teachers must contemplate the dynamic relationship that exists among content, pedagogy and content within an educational context; they must have a well developed Technological Pedagogical and Content Knowledge (TPACK).

I recommend Dorfman's and Bauer's texts for further study of TPACK; the model is extensively developed for integrating technology into music education practice.

Case Study: Technology-based Music Classrooms and the Nontraditional Music Student

To illustrate the benefits of training in music technology skills and the benefits from successfully bridging the technology adoption chasm to effect change in music classroom pedagogy, let me share one case in point. Nationwide,

80% of the students in secondary schools do not participate in the traditional performing ensembles of band, choir, and orchestra. Children begin music education in the earliest grades with everyone participating in music performance and creative activities. Following an inverted triangle, they are then selectively removed from music activities as participation becomes more specialized with performing ensembles at the secondary level.

The 80% figure comes from an analysis of several different studies, some longitudinal over 30 years to show that there has been little change in this percentage (discussed fully in Williams, 2012). Thibeault in "Shifting Locus" clearly makes this point when he observes that "music education still heavily favors a type of performance characterized by competitions and festivals, emulation of military bands and makers of traditional band and orchestra instruments along with publishers of scores for these ensembles" (p. 35).

There is a grassroots movement afoot in music education to change this. Using the technology tools richly described herein, music teachers across the county are implementing technology-based music classes that engage the nontraditional music student (NTMs) in just such participant-listeners-turned-performers-turned-composer activities described in "Shifting Locus" and embodied in the new media framework of "Landscapes." Using tools such as GarageBand, Mixcraft, Soundation, and Abelton Live, students are able to perform on instruments of their own creation and mix and compose without knowledge of traditional notation much as the characters in Powell's "Modulation" or Madlib's studio, activities that run the full range of Turino's (2008) continuum of participatory music making. Dammers (2012) research and the profiles of these teachers on the musiccreativity.org (2013) website show that these educators implement technology-based music courses typically on their own initiative. As the demand expands from successful implementation of NTM programs, administrative support often follows (cf. the profiles on NTM programs on musiccreativity.org). These are the innovators and early adopters of music curriculum reform reaching students through music experiences that most often reflected the students' personal participatory culture outside of school.

THE LAST DANCE

Clearly the three themes I proposed at the outset of this response to "Making Sense of Our Tools" come through all of the diverse and deep thinking shared in this section of *Music Education: Navigating the Future*. The technology-music dance is constantly evolving and absorbing changes in technology, the dance plays out in society at large and, hopefully, in the future, to a much greater extent in the music classroom. At certain key points in the evolution some dimension of music making is democratized and facilitates for an ever greater population of people the ability to express themselves with music as never before. The summary point I am hopeful you as the reader take away is the need for making sense of the tools from a classroom and pedagogical vantage point to ensure that what is accessible in society is also used to enable new and improved ways for all of our students to learn about and experience the multiple dimensions of music making.

In closing, as one who has been an innovator and early adopter in the technology adoption cycle for music since the mid-1960s, I'd like to offer a set of ten predictions for new technologies in the future:

1. Freedom from of the tyranny of wires: power, video, audio, MIDI cables will disappear with a common wireless technology that can handle all of these channels of information along with batteries that last weeks, not hours.

2. Ubiquitous networking and super fast network speed with a common, secure technique for logon to the Internet that is pervasive around the world. The United States was ranked 9th globally in network speed in 2013 based on an Akamai study (Gross, 2013).

3. Computing power delivered in smaller packages, even smaller than a watch. Technology will be imbedded in ever-increasingly smaller devices perhaps looking forward to a smart-baton, smart-music stands with sheet music readers synchronized wirelessly to cloud-based music libraries, tuners and metronomes on a chip embedded in anything you would care to name, and, eventually, digestible nano-chips that might, for example, redefine interfaces between musicians and machines.

4. Workstation labs will disappear and be replaced by "filling stations" for our tablets and laptops, with smart, wireless devices available as resources for printing, charging, alternative input devices, scanning, and more.

5. Small discrete apps will continue to replace the past, large Swiss-army knife solutions for music software, but apps will talk to one another like the AudioBus solution for iOS music apps. This cries for an open-source, music-classroom management solution that allows the music teacher to develop a custom curriculum for lesson planning and assessment using any music-learning app available. This trend in software deployment, as well as web-based software, will drive down the cost of software for education and expand the *a la carte* model through what the industry calls the move from licenses to subscriptions (see MusicFirst, 2013).

6. Hi-res video will be as easy to manipulate in a GarageBand-like environment and share over the Internet as MIDI, digital audio, and graphics, helping to democratize Tobias's inter- and transmedia creative activities.

7. Totally new devices (including nano-devices noted above) will enable new, more natural gestures for music expression and performance through computing devices (see Leap's Motion, 2013, and Eric Rosenbaum's Makey Makey, 2013, controllers).

8. Virtual, live participatory musicking over the Internet with an Internet-based metronome that auto adjusts for time latency will be a common component in web browsers and apps.
9. Scanning music to notation and audio recognition to music notation will *finally* work effectively for complex music events and scores.
10. Delivery of instruction at every level, driven by the catalysts of flipped classrooms, just-in-time learning (JiTT), MOOCs (massive open online courses), and more, will be accessible and managed from in or outside the classroom through tools based on the Internet "cloud" and social networking.

Quoting Buzz Lightyear from *Toy Story*, "to infinity and beyond!"

NOTES

1. References cited in the chapters will not be restated in the Reference list below and page numbers will refer to location in the respective chapter, not in the original source.
2. The term "musicking" is defined by Christopher Small (1998, p. 9) as taking part in a "musical performance, whether by performing, by listening, by rehearsing, or practicing, by providing material for performance (what is called composing), or by dancing."

REFERENCES

Bauer, W. I. (2014). *Music learning today: Digital pedagogy for creating, performing, and responding to music.* New York, NY: Oxford University Press.
Blacking, J. (1973). *How musical is man?* Seattle: University of Washington Press.
Dammers, R. J., & Phillips, S. L. (2011, October). Making the connection: A study of secondary and collegiate music technology programs. National Conference of the Association for Technology in Music Instruction (ATMI) and College Music Society (CMS). Richmond, VA.
Dammers, R. J. (2012). Technology-based music classes in high schools in the United States. *Bulletin of the Council for Research in Music Education, 194,* 73–90.
Dorfman, J. (2008). Technology in Ohio's school music programs: An exploratory study of teacher use and integration. *Contributions to Music Education, 35,* 23–46.
Dorfman, J. (2013). *Theory and practice of technology-based music instruction.* New York, NY: Oxford University Press.
Farrell, C. (2013, October 01). Why classical music is imperiled—sort of. *Bloomberg Businessweek.* Retrieved November 12, 2013, from www.businessweek.com/articles/2013–10–01/why-classical-music-is-imperiled-sort-of
Gross, D. B. (2013, July). Sloooooooow: U.S. slips to 9th in Internet speed. *CNNTech.* Retrieved from www.cnn.com/2013/07/24/tech/web/us-internet-speed
Johnston, L. D., O'Malley, P. M., Bachman, J. G., & Schulenberg, J. E. (1976–2009). Monitoring the future: A continuing study of American youth (8th, 10th, 12th grade surveys). Retrieved September 10, 2011, from www.icpsr.umich.edu/icpsrweb/ICPSR/ssvd/studies?prefix=M

Leap Motion. (2013). Retrieved November 15, 2013, from www.leapmotion.com

Makey Makey. (2013). Retrieved November 15, 2013, from www.makeymakey.com

Mishra, P., & Koehler, M. J. (2006). Technological pedagogical content knowledge: A framework for teacher knowledge. *Teachers College Record, 108*(6), 1017–54.

Moore, G. A. (2006). *Crossing the chasm: Marketing and selling disruptive products to mainstream customers.* New York, NY: Harper Business.

Musiccreativity.org. (2013). Retrieved November 15, 2013, from http://musiccreativity. org

MusicFirst: Cloud-based tools for music educators. (2013). Retrieved November 15, 2013, from www.musicfirst.com

NAMM (National Association of Music Merchants) (2003, April 21). Gallup organization reveals findings of "American attitudes toward making music" survey. Retrieved November 13, 2013, from www.namm.org/news/press-releases/gallup-organization-reveals-findings-american-atti

Reese, S. (2003). Four years of progress: Illinois teachers and schools using technology. *Illinois Music Educator, 63*(3), 78–81.

Rogers, E. M. (2003). *Diffusion of innovations* (5th Ed.). New York, NY: Free Press.

Shamoon, E. (2013, October 18). World's first live "wireless opera" baffles commuters at L.A.'s union station. *TechHive,* Retrieved November 13, 2013, from www. techhive.com/article/2056180

Sheets, H. M. (2013, October 25). Artists take up digital tools. *New York Times.* Retrieved October 25, 2013, from www.nytimes.com/2013/10/27/arts/artsspecial/artists-take-up-digital-tools.html

Small, C. (1998). *Musicking: The meanings of performing and listening.* Middletown, CT: Wesleyan University Press.

Surry, D. W. & Ely, D. P. (2007). *Adoption, diffusion, implementation, and institutionalization of educational technology.* Unpublished manuscript, College of Education, University of South Alabama, Mobile, AL. Retrieved from www.usouthal.edu/coe/bset/surry/papers/adoption/chap.htm

Tapscott, D. (1999). *Growing up digital: The rise of the net generation.* New York: Oracle Press.

Williams, D. B. (2012). The non-traditional music student in secondary schools of the United States: Engaging non-participant students in creative music activities through technology. *Journal of Music, Technology, and Education, 4*(2–3), 131–47.

Williams, D. B., & Webster, P. R. (2008). *Experiencing music technology* (3rd Ed.). Boston, MA: Cengage Learning.

Williams, D. B., & Webster, P. R. (2013, November). Defining undergraduate music technology competencies and strategies for learning: A third-year progress report. Paper delivered for The College Music Society/Association for Technology in Music Instruction National Conference, Cambridge, MA. Retrieved from http://teachmusictech.com/resources.html

10 Understanding the Tools
Technology as a Springboard for Reflective Musicking

Frank Heuser

Every January, musicians of all flavors from the wide-ranging musical sub-cultures of Southern California make a pilgrimage to Anaheim, not to visit the amusement park that made the city famous, but rather to attend the winter exhibition of the National Association of Music Merchants. Although it is intended primarily for manufactures and music retailers, the annual NAMM show is also a place where symphonic and studio performers, concert artists and music educators gather to examine the innovations the industry has developed over the previous year. Perhaps one of the most significant revelations occurred at the 1983 NAMM show when Dave Smith, the CEO of the synthesizer company Sequential Circuits Inc., publically introduced the newly standardized Musical Instrument Digital Interface by connecting a Prophet 600 with a Roland Jupiter-6 synthesizer (Chadabe, 2000; Holmes, 2003; Manning, 2013). Even at the moment of its birth, the potential of MIDI to impact and shape the future of music seemed obvious. The impending evolution of electronic media would soon blur established definitions and challenge previous understandings of how music would be created, accessed, learned, and understood as an incredible range of digital tools were developed and became increasingly available over the subsequent decades.

The three chapters in the portion of this book titled *Making Sense of our Tools* provide historical context to the changing technologies that are intertwined with all aspects of music and musicking. These chapters also challenge music educators to give careful consideration to how these tools will mediate traditional understandings and practices in the field as technologies open new avenues of creating, performing, interacting with and conceptualizing music. Technology has, of course, always influenced music. The mechanical innovations taking place as the harpsichord evolved into the fortepiano induced Haydn and Mozart to abandon the earlier instrument (Hess, 1953). Structural changes in the piano, which included an expanded range, iron framing, steel strings, and felt hammers, allowed Beethoven and subsequent composers to explore new expressive possibilities as sustaining power improved in the instrument (Erlich, 1990). Increased neck length (Rosen, 1971) changed the sound of the violin, and newly designed bows by

Francois Tourte allowed composers to write music which would have been impossible to perform had it not been for the technological evolution of this seemingly simple marriage of wood and horse hair (Ervin, n.d.). As the 19th century progressed, the emerging virtuoso performers enabled by technological enhancements in brass and woodwind instruments allowed composers to explore and challenge the technical limits of those improved instruments. However, the limits of composition were not always determined by technology. In the *Rite of Spring*, Stravinsky chose to write beyond the conventional range of the bassoon, thereby compelling future generations of performers to extend the upper limits of playing (Grymes, 1998).

In contrast to the types of technological changes that impacted how music was presented and composed in the era of performance, Matthew Thibeault provides a compelling account of how the music listener, the music listening experience, and the ways we think about music have evolved since the advent of sound recording. The jarring differences between the dichotomous musical and social worlds depicted by James Joyce and Richard Powers contextualize how new media influences the musical lives of young people currently learning in our universities. Although students come into the academy having listened to a vast amount of recorded music, the curriculum offered by most university music departments often seems as though we are still preparing students to enter the acoustical world of pianist Mary Jane and vocalist Aunt Julia, so aptly depicted by Joyce. The curricular traditions preserving this approach to music study remain beholden to practices established in early German conservatories that emphasized preparation for careers in orchestras and opera houses. It is understandable that performance faculty members, whose own rigorous conservatory training enabled achievement at a high professional level in Western art music, might have difficulty conceiving of university instruction being delivered in any other way. However, modern students often lead multiple musical lives in which their own interests in popular genres, world music, and digital media remain clandestine. By acknowledging and embracing the new media world described by Powers, the academy might develop new conceptions of musicianship that could in turn provide their students with the tools needed to creatively renew their musical ideals. By juxtaposing these two authors in his essay, Thibeault provides a view of where music has been and a glimpse of where music education must go in the future.

The fears expressed in "The Menace of Mechanical Music" were frequently echoed by acoustic musicians in the months immediately following the introduction of MIDI. Like Sousa, music educators were also concerned about what impact technology might have on the inclination of future generations to submit to the discipline required to learn the craft of live music making. Similar apprehensions have recently been articulated by former Rolling Stones bassist Bill Wyman who expressed disdain regarding technologically enabled video games such as *Rock Band* because "it encourages kids not to learn, that's the trouble. It makes less and less people dedicated to really get down and learn an instrument. I think [that] is a pity so I'm not really keen on that kind of stuff" (quoted in Masters, 2009). Reiterating this view is Pink Floyd's Nick Mason who found that *Rock Band* "irritates me having watched my kids do it—if they spent as much time practicing the guitar as learning how to press the buttons they'd be damn good by now" (Masters, 2009). It seems ironic that these artists, both of whom earned a considerable portion of their living through recording, would be echoing the sentiments of Sousa from a century earlier. There is just a hint in Thibeault's essay that current undergraduate music education students may hold views similar to these two rock musicians. Even though future music teachers have grown up in the new media era, they may not be immediately welcoming of technology in their future professional work. Their comments about the need to make musical judgments based on live performances suggest that many maintain educational ideals more in tune with the world described by Joyce than of the new media era in which they matured.

Understanding new media remains challenging because the rate of technological progress is constantly accelerating and requires a willingness to navigate a multiplicity of continuously evolving meanings. Even those deeply immersed in the digital world portrayed by Powers in "Modulation" can be confused by the plethora of constantly emerging terms associated with new media. Although a chapter titled "Inter/trans/multi/cross/new media(ting): Navigating an emerging landscape of digital media for music education" may seem intimidating, it is an accessible introduction to the terminology and cultural concepts currently associated with the relentlessly expanding arena of music technology. Evan Tobias offers a road map of newly emerging technologies and examples of how these technologies are beginning to allow music educators to reconceptualize music pedagogy and curriculum. More importantly, he urges music educators to move beyond concentrating on the medium and instead to examine the "larger contexts and systems in which media, musicking, and education exist." Tobias does this by "focusing on cultural contexts and overarching frameworks of which digital media are a part."

Music education exists in multiple cultural contexts and the chapter provides examples of how music learning might be enhanced and mediated by innovative use of new media. The opening description of audience members interacting via digital media with one another during an actual performance immediately captures our attention. The very thought of being in a concert hall in which the glow of numerous digital screens is allowed to infringe on the darkness that usually enforces singular concentration on the aesthetic products emanating from the stage is antithetical to the indoctrination regarding concert etiquette most people receive in the course of their musical education. Does encouraging individuals to communicate during a concert suggest that the importance of performance is becoming less valued, or might such interaction instead actually nurture reflective engagement with music as the sound and multiple conceptual ideas about a performance unfold in real time? Questions of this nature challenge commonly held for-malistic ideals of music as an aesthetic object.

The types of online tools available for interacting with music, analyzing music, and understanding music challenge traditional notions of how music should be learned. Traditionally, music education has compartmentalized musical elementals and placed overt importance on pitch and rhythm. At least one critic of this approach (Pratt, 1998) maintains that the focus on pitch and rhythm, which are the most prominent aspects of standard western notation, results from the ease with which those elements might be assessed and points to difficulties in evaluating understandings of musical elements such as timbre and texture. Tobias suggests that this type of analysis might be facilitated through the use of multimedia spectrograms (Thibeault, 2011) and provides descriptions of other digital tools and apps that might allow music educators to move beyond a "mono-media focus on music." How-ever, the author repeatedly warns that particular technologies and applica-tions must not be the focal point of instruction. New media should instead be used to inform instruction and develop curricula that expand musical thinking as well as enable creativity.

Using new media in the service of music learning requires the capacity to reflect on and theorize about how this might be accomplished. Just as the abil-ity to hear and identify musical structures is refined as one learns to apply specific labels acquired through the study of music theory, the capacity for understanding effective uses of digital media will be enhanced as our profes-sion cultivates a sophisticated vocabulary for describing and discussing this emerging field. The first part of the chapter's title, "Inter/trans/multi/cross/new media(ting)," suggests that we are entering an educational landscape that will require music teachers to develop proficiency in using very specific terminology for the purposes of understanding how these media are being used as well as how meaningful learning experiences can be constructed and implemented. The author provides several frameworks for understanding and theorizing about the multiple roles new or digital media might play in music education. Understanding the frameworks presented in the chapter, including the concepts of convergence culture(s) and participatory culture(s) as well as those specific to media including multimedia, intermedia, and transmedia, will become essential for interpreting and meaning making when working and teaching with new media. Fluency with these terms will allow teachers to clarify basic concepts by identifying both broad and specific categories of practice thereby facilitating analysis and theory building. This in turn should permit music educators to relate the design of instructional activities using new media to the foundational premises of music education. From my perspective, Tobias has done a masterful job of collecting and codifying the currently available vocabulary that is central to understand-ing new media from a variety of disparate sources. More importantly, he provides an example of how to think about digital media so that discussions might become nuanced in ways that allow for multiple understandings and outcomes rather than reduced to discrete characteristics or technologies.

The clearly articulated message that using new media requires critical awareness of how these tools must purposefully contribute to music learning rather than become a means of amusement is a perfect prelude to the chapter "Is It the Technology? Challenging Technological Determinism in Music Education." The essays in this chapter provide three distinct and ultimately hopeful perspectives on technological determinism. Collectively, they can be seen as a call to examine critically the ways new technologies are impacting music, music consumption, and music learning. They also serve as an appeal to apply a critical lens to traditional practices in music education so that we can develop increasingly nuanced understandings of the possibilities and limitations inherent in all instructional practices.

The concepts of affordances and constraints developed by Tobias offers a framework for examining technology critically and thereby avoiding the pitfalls that might be experienced when incorporating digital technologies in well-established educational processes. One example of the necessity to look at the affordances and constraints of technological solutions to educational issues is in the realm of piano instruction. Traditionally students have needed to practice on an excellent acoustic piano in order to acquire the touch and motor skills necessary to develop beautiful tone production. Unfortunately, the financial burden of purchasing a high quality piano precludes many learners from being able to practice regularly on such an instrument thereby placing a major constraint on their ability to develop performance skills. For learners hoping for an affordable alternative, the relatively new Yamaha DGX-650 portable grand promises the touch of an acoustic piano and the tone quality of a Yamaha concert grand. With a street price of less than one thousand dollars and advertised to build "the proper finger technique for when the time comes to perform on an acoustic piano" (Yamaha Corporation of America, 2014), this digital instrument seems like the perfect substitute for a far more expensive grand piano. However, the development of proper keyboard technique depends on learning to listen for subtle gradations and improvements in tone quality that occur as a result of increasingly effective playing mechanics. Because the tone quality of an acoustic piano varies depending on the way the fingers press the keys, the aural feedback a student receives while practicing enables refinements in finger technique. This important but somewhat unrecognized characteristic of acoustic pianos is not present in the synthesized sounds generated from digital instruments that produce a consistent tone quality regardless of playing mechanics. Without aural feedback from an instrument that allows for both good and poor tone quality, proper piano finger technique may not emerge. This suggests that although a digital piano might make excellent economic sense, it might not be the ideal instrument for a student at certain stages of the learning process.

The limitations of a specific digital instrument depicted in the foregoing discussion provide one small example of the subtle and nuanced issues that must be considered when incorporating new media and digital music making into music education. Both the affordances and constraints must be known, acknowledged, and examined with regards to how each contributes to or limits music learning. An understanding of the strengths and shortcomings of digital music making allows thoughtful teachers to guide students and their parents in a direction that will provide a meaningful musical education to each learner. All must realize that constraints may be outweighed by the affordances offered by any given pathway. Continuing with the piano example, the affordances of a digital keyboard such as the ability to record audio files or practice with recordings of popular songs may prove more valuable than the constraints synthesized tone places on the development of proper finger technique. Some learners, especially those who never plan to play on an acoustic piano, may prefer practicing on a synthesizer that has multiple built in recording and playback options even though developing the sensitivity to subtle changes that are a result of proper finger technique on an acoustic piano might nurture better playing mechanics. This comparison of synthesized and acoustically produced piano tone implies that decisions about affordances and constraints must be made in regards to all instructional tools, not just digital instruments and new media.

The degree to which the technological resources of any era influence cultural understandings and determine educational practices often remain unexamined. Just as digital natives may have little insight about how the technologies they so fluently use impact their understanding of the world, those of us who practice established forms of music education can be somewhat naive about the ways that the non-digital technologies which enable traditional music practices also can determine how music is taught, what students learn, and what becomes valued in music education. As discussed earlier in this chapter, technology has always played a vital role in music and music learning. Without the mass production of woodwind, brass and percussion instruments, the school band movement could not have become a defining feature of music education in the United States. The universal presence of large performing groups in communities throughout the country might lead to the assumption that participating in school ensembles automatically develops musical concepts and literacy. Yet the technology through which instruction is delivered, usually in the form of printed method books and sheet music, may often constrain learning to the narrow range of skills needed to decode Western notation and assume a predefined position within a school ensemble. The materials included in method books tend to develop and reinforce a very specific set of performing skills rather than nurture the broad range of musical concepts, aural skills, and creative abilities needed for informed musical citizenship (Heuser, 2007). The constraints described here are not "inherent or embedded in the technology" of instrumental method books but are instead the result of an instructional vision that values ensemble membership over the development of individual musicianship. Even traditional educational technologies can be deterministic when used unreflectively.

We have seen how the seemingly straightforward process of choosing a keyboard or using an instrumental method book may determine the nature of the musical skills a learner eventually develops. As emerging technologies find their way into instructional settings, we must critically assess what it is we want students to learn and remain cautious so that technology does not dictate how we teach or become more important than the musical values that we seek to instill. Perhaps both the best and worst aspects of technological determinism can be found in iPads as they are brought into music-learning settings. The elegant design of these tablets allows even novice musicians to easily manipulate sounds through programs like GarageBand. When used reflectively, the applications available on the iPad can become a catalyst for developing musical concepts. The kinds of discussions about aesthetic values that are rarely possible in school ensemble settings are readily facilitated by asking students to justify the stylistic or timbre choices they make when creating an arrangement in GarageBand. Understanding the rhythmic skills needed for ensemble performance can be nurtured as students compare a recording they make in real time to a quantized version of their own work. Asking the right questions changes an iPad ensemble from just a performing group into a forum for exploring musical thought processes. However, without carefully guided reflective questions, the musical escapades of iPad users might provide no deeper levels of musical knowledge than that a group of teens acquires from playing "Heart & Soul" on a camp piano. The availability of predetermined tracks in GarageBand can be used simply to create musical products that are immediately satisfying to the user but provide no basic understanding of underlying musical concepts or values. The same dangers will be present when using iPads in ensemble settings.

Presumably, tablets offer unlimited possibilities for use in music-learning settings. A quick review of the Apple App Store reveals incredible numbers of products including music-learning games for children, practice aids such as *iReal,* a wide variety of virtual instruments, to sophisticated recording and music-creation applications. When thoughtfully used for music instruction, students can form ensembles via wireless networks, practice aural skills, and compose without needing to know music notation. As enticing as these possibilities seem, music educators must, as with all technology, be critical and reflective so as to avoid using tablets and applications in deterministic ways. We must be aware that, as Jaron Lanier (2013) suggests, tablets "enforce a new power structure . . . by running . . . only programs and applications approved by a central commercial authority." Because many of the programs running on tablets are extremely enticing to young people, we must avoid succumbing to their flashiness and make sure that we use them in a way that empowers students rather than nurtures intellectual laziness. John Naughton (2013), a professor of the public understanding of technology at the Open University, critically warns that technologies such as the Macintosh computer frees users "from the need to make decisions," suggesting that the "hard determinism" described by Randles may be unavoidable when using Apple products. It is difficult to imagine music technology without the contributions that have been developed as a result of the elegant Apple operating system. However, Naughton's advice implores us to be as analytical about this family of hi-tech products as we are of all the technology creeping into the music education arena. By juxtaposing the concepts of "hard" and "soft" determinism," Randles suggests that what might be viewed as a constraint on creativity can instead become "a mechanism that assists individuals in developing their own capacities for self-expression." Although his contribution to this chapter could be read as a Festschrift for Steve Jobs, his insights regarding technological determinism along with the imaginative views of Matthew Thibeault, who explores ways determinism can make sense, provide our profession with a hopeful view of how new media and music technology might be used for the betterment of music education.

The three chapters in *Making Sense of our Tools* explore different aspects of how music is viewed, the ways technology and digital media mediate understandings of music, and how music educators must become critically reflective of technology in order to avoid potential negative possibilities. An essential step for any emerging new discipline is the creation of its own vocabulary, to which these chapters have made a substantial contribution. The terms introduced by these authors will facilitate reflection and critical assessment of the multiple roles new media will play in music education. As we moved from an era of acoustic music making to one of digital media musicking, the writers reminded us that what it once meant to be a musician and what it once meant to listen to music has and will continue to change. This suggests that our profession has an obligation to maintain critical awareness about the ways the persistent evolution of music and technology will transform the ways people will want to learn music. While reading these chapters, it is clear that the authors hope the new media we are beginning to embrace might result in greater reflection about what it means to teach music. It is my hope that such reflection will extend to all approaches toward music education, traditional as well as digital. A profession that is constantly asking questions about the nature of music, the nature of musical understanding, and the nature of music learning will, to paraphrase Matthew Thibeault, lead to more profound understandings, improved questions, and more nuanced instructional approaches that will advance our work in music education.

REFERENCES

Chadabe, J. (2000). Part IV: The seeds of the future. *Electronic Musician, XVI*(5). Retrieved November 13, 2013, from www.emusician.com/gear/0769/the-electronic-century-part-iv-the-seeds-of-the-future/145415.

Erlich, C. (1990). *The piano: A history.* New York, NY: Oxford University Press.

Ervin, (n.d.). "The Tourte model bow." Retrieved November 5, 2013, from www.ervinviolins.com/tourte_bows.shtml.

Grymes, J. A. (1998). Dispelling the myths: The opening bassoon solo to the *Rite of Spring. The Journal of the International Double Reed Society, 26.* Retrieved July 14, 2014, from www.idrs.org/publications/PublicationsIndex/recordlist.php?-skip=1238&-max=25

Hess, A. G. (1953). The transition from harpsichord to piano. *The Galpin Society Journal, 6,* 75–94. Retrieved September 12, 2013, from www.jstor.org/stable/841719.

Heuser, F. (2007). A theoretical framework for examining foundational instructional materials supporting the acquisition of performance skills. In A. Williamson & D. Coimbra (Eds.), *Proceedings of the International Symposium on Performance Science 2007.* Utrecht, Netherlands: The European Association of Conservatoires (AEC).

Holmes, T. (2003). *Electronic and experimental music: Pioneers in technology and composition.* New York, NY: Routledge.

Lanier, J. (2013). Digital Passivity. *The New York Times.* Retrieved November 30, 2013, from www.nytimes.com/2013/11/28/opinion/digital-passivity.html?ref=turningpoints2014&_r=0

Manning, P. (2013). *Electronic and computer music.* New York, NY: Oxford University Press.

Masters, T. (2009). Rock stars cool over video games. Retrieved November 30, 2013, from http://news.bbc.co.uk/2/hi/entertainment/8242749.stm

Naughton, J. (2013). The church of Apple tests the faith of its flock. Retrieved November 30, 2013, from www.theguardian.com/technology/2013/nov/17/apple-mavericks-upgrade-naughton

Pratt, G. (1998). *Aural awareness: Principles and practice.* New York, NY: Oxford University Press.

Rosen, C. (1971). *The classical style.* New York, NY: Norton.

Thibeault, M. D. (2011). Learning from looking at sound: Using multimedia spectrograms to explore world music. *General Music Today, 25,* 50. (Originally published online July 27, 2011). doi: 10.1177/1048371311414050

Yamaha Corporation of America, (2014). Portable Grand DGX-650 Digital Piano. Retrieved November 14, 2013, from http://usa.yamaha.com/products/musical-instruments/keyboards/digitalkeyboards/dgx_series/dgx-650/

Part III
Visualizing Expansion

11 Liminal or Lifelong
Leisure, Recreation, and the Future of Music Education

Roger Mantie

Navigating the future is often aided by an understanding of the past. The past is not necessarily a predictor of the future, however. As French philosopher Michel Foucault has demonstrated, history is not teleological.[1] Today was not inevitable; today is the result of choices made in the past—whether recent or distant. Valences can and do change—sometimes for obvious reasons, but often for subtle reasons little understood at the time. In this chapter I wish to draw attention to how the profession's conception of rationales for music in the schools in Anglophone North America changed over the course of the 20th century, and argue for a reconsideration of *leisure and recreation* as a worthy aim and purpose for music education, one that may hold the potential to reinvigorate music education, both in the United States and beyond, in the 21st century.

This paper derives from my work investigating the phenomenon of collegiate a cappella. For two years I conducted an in-depth study, observing rehearsals and performances and formally interviewing 22 students drawn from ten different groups at four universities in the Northeast United States. My aim is not to offer generalizable "findings," but instead to problematize music education practices, especially the connections between music making in school and music making later in life. That is, I seek to offer commentary about the present and suggest ways in which the profession might move forward in order to further the benevolent goal of a more musical, healthier society—one where music is not learned as a disembodied subject for its own sake, but as a rewarding leisure activity with which to engage throughout the lifespan.

LEISURE AND MUSIC EDUCATION: A FORGOTTEN HISTORY

As "quality of life" researcher Mark Rapley (2003) points out, leisure, in the sense of spare time and disposable income, is a Western construction (p. 52). Nevertheless, leisure has, since the ancient Greeks, helped to define how "the good life" has been understood in Western societies (e.g., Kaplan, 1978; Pieper, 1963; Winnifrith & Barrett, 1989). When considering larger life purposes, goals, and ambitions, one rarely gets too far before considering three major issues central to leisure studies: the extent to which we have control over our time (freedom and obligation), the ways we choose to use our time (responsible and irresponsible), and the quality of our life experiences and the satisfactions we derive from them. That is, leisure as a concept and as a practice is central to our way of understanding and operating in the world.

Not incidentally, the concept of leisure is historically tied to the concept of education. The online etymology dictionary indicates that our modern term *school* is derived from the Greek *scholē* (*skholē*),[2] meaning "school, lecture, discussion," but also "leisure, spare time." Sociologist of leisure, Joffre Dumazedier, for example, translates *scholē* as idleness and as school (Dumazedier, 1974, p. 15), while leisure studies authority Donald Weiskopf suggests that *scholē* means "serious activity without the pressure of necessity" (Weiskopf, 1982, p. 4). Notably, the origins refer to "a holding back" or "keeping clear," as well as a "getting" and a "holding in one's power" ("to have").

Music's connection with leisure and education dates back over two thousand years. In *Politica, Book VIII,* for example, Aristotle writes at length about music and whether or not it should be part of education, speculating about music's educative value. Elsewhere Aristotle discusses how music and contemplation are the only two activities that qualify as genuine leisure. Education for the ancient Greeks was, of course, restricted to those of noble birth fortunate enough to be able to indulge in a life of leisure (i.e., education), setting in motion a long history that connected leisure and education with privilege. Similarly, instruction in music, as a leisure activity *par excellence,* has been historically restricted to those who could afford private tutelage.

The advent of state-sponsored, compulsory schooling altered understandings of education. Although in many countries compulsory schooling arose as part of nation-building projects and reflected the desire of governments to inculcate particular skills considered advantageous to the country (e.g., literacy, numeracy) rather than ancient Greek educational ideals *per se,* there is no question that compulsory schooling brought with it an egalitarian ethos that helped to ameliorate the practice of education as exclusive or privileged; education became something that everyone could "have." The eventual inclusion of music as part of the school curriculum in the 19th century in many countries (see Cox & Stevens, 2010) similarly changed how the learning of music was viewed. No longer the sole province of those with sufficient financial resources to afford private instruction, music (or rather, singing) instruction was to be available to all. Arguably, however, music's inclusion in the curriculum was initially dependent on it fulfilling an explicit need of society rather than based on any perceived specialness about music in and of itself. In the case of Lowell Mason and the successful inclusion of music in the schools of Boston in 1838, that need was functional singing in church.

The rise of the Progressive Education movement (¯1918–1935) saw intellectual learning broadened to include social and recreational activities. Thus, music—the status of which was always somewhat ambivalent *vis-a-vis* education—was viewed by many, or at least by those with an interest in it, as holding the potential for educative value as part of state concerns over the "worthy use of leisure"—number six of the seven *Cardinal Principles of Secondary Education*, published in 1918. Consider, for example, the following rationalization statements in music education literature in the United States and Canada from the 1920s through the 1950s:

- [Music in schools can] prepare the next generation for a healthier enjoyment of their adult leisure activities.
- . . . training the student for a wise use of his leisure time.
- . . . when it is realized that education must take into account the whole man and aim at enriching his personality, and when the wise use of leisure is acknowledged as one of its chief objects, then the arts, and especially Music, are seen to deserve generous recognition.
- [O]ne of the chief aims [of school music] . . . should be to develop the child's capacity to employ his leisure properly.
- [Music in schools can be for] recreation, pleasure, and [is a] worthy use of leisure time. [No. 3 of 8 objectives for school music]
- Music education aims to contribute to recreation and to the fun of living.[3]

Clearly, in the first half of the 20th century the learning and teaching of music was connected with an appreciation of leisure and recreation, aspects viewed as central to "the good life" and the "art of living." Leisure was not necessarily conceptualized by these early music educators in its purest Aristotelian sense, of course, but, consistent with Progressive Era ideals that considered education as a developmental process aimed at both vocation *and* avocation, the learning of music in schools was very much rationalized on the basis of its potential for leisure time use. One learned music in schools, in other words, in order to *use it* (i.e., play or sing it recreationally) beyond the school years.

By the late 1950s, however, one no longer finds many references to leisure and/or recreation in the scholarly discourses relating to the rationalization or justification for teaching music. Max Kaplan's (1955) *Music in Recreation: Social Foundations and Practices* and Charles Leonhard's (1952) *Recreation through Music* appear to mark the end of scholarly concern with leisure and recreation among most music education academics. The founding of the International Society for Music Education (1955) and *Journal of Research in Music Education* (1953), and the publication of *Basic Concepts in Music Education* (Henry, 1958) and *Foundations and Principles of Music Education* (Leonhard & House, 1959), all represent a shift in emphasis, whereby music education was to be treated as a serious academic subject concerned primarily with—at least until the 1990s—"aesthetic education," not the "nice but not necessary" interests of leisure and recreation. Notably, the words *leisure* and *recreation** (* here signifying a wildcard to account for *recreational*) do not appear in the index of *Foundations and Principles of Music Education*. In *Basic Concepts in Music Education* the word *leisure* (but not *recreation*, which appears only twice in the entire book) shows up in the index under *music,* listed "as an activity of leisure." The eight appearances of the word *leisure* occur over the space of three chapters, although only once is it discussed seriously, when John Mueller (1958), in his chapter, "Music and Education: A Sociological Approach," presciently writes, "There are many who do not quite feel comfortable in the thought that music is an activity for leisure. Such a function is not quite substantial enough and still reflects a squeamish affinity with the frill" (p. 110). Although his discussion makes clear he does not necessarily agree with this, he seems to have accurately summarized prevailing thought with his appraisal.

Leisure and recreation do not currently register as the proper concerns of music educators—or many other educators for that matter. Educational discourses in the United States, especially those reflected in the popular media, emphasize such things as accountability, parental choice, and standards.[4] A JSTOR search of music education journals reveals a marked decline in the presence of the words *leisure* and *recreation** from the 1960s onwards, with almost no appearances from the year 2000 onwards. The words *leisure* and *recreation* do not appear in the *Handbook of Research on Music Teaching and Learning* (1992), *The New Handbook of Research on Music Teaching and Learning* (2002), or the two-volume *Oxford Handbook of Music Education* (2012).[5] Nor do they appear in the indices of Bennett Reimer's *A Philosophy of Music Education* (1970, 1989, 2003) or David Elliott's *Music Matters: A New Philosophy of Music Education* (1995).[6] What was once such a fundamental part of thinking about music and education up until the early1950s has almost completely disappeared from the profession's vocabulary.

It could be, of course, that societal endorsement of education for leisure and recreation growing out of the Progressive Education period was simply a product of its time, and that the rise of the Cold War and the launch of Sputnik resulted in wholesale changes in attitudes regarding schooling and education, ones where leisure was relegated to the province of private, not public, concerns. Strangely, however, the profession seems to have forgotten its own history. Many music teachers of the 1920s through the 1960s clearly understood their work as helping students prepare for a life worth living by premising their own teaching of bands, orchestras, and choirs (in the case of music educators in the United States and Canada) on at least the *possibility* of active music making outside of schooling.[7] Today's concerns, as evidenced in the pages of *Music Educators Journal* and *Journal of Research in Music Education*, show little sympathy for such a view. As I argue via my presentation of empirical analysis in the next part of the chapter, thinking of music as something *used* by people beyond K-12 graduation, rather than as simply a quasi-academic subject to be learned during the school years, provides insights into the possibilities for reviving leisure as a viable aim for music education.

COLLEGIATE A CAPPELLA, COMPETITION, AND AMATEUR MUSIC MAKING

> OMG, why am I here? Why did I waste my time coming to campus? . . . I'm struggling to make sense of this phenomenon; I can see it working in private, but on this stage it just doesn't work; it is just TOO amateurish— it feels like watching the *American Idol* audition episodes: you feel bad for the people up there.
>
> *(Field notes: Sat., Feb. 4, 2012, International Championship of Collegiate A Cappella quarterfinals)*

In previous research (Mantie, 2013) I have argued that the college years provide what should be a temporal frame of great interest for music education researchers, given that the college years are, in a sense, "liminal" (Turner, 1967). For many students the college years represent the first period of sustained living apart from direct parental care; students are no longer children but they are not quite adults, at least in the practical sense of the word (see Arnett, 2000, Blatterer, 2010). It is during these years that students exercise greater choice over their leisure, or discretionary, time. Thus, for those who believe that school music should "make a difference" (Regelski, 2005), both immediately and, more importantly, later in life, how people choose to spend their time when not influenced by authority figures (e.g., parents, teachers) provides a good measure of how successful music education has been in its mission—assuming of course that making music beyond the school years matters to the music education profession. This is not to imply that *making* music is the only, or necessarily the best, way to experience music, nor is it to dismiss the value of the experiences had by students in primary or secondary school music programs. Rather, it is to suggest that the extent to which people engage in music making beyond the school years is a significant indicator of how such an activity is regarded. What does it communicate about the effectiveness of music education if people stop making music at their first opportunity to do so?

The phenomenon of collegiate a cappella provides a fascinating case study of recreational music making during this "liminal" stage in life. An online directory of collegiate a cappella (Collegiate A Cappella Group Directory, www.collegiate-acappella.com) lists over a thousand groups at colleges and universities throughout the United States and Canada. Thanks to television shows like *Glee* and *The Sing Off*, and more recently the movie *Pitch Perfect*,[8] this form of musical activity has become more widely known in recent years.[9] Significantly—and not always evident from *The Sing Off*—these groups are most often populated by non-music majors. While the specifics vary from institution to institution, in my own research I found that most students were heavily involved in academics, with many sustaining full course loads in "serious" degrees of study, such as environmental analysis, aerospace engineering, neuroscience, bio-medical engineering, communications, human physiology, chemistry, business, international relations, and so on. It also bears mention that the phenomenon of collegiate a cappella is not limited to so-called second- or third-tier academic institutions. On the contrary, prestigious institutions like Harvard and the Massachusetts Institute of Technology boast over two-dozen groups between them. That serious students at so many colleges throughout the United States volitionally involve themselves with an intensive, time-consuming recreational activity is intriguing. Why do these students choose to participate in this leisure activity when it takes time away from their academic studies? It is one thing to enjoy singing and making music, it is quite another to do so while spending substantial money to attend college in pursuit of an academic qualification not enhanced by one's leisure time pursuits (students typically do not receive academic credit).

The majority (approximately 70–75%) of individuals I interviewed sang with their high school chorus, with a minority of these "singers" also having previously participated in high school a cappella, but only about half of these participated in a form of a cappella analogous to the collegiate pop style.[10] Interestingly, however, other members had no previous singing background, with many identifying as instrumentalists (e.g., from a saxophonist: "I'm more of a musician, less of a singer"). Surprisingly (or perhaps not), in my research I found that the Music Director, or MD—an individual elected from within and by the group, and who performs with, not in front of, the group—was often someone who identified more as an instrumentalist than as a singer. Although collegiate a cappella is a somewhat diverse musical practice,[11] most groups are student-run, comprise 12–16 members, and rehearse 4–6 hours per week (or more), 2–3 times per week. Groups usually perform two or more times per semester, with intense activity groups sometimes performing almost weekly.

Collegiate a cappella can be viewed as exemplifying many of the values and characteristics hopefully desired of an education in music. Groups are self-run, self-directed, and perform self-arranged music. As a musical performance practice, collegiate a cappella demands a level of musicianship that we might hopefully desire for all people: a good sense of pitch, part independence, rhythmic embodiment, and not least, a strong sense of musical expression. One cannot succeed as an a cappella musician without these four vital components. Indicative of previous musical training perhaps, many of the groups I observed used sheet music during at least part of the learning phase (the arrangements were generally notated), but it should be noted that reading was not necessarily a prerequisite for participation (there were some non-readers and even the occasional person with little prior formal music training or involvement).[12]

In my observations I was consistently impressed with the level of musicianship evident in rehearsals. Moreover, as a student-run and student-directed group, a cappella requires a level of social interaction and cooperation that Randall Allsup (2003) might describe as democratic. During part of each rehearsal there was some form of business meeting where function and logistics were discussed. Groups employ some form of executive, but I repeatedly witnessed a lot of cooperative decision making among all members. Musically, I was continually impressed by the level of group involvement in the process and product in rehearsals. Every single member demonstrated a vested interest in "getting it right" and making the music better.

For this study I was particularly interested in learning about the participants' perceptions of the balance between effort, excellence, and enjoyment, aspects that speak to the heart of recreational involvement in music. I would frequently challenge my interviewees: "If six hours per week gets you *this* good [visualizing with my hands] and you wish to be better than that, why not rehearse eight hours? Why not ten? Why not twenty?" In other words, I wanted people to express the importance of musical excellence in relation to their own enjoyment and the time and effort involved. Just how serious were they about what Stebbins (1992, 1998) terms "serious leisure"? Although a few participants expressed the desire for additional rehearsal time (e.g., "I wanted to do ICCAs [International Championship of Collegiate A Cappella] but the other girls aren't as committed"), the vast majority felt the current amount about right. Despite institutional variation *vis-a-vis* exact rehearsal format (e.g., 2 three-hour vs. 3 two-hour rehearsals), I found it interesting that six hours per week appeared to be the norm for all groups in spite of the absence of formalized communications between colleges regarding such matters. Six just seems to be the magic number that represents the maximum regularly scheduled time that most students are prepared to commit.

Some groups do spend more than six hours in rehearsal and related activities, however. In addition to extra time devoted to preparation for concerts, many groups record CDs.[13] The single biggest factor determining whether or not a group spends additional hours in rehearsal preparation appears to be if they decide to participate in the International Championship of Collegiate A Cappella—a national singing tournament, organized by Varsity Vocals, that occurs over a period of months with regional quarter and semifinals leading up to (at time of writing) the final competition at New York City's Lincoln Center. From what I could gather, *everyone* involved with collegiate a cappella knows about the "ICCAs," and the decision to enter the competition is a major determinant of group identity. Some groups enter every year, some never enter, and some consider it on a year-by-year basis.

What I found intriguing in my conversations was how various participants understood the very obvious pecking order that existed among groups, a reputation and performance hierarchy with serious implications for auditions and, subsequently, for how students' tenure with collegiate a cappella would play out. To explain, groups almost always stay intact. For schools with multiple groups, there is usually an unwritten (or even written) rule that stipulates that people cannot switch between groups. Thus, acceptance into a group in freshman year dictates one's fate as a participant from freshman through senior year. That is, acceptance into a competitive group means one's collegiate a cappella experience will be competitive and vice versa. Next, consider that groups are usually 12–16 in size. This usually breaks down to 3–4 people per academic year (freshman, sophomore, junior, senior). Although the number of people auditioning for the open 3–4 spots per group (i.e., replacing the graduated seniors) is a reflection of the size of the institution and number of groups at that institution, I heard numbers as high as 150 auditioning for two open spots in a group. At larger institutions, students usually audition for multiple (or all) groups to increase their chances. The goal for most students is to get into the "best" groups on campus.[14] These "best" groups usually compete in the ICCAs. Most students, however, seemed to understand that just getting into a group is an achievement, as most who audition do not make any group. In addition, while those in the lower tier groups I interviewed expressed their initial disappointment of not making it into the group(s) of their choice (e.g., "I wish we were more competitive"), they also, explicitly or implicitly, seemed to understand the outcome as reflective of their own abilities. Moreover, almost all admitted that the outcome was a blessing in disguise and that they loved their a cappella group. (Without exception, everyone *loved* his or her group.) This admission could be considered a defense mechanism of "sour grapes," but I sensed instead that it was, rather, reflective of their own satisfaction of coming to a better understanding of who they were in the world.

Listening to the "best" collegiate a cappella groups live (rehearsal and performance) can be quite exhilarating. A group at one university, for example, regularly drew an audience of a thousand screaming fans reminiscent of a rock or pop concert experience. In attending rehearsals, experiencing, in close proximity, the power of good a cappella singing frequently gave me goose bumps and sent shivers down my spine. As evident in my field notes above, however, not all groups are at this refined level. Not infrequently I experienced, according to Western performance norms, issues of pitch, balance, or expression, which, for me, raised issues of public performance and associated expectations. Just as one's listening expectations for the elementary school band or chorus are not the same as they are for the professional symphony orchestra or chorus, I was left to ponder where this left the performance efforts of recreational music making like collegiate a cappella. While I did not personally observe any groups I would consider musically unacceptable, the majority were, as public performing groups, just good or okay.

My own discomfort sitting through one of the quarterfinal competitions of the ICCAs stemmed from what I perceived as a disconnection between the purpose of the event and the *raison d'être* of collegiate a cappella. Attending this particular competition brought into stark relief the difference between what Thomas Turino (2008) describes as participatory and presentational music making. While collegiate a cappella does derive from a Western presentational aesthetic normed to "professional" performance standards, as a form of amateur, recreational music making utilizing pop and rock repertoire it is fundamentally participatory. Although the groups do perform in public, observing any rehearsal makes clear that the goods of the activity reside in the joy of singing together each week. The musical embodiment I witnessed in rehearsals was a reminder to me of what I would want for any of my own music students. Each and every member of each group exhibited an overt love of what they were doing irrespective of what more refined Western trained ears might describe as flaws detractive from listening pleasure. However, when placed on the stage of an elegant concert hall designed for presentational music, especially that of the high art music tradition, the efforts of the "weaker" groups suddenly seemed unfortunate. The musicking (Small, 1998) event of the rehearsal space—so intimate, personal, meaningful, and amateur in the best sense—suddenly took on what I considered to be the mean-spiritedness of the *American Idol* audition episodes that, for the perverse amusement of the viewer, mock the efforts of hopefuls who are apparently oblivious to the inadequacy of their amateur (in the worst sense) efforts. What seemed to me as an admirable get-together of people with a shared love of music in their rehearsal environment became, in the context of a formal performance space, a spectacle highlighting their shortcomings as performers (although not necessarily as musicians; it was their inexperience as performers that was glaring).

LIMINAL OR LIFELONG?

> The thing about collegiate a cappella is, no one wants the party to end.
> —Mickey Rapkin, *Pitch Perfect*

Commentators (e.g., Booth, 1999; Regelski, 2007) have lamented how the expectation for professional level performance norms has been detrimental for amateur music making—"amateuring" here meant in its sense of *amare*, or "to love." What is intriguing about collegiate a cappella is that the level of passion exhibited by the students was uncorrelated with the performing level of their group. While most students interested in collegiate a cappella desire at the outset of their college experience to be in the high-level competitive groups, the reality is that only a handful of available spots exist; the majority end up in groups that vary from pretty good to just okay. This, however, did not seem to affect their level of interest or commitment, which appeared to me relatively consistent from group to group. Everyone involved with collegiate a cappella, it seems, enthusiastically participates, as Wayne Booth (1999) might put it, "for the love of it."

And yet, this apparent love for what they do seems to blur an issue that I believe speaks to a vitally important issue in recreational music making. I discerned in my interviews a lot of what Isbell and Stanley (2011) describe as "the competition paradox." Participants generally were not willing to sacrifice the hours necessary for the pursuit of a higher level of performance, and were content with their group's present level (e.g., "I don't want to suck, but I don't want to put in a ton of hours to be just a little bit better"). As the majority of participants pointed out to me, however, competition was a regarded as a good thing and competitive performance events such as the ICCAs serve as a necessary goal toward which groups can orient their efforts (e.g., "you can only get so good without competition"). The paradoxical nature of this rang through repeatedly, however. Not infrequently did people tell me that the ICCAs were a necessary goal but that they participated for fun, not because of the competition. As one person phrased it, "I like to be good, but not at the expense of happiness." The issue this raises, however, is why a competitive goal is necessary in the first place. Is recreational participation alone—in this case, regular rehearsing and presenting the occasional performance—considered insufficient? Are competitive events really necessary for improvement and effort? Is recreational participation for its own sake—doing something for the love of it—just a fictive notion masking a deep-seated desire to be number one? Or, to put it in rather grand terms, is the desire for competition driven by a conditioned, capitalistic ethic pervasive in Western society—one that, in its pursuit of besting others, stands in the way of enjoying activities for their own sake?

In part, I believe the answer to this question is addressed by considering whether individuals as their participation regarded part of a lifelong involvement with music or merely as a transitional college activity. A defining moment for me in almost every interview was the answer to my question, "What happens after you graduate?" When coupled with the participants' responses to my earlier question, "Why do this?" their description of future plans inevitably laid bare whether participants viewed music making as a lifelong activity or merely something one did during the college years. That is, when I asked people why they auditioned for a cappella, most responded by saying how much they loved music or loved singing (e.g., "I just want to be able to sing out loud and have it not be weird"), or that they had always been part of music groups and could not imagine not continuing to be in a music group. Others said that they thought joining a cappella would be a good way to transition to college, as they were likely to meet people with similar interests.

When asked about the prospect of collegiate a cappella coming to an end, however, slightly over half of those I interviewed responded by saying that they were scared or terrified (their words), although one or two of the freshmen and sophomores feigned ignorance of the time-bound nature of the activity: e.g., "I haven't thought about it; I've concentrated on this lasting forever."[15] Clearly, however, most had thought about it to some degree.

Some pointed out that current collegiate a cappella members are more fortunate than those of 5–10 years ago thanks to the rise in what participants referred to as "post-collegiate a cappella." One person mentioned that she would eventually become like several of her friends, who "are now trolling for post-collegiate a cappella." And while some people expressed possibilities for future involvement (e.g., musical theatre, starting a band, songwriting) and emphasized their passion for music making ("I can't live without singing; if I can't be part of a cappella I'll take singing lessons"), what disturbed me, as a music educator, were the number of people who saw their music making lives ending (e.g., "I think singing ends for me") and the number who had virtually no clue about the ways they might continue to be musically active post-graduation. One interviewee, confessing her frustration at the thought of not being able to continue with something she loved so much, commented, "it would be awesome if there was some after college group out there."

A minority, about one in three, felt that collegiate a cappella was an activity intended for and bounded by the college years. As a member of a highly competitive group remarked, "Last year the thought [of this ending] would have destroyed me, but now I'm okay with it. I've had my run." Or as another person put it, "You have your time and then you should move on," a comment that serves as a reminder that, in the minds of some, collegiate a cappella is indeed a college activity akin to student government, the student newspaper, other student clubs, or college rituals such as Greek life or attending sporting events on campus. Graduation, like the Jewish bar and bat mitzvah, marks the end of this liminal period in one's life;[16] the time for frivolous playful activities, like recreational singing, is over.

IMPLICATIONS

Arguably, that so many people participate in collegiate a cappella speaks to the potential success of school music programs. As I point out in previous research (Mantie, 2013), however, this is a suspect conclusion. My previous research suggests instead that recreational music making at the college/university level is much more a reflection of students' personal backgrounds— their *habitus*, in Bourdieu's (1984) formulation—than their school music experiences alone. This finding, however, does not discount the possibility of school music playing a greater role in fostering recreational music making in the future. As presented in this chapter, I suggest that collegiate a cappella is a quintessential example of recreational music making that represents so much of what the music education profession (hopefully) cares about: the volitional engagement, beyond the school years, with music making in a social musical form. The challenge is in finding ways for the profession to improve its efforts.

I believe there are at least three big takeaways from this study of collegiate a cappella. First is the importance of understanding the structural factors and conditions that enable or disable recreational participation in music. For example, one of my questions to those in leadership roles (those of my participants who were on the executive or who were the musical director) was, "If you have so many people auditioning for so few spots, why not have more groups to meet the demand?" As I learned, this was frequently a problem of institutional rules and regulations. At two of the four institutions I researched, club rules were very strict. At one, for example, regulations stipulated that no new club could be formed that duplicated the function of an existing club. Hence, the number of formally recognized a cappella groups was capped by this restriction. (Groups without club status would not have access to rehearsal space and other logistical requirements and thus face an almost impossible existence.) Conversely, I also learned how the growth and expansion of multiple a cappella groups at another institution reflected intergroup cooperation with formal rules that, while they, intentionally or not, help to ensure that the better groups stay the best and the weaker groups stay weak, also help to ensure the long-term stability and longevity of a cappella by avoiding potentially damaging conflicts and practices, such as stealing members from rival groups and so on. Additionally, many a cappella groups have established alumni associations in order to sustain both the legacy and longer-term social cohesion of participation. Although likely logistically somewhat unwieldy for high school music teachers years ago, one can only speculate on the tremendous potential such a practice might hold if instituted on a widespread basis today.[18] My point is that increasing lifelong participation in music is not simply a matter of, as some have argued, substituting rock and pop groups in schools for anachronistic concert bands. If music education is serious about increasing lifelong participation it needs to involve itself to a much greater extent with helping students negotiate such things as spaces, equipment, rules, policies, and so on. Lack of participation, in other words, cannot be solely attributed to insufficient motivation or musicianship.

The second takeaway is the matter of our obligations as music educators to educate students, and perhaps ourselves, about musical options beyond K–12 graduation. That so few of my participants could articulate future musical possibilities for engagement speaks to our failure as a profession to make people aware of the range of human musical activity. I grew increasingly frustrated when the only thing that participants could name as a future activity was taking more lessons. A love of learning for its own sake is fine, but surely, given their school experiences as former band, orchestra, or choir members, it might have been expected that more would name community ensembles of this variety, but those responses were rarely forthcoming. Far too many, it seemed to me, viewed their participation simply as an extension of their high school music experience. There is certainly nothing wrong with students' desire for a transitional activity, one with a strong social component. However, the lack of knowledge about future possibilities among so many suggests that there are likely many people in society who wish to be musically active but who are simply unaware of the options available to them (see also Mantie & Tucker, 2008).

Finally, based on the opinions and attitudes expressed by the participants, it appears that a more nuanced understanding of competition is necessary in order for people to see musical participation as healthy in the way that, for example, exercise is healthy. This is in no way to suggest that competition is necessarily bad or unhealthy. Rather, it is to emphasize that when competition becomes the sole *raison d'être,* participation ends when the competition ends. If one's participation in a collegiate a cappella group becomes only about competing in the ICCAs, then it becomes a temporary rather than lifelong activity. The value of participation under a competition orientation resides in external recognition (e.g., "we're kind of like rock stars on campus") rather than in, as Robert Stebbins (1992) describes with his term *serious leisure,* the benefits that accrue germane to the activity as a calling, life passion, or form of recreation—benefits analogous to what regular exercise is to physical health.

CONCLUSION

We cannot undo the present state of the music education profession, but we can make choices with the potential to change the future. We can choose to resurrect leisure and recreation, long a fundamental rationale for school music, as a legitimate aim and purpose for music education. Rather than viewing "leisure" negatively, associating the word with privilege or frivolity, we can restore its noble origins as the very definition of "the good life." Furthermore, we can restore recreational participation as a legitimate goal for school music instruction. Appreciating music is fine; *doing* music, however, holds greater potential for realizing more of music's goodness as a healthy and worthy use of leisure time.

Collegiate a cappella is but one example of how music is currently engaged with recreationally for the purpose of leisure. It provides an interesting case study because it occurs at a stage in life when young adults have the autonomy to make individual choices over their use of time. That so many choose to continue making music rather than stop at their first opportunity is encouraging. Whether or not they continue to do so after they graduate from college will be the real litmus test of their commitment to lifelong recreational music making, however. By continuing to study those who remain musically active we can hopefully generate better understandings that can help to orient our curricular and instructional efforts so as to ensure that more people are able to make music a meaningful and desirable part of their life throughout the lifespan.

NOTES

1. See, for example, Foucault's essays "On the Ways of Writing History," "Nietzsche, Genealogy, History," and "Return to History" in *Aesthetics, Method, and Epistemology,* edited by James D. Faubion (New York: New Press, 1998). Foucault's entire *oeuvre,* however, tends to emphasize this message.
2. The Greek word uses *chi,* hence the variations in Anglicized spellings (k vs. ch vs. kh). Moreover, in contemporary Greek the meaning of *skholē* depends on the accent: stressing the first syllable means school, stressing the second means leisure.
3. The first three of these are taken from Diana Brault's (1977) dissertation, "A History Of The Ontario Music Educators' Association (1919–1974)" (The University of Rochester). The first is from Roy Fenwick's 1935 address to music teachers (p. 167), the second from the 1935 *Canadian School Journal* (p. 171), and the third from the Ontario government's *Chief Inspector's Report* for 1930 (p. 505). The fourth example is from Alice Rogers', "The Junior High School Music Program and Some of Its Problems," *Music Supervisors' Journal,* no. 13(1) (1926): 27. The fifth is from Joseph Leeder and William Haynie, *Music Education in the High School* (Englewood Cliffs, NJ: Prentice-Hall, 1958), 100–101. The last is from a 1952 MENC publication, *The Function of Music in the Secondary-School Curriculum,* 6.
4. These types of neoliberal discourses are not unique to the United States; it is simply a context with which I am more familiar.
5. There are two very incidental references to leisure sociology (pp. 203 and 573) in *The New Handbook of Music Teaching and Learning.* One, in passing, mentions Max Kaplan and his interest in leisure; the other simply mentions leisure sociology as a field of study.
6. On page 7 of the first edition of Reimer's *A Philosophy of Music Education* there is a very brief mention of leisure in connection to the Progressive Education movement.
7. As I have documented elsewhere (Mantie, 2013), this was often referred to in the literature as "carry over."
8. *Pitch Perfect* is based on a book of the same name by Mickey Rapkin, a journalist who studied three collegiate a cappella groups in the early to mid-2000s. A similar project, but more academic in tone, is Duchan's (2012) *Powerful Voices: The Musical and Social World of Collegiate A Cappella.*
9. Contemporary interest in collegiate a cappella dates to the 1990s. Thus, it is likely that in this case popular culture capitalized on existing social practices before (arguably) fueling them.
10. Collegiate a cappella is technically over one hundred years old, dating back to such groups as the Yale Whiffenpoofs. The current resurgence of interest from the 1990s onwards, however, differs in that groups began to focus on "popular" music (i.e., of the Billboard charts and the like) rather than, as had been the tradition up to that point, singing published choral arrangements or emulating barbershop or doo-wop styles. The term "collegiate a cappella" is usually reserved for groups performing today's "popular" music (although many groups show great latitude in what they consider popular).
11. As per my previous note, I investigated mainstream collegiate a cappella. Many specialized varieties, for example religious or culturally based, exist and provide yet another potential layer of interest for researchers. My own concern was restricted to mainstream groups without special motivators or agendas at play. It should be noted that other forms of a cappella, such as barbershop based or "glee" style, also exist, but represent more of a subcultural involvement compared to the broadly based participation of mainstream collegiate a cappella.

12. Clearly, however, people with no formal training must possess the requisite musicianship: they must, in their auditions, exhibit a good sense of pitch, rhythm, and musical expression.
13. There are websites devoted to collegiate a cappella recordings, such as www. acatunes.com.
14. The gendered aspects of this are fascinating, insofar as the best group on campus is often all male. The all-female groups tend to lie at the bottom of the pecking order. Alas, this aspect of collegiate a cappella requires an article of its own and cannot be discussed here.
15. One needs to be an enrolled student to be a member. Although there are exceptions, collegiate a cappella is generally considered an undergraduate activity.
16. I am alluding here to the sense of liminality as a threshold, especially in relation to ceremonial markers (*a la* Arnold van Gennep's "rites of passage"). The Jewish mitzvahs, for example, ceremoniously mark the end of childhood.
17. Space does not allow for elaboration, but I have based my discussion on Patricia Stokowski, *Leisure in Society: A Network Structural Perspective* (New York: Mansell Publishers, 1994).
18. I am thinking here especially of possible variations on sites like Facebook or meetup.com.

REFERENCES

Allsup, R. (2003). Mutual learning and democratic action in instrumental music education. *Journal of Research in Music Education, 51*(1), 24–37.
Arnett, J. J. (2000). Emerging adulthood: A theory of development from the late teens through the twenties. *American Psychologist, 55*(5), 469–80. doi: 10.1037//0003–066X.55.5.469.
Blatterer, H. (2010). The changing semantics of youth and adulthood. *Cultural Sociology, 4*(1), 63–79. doi: 10.1177/1749975509356755.
Booth, W. C. (1999). *For the love of it: Amateuring and its rivals.* Chicago, IL: University of Chicago Press.
Bourdieu, P. (1984). *Distinction: A social critique of the judgement of taste.* Cambridge, MA: Harvard University Press.
Cox, G., & Stevens, R. S. (2010). *The origins and foundations of music education: Cross-cultural historical studies of music in compulsory schooling.* New York, NY: Continuum.
Duchan, J. S. (2012). *Powerful voices: The musical and social world of collegiate a cappella.* Ann Arbor: University of Michigan Press. Retrieved from http://site. ebrary.com.ezproxy.bu.edu/lib/bostonuniv/docDetail.action?docID = 10547403.
Dumazedier, J. (1974). *Sociology of leisure.* New York, NY: Elsevier Scientific Publ. Co.
Isbell, D., & Stanley, A. M. (2011). Keeping instruments out of the attic: The concert band experiences of the non-music major. Paper presented at American Educational Research Association Conference. New Orleans, LA.
Kaplan, M. (1978). *Leisure: Perspectives on education and policy aspects of learning.* Washington, DC: National Education Association.
Mantie, R. (2013). Structure and agency in university-level recreational music making. *Music Education Research, 15*(1), 39–58. doi: 10.1080/14613808.2012.722076.
Mantie, R., & Tucker, L. (2008). Closing the gap: Does music-making have to stop upon graduation? *International Journal of Community Music, 1*(2), 217–27.
Mueller, J. (1958). Music and education: A sociological approach. In N. B. Henry (Ed.), *Basic concepts in music education* (pp. 88–122). Chicago, IL: NSSE. (Distributed by the University of Chicago Press)

Pieper, J. (1963). *Leisure, the basis of culture*. New York, NY: New American Library.

Rapley, M. (2003). *Quality of life research: A critical introduction*. Thousand Oaks, CA: SAGE Publications.

Regelski, T. (2005). Music and music education: Theory and praxis for "making a difference." *Educational Philosophy and Theory, 37*(1), 7–27.

Regelski, T. (2007). Amateuring in music and its rivals. *Action, Criticism & Theory for Music Education, 6*(3), 22–50.

Small, C. (1998). *Musicking: The meanings of performing and listening*. Middletown, CT: Wesleyan University Press.

Stebbins, R. A. (1992). *Amateurs, professionals, and serious leisure*. Montreal, CA: McGill-Queen's University Press.

Stebbins, R. A. (1998). *After work: The search for an optimal leisure lifestyle*. Calgary, AB, Canada: Detselig Enterprises.

Turino, T. (2008). *Music as social life: The politics of participation, Chicago studies in ethnomusicology*. Chicago, IL: University of Chicago Press.

Turner, V. W. (1967). *The forest of symbols; Aspects of Ndembu ritual*. Ithaca, NY: Cornell University Press.

Weiskopf, D. C. (1982). *Recreation and leisure: Improving the quality of life* (2nd Ed.). Boston, MA: Allyn and Bacon.

Winnifrith, T. & Barrett, C. (1989). *The philosophy of leisure*. New York, NY: St. Martin's Press.

12 Seeking "Success" in Popular Music

Gareth Dylan Smith

INTRODUCTION

This chapter was written in response to the call-for-papers for the 2013 Suncoast Music Education Research Symposium (SMERS IX), which had the theme of "navigating the future"—an inherently unknowable domain. In order to negotiate the unpredictable, it seems prudent to take time to reflect critically upon the present. To do this, I discuss three interrelated areas in which I work as a practitioner—popular music performance, popular music education, and scholarship in these related areas. This paper reflects my own perspective on, and experiences in, the fields about which I write and the issues that I discuss. It is a truism that an "invisible" authorial voice is present in most scholarly writing; by foregrounding my own voice I wish to highlight its centrality to my work. I could not write this paper without my discrete positionality, so I invite readers to critique this in concert with the other subject matter. Any assumptions that I make in this text are, therefore, included as part of a consciously reflective autoethnographic approach (Chang, 2008). To exclude my subjective voice "would have been dishonest" (de Rond, 2008, p. xii).

I have been a drummer for 25 years, and have been self-employed as such part-time since 1999. I have mostly performed and recorded in musical theatre "pit" bands, punk, rock, folk, blues, and jazz bands, and with singer/songwriters of many a hue. I also began teaching in 1999. I taught mostly drum set, guitar, clarinet, and general music in elementary and secondary schools for a decade before I began working at a college of further and higher music education—the Institute of Contemporary Music Performance (hereafter, the Institute) in London, England. At the Institute I teach drum set performance to undergraduates in a range of styles such as blues, rock, and jazz; I teach ensemble classes including Creative Ensemble, Rhythm Section Workshop, and Advanced Performance Workshop; I taught Harmony and Theory for two years, and increasingly I teach popular music studies courses including Music in Context, Music and Society, Cultural and Philosophical Studies, and History of Popular Music. I also teach Research Skills and supervise around fifteen students annually through undergraduate

Dissertation courses, one of which I also lead. My work as a performer continues to inform my work as an educator, and vice versa, in a symbiosis that breathed life to this chapter.

The Institute where I work could arguably be seen as an example of an extension of the northern European "fait accompli," in which popular music is included and valued in the U.K.'s music education system (Hebert, 2011, p. 13; Mantie, 2013, p. 342). However, the Institute is a post-compulsory, higher education institution, broadly modeled, since its inception almost 30 years ago, on U.S. (Los Angeles) college, Musicians Institute. The pedagogical model has tended, perhaps out of a perceived need, to overtly and rigorously systemize and legitimize its provision, to "formalize the informal" learning practices (Smith & Shafighian 2013, p. 257) that are typically identified as being native to popular music (Green, 2002). As the Institute's full name implies, the primary focus for student activity is performance of popular music (I critique the conflation of terms "popular," "contemporary," and others in Smith, in press). Given that education programs in popular music are considered (even assumed) in this context to be worthwhile—they are the school's *raison d'être*—I turn my attention to assumptions that may underlie and inform educational practice, and the potential implications of these assumptions in and beyond higher popular music performance education (hereafter, HPMPE).

My emic perspective is a limiting factor in this paper, and also a strength. Bresler and Stake (2006) advise that "in music education, we have a need for . . . experiential understandings of particular situations" (p. 278). Muncey (2010) adds that "subjectivity doesn't infect your work, it enhances it. Making links between your own experience and your [scholarly] work is healthy" (p. 8). Muncey's work comes from the field of health care studies, but it is clear that her observations regarding the value of reflexive, autoethnograhpic writing speak also to the ongoing experiences of those working in music education, and perhaps especially in the emerging, less well-established domain of popular music education. I stand at the intersection of current directions in scholarly practice and music education and find, as Muncey affirms, "there is no distinction between doing research and living a life" (2010, p. 3).

AIMS OF THIS PAPER

Jorgensen (2009) advises us that "the field [of music education] is in need of robust conceptual theories of music education" derived from research that includes "systematically describing the field" (p. 415). I offer nothing here so bold as a conceptual theory of this broad field. Instead, this paper may be viewed as the type of descriptive work sought by Jorgensen, and as a response to Mantie's invitation in his remark that, "Researchers may wish to document practices . . . outside of the United States to more adequately determine the actual extent and forms of engagement with popular musics" in music education (Mantie, 2013, p. 347). Hopefully this paper may thus contribute to the valuable work of colleagues attempting to construct much-needed theories of our profession.

Williamson, Cloonan, and Frith (2011) describe a lack of trust between professional academics who value scholarly knowledge in or from academia, and professional musicians and others in the music business who value music knowledge in or from the popular music industry. They state that "academics have a vital role to play in keeping the public informed in ways that are not processed by PR companies or designed to serve corporate ends" (Williamson, Cloonan, & Frith, 2010, p. 470). Equally important, of course, is that scholars in music and education are able to accommodate the knowledge of those "on the ground" in popular music performance. As I hope to illustrate, in order to navigate the future, scholars, performers, and educators need to share expertise in a broad dialogue that embraces the overlapping boundaries of music performance, scholarship, and education. As is indicated by the literature on learning in popular music (e.g., Green, 2002, 2008; Smith, 2013a), there is often little or no distinction between musician, educator, and learner—between music practices and music education—in popular music. Few writers appear to be directly involved with knowledge from these three domains; the world of HPMPE is at the crossroads. In such a broad and under-researched field as popular music education (Mantie, 2013; Smith, 2013a), it is especially vital that all proceed with open ears, eyes, and minds.

I seek in the following pages to describe and explore two related problems. The first of these is that HPMPE programs, courses, and institutions may be in danger of de-valuing many popular musicians (including the overwhelming majority of their own students, faculty, and alumni) and those musicians' work through adherence to a tacit and under-interrogated epistemology of "success." Bennett explains how this situation exists across higher music education: "The learning cultures within music are unlikely . . . to encourage broad purviews of career or broad definitions of what it is to be a successful musician" (Bennett, 2013, p. 236). As HPMPE programs proliferate, this situation is becoming untenable, and serves our students poorly, since "building a successful career depends on entrepreneurial activities and carving out a niche market" (Bennett, 2013, p. 235). The second problem is that this potential epistemological deficit is accompanied and exacerbated by the adherence to similar prohibitively exclusive assumptions regarding success in popular music, both by scholars in the field of popular music studies, and by commentators in the wider public consciousness and the mainstream media. The overall aim of this paper is, thus, to challenge, broaden, or recontextualize perspectives of colleagues in HPMPE and beyond, by exploring what appear from my perspective and context to be salient issues regarding how the HPMPE community and others construe success in popular music.

POPULAR MUSIC IN EDUCATION

Popular music performance has a steadily growing presence in education—from elementary school to Master's programs—in many countries including the U.K., Argentina, Finland, Sweden, Australia, United States, and South Korea (see, for example, Abramo, 2011; Allsup, 2008; Feichas, 2010; Green, 2008; Krikun, 2009; Mantie, 2013; Partti, 2012; Randles & Smith, 2012; Smith, 2013a, 2013b; Westerlund, 2006). While in the U.K. and much of northern Europe popular music and education could arguably be seen as relatively comfortable companions, the music education system in the United States—the country that spawned many of the most commercially successful popular music artists and styles of the last century—has largely been reluctant to adopt curricula that include popular music of musics (Hebert, 2011).

In the United States, however, the situation appears to be changing, albeit gradually and only at the margins of the mainstream. In 2007, John Kratus wrote provocatively that the country's school music education was at a "tipping point" (Kratus, 2007, p. 42), about to undergo systemic change following a beginning trend toward new models of classroom music education. This shift looks set to include a greater incorporation of popular music in curricula (Allsup, 2008), as championed by the iconoclastic leadership of the Music Education area at the University of South Florida (Williams, 2007). In 2012/13, a handful of the advertisements for vacancies for music education faculty members at U.S. universities included mention of popular music among the specialisms welcome in applicants; while unprecedented, this is not (yet?) indicative of a broad national trend.

There has been a notable increase in scholarly activity around popular music in education in recent years (Mantie, 2013), including conferences in 2010 and 2012 at London's Institute of Contemporary Music Performance: "The Place and Purpose of Popular Music Education" and "Sociology and Philosophy of Popular Music Education," the 2011 Suncoast Music Education Research Symposium on "Popular Music Pedagogy," and the 2011 formation of the Association for Popular Music Education (A.P.M.E.) in the United States, led by Christopher Sampson at University of Southern California's Thornton School of Music (as I finish this chapter, A.P.M.E.'s second quarterly *Newsletter* has just been published). With the fast pace at which (inherently trend-based) popular music moves, and with the desire that music educators often feel—perhaps necessarily—to write and publish curricula and "methods" text books that can be of some use at and beyond their publication date, I am keen that this paper be viewed as the product of a very particular set of experiences at a specific point in time. As Allsup (2008) underlines, there is a danger of approaches or perspectives becoming reified or overstated. Restlessly evolving, genre-defying contemporary musician Robert Glasper says: "Some people say, 'You're the future of jazz.' I'm not the future—I'm just now. Jazz is so far behind that the present actually looks like the future" (Glasper, cited in Aveling, 2012, p. 112). Substituting the words "music education" for "jazz," I would rephrase Glasper's assertion thus: "I'm not the future—I'm just now. [Music education] is so far behind that the present actually looks like the future." We in the music education professions, whether already heavily invested in the paradigm of HPMPE or edging towards popular music/s in compulsory school settings, cannot afford to stand still.

POPULAR MUSIC STUDIES AND POPULAR MUSIC PERFORMANCE

The fields of popular music performance and popular music studies have infrequently collided in the extant literature. In discussing "popular music studies," I refer to that wide branch of scholarship championed by the International Association for the Study of Popular Music (IASPM) that investigates popular music textually, contextually, historically, culturally, and sociologically, having no explicit concern with music education. Popular music studies (as it is thus defined for this paper) also tends largely to exclude popular music performance as an area of interest. Indeed, when I have, at various IASPM conferences over the last five years, presented papers on learning and identity in popular music education, and on the embodied experience of performing popular music, I have found my studies to be somewhat anomalous (although of sufficient interest to be accepted for presentation).

In late summer 2012, I received a call-for-papers from @*IASPM*, IASPM's online peer-reviewed journal, for a special edition that would explore popular music performance. Isolating performance in this way underlined for me the "orthodox" assumption that when one studies popular music one is not studying performance. A week later, as if to underscore this dichotomy, an editorial piece in the newly reinstated IASPM U.K. and Ireland newsletter declared that "every issue now we intend to let the other side of the fence have their say—in each edition we will be asking a practicing musician for their perspective and opinion on popular music studies" (McLaughlin, 2012, p. 12). In that edition of the newsletter, Rod Jones of Scottish rock band Idlewild gives a 245-word response to this invitation, in which he talks only about the pros and cons of popular music *performance* programs in the U.K.; he clearly appears to misunderstand the question, believing "popular music studies" to refer to the study of popular music performance, in the sense of working hard at being a performer. This is quite an understandable error, and underlines the centrality of performance in popular music to those who perform it—this does look like the most obvious way to study popular music. However, to bifurcate the two fields of "performance" and "studies" creates a false duality that is misleading because it is at odds with the experiences of popular musicians.

I have always found difficulty in conceptually separating "popular music" from "popular music performance," since to me the former implies the latter. Without the performance there would be very little popular music (and historically, most popular music has been performed). While this is a gross over-simplification and could engender volumes of discussion, it is from this perspective that I write; being a professional drummer, I have always approached the teaching of music and writing about music and musicians as a drummer, first and foremost. I have not, as it were, left my musicianship at the door when entering the office to write or the performance classroom to teach.

Attending the inaugural meeting of the U.K. Punk Scholars Network in late 2012, it struck me that those of us who straddle McLaughlin's "fence" are growing in number. We are reaching a point where it is no longer healthy or tenable—if it ever was—to maintain the epistemological barrier between performers and scholars. This is not to say that scholars need to be performers; but rather that academia could consider using a less divisive lens. Berger (2002) observes "a huge gap between the experience of living a normal life at this moment on the planet and the public narratives being offered to give a sense to that life" (p. 176). Musicians increasingly lead protean or portfolio careers (Bennett, 2008, 2013; Hallam & Gaunt 2012; Partti, 2012) that Burnard (2013) identifies as "boundary-less careers"; those of us working in HPMPE need to recognize this as soon as possible, or else risk holding the frame up quite a long way from the picture. Our institutions need to recognize diverse manifestations of success for musicians, and to reflect these back, through curriculum and pedagogy, to our students so that they are all the better prepared for navigating the future. Bennett (2013) asserts that students across higher music education "need to form themselves for entrepreneurship even while they are studying. This requires a future-oriented epistemology developed within a safe study environment that rewards leading as well as learning, such that the 'future self' is self-defined as one who combines knowledge and action in the creation of the new" (p. 238).

CONSTRUING "SUCCESS" IN PARLIAMENT[1]

In April 2012 I attended a debate in a committee room at the House of Commons in London, where the question under discussion was "Where are the musicians of tomorrow coming from?" Present at this 90-minute debate, along with several elected Members of Parliament, were representatives of the Music Industries Association, the Youth Music charity, the British Phonographic Industry, and the Institute. I attended with four students and our Managing Director. The representatives of these various institutions (including the Institute's Managing Director) had each prepared a response of five to ten minutes that they read aloud, prior to the general debate. I was surprised that each response, without exception, was only addressing the same tiny part of the tabled question; presenters appeared to be answering the related—but wholly different—question: "Where are the *professional* musicians of tomorrow coming from?" This is an important question, and worthy of debate at the House of Commons. However, it is not the question that I was expecting to hear discussed.

As debate followed the prepared speeches, the tone of the session took on a still narrower focus. Attendees were trading answers to the yet-further-removed question, "Where are the *famous* musicians of tomorrow coming from?" The Right Honourable Member of Parliament chairing the session allowed the debate to proceed for almost its full term before I interjected to express my concern that we appeared to have been distracted by a different matter from the one that we had been asked to discuss. My remarks failed to alter the course of the dialogue. I wonder if the apparent underlying assumptions of this debate are indicative of those of a majority of people across the education and music sectors. In our commercialized, media-rich world, have we become enculturated to equate "musician" with "celebrity performer"? My answer to the question initially posed ("Where are the musicians of the future coming from?") is this: the musicians of the future are coming from a *substantially changed cultural understanding of what it means to be a musician.*

CONSTRUING "SUCCESS" IN MUSIC EDUCATION

Popular public mythologies are aggressively perpetuated with regard to musicianship and musical "ability" and "talent" via the celebrity-saturated charade of television shows like *The X-Factor* and *The Voice* touting a false and transparent made-for-television meritocracy. These myths are compounded by the work of scholars in education who espouse a different notion of what it is to be musical than is mostly prevalent in the contemporary literature. Narrow and potentially misleading views of what it is to be "naturally" musically able can be found in such constraining models as Gagné's "Differentiated Model of Giftedness and Talent" (Gagné, 1998, p. 39). I discuss the problems inherent in such models in Smith and Durrant (2006).

Welch (2001) writes that "the limiting concept of humankind as either musical or unmusical is untenable. The neuropsychobiological research evidence indicates that everyone is musical (assuming normal anatomy and physiology)" (p. 22). This being the case, the science is very much at odds with the tone of (and undertones of) the debate in the English Houses of Parliament. Durrant (2003), echoing Welch, explains that it is up to society—including but not exclusive to the formal education system—to realize each person's inherent musicality:

> Although we have capabilities, this does not necessarily mean that abilities will be learned. Abilities are learned and elaborated only if the people, places, things, and events in our surroundings support that learning. Our experiences, therefore, determine the extent to which our human capabilities will be converted into increasingly refined abilities.
>
> (p. 13)

While the job of the music educator may be construed broadly (or maybe narrowly) as to actualize the musical abilities of those in his or her care, these abilities may not necessarily fit into the existing categories prescribed by, for instance, extant curricula or the criteria for assessing excellence in performance at a wind band, chamber string, or punk rock performance.

Attempts are being made to incorporate a broad range of musics and musical experiences into the world's music classrooms (e.g., Burton, ed., 2012; Green, 2008) that are meaningful to the students involved. As Jorgensen (2009) and Mantie (2013) advise above, a key challenge is for music educators in institutions to remain responsive to what we see around us. Partti (2012) challenges the status quo, thus:

> Formal music education, if operating from a place of fear and defensiveness, turns inward by advancing the development of a compartmentalised musicianship that is firmly rooted in particular genres, styles and communities, and conforms to a reactive role in the midst of the supercomplex cultural landscape. . . . This stance seems not only unsustainable as a way forward for 21st century music education, but also utterly irresponsible."
>
> (p. 90)

Partti's words are as salient to compulsory education as they are in HPMPE. Following Burnard's (2012) acknowledgement of humans' numerous and varied musical "creativities" (pp. 17–18), I contend that it is incumbent upon music educators to embrace a pluralistic view of multiple (perhaps infinite) potential "musicalities." We should be asking our students and ourselves, "How can my musicality help you more fully to realize (in both senses of the word) yours?" We must commit to what Partti (2012) describes as "the school (or college) as an institution that guides students towards increasing agency" (p. 88), including musically.

In the music education community there is broad agreement with the view that all people are musical, that musical experiences should be available to all and that, by extension, all should therefore have access to meaningful music education. The website of the International Society for Music Education (ISME) states: "We believe that lived experiences of music, in all their aspects, are a vital part of the life of all people" (International Society for Music Education, 2012). Similarly, the mission of the National Association for Music Education (NAfME) in the United States is: "To advance music education by encouraging the study and making of music by all" (National Association for Music Education, 2012). Wright (2012) suggests, "We can surmise that many children and young people who fail and drop out of formal education, far from being either uninterested (or unmusical) simply do not respond to the kind of music instruction it offers," bringing to bear upon music educators a weight of social responsibility, engaging young people with music so that they can develop into empowered and actualized members of the society. This does not need to have anything to do with winning high school band competitions or getting through to the final round of a made-for-television "reality" talent contest. These should not be taken off the table either, but a broader vision is required of *what being a musician is*—from the first years of music education, through college or university, and beyond (Mantie, in press).

CONSTRUING "SUCCESS" AT THE INSTITUTE

Students beginning programs at the Institute usually want music to play a significant role in their futures. For the vast majority this means seeking careers in music. A browse through the promotional literature of the Institute reveals that, "At the Institute, we are constantly focused on the needs of our students . . . our goal is their success!" (Institute of Contemporary Music Performance, 2012a, p. 33). Laudable though this sentiment is, defining success for all current and potential students is no straightforward task. Success may reasonably be construed in terms of making a career and a living from and/or in performing music; the Institute emphasizes this view throughout its publicity materials (Institute of Contemporary Music Performance, 2012b, 2012c). I have written elsewhere (Smith, 2013b) about the "pedagogy for employability" (p. 1) that is a pervasive theme at the Institute, in current literature, and at recent conferences (such as the College Music Society's Annual Conferences in the United States).

In the music education literature there is currently a strong focus on the employability of music college graduates (e.g., Bennett, 2013; Smith, 2013b; Smith & Shafighian, 2013). In the U.K. this has been especially heightened recently in the face of the economic recession and the concomitant huge rise in tuition fees for higher education; customers (students and their parents) want more "bang for their buck," including a job at the other end. Bennett (2013) tells us that music educators (particularly in higher education) face "an ethical and moral imperative" to adopt creative practices, affording "pedagogies that encourage students to redefine the term 'musician' for themselves . . . (enabling) creative learners who explore individual strengths and talents, and the intrinsic and extrinsic influences driving their passion for music" (p. 240).

Curricula at the Institute embody broadly two pedagogies for employability in respective undergraduate study programs (Smith, 2013b; Smith & Shafighian, 2013). The Bachelor of Music in Popular Music Performance program aims to equip students with a sort of tool-kit of skills useful to the jobbing, craftsperson musician. The Bachelor of Arts in Creative Musicianship program seeks to develop the unique creative, collaborative skills of individual artist musicians, with a particular focus on the importance of collaboration for the entrepreneurial musician (Burnard, 2012; Smith, 2013b); and the Bachelor of Arts in Songwriting combines these approaches (Institute of Contemporary Music

Performance, 2012d, 2012e, 2012f). These latter two programs are new, and have yet to gather data on graduate employment; Bachelor of Music alumni are working in a wide variety of full-time and portfolio occupations, from beauty therapy, marketing, and teaching, to working full-time in a well-known pop-punk band. Which of these has achieved "success," and to what degree? Perhaps, as Partti (2012) suggests, any student is successful who has been guided towards increasing agency.

Arguably the most common way to construe success in music today, in HPMPE and the media, is in terms of fame or commercial success. Rhetoric from the Institute and other similar institutions, such as the Academy of Contemporary Music Performance in the U.K. (Institute of Contemporary Music Performance, 2012b; Academy of Contemporary Music, 2012), mentions "connectivity" to the "the industry" as though the music industry is a separate entity that exists beyond the walls of the college—an esoteric arena to which the colleges can help students gain access. The Institute lists alumni in its publicity materials, but only those who are in or affiliated with bands and artists who have achieved a degree of fame in performance or music production. Around 300 students graduate annually from the Institute, and most of these do not go on to become headline news or, therefore, to make the list of selected alumni that ignores the vast majority of possibilities for construing success. Wherefore this endemic resistance to acknowledging a wider conception of success?

CONSTRUING "SUCCESS" IN POPULAR MUSIC STUDIES

Rodriguez (2004) observes that popular music benefits from "a rich history that is tied to our social, political, cultural, and economic history. What it lacks, in comparison to, say, Western European music, is the passage of sufficient time to determine which practices, structures, persons, and places have most influenced the genre" (p. 17). Rodriguez's denial of a canon in popular music, however, runs contrary to my experience as an educator and scholar working in HPMPE. Students at the Institute are required to take a course in the history of popular music, part of "popular music studies" misunderstood above by Rod Jones (McLaughlin, 2012). Literature in popular music studies has tended to focus on the work of famous and commercially successful musicians, with few exceptions. This is not unreasonable, as bands or artists that have sold millions of albums and become recognized internationally are, by definition, very popular. Popular music scholars have thus arguably (although perhaps inadvertently) established a canon of Great Works and Great Masters in popular music to parallel those of the Western Classical and (more recently) Jazz traditions (e.g., Frith, 1996; Gracyk, 1996, 2007; McLaughlin & McLoone, 2012; Moore, 2001, 2012). Those of us in popular music education risk embedding this view as an orthodoxy which ignores the 21st-century "reemergence of grassroots creativity" that continues increasingly to characterize artists' and musicians' modes of production and distribution of their creative products (Jenkins, 2006, p. 136). Indeed, Reynolds (2011) argues compellingly that the obsession with its past threatens popular music's very survival as a paradigm; this threat is perhaps nowhere in more urgent need of consideration than at institutions such as the Institute, whose students, alumni, and faculty can only ever hope to have careers in the present and the future.

One of the key foci in creation and distribution of popular music has always been the "new," the current, music that has changed sometimes by revolution, at others by evolution, with artists and craftspeople striving to be novel and exciting by assimilating, synthesizing, replacing, and displacing various gestures—musical, corporeal, attitudinal, social—of preceding styles or movements that have spawned today's plethora of musics in the "popular" realm. Those creating and producing the music may wish for high-profile commercial longevity, but that is not the prevalent model in popular music, although the media have a habit of wheeling out and reifying, even deifying, popular music iconic heritage acts of a former age such as Paul McCartney and the Rolling Stones; the mind boggles at the thought of what fate might today have befallen a withering Elvis Presley, had he survived to the present day. There is not much room on the tiny pedestal at the top of the media industry "tree" for musicians and bands. However, in the "creative revolution" taking place around us and amongst us, the dialogue and boundaries between "participatory culture and commercial culture" (Jenkins, 2006, pp. 136–37) are becoming ever more blurred. The tacit overarching epistemology in popular music studies needs to change and to acknowledge this or else, as Hoskyns (2012) warns, "the most authentic scenes will be those we know nothing about."

Messages from mainstream media are often reductive and sometimes wholly misleading, such as when the *New Musical Express* in 2002 announced the "New Rock Revolution" (New Musical Express/Ignite!, 2002). I recall my disbelief at the allegation that a handful of bands selected for coverage by a high-profile publication were suddenly rediscovering and re-inventing a genre that had been alive and well since its inception. As far as I (along with the scores of people I frequently encountered on London's less well-publicized rock scene) was concerned, there was no revolution, just a shift in the attention of mainstream media to a style that had been ignored for a season while indie bands, divas, and (in the U.K.) Welsh musicians were the flavor of the day. Similarly, "the most important acts who are shaping music today" (Q, 2011)[2] include hip-hop and alternative rock artists, with a particularly high level of attention paid to folk music musicians Laura Marling and Mumford & Sons. These artists are not unworthy of attention, but then neither are dozens, scores, or hundreds of comparably "good" acts. I and many of my peers have been playing folk music for over twenty years, and will continue to do so after the cameras have turned elsewhere for the next "new" style that will likely have long preexisted and will long outlast the fickle media hype. Instances such as these are typical of what Hoskyns (2012) describes as the mainstream media's propensity for "deification and demolition—build 'em up and knock 'em down."

When I teach undergraduate popular music history I begin by telling the students that I will not be giving them an accurate or complete history. Notions of "popular," "music," and "history" are so complex that to attempt to fool students that I could comprehensively fill them in on all the details would be arrogant, at best. I am always very nervous to canonize and to reify the songs, albums, artists, genres, movements, and events that we discuss, although I realize that by discussing them I risk canonizing them all the more, in the minds of one class of undergraduate students at a time. At best, I can aim to augment students' existing—usually substantial—knowledge of music that has gone before, and, my main task, perhaps to encourage them to question the histories and messages that they encounter. I discuss with the class our inevitable ignorance of the majority of music being made in the world or even just in London at present, and, by extension, the futility of trying to identify a definitive history of popular music.

I like to try the following exercise with my classes: I ask how many of the students in the class are in bands making original popular music, and every hand in the room goes up. I then ask students to keep their hands up if their band is "any good." Most hands remain up. Finally I ask who is in a band of which I would have heard. Hands then all go down (apart from the occasional hand belonging to someone who sings backup vocals or plays drums for a high-profile pop artist on tour). These young musicians are just beginning to find their niches in the "long tail" of the music business (Anderson, 2006), where the traditional music industry model of selling as much as possible of as little as possible (Cartwright & Smith, in press) is incompatible with a now-normative, more flexible, portfolio career model. As Cartwright and Smith (in press) point out, "Whereas once upon time such an existence would have been construed as a paying one's dues *en route* to success, for a considerable majority of excellent, professional musicians in the contemporary socio-musical business environment, *this is success*. It is just not widely recognized and valued as such." Popular music studies' prevailing focus on musicians who have been afforded (and in the very rarest of cases may themselves have achieved) significant mainstream and commercial success risks miss-construal by educators, students, and the public as reflective of popular music in the present, when it is distinctly at odds with the perspectives of musicians making the vast majority of the world's popular music today, that is, the very ways in which popular music *is popular* in a 21st-century paradigm.

CONCLUSIONS AND IMPLICATIONS: CONSTRUCTING AND CONSTRUING CAREER "SUCCESS"

My fellow tutors and I at the Institute play music that, although in similar styles, and using virtually all of the same gestures as more commercially successful artists, is (if we take traditional indicators like album sales and fame as the yardsticks of success) wholly *un*popular. However, the ways that it sounds and is created are entirely consistent with notions of popular music (e.g., Frith, 1996; Green, 2002; Hoskyns, 2012). We all have portfolio careers, pieced together from a mixture of high-profile performances, low-profile gigs, teaching, journalism, composition, and all manner of music-related and non-music-related work. Similar work patterns are described in detail in the work of Cottrell (2004), who studies the working lives of musicians in London, Bennett (2008), who explores the practices of musicians in Australia, and Smith (2013a), where I describe the identities and practices of drummers in and around London. This is the *modus operandi* of many a successful musician.

I consider myself to be a successful musician. I have accomplished things of which I am proud and for which I have received praise from respected peers; I have a secure job in HPMPE, and many "irons in the fire" for current and future projects. This being said, I am not famous, and my income derives largely from things other than performing. Most of the music that I make and that I would consider truly successful in artistic and technical terms, pays me very little. Indeed, the music that I have been paid the most to play has frequently (although not always) been what I consider to have been some of the least successful music, musically. In terms of the aspirations of ISME and NAfME, my life would probably be judged to be an ongoing story of success. In the tacit, unwritten terms of the discussion in the House of Commons, I would probably be barely recognized as a "musician." My performance and recording career to date will certainly be ignored by the overwhelming majority of IASPM-ites (as the Association's popular music scholars affectionately refer to ourselves).

Successful musicians today occupy unique niches as multifaceted entrepreneurs, operating in numerous intra- and inter-disciplinary networks of contacts with artists, writers, and colleagues from all over the world—what Gloor (2006) in his book *Swarm Creativity* terms "COINs . . . collaborative innovation networks" (p. 3). Work patterns like this are increasingly common and increasingly encouraged across creative industries and other domains—including the academia—with members of COINs collaborating for individual as well as mutual benefit toward outcomes only achievable with collaborative, group efforts. Gloor (2006) writes that, "In a COIN, knowledge workers collaborate and share in internal transparency. They communicate directly rather than through hierarchies. And they innovate and work toward common goals in self-organization instead of being ordered to do so" (p. 4). While this type of career is not new, the literature indicates a general shift toward a significantly higher level of people's experiences of work happening in these ways (Gloor, 2006; Partti, 2012; Sennett, 2012; Netto, 2012; Smith & Shafighian, 2013). It is in collaborative networks that most musicians in popular and other musics construct their continued success, through a process that Cartwright, Gillett, and Smith (in press) identify as "orchestration . . . defined in terms of efforts to achieve success by finding and managing creative combinations for value."

Many in higher music education are tuning in to the changing shape of success in music (e.g., Hallam & Gaunt 2012). Partti (2012) advocates integration of networks akin to Gloor's COINs into the music education experience at and across every level, to the mutual benefit of all stakeholders:

> Institutions of formal education could and *should* [emphasis in original] actively construct various kinds of inter-generational (and even international and inter-institutional) communities and networks of communities between students, between teachers, and between students and teacher(s), cooperating within systems of exchange based on generalized reciprocity at the junction of generosity and self-interest.
>
> (p. 98)

The challenge for those of us working in music education is to recognize and incorporate contemporary understandings of the work patterns of successful music professionals and, where necessary, to alter discourses accordingly. As teachers, the personal narratives that we offer our students about life as musicians are thus essential, reflecting success for the majority of musicians in our culture and supportively guiding students towards realistic expectations of how they will likely work (Bennett 2013).

Echoing Burnard's construal of musicians' multifaceted careers as "boundary-less," Netto (2012) finds normative discourse in terms of the "core industries" of the music business and "related industries" to be outmoded, seeking a re-construal of stakeholders' roles and practices. An emerging trend in cross-disciplinary research between Management, Economics, and Music fields reflects and underpins a need to recognize the centrality of these "other" industries and domains to our own work in Music Education and HPMPE. Groups such as the Centre for the Study of Working Lives (Gillett & Smith 2013) and the Art of Management and Organization (2013), whose biennial conferences bring together current thinking and practices in and across arts, management, and organizational behavior, are taking a keen interest in how musicians construct careers. Similar critical engagement with the "business of doing business" as musicians (Cartwright & Smith, in press) is necessary in HPMPE.

"Success" for most musicians has yet to be determined; what seems certain is that it will not follow the patterns of the first 100 years of commercially available recorded music or the stories offered up by the mainstream media and many scholarly studies to describe it. Success will be based upon involvement in COINs of all shapes and sizes. Institutions and organizations need to embrace a new, flexible, dynamic epistemology of popular music that incorporates real-life scenarios for multiple musicalities, careers, and notions of success. This will include recognition that musicians and music practices in popular idioms beneath the fickle radar of the mainstream media are, at the very least, relevant and important, and that recognition and understanding of them as central to the popular "canon" will prove vital to successful navigation of the future in music education. I call upon scholars in higher education institutions to utilize their influence to begin to effect empowering social-cultural change: if asked, "Where are the musicians of the future coming from?" those in the music and music education professions need to have answers that reflect a critical and reflexive engagement with the diverse and changing present. To alter (again) Glasper's observation, we in the music education professions should aspire to a future where we can say:

good quote

Some people say, "You're the future of music education." We're not the future—we're just now, but, because of our relentless critical interrogation of our culture, our practices, and the needs of our students, the present actually looks like the future.

NOTES

1. The Houses of Parliament (often referred to as just "Parliament") are the two debating houses of the U.K. government. In the House of Commons, democratically elected representatives, "Members of Parliament" (or "MPs"), debate and pass laws on behalf of the populace. The House of Commons functions in conjunction with the House of Lords, whose members ("Peers") are not democratically elected. MPs in the House of Commons refer to one another in the third person as "the Right Honourable Member."
2. *Q* is a monthly U.K.-based journalistic publication advertising and discussing current "popular" music.

REFERENCES

Abramo, J. M. (2011). Gender difference of popular music production in secondary schools. *Journal of Research in Music Education, 59*(1), 21–43.
Academy of Contemporary Music. (2012). Retrieved from www.acm.ac.uk/
Allsup, R. (2008). Creating an educational framework for popular music in public schools: Anticipating the second-wave. *Visions of Research in Music Education, 12,* 1–12.
Anderson, C. (2006). *The long tail: Why the future of business is selling less of more.* New York, NY: Hyperion.
The Art of Management and Organization. (2013). Retrieved from www.artofmanagement.org
Aveling, M. (2012). Present tense. *Wax Poetics, 51,* 110–14.
Bennett, D. E. (2008). *Understanding the classical music profession: The past, the present and strategies for the future.* Aldershot, United Kingdom: Ashgate.
Bennett, D. E. (2013). The role of career creatives in developing identity and becoming expert selves. In P. Burnard (Ed.), *Developing creativities in higher music education: International perspectives and practices* (pp. 224–44). London, United Kingdom: Routledge.
Berger, J. (2002). *The shape of a pocket.* London, United Kingdom: Bloomsbury.
Bresler, L., & Stake, R. (2006). Qualitative research methodology in music education. In R. Colwell (Ed.), *MENC handbook of research methodologies* (pp. 270–311). New York, NY: Oxford University Press.

198   *Gareth Dylan Smith*

Burnard, P. (2012). *Musical creativities in practice*. Oxford, United Kingdom: Oxford University Press.

Burnard, P. (2013). Addressing the politics of practice-based research and its potential contribution to higher music education. In S. Harrison (Ed.), *Research and research education in music performance and pedagogy*. Dordrecht, Netherlands: Springer.

Burton S. (Ed.). (2012). *Engaging musical practices: A sourcebook for middle school general music*. Lanham, MD: Rowman and Littlefield.

Cartwright, P. A., & Smith, G. D. (in press). Innovation and value in networks for emerging musicians. In M. Hülsmann, N. Pfeffermann, T. Marshall, & L. Mortara (Eds.), *Strategies and communications for innovation: An integrative management view for companies and networks*. New York, NY: Springer.

Cartwright, P. A., Gillett, A., & Smith, G. D. (in press). Valuing networks for emerging musicians. In V. Lejeune (Ed.), *Les tendances technico-économiques de la Valeur*. Paris, France: 'l'Harmattan.

Chang, H. (2008). *Autoethnography as method*. Walnut Creek, CA: Left Coast Press.

Cottrell, D. M. (2004). *Secrets of life: Unique insight into the workings of your soul by the most powerful intuitive of our time*. London, UK: K. Cottrell Incorporated.

De Rond, M. (2008). *The last amateurs: To hell and back with the Cambridge boat race crew*. Cambridge, United Kingdom: Icon Books.

Durrant, C. (2003). *Choral conducting: Philosophy and practice*. London, United Kingdom: Routledge.

Feichas, H. (2010). Bridging the gap: Informal learning practices as a pedagogy of integration. *British Journal of Music Education, 27*(1), 47–58.

Frith, S. (1996). *Performing rites: Evaluating popular music*. Oxford, United Kingdom: Oxford University Press.

Gagné, F. (1998). Nature or nurture: A re-examination of Sloboda and Howe's (1991) interview study on talent development in music. *Psychology of Music, 27*, 38–51.

Gillett, A., & Smith, G. D. (2013). Swarm creativity and relationship marketing in punk and post-punk: A case study of the Eruptörs. CEGBI/CSWL Summer Conference, York Management School, University of York, York, United Kingdom. Available online at: www.youtube.com/watch?v=EokzYOdRP64.

Gloor, P. (2006). *Swarm creativity: Competitive advantage through collaborative innovation networks*. New York, NY: Oxford University Press.

Gracyk, T. (1996). *Rhythm and noise: An aesthetics of rock*. London, United Kingdom: I.B. Tauris.

Gracyk, T. (2007). *Listening to popular music: Or, how I learned to stop worrying and love Led Zeppelin*. Ann Arbor: University of Michigan Press.

Green, L. (2002). *How popular musicians learn: A way ahead for music education*. Aldershot, United Kingdom: Ashgate.

Hallam, S., & Gaunt, H. (2012). *Preparing for success: A practical guide for young musicians*. London, United Kingdom: Institute of Education Press.

Hebert, D. G. (2011). Originality and institutionalization: Factors engendering resistance to popular music pedagogy in the U.S.A. *Music Education Research International, 5*, 12–21.

Hoskyns, B. (2012). This must be the place: Holy grails and musical Meccas. Paper presented at the International Association for the Study of Popular Music (U.K. and Ireland) Conference, Salford, UK (October, 2012).

International Society for Music Education. (2012). Retrieved from www.isme.org.

Institute of Contemporary Music Performance. (2012a). Programme: *Rock and roles conference 2012. Philosophy and sociology of popular music education*. London, United Kingdom: Institute of Contemporary Music Performance.

Institute of Contemporary Music Performance. (2012b). Retrieved from www.icmp. co.uk.

Institute of Contemporary Music Performance. (2012c). *Prospectus 2012.* London, United Kingdom: Institute of Contemporary Music Performance.

Institute of Contemporary Music Performance. (2012d). *Programme handbook BMus popular music performance 2012–2013.* London, United Kingdom: Institute of Contemporary Music Performance.

Institute of Contemporary Music Performance. (2012e). *Programme handbook BA Creative musicianship 2012–2013.* London, United Kingdom: Institute of Contemporary Music Performance.

Institute of Contemporary Music Performance. (2012f). *Programme handbook BA songwriting 2012–2013.* London, United Kingdom: Institute of Contemporary Music Performance.

Jenkins, H. (2006). *Convergence culture: Where old and new media collide.* New York: New York University Press.

Jorgensen, E. R. (2009). A philosophical view of research in music education. *Music Education Research, 11*(4), 405–24.

McLaughlin, N., & McLoone, M. (2012). *Rock and popular music in Ireland: Before and after U2.* Dublin: Irish Academic Press.

McLaughlin, S. (2012). *International association for the study of popular music UK and Ireland Newsletter, 28*(1).

Kratus, J. (2007). Music education at the tipping point. *Music Educators Journal, 94*(2), 42–8.

Krikun, A. (2009). Mixing Memphis soul into the community college curriculum stew. *Journal of Popular Music Studies, 21*(1), 76–89.

Mantie, R. (2013). A comparison of "popular music pedagogy" discourses. *Journal of Research in Music Education, 61*(3), 334–52.

Mantie, R. (in press). Liminal or lifelong: Leisure, recreation, and the future of music education. In C. Randles (Ed.), *Music education: Navigating the future* (pp. __-__). New York, NY: Routledge.

Moore, A. F. (2001). *Rock: The primary text. Developing a musicology of rock* (2nd Ed.). Aldershot, United Kingdom: Ashgate.

Moore, A. F. (2012). *Song means: Analysing and interpreting recorded popular song.* Farnham, United Kingdom: Ashgate.

Muncey, T. (2010). *Creating autoethnographies.* London, United Kingdom: SAGE Publications.

National Association for Music Education. (2012). Retrieved from http://musiced. nafme.org/about/mission-statement/

Netto, M. (2012). Monetising the music: The new characteristics of the recorded music field. In A.-V. Kärjä, L. Marshall, & J. Brusila (Eds.), *Popular music and the Nordic region in global dynamics.* Helsinki, Finland: International Institute for Popular Culture.

New Musical Express/Ignite! (2002). *NME presents the sound of the new rock revolution: 15 tracks of fuzzed-up mayhem.* Various artists. NME NRR1.

Partti, H. (2012). *Learning from cosmopolitan digital musicians: Identity, musicianship, and changing values in (in)formal music communities.* Helsinki, Finland: Sibelius Academy.

Q (2012). Retrieved from http://news.qthemusic.com/2011/09/muse_killers_noel _liam_jay-z_t.html.

Randles, C., & Smith, G. D. (2012). A first comparison of pre-service music teachers' identities as creative musicians in the United States and England. *Research Studies in Music Education, 34*(2), 173–87.

Reynolds, S. (2011). *Retromania: Pop culture's addiction to its own past.* London, United Kingdom: Faber and Faber.

Rodriguez, C.X. (2004). The broader perspective. In C. X. Rodriguez (Ed.), *Bridging the gap: Popular music and music education.* Reston, VA: The National Association for Music Education.

Sennett, R. (2012). *Together: The rituals, pleasures and politics of cooperation.* New York, NY: Penguin Books.

Smith, G.D. (2013a). *I drum, therefore I am: Being and becoming a drummer.* Farnham, United Kingdom: Ashgate.

Smith, G.D. (2013b). Pedagogy for employability in a foundation degree (FdA) in creative musicianship: Introducing peer collaboration. In H. Gaunt & H. Westerlund (Eds.), *Collaboration in higher music education* (pp. 193–98). Farnham, United Kingdom: Ashgate.

Smith, G.D. (in press). Popular music in higher education. In G. Welch and I. Papageorgi (Eds.), *Investigating music performance.* Farnham, United Kingdom: Ashgate.

Smith, G.D., & Durrant, C. (2006). Mind styles and paradiddles—beyond the bell curve: Towards an understanding of learning preferences, and implications for teachers. *Research Studies in Music Education, 26,* 51–62.

Smith, G.D., & Shafighian, A. (2013). Creative space and the "silent power of traditions" in popular music performance education. In P. Burnard (Ed.), *Developing creativities in higher music education: International perspectives and practices* (pp. 256–67). London, United Kingdom: Routledge.

Welch, G. (2001). *The misunderstanding of music: An inaugural lecture.* London, United Kingdom: Institute of Education.

Westerlund, H. (2006). Garage rock band: A future model for developing musical expertise? *International Journal of Music Education, 24* (2), 119–25.

Williams, D.A. (2007). What are music educators doing and how well are we doing it? *Music Educators Journal, 94*(1), 18–23.

Williamson, J., Cloonan, M., & Frith, S. (2011). Having an impact? Academics, the music industries and the problem of knowledge. *International Journal of Cultural Policy, 17*(5), 459–74.

Wright, R. (2012). Art for art's sake, music for whose sake: Democracy, social stratification, social exclusion and music education. Paper presented at the Institute of Contemporary Music Performance Rock and Roles Conference, London, United Kingdom. (October, 2012)

13 "Pssst . . . Over Here!"

Young Children Shaping the Future of Music Education

Alison M. Reynolds, Kerry B. Renzoni, Pamela L. Turowski, and Heather D. Waters

---

PSSST . . . OVER HERE!

A narrative in one scene

Setting and Characters: Co-constructivist preschool in the not-so-distant past. Nate, a preschool child, is playing with a few of his friends. Teacher Catie and Teacher Amy, when called on, facilitate their morning's activities. Teacher Alison is an early childhood music specialist.

(Based on real stories and real music activities.)

Time: 9:40–10:00 AM on "music day."

My name is Nate. I'm four years old. My dad and I get out of our red car. We're at my favorite place—preschool! "Dad, can I ring the buzzer?" "Sure!" he says. He lifts me up because the buzzer is high up for grownups. I run up the stairs.

"Good morning!" Teacher Catie says. She bends down and gives me a hug. I like Teacher Catie. She looks at what I'm holding in my hand. "What have you brought to share today?"
"It's a recorder! My sister is learning how to play it in school!"

I'm going to go cook in the kitchen. I hear Teacher Catie call to me, "Oh, you should show your recorder to Miss Alison when she gets here." "Okay," I say.

I'm Alison. I've been a music teacher for many years. It's my day to travel to a local preschool for its weekly music class. As I walk to the front door I see Nate and his dad, headed into the preschool. I scurry to reach the front door before it closes, but I'm too late.

The door clicks shut.

I ring the doorbell.

After a brief silence, I am "buzzed in." I shift the gathering drum filled with bags of props to my hip, open the door, and climb the stairs. I linger in the stairway to read the information the teachers prepare for parents.

As I enter the hallway, I see Nate disappear, and exchange hellos with Nate's dad as he's leaving. Teacher Amy greets me, "Good morning! You're an early bird today!"

All my friends are in the kitchen! They run and give me a big hug! "Nate! We missed you!" says my friend Nadine. I didn't see her yesterday because that was a home day for me.

I'm so excited. Miss Alison is coming today! She likes to sing. I like to sing, too. I like to sing like this:

Oh, there's my friend Noura. She's cooking something on our stove. "Hey, Noura," I say. "Can I play with you?" "Okay!" says Noura. We cook next to each other in the kitchen. I sing while I cook some eggs.

Noura is making the toast. She's singing, too.

I giggle. "Noura, you're singing my song!"

"Teacher Catie!!! Teacher Catie!!! Noura's singing my song!" "Oh, that's nice," she says.

I keep making my eggs and then my teacher comes over to me.

As I enter the hallway, several children approach, curious to learn who's arrived. We exchange smiles, hugs, and my greeting song, which invites their singsong hellos. Teacher Amy continues, "The children have been checking if you would be here today—you know how much we all love music play time. You're welcome to set up if you'd like. We'll call the children together for music in about 20 minutes, okay?"

"Okay, thank you!"

Children already are asking to help carry bags of props to the space for music time. We make our way through the big room with the art studio, weaving through the empty spaces among children and their play. We place the props in the corner of the activity space. I thank the children, saying Teachers Catie and Amy will call them when it's music playtime. They skip away.

As I unpack for the morning's class, I realize I'm already humming a song from last week's class. Meanwhile, children bound in and out—some to share with me what they have been playing, others to see what I'm doing.

During the in-between moments of solitude, I open my notebook to review my observations of children's expressive music making in past music classes. What a list! Children have shared their singing, chanting, moving, improvising—even listening! The children's capacity is at once unexpected and not surprising.

I sing to Teacher Catie. "Thank you," *she says.* "Oh these are delicious!" *she says.*

That's weird. Why didn't she sing back to me?

Noura sings,

and I sing back to her,

Noura and I sit down next to Teacher Catie and hum while we eat. Teacher Catie isn't humming. How silly.

Teacher Catie gets up and leaves. I keep eating my eggs and remember the beautiful painting I made the last time I was at school. It was blue and yellow and red and had really cool swirls all over it! I remember Teacher Catie coming over and saying, "Oh! That's a beautiful picture, Nate! I love how you blend the green and the blue together. And your brush strokes give the swirls on your painting a beautiful texture." Then I tell her all about my picture, about the storm with the little dog that was lost in the green fog and how a dolphin saves the dog. She said my picture was so beautiful that I should share it at our afternoon meeting. And I did!! Teacher Amy was really excited. The other kids were getting really excited!

Humming again, I check the clock, eager for music time. 15 minutes. I review the repertoire of songs I've prepared for the morning's class, and realize the tune I'm humming now is one I heard the first time I ever participated in a preschool music class. When was that? 1988? I'm grinning. The novelty of being astounded by the music making and young children's expressive musicianship hasn't worn off. I remember thinking, "Where has the secret of very young children's expressive music been hiding?"

No secret now! I think of the past 25 years. Early childhood music education has enjoyed increased attention. I consider how my perspectives both of very young children and "music learning" have changed—more than once! The young children—babies, even—have been my teachers as frequently and meaningfully as my colleagues. I consider, too, how young children have changed my perspectives about what it means to be a "music teacher."

Has it really been 25 years? Plenty of time for change. Memories pass by in an instant, real time rushes nearly as quickly. I grin again. Recently, one of those "young children" approached me after an undergraduate music education class, exclaiming, "Hey! You were the music teacher in the early childhood music class my mom took me to when I was a little boy."

Oh no! My eggs are burning! I better pay attention. I stir the eggs and add some salt.

Why didn't Teacher Catie ask me to sing my song at meeting today? Maybe she didn't hear my song.

"Teacher Catie!! Listen to my song!"

"That's nice," *she says again.*

Hmm, I guess she doesn't like my song. Noura likes it, though.

I bet Miss Alison will like my song. She sings all the time. I say . . .

The buzzer rings again, and I'm startled out of the past. I glance at my watch: 13 more minutes. Because I'm prepared for music playtime when the children enter.

I leave the music space.

So I thought. Moments after stepping out into the hub of activity, I hear it . . .

"Pssst . . . over here! Listen to my song!"

Alison: *I listen to Nate's song, smiling as I enjoy seeing his sparkling eyes and expressive face and the way he moves as he sings.* "Wow, Nate, what a beautiful song!"

Nate: "I knew you'd like it!" *I say to Miss Alison.*
Alison: "Can you sing it to me again?"
Nate: *I hum*

Alison: "Wow, I really like when you sing . . .

Nate: [singing]

Alison: [singing]

Nate: [singing]

Alison: "Oh you changed the ending that time to

I like that ending. So your song sounds like this?" *I sing Nate's song.* "Is that right?"

Nate: *I smile a big smile. You know, the kind where you show all your teeth.* "Uh uh, Teacher Alison. That's my song!"

Alison and Nate: *We sing the song together.*
Noura: "Hey, that's Nate's song!"

Alison: "Yes, he's letting me share it with him. It's a shared tune."

Noura: "Yay! I know it too!"

Nate: *I remember my recorder, and find it on the kitchen counter. I run back over to Noura and Alison, showing them the recorder.* "I can play it on my recorder, you know."

Alison: *Nate plays his song on his recorder as Noura sings and I move. Other kids are running over to join in. Max grabs a drum and joins in on the fun. Andrea finds some maracas and adds another rhythmic layer. Pretty soon all of the children have joined in our band. Some are playing instruments, some are dancing, some are singing, and some are listening. Soon, teachers Catie and Amy also join in.*

Nate: "Okay, we need a rehearsal!! One, two, three, four!!" *My friends begin performing my song. They sound great. I tell them when it's time to stop.*

> Alison: *I wonder if this is like what the child in the Pillsbury Foundation School had experienced when he said,* "Everybody stand up and raise your hands to the sky. That means you're all members of this music; we're all members of that tune we were playing."[1]
>
> *I thought I was ready for music playtime! But, children's music making began long before I rang that doorbell.*

Stepping out of that setting, we ask you to stop and reflect.

When the noise of the past settles into relative stillness within the present, articulate your current view of young children, and how young children—particularly very young children—fit in your descriptions and definitions of *"the study and making of music by all."*[2]

   Next, we ask you to reflect on music moments that were also transformative moments in your lives as musicians, parents, teachers, researchers, or policy makers.

   Do any of the following relate to your reflections?

   Context. Culture. Identity. Expression. Listening. Play. Creativity. Improvisation. Composition. Social interactions. Empathy. Collaboration. Community. Informal music learning. Life-long music learning.

   Increasingly, we note music educators are seeking to place those ideas at the forefront of their ways of interacting with students. We note, too, that young children are ahead of that curve. Researchers, teachers, and parents continue to offer mounting evidence of young children's capacities for music making, particularly in social contexts (e.g., home, playgrounds, care or school settings). Long before they ring the doorbell in preschool, and long before they become adolescents and young adults, young children use music in socially interactive ways.[3] Indeed, when adults have actually stopped to ask *and listen* to the youngest children able to talk about their musicking, young children have shared the myriad of ways music resides in them (e.g., Campbell, 2010; Filsinger, 2011; Reynolds, Cancemi, et al., 2012; Reynolds, Filsinger, et al., 2012) In this chapter, we advocate on behalf of 40.5 million young children in the United States ages nine years and younger—approximately 13% of the nation's total population (U.S. Census Bureau, 2010). We advocate halting unproductive parallel play among early childhood music educators, music educators, early childhood caregivers, researchers, parents, and policy makers in favor of their integrated play. For this to happen, we urge each of you to assimilate all of the nation's youngest children into your professional mindset.

As the profession joins together, the youngest children will be folded into the National Association for Music Education's mission to *encourage the study and making of music by all.* However, the diverse contexts in which children reside and the diverse types of primary and secondary caregivers challenge our access to the youngest musickers. We acknowledge that, as a profession, our ability to extend intentions to the youngest musickers depends in part on ways our nation focuses its broader intentions on young children's health, education, and welfare. The enormity of that implication looms.

On February 12, 2013, the President asserted, ". . . expanding access to high quality early childhood education is among the smartest investments that we can make" ("Early Childhood Education," 2013, para. 1). He has proposed a plan for universal access to preschool for children from low and moderate income families, justifying the expense: "Every dollar we invest in high-quality early childhood education can save more than seven dollars later on—by boosting graduation rates, reducing teen pregnancy, even reducing violent crime" ("Remarks by the President," 2013, para. 40). In the broadest sense, investing *funding* in a young child's education holds promise as a fiscally sound choice. Placing dollar amounts on economic returns perhaps sparks action among policy makers, but it alone is insufficient, and negates a human view of the child. We advocate that investing of *ourselves* in our nation's youngest children's education holds promise as socially and culturally sound choices.

Together, those investments lay the groundwork to support our youngest children. Specifically, evidence continues to mount that adults play critical roles each time they interact socially with young children. From the start, adults' fluency with language during loving and playful interactions with infants provides a strong foundation that offers children advantages as they move into school settings (e.g., Hirsh-Pasek, Golinkoff, & Eyer, 2003). While researchers have documented that many adults comfortably use music with very young children, researchers also have documented that, sadly, many adults do not (Nardo, Custodero, et al., 2006). As a profession, we've lacked longitudinal research to chronicle long-term benefits of adults' loving interactions with infants that include play and music. Even so, what could be the harm in working to ensure every adult can interact with musical fluency with the nation's youngest children, and ensuring young children's equal access to those adults?

Modifying President Obama's statement, we suggest that expanding access to high quality early childhood music education is among the smartest investments that *music educators* can make. We ask a few questions of our profession:

What are we doing to ensure we are investing fiscally, and of ourselves socially and culturally, in young children's music education? What evidence do we have that the level of music-based interactions in the earliest years of life contributes significantly to children's relative study and making of music once in school? How might we ensure answers to those questions? Are we, as a profession, able to prioritize an effective national action plan for early childhood music education? The enormity of those possibilities is exciting Each of us is in a position to make a difference.

In the current political climate, there are many persons and agencies working on behalf of children younger than nine years of age. Globally, the *Association for Childhood Education International* and the *Alliance for Childhood* have joined efforts to intensify support of children between 2012 and 2022. In sum, they work to ensure each child has the brightest possible future. Boldly, the affiliates state:

> Indeed, all nations and communities should listen to the voices of their youngest citizens. Children can offer critical insights that support myriad societal developments. We must ask the question: What do the children say they need in order to lead successful and fulfilled lives?
>
> ("Children Investing in Childhood," 2013, para. 2)

> We can no longer afford to ignore the current state of childhood. The long-term effects of an unhealthy childhood will weaken societies that need creative and compassionate individuals with mature insights who are able to solve complex human problems. We have the collective strength to create a more robust and creative childhood for all children.
>
> ("The State of Childhood," 2013, para. 4)

The affiliates offer five statements that can frame broad perspectives for the music education profession's views of young children as music makers:

1. Promote and protect childhood as a unique and critical stage of human development
2. Explore childhood from interdisciplinary and cross-cultural perspectives
3. Identify issues that erode childhood
4. Advocate for children's rights as a vital element of childhood
5. Translate the "Ten Pillars of a Good Childhood" into policies and practices that benefit all children ("Goals of the Decade," 2013, para. 3)

"The Ten Pillars of a Good Childhood" ("Embracing the Human Future," 2013, para. 3), constructed by members of the Association for Childhood Education International and the Alliance for Childhood, resonate with us. The Pillars seem reasonable to consider as functioning at the heart of all education initiatives in the United States, and aligning well within our profession's early childhood music education initiatives:

1. Safe and secure places for living and learning, with access to health care, clothing, and nutritious food
2. Strong families and loving, consistent caregivers
3. Social interactions and friendships

4. Creative play and physical activity
5. Appreciation and stewardship of the natural environment
6. Creative expression through music, dance, drama, and the other arts
7. Education that develops the full capacities of the child—cognitive, physical, social, emotional, and ethical
8. Supportive, nurturing, child-friendly communities
9. Growing independence and decision making
10. Children and youth participating in community life.

> Every child in every nation deserves a childhood full of hope, joy, freedom, and promise for the future.
>
> ("Embracing the Human Future," 2013, para. 3)

Within the United States, federal and state initiatives, credentialing agencies for education certification, curricula in higher education, and organizations in education and music education from national to local levels make policy that eventually affect young children and their music capacities. Specifically within our profession, early childhood music educators have documented steadily increasing attention to early childhood music education research, practice, and policy. Officially, the National Association for Music Education (NAfME) wraps its arms around all young children, advocating for music interactions from birth. In *The School Music Program: A New Vision* (NAfME, 2013), the profession states:

> The years before children enter kindergarten are critical for their musical development. Young children need a rich musical environment in which to grow. The increasing number of day-care centers, nursery schools, and early-intervention programs for children with disabilities and children at risk suggests that information should be available about the musical needs of infants and young children and that standards for music should be established for these learning environments as well as for K–12 settings.

> The standards outlined in this section reflect the following beliefs concerning the musical learning of young children:
>
> 1. All children have musical potential
> 2. Children bring their own unique interests and abilities to the music-learning environment
> 3. Very young children are capable of developing critical thinking skills through musical ideas
> 4. Children come to early-childhood music experiences from diverse backgrounds
> 5. Children should experience exemplary musical sounds, activities, and materials

6. Children should not be encumbered with the need to meet performance goals
7. Children's play is their work
8. Children learn best in pleasant physical and social environments
9. Diverse learning environments are needed to serve the developmental needs of many individual children
10. Children need effective adult models ("The School Music Program: A New Vision," NAfME, 2013, para. 1–2)

NAfME's current standards offer guidelines for music with infants and toddlers, and standards for interacting with children from two to four years old. Music standards for children K–4 encompass the remaining ages that we advocate for in this chapter.

Early childhood music educators, no doubt, applaud the profession's advocacy efforts to date. Yet, the need for increased dialogue and integrated play among stakeholders within and beyond the profession and academies persists. Prioritizing the role the future of early childhood music education plays relative to the future of all of music education seems critical to our profession's next steps.

> We cannot underestimate children's musical capacity or their own musical repertoire, behaviors, and values. Children's musical selves are enculturated early on and continue to develop even as the children participate in our school music programs. While we must step with caution and be wary of over-generalizing about children and their musical development, we must also consider emergent arguments in favor of a species-specific musical competence. No child is without the capacity for musical expression, and every child may find safe harbor in his or her preferred tones and personal musical time. *The musical development of children may depend on the emphasis given by a society to musical activity and on the opportunities that we offer them to make music* [emphasis added].
>
> (Campbell, 1999, p. 13)

What if we decided as a profession to focus intentions on music interactions with our nation's youngest children, regardless of their care settings or access to early education? As our nation grapples with ways to bolster its economy, we could consider initiatives that would apply our profession's diverse expertise in settings with the youngest children. Following are eight recommendations for navigating the future of early childhood music education together. They echo and extend recommendations of those who have come before us.[4]

1. Honor children's music capacities while honoring their humanity.

   a. Increase use of mechanisms beyond text and numbers to communicate children's music development.

    b. Apply techniques learned from Reggio Emilia-inspired educators about becoming co-researchers with young children.

    c. Apply innovative ways to document evidence of young children and adults' creative music capacities.

    d. Continue to reconfigure journal structures and submission guidelines to accommodate innovative representations of co-constructed documentations.

2. Increase visibility of early childhood music education within NAfME.

    a. Integrate early childhood music education for children from at least birth to age eight systematically into the NAfME website.

    b. Increase ease of access to early childhood music advocacy and information on the NAfME website.

3. Continue to create spaces in higher education that generally honor *Context. Culture. Identity. Expression. Listening. Play. Creativity. Improvisation. Composition. Social interactions. Empathy. Collaboration. Community. Informal music learning. Life-long music learning.*

    a. Design innovative music education curriculum in higher education that, at their core, integrate adults' capabilities for playing musically with young children. Integrating preservice teachers' experiences with young children systematically could prepare them to empower children to drive curricular revisions the profession seeks in K–12 music programs.

    b. Introduce preservice music teachers and faculty to live or video-recorded interactions with children that feature children's creative music voices.

    c. Create meaningful and systematic opportunities for preservice and graduate music education students to interact musically with young children—regardless of the absence or presence of Pre-K on states' music certifications or students' initially selected specialization areas. As the *President's Preschool for All Initiative* ("Early Childhood Education," 2013, para. 4) takes hold,[5] universities should have increased systematic access to four-year-old children.

    d. Create interdisciplinary degrees that integrate specialties in music education, business, technology, and communication and focus on young children. Graduates could push innovative markets for jobs in private sectors.

    e. Include children Kindergarten to 3rd grade in early childhood initiatives. Though tempting to rely on a school's systematic commitments to elementary school music programs, we advocate ensuring that age group continues to have access to high quality music interactions.

4. Apply the profession's collective expertise to innovative professional development for early childhood and early childhood music specialists. Their increased capacities could empower their own music identities.
5. Form collaborative partnerships between music faculty and ensembles (of *all* types) and young children directly. Partnering with health care-givers, social workers, and community-based centers could help our profession reach expecting parents and families with young children regardless of families' economic status, gender, or age.
6. Focus on ways music faculty can help with outreach to all young children, particularly those in underserved communities. Partner with existing child care facilities, requesting space in community centers and senior citizen centers for family-oriented, musically interactive gatherings.

Our penultimate recommendation: all we learn and accomplish must be disseminated outward. We must lift our heads out of our scores, and preach beyond our choirs. As we increase our music interactions with young children, we must unify efforts to systematically collect, store, and communicate long-term documentation of ways musical interactions from the earliest ages benefit children and shape our profession. Parents, taxpayers, and policy makers need to hear from each of us.

We save our chief recommendation for last: pay attention to young children. Notice their expressive and creative singing, chanting, and movement. Listen for the melodies they sing as they play. See and hear their rhythmic movement as they skip down the hallway. Smile and let them know you're listening and watching. Sing, chant, move, improvise, and create with them. Share with them what you like about their music making. Share music you like so they can continue expanding their music vocabulary.

Give a child's music the same importance you do her painting, block building, crying, and hunger. And don't just pay attention to one child, pay attention to all the children making music around you—even the babies. Listen for the melody in babies' coos and gurgles. Notice the tempo in a child's coordinated breathing and movement. Consider all of those as topics of musical conversations, and as invitations to join in. Echo the melodies. Match the tempo and movements. Sing. Improvise! Prepare to be amazed by the effects of your joint music attention.

Now, imagine the ripple effect.

Other teachers and parents notice you interacting musically with children, and valuing their musical expression. They start doing the same things. Next, other teachers and parents change their music expectations. They become empowered to provide high quality music interactions for children. As children travel through Pre-K and beyond, imagine. They grow up to be autonomous music makers. They also grow up to be taxpayers, policy makers, parents, teachers. As grown ups, they, in turn, make music with children. They meaningfully express themselves through one of our birthrights: music.

The young children you interact with define the future. That is why, in the words of Nate, we say, "Pssst ... over here!" The future begins with you. The future begins each time you interact musically with the youngest child.

NOTES

1. Donald Pond quoted the child in Wilson, 1981, page 20.
2. The National Association for Music Education mission statement http://musiced.nafme.org/about/mission-statement/.
3. A few recent examples: Barrett, 2011; Berger & Cooper, 2003; Campbell, 2010; Custodero, 2009; Filsinger, 2011; Marsh, 2008; McCarthy, 2010; Moorhead & Pond, 1978; Reynolds, 2014; Reynolds, Cancemi, et al., 2012; Reynolds, Filsinger, et al., 2012; Valerio, 2009.
4. Examples: Nardo, Custodero, et al., 2006; Overland & Reynolds, 2010; Persellin, 2007; Runfola & Swanwick, 2002; Scott-Kassner, 1992.
5. February 13, 2013, President Obama introduced his initiative for universal preschool. The several-point plan includes initiatives to reach all children birth to four years old.

REFERENCES

Barrett, M. S. (Ed.) (2011). *A cultural psychology of music education*. Oxford, United Kingdom: Oxford University Press.

Berger, A. A., & Cooper, S. (2003). Musical play: A case study of preschool children and parents. *Journal of Research in Music Education, 51*(2), 151–65.

Campbell, P. S. (1999). The many-splendored worlds of our musical children. *Update: Applications of Research in Music Education, 18*(1), 7–14.

Campbell, P. S. (2010). *Songs in their heads: Music and its meaning in children's lives* (2nd Ed.). Oxford, United Kingdom: Oxford University Press.

Custodero, L. A. (2009). Musical portraits, musical pathways: Stories of meaning making in the lives of six families. In J. L. Kerchner & C. R. Abril (Eds.), *Musical experiences in our lives: Things we learn and meanings we make* (pp. 77–92). Lanham, MD: Rowman and Littlefield.

Decade for Childhood. (2013). Investing in Childhood. Retrieved from http://decadeforchildhood.org/home/investinginchildhood.html

Decade for Childhood. (2013). Embracing the Human Future. Retrieved from http://decadeforchildhood.org/home.html

Decade for Childhood. (2013). Goals of the Decade. Retrieved from http://decadeforchildhood.org/home/investinginchildhood.html

Decade for Childhood. (2013). The State of Childhood. Retrieved from http://decadeforchildhood.org/home/thestateofchildhood.html

Early Childhood Education. (2013). The White House President Barack Obama. Retrieved from www.whitehouse.gov/issues/education/early-childhood

Filsinger, K. B. (2011, December). *Side-by-side: Guiding young composers*. Research-based workshop co-presented with research participants at the NYSSMA Winter Conference, Rochester, NY.

Hirsh-Pasek, K., Golinkoff, R. M., & Eyer, D. (2003). *Einstein never used flashcards*. Emmaus, PA: Rodale.

Marsh, K. (2008). *The musical playground: Global tradition and change in children's songs and games*. New York, NY: Oxford University Press.

McCarthy, M. (2010). Researching children's musical culture: Historical and contemporary perspectives. *Music Education Research, 12*(1), 1–12.

Mission Statement of the National Association for Music Education. (2013). Retrieved from http://musiced.nafme.org/about/mission-statement/

Moorhead, G. E., & Pond, D. (1978). *Music of young children.* Santa Barbara, CA: Pillsbury Foundation for Advancement of Music Education.

NAfME. (2013). The School Music Program. Retrieved on November, 15, 2013, at: http://musiced.nafme.org/resources/the-school-music-program-a-new-vision/

Nardo, R. L., Custodero, L. A., Persellin, D. C., & Fox, D. B. (2006). Looking back, looking forward: A report on early childhood music education in accredited American preschools. *Journal of Research in Music Education, 54*(4), 278–92.

Overland, C., & Reynolds, A. M. (2010). The role of MENC: The National Association for Music Education in early childhood music education, 1980–2007. *Journal of Historical Research in Music Education, 32*(2), 99–117.

Persellin, D. C. (2007). Policies, practices, and promises: Challenges to early childhood music education in the United States. *Arts Education Policy Review, 109*(2), 54–61.

Remarks by the President in the State of the Union Address. (2013). The White House, President Barack Obama. Retrieved from www.whitehouse.gov/the-press-office/2013/02/12/remarks-president-state-union-address

Reynolds, A. M. (2014). Qualitative research in early childhood music education. In C. M. Conway (Ed.), *Handbook of qualitative research in music education.* Oxford, United Kingdom: Oxford University Press.

Reynolds, A. M., Cancemi, J., Weston, C., Folliott, B., & Children at the Early Learning Center, Yokohama International School. (2012). *The Oxford handbook of qualitative research in American music education* (pp. 339–361). New York: Oxford University Press.

Reynolds, A. M., Filsinger, K. R., Chayot, K., Goldenberg, K., & Children at Project P.L.A.Y. School. (2012, July). Co-constructing music-rich environments. In A. Niland & J. Rutkowski (Eds.), *Passing on the flame: Making the world a better place through music. International Society for Music Education, Early Childhood Music Education Commission seminar proceedings* (pp. 94–5). Nedlands, Western Australia: ISME.

Runfola, M., & Swanwick, K. (2002). Developmental characteristics of music learners. In R. Colwell & C. Richardson (Eds.), *The new handbook of research in music teaching and learning* (pp. 373–97). New York, NY: Oxford University Press.

Scott-Kassner, C. (1992). Research on music in early childhood. In R. Colwell (Ed.), *Handbook of research on music teaching and learning* (pp. 633–50). New York, NY: Schirmer Books.

U.S. Census Bureau. (2010). *United States census 2010.* Retrieved from www.census.gov/2010census/

Valerio, W. H. (2009). From the teacher's view: Observations of toddlers' musical development. In J. L. Kerchner & C. R. Abril (Eds.), *Musical experiences in our lives: Things we learn and meanings we make* (pp. 39–58). Lanham, MD: Rowman and Littlefield.

Wilson, B. (1981). Implications of the Pillsbury Foundation School of Santa Barbara in perspective. *Bulletin of the Council for Research in Music Education, 68,* 13–25.

14 Identity and Transformation
(Re)claiming an Inner Musician

Karen Salvador

One problem with the title "musician" is that people are afraid to use it. They fear that other people will disagree with this term. They compare themselves to other musicians that they feel are more talented. Just because you aren't the master of your craft does not mean you aren't considered part of that craft. I am a student. I may not go to Harvard, 4.0 every assignment, and study tirelessly, but I am a student nonetheless. . . .

I am a musician because I am the best shower singer you ever heard. I am a musician because I sing at the top of my lungs in the car. I am a musician because I love music so much I cannot study, sit in my room, car, or get ready without it. I am a musician because going to concerts is one of my favorite things to do. I am a musician because I know that music can often say what words cannot.

(Essay 22)

For two semesters during graduate school, I taught *Music for the Classroom Teacher*,[1] a 4-credit, 400-level course for elementary education majors. Most students in the course had participated in school music programs, at least in elementary general music. Many students had taken band or choir in middle school, and some continued in school music (instrumental and/or vocal) throughout high school. Several students participated in music outside of school, through private lessons, camps, or additional performance ensembles such as church choirs or garage bands. All of the students interacted with music socially (e.g., going to clubs or concerts, sharing music with friends) and individually (nearly omnipresent iPods). However, very few students would say they were "musical" or "a musician."

In class, we debated possible definitions of the word "musician" and briefly discussed musician identity development in early childhood through adolescence. We had this discussion for three reasons: (1) to advance my assertions from earlier in the course regarding the inherent musicality of young children, (2) to further position music integration in the elementary classroom as natural and likely to be beneficial for students, and (3) to help students think about the effect their own music identity (often a negative one) could have on their students. This discussion took place in week 12 of the 14-week semester. As the culmination of this discussion, each student wrote a description of his or her current music identity and its development over time. As I graded these essays, I found them poignant and powerful as a music teacher and music teacher educator. I wanted to analyze and share the insights they contained.

IDENTITY AND MUSIC

A significant body of research has accumulated regarding identity and music, and this research has been the source of vigorous debate in the music education community. Some main threads from this research indicate that musical identities are socially constructed: "The term 'musical' is not based upon the achievement of a set of prescribed technical abilities but rather on a social construction that involves self-assessment with regard to significant others" (MacDonald, Hargreaves, & Miell, 2003, p. 3). Music and identity are reflexive: Music can be a vehicle for exploration and development of other (non-music) identities such as feminism, queerness, ethnicity, and social class (Lamb, 2003), and musical identities are influenced by these and other identities such as gender, (dis)ability, and nationality (MacDonald, Hargreaves, & Miell, 2002). Because identity and music are so interwoven, the study of musician identity is "murky and muddy" (Lamb, 2003, p. 6). Musician identities have been conceptualized as personal (individual and idiosyncratic characteristics) and social (comparisons to others and group characteristics) (Lamont, 2002, p. 42). Musician identity is situated: "When I am on stage singing Tamino, I am not giving much time to worrying over *tas* and *titis* from my methods class" (Roberts, 2006, p. 3). Finally, these socially constructed, messy, reflexive, interwoven, personal, social, situated identities are fluid and evolving, so that any single person at one time may have several musician identities in different contexts, and over time, these identities can (and probably should) change.

In studying music identity through the lifespan, there is evidence that humans across cultures are musical from birth (e.g., Trehub, Unyk, & Trainor, 1993), and that engagement in a variety of musical behaviors is important to infants' cognitive, social, emotional, and physical development (for review see Trevarthan, 2002). It is difficult to ascertain if and how children younger than four or five conceptualize identity—as a musician or anything else (Marsh, Debus, & Barnholt, 2006). However, the idea that very young children need to sing, dance, and play instruments is so widely accepted that musical interactions are included in accreditation standards by the National Association for the Education of Young Children (NAEYC) (NAEYC, 2012, e.g., p. 4, p. 13). By school age and through adolescence, children become increasingly less likely to call themselves "musicians," girls are more likely than boys to claim the label "musician," and children and adolescents are most likely to define a "musician" as someone who plays an instrument (Lamont, 2002; Randles,

2010). Child and adolescent musician identities seem sensitive to parental and sibling influences (e.g., Borthwick & Davidson, 2002; McPherson, 2009) and peer influences (e.g., Lamont, 2002; O'Neill 2002). It is intriguing to note that the influence of elementary and/or secondary school music teachers on musician identity in children and adolescents has not been specifically addressed in research, although it is mentioned as an emergent theme in a few studies (e.g., Campbell, Connell, & Beegle, 2007).

With regard to participant/subject populations, the bulk of recent identity research in music education has focused on undergraduate music majors (performance and education), in-service music teachers, and professional musicians (see Scheib et al., 2007). Studies also investigate musician identity in high school students who play instruments (e.g., Borthwick & Davidson, 2002). In choosing populations, it seems that researchers investigating musician identity often define a musician as someone who plays an instrument, as studies of non-instrumentalists are comparably rare.

But what of the voices of those who have opted not to participate in school music, formally study an instrument, major in music, or have a career in music? Those who do not pursue school or private music instruction or some other music performance activity are often labeled as "non-musicians" by educators and researchers, and this population has been largely ignored in music education identity research. Some studies have surveyed entire school populations about how they define a musician (Lamont, 2002; Randles, 2010). In other studies, subject pools may have included "non-musicians," but a respondent's musician or non-musician status was not explicit in the data (e.g., Campbell, Connell, & Beegle, 2007). Abril (2007) worked with three undergraduate women who self-identified as non-singers. He found that the roots of their anxiety about singing traced back to negative experiences in school music programs. If others have had similar experiences, "non-musicians" may be an important population for music teacher educators to study. We all know people whose expressions of musical identity are primarily characterized by negative statements like "I am not musical" or "I can't sing" who nevertheless proclaim a love of music and/or engage in musicking behaviors such as attending concerts, dancing and/or singing when alone, and selecting specific music to complement or change their moods. Given the role of music in infancy and early childhood, and the importance of music in the lives of adolescents—including "non musicians" (North, Hargreaves, and O'Neill, 2000), understanding the development of this "negative identity" (Lamont, 2002; Lee, 2003), may help music educators as they strive to be more inclusive and serve a broader spectrum of students.

Purpose

The purpose of this qualitative study was to explore essays on music identity development written by undergraduate students who were not music majors or minors. Further, my intent was to analyze findings specifically with regard to their implications for school music instruction and music teacher education. My guiding questions were: How did the students describe their musical identity from childhood through their lifespan? What experiences did students describe as having positive or negative influences on their musician identity? *↓ great Research topic*

DESIGN

Participants and Data Collection

All the students I taught in *Music for the Classroom Teacher* over two semesters (N = 48) were invited to participate in this study. Via email after grades had been submitted, I asked each student to resubmit his or her musician identity essay along with a consent form, which included some basic demographic information (age, year in school, major, gender). Upon receipt, demographic information was separated from the essay content. Thirty-five students (73%) sent their essays, which comprised 47 pages of single-spaced text when empty space was removed. Participants included 4 males and 31 females, whose ages ranged from 19–28 years at the time of the study (average age 21.1 years). Nearly all participants were traditional undergraduate students at the sophomore- to senior-level of study.

Data Analysis

For this qualitative content study, I used deductive analysis related to my guiding questions as well as general inductive data analysis as described by Thomas (2003). This analysis involved cleaning the data (removing identifiers and empty space, unifying fonts, etc.), close reading of the text, creation of categories, and continually revising and refining these categories through multiple sets of coding, allowing overlapping coding and uncoded text. The trustworthiness of the data was established through triangulation within the project (among the 35 essays), comparison with other findings in the literature, and peer review (Creswell, 2012). In this deductive and inductive analysis, my assumptions and experiences inevitably informed both how I conducted the research and how I analyzed the data (Peshkin, 1994). Therefore, my thoughts with regard to musician identity and "non-musicians" become the lens through which the data is viewed, and it is important to the trustworthiness of this study that I describe my biases with regard to musician identity.

Researcher Lens

Although I am now an assistant professor who specializes in music teacher education, my views are informed by my previous identity as an elementary general music teacher, and by my continued practice as an early childhood music teacher. I acknowledge that my background as a classically trained musician means that I see music and musicianship differently than the general population who do not have that background. Therefore, as I read these essays, I was an "Other" or outsider. Moreover, I believe that every person has the potential to be musical: music is the birthright of every human. I believe that participatory musicianship is good for individuals of all ages, communities, and society, and that musicking[2] can take a variety of forms. My idea of a musician is not limited to people who engage regularly in music performance, and I do not think that the label "musician" is limited to those with "talent" or who have high levels of expertise. These beliefs were likely evident as I taught the classes, designed this study, analyzed the data, and wrote this paper.

FINDINGS

Most essays followed a common rhetorical structure based on the assignment: Reflect on your own musical identity. Has it changed since you were a child or since you have taken this class? How will your musical identity play a role in your own classroom?[3] This question resulted in a shared beginning point for the narrative arc of most essays: when I was a small child I felt like a musician, someone who loves music. After this beginning, however, students' descriptions of their musical lives and identity formation varied widely. One student, who grew up in China, was tracked into a school for the musically gifted at five years of age. Another student received so many negative messages regarding her[4] musical play at home that she gave up on singing before she entered kindergarten. A few students did not remember any involvement in music classes or activities at any point, while some had vague recollections of elementary music, but did not participate in school music or any other organized musical activity after that. Other participants sang and/or played instruments in school ensembles all the way through middle school and high school. A few students mentioned private study and/or musical groups outside of school, such as church choirs and garage bands. Many students reported a change in how they viewed their musical identity as a result of some component of *Music for the Classroom Teacher*. This presentation of findings will begin with a deductive analysis of data related to my guiding questions, presented in two sections: (1) Factors contributing to positive musician identity and (2) Factors contributing to a negative musician identity. Then, I will present the results of my inductive analysis, which resulted in three emergent themes: (1) Defining and redefining "musician," (2) Self-efficacy beliefs and (3) Transformation/reclaiming.

Factors Contributing to Positive Musician Identity

Many students described "feeling like a musician" at various times in life. Nearly all students recalled a childhood filled with singing and/or dancing along with parents, siblings, and/or recordings. Further, most students recalled feeling like musicians in elementary general music. "I always enjoyed music and would practice the recorder at home, where I would experiment with the different sounds and pretend I was a rock star" (Essay 24). "When I was younger I used to think I was the next Brittany Spears. I would sing my answers to a question instead of just talking, [and] I would sing as loud as I could in music class . . . " (Essay 11). However, only a few students maintained positive musician identity through adolescence and into young adulthood. Factors that contributed to a persistent positive musician identity were interrelated and included music at school, music outside of school, family influence, and talent attributions/competition.

Music at School

Several students related positive experiences with secondary school music ensembles and teachers, and cited these as reasons that they viewed themselves as musicians. These school music experiences were rarely mentioned separately from how they interrelated with music experiences outside of school.

> Using my formal knowledge from playing the trombone in band class for 3 or 4 years, I began to teach myself drums. Eventually, I started playing with bands and even began playing gigs in high school. My band played at local venues and in venues around the state and the country. . . . During this time I became on avid blues fan, eventually giving way to my love of jazz music. Also around this time, I had the opportunity to take a music history class . . . at my high school. This class opened my ears to music that I had never really given much time. I began listening to Chopin, Vivaldi, Beethoven and others. . . . Music has become a driving force in my life. I am an avid player, listener, and researcher of music.
>
> (Essay 19)

It seems that for some people, "traditional" secondary school ensembles and nonperformance classes can be a place in which strong musician identities are maintained and developed.

Music Outside of School

Music participation outside of school was another important factor in persistently positive musician identity. Settings for music outside of school included private lessons, church music, and garage bands. For many (but not all) students, these experiences were informed by experiences in school music and vice versa.

> The choir was about to sing at church and my ten-year-old self was the only soprano there. I was absolutely terrified but I knew that I knew the song. . . . The director got to the bridge and had each part sing the part alone. It gets to be my turn and I'm singing and crying at the same

time but it sounded really good. After that, singing and music became the thing that made everything else OK.

(Essay 2)

My mother was the choir director and later minister of music. . . . I started singing in a church choir before I can remember and I did not know that people thought it was a skill. I saw my mother dance around singing and praising God all the time so of course I did the same.

(Essay 6)

Family Influence

The influence of family members also sometimes supported a persistently positive musician identity. The author who described being ten and the only soprano in choir one day (Essay 2, see above) mentioned elsewhere in her essay that her grandfather was minister for music at the church, and her dad played drums for the choir. Many students mentioned parents who played instruments (especially guitar and piano), and siblings who preceded them in school music programs as supporting their musician identity.

I liked it [playing cornet] because I remember the support I got from my parents, not because I enjoyed playing it.

(Essay 24)

I sang everywhere from church to the shower, and I sang everything. My grandparents saw this and put me in voice lessons and piano lessons. . . . With this under my belt, I could read music with the best of them and excelled in high school choir. . . . I also received a scholarship to go to Blue Lake Fine Arts Camp. I was proud and very confident in my musical ability and the ability to teach other people music because I also led the children's choir and played the organ in church. Having all this musical background, my identity is: a musician. I enjoy music, and I also can perform adequately.

(Essay 12)

While the influence of family is clear, the author of Essay 12 seemed also to indicate that her musician identity was strengthened by competition.

Competition/Talent

For some students, it was competition (in school and/or out) or a perception that they had a special talent, which led them to see themselves as musical.

I think that in high school I was a Musician [sic[5]] as I was very serious about learning music and improving my instrument. By my sophomore year, I was a part of the chamber choir, and I competed in both Choral and Solo & Ensemble Festivals, singing with the choir and as a soloist, reaching the state level in both areas. I also auditioned for and performed with the MSVMA regional, state, and all-state Honors Choirs.

(Essay 3)

I have always been identified as a "talented" child in the field of music. . . . I remember I was confident and self-satisfied most of the time in music class. All the music teachers liked me and set me as a perfect example in front of the class. . . . Due to such experience, I feel very comfortable singing or performing in public. . . . [However,] while I am being praised and set up as an example other students might feel stressed and start to have the fear to sing out loud. I have noticed that not many people . . . liked the music class . . . since the teacher gives them a feeling, which they cannot sing and it cannot be improved. It is obvious that teachers have more focus on those who can sing and leave the rest aside.

(Essay 14)

Although this student's musical identity was strengthened by being seen as "talented," she also observed how her teachers' recognition of her "talent" set her apart and may have diminished the music identity of other students.

Factors Contributing to a Negative Musician Identity

Despite nearly all respondents describing a positive musician identity in young childhood, most students reported entering *Music for the Classroom Teacher* with feelings of trepidation because they no longer viewed themselves as musicians. A number of factors contributed to this negative identity, including music at school, competing identities, talent attributions/competition, and influence of family.

Music at School

Some participants indicated secondary school music instruction as a main reason they stopped seeing themselves as musicians. Sometimes, it seemed that the band/choir director either would not or could not teach them how to succeed in school music:

Joining choir was a lot of fun for me. I got to sing every day and I even mustered the courage to try out for a solo. However . . . my choir teacher said that I did not have a voice that was "special" enough. This comment made me reconsider singing out loud in front of people and for the next few years I only sang to myself.

(Essay 13)

I was pushed around to many different instruments [because] I was not performing the way they wanted me to. So I decided I was done with band. . . . I was so devastated by my experience that I decided I wanted to stay away from anything that would identify me as a musician.

(Essay 27)

In other essays, it seemed that some teachers were willing to sacrifice the needs of one student for the needs of the group:

I was in the boys' section of the choir for a while and I liked to tell myself that I didn't mind, but sometimes looking back I think I did. . . . I wish that someone, such as my choir teacher, would have told me why she put me in the boy's section of the choir. I look back now and I know it is because my voice could reach lower pitches and I showed a confidence that a lot of other girls didn't necessarily show at that age. By the time eighth grade was over, that confidence in choir was pretty much gone.

(Essay 7)

I wanted to play it [percussion] when I got older. When it came my time to join the band I was *given* a cornet by the band instructor [italics in original].

(Essay 24)

Competing Identities

Some students linked a weak or negative musician identity to a stronger identity in some other pursuit. "I grew up as an athlete and never wanted anything to do with music" (Essay 8). However, other students—who enjoyed music, felt musical as young children, and may have maintained a positive identity if they continued to play and/or sing—quit because of time constraints. "[At age ten] I started to play the flute. I played for three years and I really loved it. However, in high school I had to choose between music class and visual arts" (Essay 30). Overall, there seemed to be an impression among the students that they should focus on one role: "I was more of an athlete than a musician" (Essay 15).

Talent Attribution/Competition

Just as being identified as "talented" and doing well in comparison to others helped some participants to develop and maintain a positive musician identity, competition and the perception of lacking "talent" contributed to negative musician identity in other students. Sometimes, music teachers contributed directly to these feelings:

[M]y director used the chair system and had quizzes where we played in front of the entire class. . . . I cried a lot in band on those days because I knew how bad I would be.

(Essay 2)

Other times, the student's sense of needing to be the best, or to be perfect, came from within:

> This frustration caused me to give up my piano and my singing voice, and I would claim to others that I was a terrible singer and not so good at piano. I think the reasons why I made these bold statements [were] because most of my musical identity was developed around a competitive edge. In regards to piano, I was always preparing for the upcoming competition, and for choir I was always fighting for solos. . . . [I stopped practicing] and once I lost some of the skills that made me a *good* singer or *good* piano player I no longer considered myself a musician [italics in original].
>
> (Essay 33)

> [B]efore elementary school I used to sing a lot because my mom was always singing. When I entered formal schooling [elementary], singing became something serious, something that I needed to be perfect at or not try at all. . . . When I was in band, I used to practice my trombone for hours before auditions. When I got first chair my sophomore year, I attributed it to my section mates having a bad day, not to my own performance. I quit band after my sophomore year because the pressure of being first chair was too much. I was so worried about maintaining a level of performance I felt like I was incapable of achieving in the first place that I made myself physically ill.
>
> (Essay 23)

Influence of Family

Similar to competition and talent attributions functioning as factors that both supported musician identity and also contributed to a negative musician identity, family influences could be positive or negative. One student recalled being "heckled" by siblings as she tried to practice saxophone at home and explained further, "I was in the school choir for three years, and loved to sing quite a bit, but was always encouraged to quit and stop singing by my three older sisters who thought that my singing voice was pretty bad" (Essay 34). Another participant mentioned that part of the reason she did not view herself as a musician was that her older brother was always so much more accomplished (Essay 23). Parental influences also sometimes factored into negative identity: "My parents were never heavily involved in music, but they had a lot of involvement in sports. . . . My childhood did not have much music in it at all" (Essay 18).

Defining and Redefining "Musician"

One student began her essay by quoting *Webster's Dictionary:* "Musician: One who composes, conducts, or performs music, especially instrumental music" (Essay 22). Many students stated that before *Music for the*

Classroom Teacher, they would have defined "musician" as an expert performer (particularly on an instrument). As I revealed in my "Researcher Lens," I do not agree with that definition, and I know that throughout class and especially when I lectured on identity, I shared my beliefs with students. Perhaps because of this, many of the participants formulated new definitions of the word "musician" in their musician identity essays. These new definitions took into account that not every musician will achieve at the highest level, and rejected previous definitions based on competition:

> I see myself as a musician both vocally and instrumentally with the knowledge that there are people better than me and there is always room for improvement. When I was younger I didn't view my musicianship that way. I felt that since I wasn't first chair and I am naturally competitive, or since I always got passed over for leads in the musicals that I wasn't one [a musician].
>
> (Essay 2)

In redefining "musician," students were able to broaden their idea of what it meant to be musical, and thus claim the (often coveted) identity "musician."

Self-Efficacy Beliefs

Although the essays were ostensibly focused on musician identity, many essays revolved around the related concept of self-efficacy beliefs. Self-efficacy is a person's judgments of her ability to achieve a particular task—not simply an assessment of skill level, but rather an individual's judgments of what she can do with the skills she possesses (Bandura, 1986).

> . . . this class made me realize knowing notes [music literacy] is not the only thing that makes a musician. It has inspired me to try to learn [guitar] again. . . . If I practice hard, and really try, I know I can learn, I may be no Led Zeppelin (who has time for that????) but that doesn't mean I can't be a musician in my own right.
>
> (Essay 22)

> I have never thought of myself as much of a singer. After a terrifying experience with a solo during a play in fifth grade, you will only find me belting out lyrics in the car or in the shower where no one else can hear me. . . . But after you told me that I have a sweet singing voice, I regained some confidence. I may not be gracing American Idol with my presence anytime soon, but this class has given me the reassurance that when I sing "Fifty Nifty" to a group of seventh graders, they won't go running to the door with their hands over their ears.
>
> (Essay 29)

As was evident in these excerpts, students' statements of self-efficacy beliefs were informed by their redefinitions of musician identity and their experiences in class.

Transformation/(Re)Claiming

Many of these students had loved music and musicking throughout their lives, but had denied themselves an identity of "musician" because their definitions of the term were limited. When they redefined the word, it seemed to allow some of them to (re)claim an identity they had yearned for: that of "musician." Taking up this mantle seems to have been transformative for some students.

> Instead of looking at music as a solo and another trophy, I wish I [were] taught more of a community aspect of music identity. This concept broadens the idea of "musician.". . . Now I look at my music identity completely different[ly]. I feel as if I am still a musician and although my skills are rusty and I might not be as consistent as I once was, this does not mean that I am no longer a musician. I still sing in the car to the radio. I still sit down at the piano and play what I can remember. Before when I did these things, I would be critical of myself and stop [musicking], but now I second guess this initial reaction and continue. This is what I would like to teach my students: music is not a competition, like I had learned. Music is something that everyone can participate in, no matter what level . . . if students are interacting exploring, experiencing, and manipulating music then they are musicians.
>
> (Essay 33)

Some of the students seemed to relate their new identity directly to teaching, creating an "identity for" integrating music in their future classroom, or in essence stating they could be "musician enough" for their students.

> My musical confidence has not necessarily changed as a result of this course. I believe now that everyone possesses a musical identity—whether it is positive or negative. I have learned that just because I am not Beyoncé, I can still enjoy music as well as teach it in the future. . . . I can have fun with music, be confident in it, and use it within my classroom curriculum. My musical identity has now changed from just goofing around to something that can be more impactful and productive with my future students and future children.
>
> (Essay 7)

> I have now gone from wanting no musical identity to a future teacher who is excited to use music in my classroom daily. . . . I am no longer afraid to sing and share what I know and love about music with my

students. I know that there is so much more I can learn and that is why I am excited to be the "musical ladder⁶" that my students will be able to climb up with me.

(Essay 27)

Several students attributed (re)claiming a musician identity directly to participation in *Music for the Classroom Teacher.*

Although I do have some history singing, and playing instruments, I haven't stuck with these things and have trouble labeling myself as a "musician" in that sense. . . . [Later,] even though I knew I loved music, all I saw was that I was not "good" at singing and wasn't instrumentally committed, so therefore was not a good musician. I now realize that I am competent, and can definitely lead a group of lower elementary students in song.

(Essay 30)

[M]y musical identity has changed from my elementary years. I began with enthusiasm about music and slowly lost that as I went into high school. Luckily for me, this course has brought me back to the realm of music and I am eager to learn more so that I can successfully apply music in my classroom.

(Essay 1)

(Re)claiming an identity as a musician seemed to stem from intertwining threads of redefining what it means to be a musician, being more specific about the musicianship role being proposed (using music in a classroom setting with elementary children), and increased self-efficacy beliefs. For many respondents, participation in *Music for the Classroom Teacher* functioned as a catalyst for these transformative experiences.

Further Context for Findings

When interpreting these findings for appropriation to similar settings or application to other practices, further context might be helpful to the reader. I taught *Music for the Classroom Teacher,* and the essays used as data in this study were graded assignments. Although participants were not asked to submit essays for this study until final grades for the semester had been calculated, there is a chance the students wrote what they thought I wanted to hear. Furthermore, *Music for the Classroom Teacher* was elective, and students who chose this course may have done so because music was important in their lives and/or they thought it was likely to be important in the lives of their students. Moreover, most participants described childhoods that seemed relatively privileged in terms of access to music instruction. Participants were almost exclusively white middle-class suburban females, who (as a group) have been better served in school music programs than those from other socioeconomic, racial, or ethnic groups (Gustafson, 2009). Finally, the narrative arc and richness of some of the essays suggested further investigation (35 case studies) or, conversely, simply publishing each complete essay for music teachers and music teacher educators to read.

DISCUSSION

Thirty-five undergraduate students submitted essays regarding the development of their musician identity for this qualitative content analysis. Deductive findings related to my guiding questions confirmed previous findings in the literature. Similar to findings in Lamont (2002) and Randles (2010), most participants described identifying as a musician when they were very young and then gradually losing this identity with the onset of formal schooling, and through adolescence, until it gave way to sentiments like, "In no way, shape or form would I consider myself a musician" (Essay 16). However, the qualitative nature of this data showed some nuance not apparent in these earlier studies: many of the students with negative musician identities participated in music performance classes at school (i.e., they played an instrument and/or sang). For the students who maintained a positive musician identity through adolescence, important factors seem to have been involvement in school music programs, involvement in music performance outside of school (as in O'Neil, 2002), family influences (similar to Borthwick & Davidson, 2002), and competition/talent attribution (e.g., being the best, getting solos, having others recognize their "talent"). Factors that seem to have led to negative musician identity included school music programs (as in Abril, 2007), competing identities, and competition/talent attributions (for students who did not win and/or were not labeled as "talented").

Emergent themes that resulted from inductive analysis were not as easy to confirm or disconfirm in previous literature. Therefore, the remainder of this discussion will focus on interpretation of results in terms of what music educators and music teacher educators might do to help students maintain or (re)claim a positive musician identity.

(Re)Defining of "Musician"

everyone's definition is different/unique

Many respondents stated that they had not considered what defined a musician until they were asked. Perhaps music teachers could ask this question, and propose inclusive and flexible definitions of "musician" to help students see the myriad of ways that someone might musick. The redefinitions of "musician" that contributed to some students (re)claiming a musician identity reflected my core beliefs, which must have been consistently apparent in *Music for the Classroom Teacher*. I positioned singing as a valid form of musicianship alongside playing instruments. I stated that musicianship can exist at a variety of levels of proficiency. I explicitly valued other musics alongside "classical" music and other forms of musicking along with performing. With regard to children's musical development, I taught that no one is completely lacking in music aptitude. Finally, I reinforced that many components of musicking that students seemed to think required "talent" (playing, singing, moving, having a "good ear") are skills that can be learned with effort and practice.

Although none of this is likely to be viewed as revolutionary to music education researchers, some student "non musicians" responded to these messages with apparent surprise and pleasure. Essentially, students seemed loath to own their musician identity because they were not "good enough" or "talented enough" in comparison to others. This negative musician identity was constraining some students from pursuing music activities they wanted to engage in, such as learning to play guitar. It was as though they needed permission to be "musician enough" to use music to teach, to learn instruments, to dance and to sing. Roberts (2006) found that music majors worked to create the proficiencies they needed to support their identity. However, these students were already accepted as music majors, and had the support of the academy in claiming a musician identity. Perhaps one way to extrapolate Roberts's findings could be that once "non musicians" realize that they may (re)claim an identity as a musician, they will feel freer to behave in the ways a musician does. An unintended consequence of this identity reflection essay assignment may have been that, in asking students to consider their current beliefs, giving information, and allowing for redefinition, I essentially engaged students in "reframing," a technique therapists use to change thoughts and behavior (Beck, 1997). Furthermore, the act of constructing a narrative of musician identity may have been a powerful act, as writing is thought to provide a space for the formation and reformation of thought (Menary, 2007).

Increasing Musician Self-Efficacy

An increase in self-efficacy beliefs was an unexpected finding in this study. My goal as an instructor was to build my students' musicianship skills so that they could engage in authentic and enriching integration of music in classroom instruction. Although I did not intentionally work to increase self-efficacy beliefs, the way that I taught mirrored some of the practices that Vanatta-Hall (2010) found to increase music teacher self-efficacy in early childhood educators. In every class, students served as my demonstration group: moving, playing classroom instruments, and singing (first as a whole group, and then in smaller groups and individually). Eventually, each student taught a set of movement activities to the class, and later in the semester, taught a song and a chant to a small group. Within the construct of building self-efficacy (Bandura, 1986) this participatory musicking could be considered a form of enactive mastery experience.

Observing and participating in my demonstrations, and then observing and participating as peers succeeded in music teaching tasks may also have strengthened self-efficacy as a form of vicarious experience, which is the establishment of self-efficacy beliefs based on the success of similar others (Vanatta-Hall, 2010). I also gave specific feedback that was supportive and honest. This "verbal persuasion" is another way to build self-efficacy beliefs, and consists of a combination of persuasive communication and evaluative feedback. This persuasion is most effective when the person delivering it is considered knowledgeable and credible (Vanatta-Hall, 2010). According to Bandura's (1986) theory, by providing enactive mastery experience, vicarious experience, and verbal persuasion, I may have helped some students increase their self-efficacy so they felt "musician-enough" to teach songs, chants, and movement activities to their elementary students. Other researchers have reported similar findings (e.g., Heyning, 2011; Vanatta-Hall, 2010).

CONCLUSION

Although a few of the 35 participants in this study could be described as having a persistently positive musician identity, most identified themselves as "non musicians" by the time they took *Music for the Classroom Teacher* in college. Nearly all the students recalled loving music and feeling musical as a small child, and most of them participated in school music performance ensembles for at least some of their adolescence. This participation had a positive influence on the musician identity of a few students. However, for many students, participation in school music convinced them they were not musicians, even though they recalled wanting this identity. These students were the ones who did not get solos, were always in last or second-to-last chair, were told their voices were not "special," were asked to mouth the words, and so on. Thus, school music became an exclusive space, in which a student was identified and/or identified herself by a non-quality or a negative: in terms of what she was not. "[I]t is that emphasis on serious music and trained musicianship . . . that privileges the musical activities of a small (and shrinking) elite, frustrating the very search for community that underlies the human drive to make music" (Gracyk, 2003, p. 5). Thus, explicit and implicit messages from home combined with school music instruction to position music class as an environment in which a child or adolescent's identity was characterized by a negative: I am not a musician. Is it any wonder that, when given the option to opt out of school music, many students (at least 79%; Elpus & Abril, 2011) choose to do so? By reconsidering definitions of "musician," considering the role of self-efficacy, and being willing to engage students at a variety of levels of proficiency (without competition or exclusion), perhaps music teachers and music teacher educators can better support positive musician identity in elementary and secondary school music.

NOTES

1. To preserve confidentiality, this is not the actual course title.
2. Intentionally using Small's (1998) catholic notion of "musicking."
3. Taken from the *Music for the Classroom Teacher* syllabus.
4. Because participants were nearly all female, I will say "she" and "her" unless the author identifies himself as male.
5. In class, we discussed the possibility that there could be Musicians and musicians.
6. The "ladder" was one of a set of metaphors for instruction we discussed earlier in the semester. These metaphors included: teacher as a work of art to be observed; teacher as a vessel of water to be poured out to students; and teacher as a ladder that students could climb.

REFERENCES

Abril, C. (2007). I have a voice but I just can't sing: A narrative investigation of singing and social anxiety. *Music Education Research, 9*(1), 1–15. doi:10.1080/14613800601127494

Bandura, A. (1986). The explanatory and predictive scope of self-efficacy theory. *Journal of Social and Clinical Psychology, 4*, 359–73.

Beck, A. (1997). The past and the future of cognitive therapy. *Journal of Psychotherapy Practice and Research, 6*, 276–84.

Borthwick, S. J., & Davidson, J. W. (2002). Developing a child's identity as a musician: A family script perspective. In R. A. MacDonald, D. J. Hargreaves, & D. Miell (Eds.), *Musical identities* (pp. 60–78). New York, NY: Oxford University Press.

Campbell, P. S., Connell, C., & Beegle, A. (2007). Adolescents' expressed meanings of music in and out of school. *Journal of Research in Music Education, 55*, 220–36. doi: 10.1177/002242940705500304

Creswell, J. W. (2012). *Qualitative inquiry and research design: Choosing among five approaches* 3rd Ed.). Los Angeles, CA: Sage Publications.

Elpus, K., & Abril, C. R. (2011). High school music ensemble students in the United States: A demographic profile. *Journal of Research in Music Education, 59*(2), 128–45. doi: 10.1177/0022429411405207

Gracyk, T. (2003). Does everyone have a musical identity? Reflections on *Musical Identities. Action, Criticism, and Theory for Music Education, 3*(1). Retrieved from http://act.maydaygroup.org/php/archives_v3.php#3_1

Gustafson, R. I. (2009). *Race and curriculum: Music in childhood education.* New York, NY: Palgrave Macmillan.

Heyning, L. (2011). "I can't sing!" The concept of teacher confidence in singing and the use within their classroom. *International Journal of Education & the Arts, 12*(13). Retrieved February 2, 2013, from www.ijea.org/v12n13/

Lamb, R. (2003). Talkin' musical identities blues. *Action, Criticism, and Theory for Music Education, 3*(1). Retrieved from http://mas.siue.edu/ACT/v3/Lamb04.pdf

Lamont, A. (2002). Musical identities and the school environment. In R. A. MacDonald, D. J. Hargreaves, & D. Miell (Eds.), *Musical identities* (pp. 41–59). New York, NY: Oxford University Press.

Lee, K. (2003). Nothing new: Lots of gel? *Action, Criticism, and Theory for Music Education, 3*(1). Retrieved from http://act.maydaygroup.org/articles//Lee3_1.pdf

MacDonald, R. A., Hargreaves, D. J., & Miell, D. (2003). Editors' response: The sound of ideologies clashing. *Action, Criticism, and Theory for Music Education, 3*(1). Retrieved from http://act.maydaygroup.org/articles/EditorResponse3_1.pdf

MacDonald, R. A., Hargreaves, D. J., & Miell, D. (Eds.) (2002). *Musical identities.* New York, NY: Oxford University Press.

Marsh, H., Debus, R., & Barnholt, L. (2006). Validating young children's self-concept responses. In D. Teti (Ed.), *Handbook of research methods in developmental science* (pp. 138–60). New York, NY: Wiley Blackwell.

McPherson, G. E. (2009). The role of parents in children's musical development. *Psychology of Music 37*(1), 91–110. doi: 10.1177/0305735607086049

Menary, R. (2007). Writing as thinking. *Language Sciences 29*(1), 621–32.

National Association for the Education of Young Children (NAEYC). (2012). *NAEYC Accreditation: All Criteria Document.* Downloaded January 26, 2013, from www.naeyc.org/files/academy/file/AllCriteriaDocument.pdf

North, A. C., Hargreaves, D. J., & O'Neill, S. A. (2000). The importance of music to adolescents. *British Journal of Educational Psychology, 70*(2), 255–72.

O'Neill, S. A. (2002). The self-identity of young musicians. In R. A. MacDonald, D. J. Hargreaves, & D. Miell (Eds.), *Musical identities.* New York, NY: Oxford University Press.

Peshkin, A. (1994). The presence of self: Subjectivity in the conduct of qualitative research. *Bulletin of the Council for Research in Music Education, 122,* 45–56.

Randles, C. (2010). What is a "good musician"? An analysis of student beliefs. *Arts Education Policy Review 112*(1), 1–8. doi: 10.1080/10632913.2010.490774

Roberts, B. (2006) Music making, making selves, making it might: A counterpoint to Rhoda Bernard. *Action, Criticism, and Theory for Music Education, 6*(2). Retrieved January 13, 2013, from http://act.maydaygroup.org/articles/Roberts6_2.pdf

Scheib, J. W., Albert, K., Haston, W., Hellman, D., Hourigan, R., Miksza, P., Moore, M. W. (2007). Roles, identity, socialization, and conflict: The transition from music student to music teacher (a literature review). *Society for Music Teacher Education.* Retrieved January 26, 2013, from http://smte.us/wp-content/uploads/2007/02/rolesidentitysocializationconflict.pdf

Small, C. (1998). *Musicking: The meanings of performing and listening.* Middletown, CT: Wesleyan University Press.

Thomas, D. R. (2003). A general inductive approach for qualitative data analysis. Retrieved January 26, 2013, from www.fmhs.auckland.ac.nz/soph/centres/hrmas/_docs/Inductive2003.pdf

Trehub, S. E., Unyk, A. M., & Trainor, L. J. (1993). Adults identify infant-directed music across cultures. *Infant Behavior and Development, 16,* 285–95.

Trevarthan, C. (2002). Origins of musical identity: Evidence from infancy for musical social awareness. In R. A. MacDonald, D. J. Hargreaves, & D. Miell (Eds.), *Musical identities.* New York, NY: Oxford University Press.

Vanatta-Hall, J. E. (2010). *Music education in early childhood teacher education: The impact of a music methods course on pre-service teachers' perceived confidence and competence to teach music.* (Unpublished doctoral dissertation). University of Illinois, Urbana-Champaign.

Part IV
Guiding Researchers

15 Methodological Trends in Music Education Research

Michael S. Zelenak

Published research articles provide information on several levels. On one level, they contribute to the knowledge base of a particular field. On another level, they identify topics of interest. And on a third level, they provide evidence of the investigative processes, or methodologies, used by researchers. An empirical evaluation of these methodologies has the potential to provide reflective information to researchers free of the contextual influences of the research itself. Such an evaluation would allow researchers to reflect upon the evolution of methodologies from past to present, to determine the appropriateness of methodologies currently in use, and to determine the methodological needs of the future. Gall, Gall, and Borg (2007) posed a question in the preface to the eighth edition of their research methods textbook: "Does research methodology change rapidly enough to warrant so many revisions?" (p. xxvii). They answered affirmatively and cited several influences on research methodologies in the early 21st century such as the increased availability of electronic resources, advances in quantitative analytical techniques, and the refinement of qualitative perspectives. Since research in music education utilizes the same methodologies as education, it is subject to the same influences. Therefore, an analysis of research methodologies in music education would produce understandings regarding the impact of these influences, elicit evidence of methodological trends, and provide insights for guiding research in the future.

Music educators have a history of conducting research. Mark (1992) provided a timeline for tracking the chronological changes of research in music education. He summarized that music educators in the 19th century wrote academic papers describing their successful teaching practices and shared those ideas with colleagues. In the early 20th century however, music educators adopted a more deliberate approach and began identifying specific problems and issues in the field. They recognized the advantages of working collaboratively and formed committees to address the issues of the day. In the 1910s and 1920s, educational trends pointed toward greater efficiency and standardization in the classroom. To achieve these goals, music educators developed objective measurement instruments and embraced scientific statistical techniques to measure and analyze the physiological and psychological processes related to music performance. Examples of instruments from this period include the Seashore Measure of Musical Talents, which was designed to measure music aptitude, and the Kwalwasser-Ruch Test of Musical Accomplishment, which was designed to measure music achievement. The development of these types of instruments provides evidence of a shift from the personal experienced-based research of the late 19th century to the acceptance of the positivist paradigm in music education research.

Research activities escalated in the second half of the 20th century and focused on a wider range of topics using increasingly diverse investigative approaches. In the 1950s, Jones (1957) documented the use of questionnaires, correlation studies, and action research. In the 1960s, Choate (1965) identified a sufficient quantity of research articles to warrant the organization of research related to music education into specific categories. His categories included historical; philosophical inquiry and speculation; curriculum content; processes and aids for improvement of instruction; and other studies. Other researchers looked toward qualitative forms of research as plausible alternatives to the quantitative approach. Heller (1985) promoted the advantages of historical research and Krueger (1987) advocated for the use of ethnographic research in music education. More recently, Flinders and Richardson (2002) documented an upsurge in qualitative investigations and posed arguments for redefining the usefulness of research methods and findings.

Researchers have acknowledged trends in music education research from macro and micro perspectives. Bartel and Radocy (2002) identified the use of technology and increasing complexity as two mega-trends. They recommended using multiple data sources or a varied method approach to address the complexity in contemporary research and strengthen the rigor in these investigations. Jere Humphreys (2006) supported this view, stating, "We need to try harder to apply combinations of research methodologies" (p. 190). Abeles and Conway (2010) suggested that assimilating findings from multiple perspectives builds confidence in those findings. From a micro perspective, researchers have investigated specific elements of the research process and the ways in which it is disseminated. They have examined study participants (Draves, Cruse, Mills, & Sweet, 2008; Ebie, 2002), citations (Kratus, 1993; Randles, Hagen, Gottlieb, & Salvador, 2010; Hamann & Lucas, 1998; Sample, 1992; Schmidt & Zdzinski, 1993), and journal histories (Yarbrough, 1984, 2002). Although these researchers have uncovered valuable information, there has not been a recent (i.e., conducted in the past 20 years), broad (i.e., drawn from multiple journals), and comprehensive (i.e., included multiple perspectives) examination of the methodological trends in music education research.

The purpose of this study, therefore, was to identify trends in the methodologies used by music education researchers and to determine differences in methodologies found in articles published by eminent journals. Research questions were:

1. What changes have taken place in the methodologies used by music education researchers?
2. What methodological differences have appeared in articles published by eminent music education journals?

METHOD

In this study, I conducted a content analysis of eminent peer-reviewed journals. Hamann and Lucas (1998) tallied citations across a broad spectrum of music education journals and identified three journals that accounted for 80% of the citations. They proposed that these eminent journals be considered "first-tier" journals in music education research. The journals were the *Journal of Research in Music Education* (*JRME*), the *Bulletin of the Council for Research in Music Education* (*Bulletin*) and *Psychology of Music* (*POM*). I examined articles in these journals in two-year increments every ten years over a 21-year period (i.e., 1988–89, 1998–99, and 2008–09). This approach incorporated articles that were recent, provided practical and realistic limitations for the breadth of the study, and included a substantially large number of articles from each time period. In addition, this 21-year period coincided with changes in the analysis and distribution of information brought on by the increasingly widespread use of personal computers and the Internet. During this period, Internet World Stats (2013) reported a 566% increase in worldwide Internet usage between the years of 2000 and 2012.

Definitions from Gall, Gall, and Borg's (2007) textbook *Educational Research: An Introduction* were used as the theoretical framework for the study. This textbook had been in print since 1963 and was in its 8th edition. Gall, Gall, and Borg (2007) defined educational research as

> a form of inquiry in which (1) key concepts and procedures are carefully defined in such a way that the inquiry can be replicated and possibly refuted, (2) controls are in place to minimize error and bias, (3) the generalizability limits of the study's results are made explicit, and (4) the results of the study are interpreted in terms of what they contribute to the cumulative body of knowledge about the object of inquiry.
>
> (p. 35)

I included only those articles that met these criteria. Articles such as essays, position papers, letters, rebuttals, speeches, symposium abstracts, book reviews, and dissertation critiques, were excluded.

Methodological Elements

Gall, Gall, and Borg described the investigative process used by educational researchers and provided definitions of each aspect of that process. From their description and definitions, I extracted five primary methodological elements: (a) form of inquiry, (b) design, (c) sampling technique, (d) data collection, and (e) data analysis (Figure 15.1). The specific type or variation of each element was then considered a subcategory. As I read each article, I tallied the subcategories and these tallies became the data used for comparison and statistical analysis.

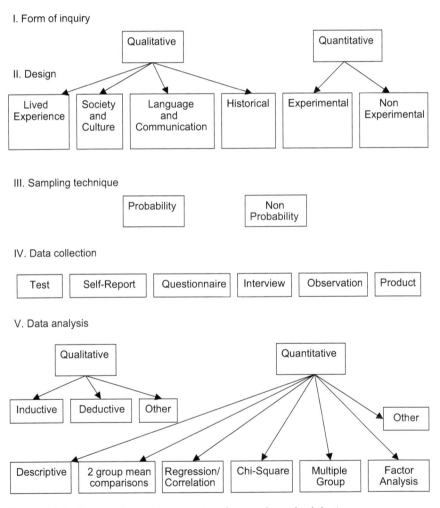

Figure 15.1　Perspectives and categories of research methodologies.

Element 1: Form of Inquiry

Gall, Gall, and Borg identified two forms of inquiry, quantitative and qualitative. Although several articles ($n = 8$) utilized a mixed methods approach (i.e., combination of quantitative and qualitative), these articles were included only in those analyses that treated the article as a single entity such as the frequency of articles published in a year. They were excluded from analyses that compared subcategories of any element such as quantitative or qualitative forms of inquiry. Including mixed method studies in these comparisons violated the assumption of independence needed for chi-square analyses (Glass & Hopkins, 1996, p. 338).

Gall, Gall, and Borg provided detailed descriptions of the two forms of inquiry. They described the qualitative form of inquiry as

> grounded in the assumption that individuals construct social reality in the form of meanings and interpretations, and that these constructions tend to be transitory and situational. The dominant methodology is to discover these meanings and interpretations by studying cases intensively in natural settings and by subjecting the resulting data to analytic induction.
>
> (p. 650)

In turn, they described the quantitative form of inquiry as

> grounded in the assumption that features of the social environment constitute an objective reality that is relatively constant across time and settings. The dominant methodology is to describe and explain features of this reality by collecting numerical data on observable behaviors of samples and by subjecting these data to statistical analysis.
>
> (p. 650)

These definitions provided a basis for determining the form of inquiry in each article.

Element 2: Design

To accommodate diverse forms of qualitative designs, Gall, Gall, and Borg recommended differentiating qualitative research based on research traditions (p. 490). They identified three traditions of investigation in qualitative : (a) lived experience, (b) society and culture, and (c) language and communication. Studies in the lived experience tradition included those pertaining to cognitive psychology and phenomenology; studies in the society and culture tradition included action research and ethnography; and studies in the language and communication tradition included narratives, hermeneutics and semiotics (p. 491). Along with these three traditions, historical research was included as a fourth category of qualitative design. Gall, Gall, and Borg devoted an entire chapter (Chapter 16, p. 528) to this topic asserting the importance of historical research as a unique form of qualitative investigation.

In studies following a quantitative form of inquiry, the design element was divided into experimental and non-experimental subcategories. In an experimental design, the researcher introduced an intervention and studied the impact of that intervention on treatment and control groups. Common experimental designs included pretest-posttest control-group design and quasi-experimental design. In a non-experimental design, the researcher does not introduce an intervention but rather examines and describes phenomena. Typical non-experimental designs include descriptive, causal-comparative, and correlational designs.

Element 3: Sampling Technique

Although many sampling techniques were used, I categorized them as either probability or non-probability. In probability sampling, the researcher assumes that "each individual in the population has a known probability of being selected. The probabilities are known because the individuals are chosen by chance" (Gall et al., 2007, p. 170). Specific types of probability sampling include simple random sampling and cluster sampling. Non-probability sampling, on the other hand, implies that the participants were chosen by other means. Types of non-probability sampling include convenience samples and volunteers. Patton (2002) acknowledged the differences between probability and non-probability sampling in qualitative research. In place of the term "non-probability," he preferred using the word "purposeful" (p. 243). In order to remain consistent with the definitions provided by Gall, Gall, and Borg (2007), I used the terms probability and non-probability in this study.

Element 4: Data Collection

Although researchers have used numerous techniques to collect data, data collection methodologies in this study were organized into six subcategories: (a) test, (b) self-report, (c) questionnaire, (d) interview, (e) observation, and (f) product. Decisions related to the categorization of data collection methodologies were based on definitions provided by Gall, Gall, and Borg (2007):

- Test—"A structured performance situation that can be analyzed to yield numerical scores, from which inferences are made about how individuals differ in the construct measured by the test" (p. 656). In music education, numerical data could come from performance measures as well as paper and pencil tests.
- Self-report measure—"A paper and pencil instrument whose items yield numerical scores from which inferences can be made about various

aspects of self" (p. 652). Although Gall, Gall, and Borg restricted the response process in a self-report measure to numerical data, I determined the difference between self-reports and questionnaires based on the content of the information being collected. Self-report measures collect information about thoughts, feelings, and preferences, while questionnaires collect information about elements outside of the individual's perception of self.

- Questionnaire—"A measure that presents a set of written questions to which all individuals in a sample respond" (p. 650). In this study, the category of questionnaire included collection techniques such as paper and pencil questionnaires, rating scales, and written evaluations. The response formats ranged from open-ended questions to Likert-type responses. On a questionnaire, participants may be asked to evaluate the technical qualities of a musical performance, but on a self-report measure, the participant would be asked to assess how they felt emotionally at the time they were making the evaluation.
- Interview—"A form of data collection involving direct interaction between the researcher and the research participant, using oral questions by the interviewer and oral responses by the participants" (p. 643). Informal oral comments and focus group discussions were also included in this category.
- Observation—the researcher collects information in the setting being studied. The experience is usually collected in the form of video recordings or field notes.
- Product—This category included those products that are evaluated as representations of an outcome from an individual's activity. They may include audio or video recordings, compositions, and MIDI file data. Artifacts, publications, and reflective journals were also viewed as products and included in this category.

Unlike research design and data analysis, data collection methods were not linked to the form of inquiry. Questionnaires, for example, can be used in studies based on quantitative or qualitative forms of inquiry. There were many types of data collection techniques used throughout the articles and it is important to note that I used the definitions stated above to determine the categorization. Some techniques, however, did not fall neatly into any of the subcategories. In these cases, I based my categorization on the intent of the authors and their use of the data.

Element 5: Data Analysis

Researchers analyze data using a variety of techniques and those techniques are often associated with the qualitative or quantitative forms of inquiry. The techniques associated with the qualitative form of inquiry are inductive, deductive, and other-qualitative. Patton (2002) described inductive analysis as "immersion in the details and specifics of the data to discover important patterns, themes, and interrelationships" (p. 41). Inductive analyses often result in the identification of emergent themes, which are synthesized into a broader theoretical framework. In contrast, deductive analyses use data to support a unifying theoretical framework. Conceptually, deductive analysis uses a top-down perspective in which the data becomes evidence of the broader framework. The other-qualitative subcategory includes techniques that provide a summary of research findings without communicating theoretical implications. These techniques included summaries, reviews, and simple categorizations.

There were seven subcategories of quantitative data analysis methodologies. I based these subcategories on general concepts and statistical procedures presented in Glass and Hopkin's (1996) *Statistical Methods in Education and Psychology*. This textbook was recommended by a statistics professor from a major research university as an accurate resource. The seven subcategories were: (a) descriptive, (b) mean difference between two groups, (c) correlation and regression, (d) chi-square, (e) analyses of variance between multiple groups, (f) factor analyses, and (g) other-quantitative. Descriptive techniques included the calculation of means, standard deviations, frequencies and percentages. Mean differences between two groups included parametric techniques such as the *t*-test and nonparametric techniques such as the Mann-Whitney *U*-test. Correlation and regression procedures included bivariate and multivariate correlations as well as simple and multivariate forms of regression. Chi-square techniques included proportional goodness of fit, association, and independence tests. Analyses of variance procedures included ANOVA, MANOVA, ANCOVA and similar techniques. Factor analysis included exploratory, confirmatory, and principal component analyses. A few techniques did not fit neatly into these categories, such as multidimensional scaling, multitrait-multimethod analysis, and structural equation modeling. These techniques were included in the other-quantitative subcategory.

Data Analysis

I read all articles and coded for each of the methodological elements. The resulting data were then entered into the Statistical Analysis Software (SAS) program for analysis. Since the articles were analyzed ten different ways, two times (time and journal) for each of the five methodological perspectives, a Bonferroni adjusted *p* value of .005 was used to determine significance. To provide evidence of reliability in coding, a colleague holding a PhD in music education coded 10% (*n* = 32) of the articles. The proportion of agreement, Cohen's kappa, was calculated for each category. According to descriptive interpretations provided by Landis and Koch (1977), results indicated almost perfect agreement in coding forms of inquiry (κ = .81 [0.63, 0.98]), substantial agreement in research design (κ = .80 [0.63, 0.98]), perfect agreement in sampling technique (κ = 1.00 [1.00, 1.00]), substantial agreement in data collection ($\kappa = 0.70$ [0.55, 0.86]), substantial agreement in quantitative data analysis ($\kappa = 0.76$ [0.60, 0.92]), and poor agreement in qualitative data analysis ($\kappa = -0.03$ [-0.51, 0.45]). The poor level of agreement in coding the qualitative analysis techniques (50% agreement) may be attributed to incongruent definitions of the terms inductive, deductive, and other. Although most of the coding was highly reliable, the reader should approach conclusions related to qualitative data analysis methodologies with caution.

RESULTS

Descriptive statistics appear in Table 15.1. Three hundred twenty-two studies met Gall, Gall, and Borg's (2007) criteria for research. Overall, *JRME* published the greatest number of articles ($n = 141$) while *POM* published the fewest number ($n = 80$). The total number of articles per time period increased from 1988–89 ($n = 65$) to 2008–09 ($n = 130$). Individually, all journals increased their publication of research articles per time period. The *Bulletin* increased from 14 (1988–89) to 47 (2008–09) and *POM* grew from 16 (1988–89) to 43 (2008–09). *JRME* increased from 35 (1988–89) to 66 (1998–99) and then decreased to 40 (2008–09).

The journals did not publish the same number of articles in each time period. There was a significant difference in the proportions of research articles published by the journals per time period χ^2 (4, $N = 322$) = 18.50, $p < .001$). This difference exhibited a moderately small effect size ($w = .24$) (Table 15.2). The most extreme difference in proportions occurred in 1988–89 when *POM* published 16 articles while *JRME* published 35 articles. In 2008–09 however, the number of research articles among journals was very similar ranging from 40 (*JRME*) to 47 (*Bulletin*).

Table 15.1 Descriptive Statistics

| Journal | Number of Research Articles[a] | | | Total | M (SD) |
	1988–89	1998–99	2008–09		
Bulletin	14	40	47	101	33.67(17.39)
JRME	35	66	40[b]	141	47.00(16.64)
POM	16	21	43[c]	80	26.67(14.36)
Total	65	127	130	322	107.33(36.69)
M (SD)	21.67(11.59)	42.33(22.59)	43.33(3.51)	107.33(30.99)	

a. Research as defined by Gall, Gall, and Borg (2007).
b. Due to changes in publishing schedule, only 3 journals were published in 2008.
c. Publication changed from semiannual to quarterly.

Table 15.2   Research Articles Published in Eminent Music Education Journals by Time Period*

Frequency Percent Row Pct Column Pct	1988–89	1998–99	2008–09	Total
Bulletin	14	40	47	101
	4.35	12.42	14.60	31.37
	13.86	39.60	46.53	
	21.54	31.50	36.15	
JRME	35	66	40	141
	10.87	20.50	12.42	43.79
	24.82	46.81	28.37	
	53.85	51.97	30.77	
POM	16	21	43	80
	4.97	6.52	13.35	24.84
	20.00	26.25	53.75	
	24.62	16.54	33.08	
Total	65	127	130	322
	20.19	39.44	40.37	100.00

* Significant difference among proportions of journal by time period, χ^2 (4, N = 322) = 18.50, $p < .001$.

Chi-square tests of association were used to compare the proportions of the categories in each element by time period (Table 15.3). As mentioned above, I removed the mixed method studies from these analyses to maintain the independence of the articles in analysis. The proportion of qualitative and quantitative studies did not change significantly over time. In addition, no significant change was found in the proportions of the subcategories of design, sampling techniques, or data analysis. A significant difference, however, was found among the data collection subcategories, χ^2 (10, N = 314) = 27.09, $p < .005$, $w = .24$. The greatest changes in proportions were in the subcategory of test which decreased from 31.71% in 1988–89 to 14.08% in 2008–09 and in the subcategory of questionnaires which increased from 8.54% in 1988–89 to 24.27% in 2008–09.

To address the second research question, I compared the five elements among the journals. The results of these tests indicated significant differences among the journals in all elements (Table 15.4). There was a significant difference in the proportions of qualitative and quantitative forms of inquiry among journals χ^2 = (2, N = 314) = 38.14, $p < .005$). *JRME* exhibited the most extreme difference in proportions between quantitative (84.40%) and qualitative studies (15.60%) while the proportions were more evenly distributed in the *Bulletin*, quantitative (48.98%) and qualitative (51.02%). The effect size of this comparison was $w = .35$, indicating a moderate level of practical significance.

Table 15.3 Frequencies and Percentages of Methodologies Used by Time Period

Perspective Category	Frequency(Column Percentage)			
	1988–89	1998–99	2008–09	Total
Forms of inquiry				
Qualitative	19(29.23)	34(27.20)	35(28.23)	88(28.03)
Quantitative	46(70.77)	91(72.80)	89(71.77)	226(71.97)
Design (Qualitative)				
Lived Experiences	6(9.23)	10(8.00)	12(9.68)	28(8.92)
Society & Culture	1(1.54)	7(5.60)	14(11.29)	22(7.01)
Language & Communication	2(3.08)	3(2.40)	4(3.23)	9(2.87)
Historical (Quantitative)	10(15.38)	14(11.20)	5(4.03)	29(9.24)
Experimental	14(21.54)	16(12.80)	18(14.52)	48(15.29)
Non Experimental	32(49.23)	75(60.00)	71(57.26)	178(56.69)
Sampling Technique				
Non-Probability	49(75.38)	112(89.60)	112(90.23)	273(86.94)
Probability	16(24.62)	13(10.40)	12(9.68)	41(13.06)
Data Collection*				
Test	26(31.71)	40(22.86)	29(14.08)	95(20.52)
Self-Report	14(17.07)	20(11.43)	33(16.02)	67(14.47)
Questionnaire	7(8.54)	28(16.00)	50(24.27)	85(18.36)
Interview	3(3.66)	20(11.43)	26(12.62)	49(10.58)
Observation	7(8.54)	16(9.14)	21(10.19)	44(9.50)
Product	25(30.49)	51(29.14)	47(22.82)	123(26.57)
Data Analysis (Qualitative)[a]				
Inductive	2(1.34)	10(3.61)	19(6.60)	31(4.34)
Deductive	1(0.67)	3(1.08)	3(1.04)	7(0.98)
Other-Qualitative	16(10.74)	21(7.58)	13(4.51)	50(7.00)
(Quantitative)				
Descriptive	41(27.52)	86(31.05)	85(29.51)	212(29.69)
2 Group Comparisons	21(14.09)	31(11.19)	38(13.19)	90(12.61)
Regression/Correlation	19(12.75)	38(13.72)	43(14.93)	100(14.01)
Chi-Square	15(10.07)	16(5.78)	19(6.60)	50(7.00)
Multiple Group	31(20.81)	59(21.30)	51(17.71)	141(19.75)
Factor Analysis	0 (0.00)	8(2.89)	14(4.86)	22(3.08)
Other-Quantitative	3(2.01)	5(1.81)	3(1.04)	11(1.54)

a. Many studies used more than one data collection and analysis technique. Frequency totals for data collection and analysis techniques were greater than total number of studies investigated.

* Significant difference in methodology used by time periods, χ^2 (10, N = 314) = 27.09, p < .005.

Table 15.4 Frequencies and Percentages of Methodologies Used by Journals

Perspective Category	Frequency(Column Percentage)			Total
	Bulletin	*JRME*	*POM*	
Forms of inquiry*				
Qualitative	50(51.02)	22(15.60)	16(21.33)	88(28.03)
Quantitative	48(48.98)	119(84.40)	59(78.67)	226(71.97)
Design* (Qualitative)				
Lived Experiences	14(14.29)	6(4.26)	8(10.67)	28(8.92)
Society & Culture	15(15.31)	5(3.55)	2(2.67)	22(7.01)
Language & Communication	7(7.14)	0(0.00)	2(2.67)	9(2.87)
Historical (Quantitative)	14(14.29)	11(7.80)	4(5.33)	29(9.24)
Experimental	5(5.10)	25(17.73)	18(24.00)	48(15.29)
Non Experimental	43(43.88)	94(66.67)	41(54.67)	178(56.69)
Sampling Technique*				
Non-Probability	91(92.86)	110(78.01)	72(96.00)	273(86.94)
Probability	7(7.14)	31(21.99)	3(4.00)	41(13.06)
Data Collection*				
Test	19(13.67)	51(25.12)	25(20.66)	95(20.52)
Self-Report	14(10.07)	31(15.27)	22(18.18)	67(14.47)
Questionnaire	16(11.51)	36(17.73)	33(27.27)	85(18.36)
Interview	26(18.71)	15(7.39)	8(6.61)	49(10.58)
Observation	17(12.23)	17(8.37)	10(8.26)	44(9.50)
Product	47(33.81)	53(26.11)	23(19.01)	123(26.57)
Data Analysis* (Qualitative)				
Inductive	20(11.98)	4(1.11)	7(3.72)	31(4.34)
Deductive	3(1.80)	3(0.84)	1(0.53)	7(0.98)
Other	27(16.17)	15(4.18)	8(4.26)	50(7.00)
(Quantitative)				
Descriptive	41(24.55)	114(31.75)	57(30.32)	212(29.69)
2 Group Comparisons	12(7.19)	51(14.21)	27(14.36)	90(12.61)
Regression/Correlation	20(11.98)	56(15.60)	24(12.77)	100(14.01)
Chi-Square	11(6.59)	26(7.24)	13(6.91)	50(7.00)
Multiple Group	25(14.97)	74(20.61)	42(22.34)	141(19.75)
Factor Analysis	6(3.59)	11(3.06)	5(2.66)	22(3.08)
Other-Quan	2(1.20)	5(1.39)	4(2.13)	11(1.54)

* Significant differences in proportions among journals ($p < .005$).

There was also a significant difference among the design subcategories $\chi^2 = (10, N = 314) = 51.78, p < .005, w = .41$. *JRME* published a large percentage of articles with non-experimental designs (66.67%) and much smaller percentages of the other designs. The *Bulletin* published articles representing an almost even distribution of design categories. As for the element sampling techniques, there was a significant difference among journals in the publishing of articles using probability and non-probability techniques $\chi^2 (2, N = 314) = 18.34, p < .005, w = .24$. In this element, *POM* and the *Bulletin* exhibited the greatest difference in proportions. Both published large percentages of studies using non-probability sampling, 96.00% and 92.86% respectively. *JRME* published many studies with non-probability sampling, but more studies with probability sampling than the other two journals combined. In addition, there was a significant difference in the proportions of the various data collection techniques reported in the journals $\chi^2 (10, N = 314) = 36.55, p < .005, w = .28$. The *Bulletin* published the largest proportion of articles using product-based data collection (33.81%), while *POM* published the smallest proportion of studies using interviews (6.61%). Finally, there was a significant difference among the proportions of data analysis techniques reported by the journals $\chi^2 (18, N = 314) = 71.02, p < .005, w = .31$. *JRME* published more articles using quantitative analysis techniques while the *Bulletin* published more articles using qualitative analytical techniques.

Limitations

The findings of this study must be approached with caution. Since I examined only a small proportion of the published articles in these journals, the findings do not represent all published articles in these journals for the 21-year time period. In addition, the articles reviewed in this study may not be representative of all work done in music education research. Some researchers may have sought publication in other journals specializing in particular types of research such as historical journals. Finally, the categorization process in this study was ultimately based on the interpretation of the methodological elements by this researcher. Although I used Gall, Gall, and Borg's (2007) definitions and Glass and Hopkins's (1996) explanations as objective measures, the categorical decisions were subject to my personal interpretations.

DISCUSSION

This study uncovered several trends in music education research. First, the number of research studies published in eminent journals increased from 1988 to 2009. This increase may be attributed to several factors. *Psychology of Music* was published semiannually in 1988–89 and 1998–99, and then quarterly in 2008–09. This change doubled the number of articles published per year by *POM*. The *Bulletin* also increased its publication of research articles in 2008–09 by removing book reviews and dissertation critiques from its pages. As for *JRME*, the total increase in article publication would have been even greater had *JRME* continued with its pre-2008 publishing schedule. *JRME* shifted the publication of its December 2008 issue to January 2009, resulting in a calendar year (2008) with only three issues instead of four.

The second trend was a significant change in the data collection techniques used from 1988 to 2009. Although there were minor changes in all of the methodological elements over the 21-year period, only the element data collection exhibited a significant difference among its subcategories. This difference was brought about by a decrease in the use of tests and an increased use of questionnaires and interviews. The increase in the number of qualitative studies conducted from 1988–89 ($n = 19$) and in 2008–09 ($n = 35$) may have been responsible for this change. Questionnaires and interviews are common data collection methods in qualitative studies.

Although each journal published research articles in music education, there were significant differences in the methodologies published in the journals. Comparisons of the subcategories of all five methodological elements revealed significant differences among the journals. In most cases, the difference in the last four elements can be linked to the form of inquiry in each article. It did not appear unusual to find differences in the design, sampling technique, data collection, and data analysis methodologies since *JRME* and *POM* published a greater proportion of quantitative articles (84.40% and 78.67%, respectively) than the *Bulletin* (48.98%). Although the form of inquiry does not prescribe specific methodologies, there are certain practices that are consistent with the positivist epistemology and its investigative processes.

Although the number of qualitative studies increased, it is important to note that the proportion of qualitative to quantitative studies remained consistent across the years. Researchers have recognized the advantages of qualitative inquiry (Flinders & Richardson, 2002) but there remains a strong quantitative orientation as exemplified by the data from the journals *JRME* and *POM*. In addition, I was unable to find any articles in the time periods examined based on the qualitative language and communication tradition in *JRME*. Although *JRME* publishes qualitative articles, this study has documented its inclination to publish quantitative research. This inclination may have resulted from *JRME* being the oldest publication among the journals. Historically, research in music education has been built on quantitative traditions.

The results of this study were consistent with findings from other studies. Yarbrough (2002) reported a decrease in the publication of historical research from 1953–2002 in *JRME*. She also noted a small increase in the use of qualitative methodologies. In this study, the publication of historical research declined from 10 articles in 1988–89 to 5 articles in 2008–09. One possible explanation may be that authors of historical articles have found other publications in which to publish their work. In a separate review of the literature, Bartel and Radocy (2002) identified seven trends in music education research. Four of the seven trends were within the scope of this study: (a) methodological complexity, (b) data complexity, (c) analytical complexity, and (d) representation complexity. The significant change in data collection methodologies provided the most direct support of Bartel and Radocy's (2002) trend of increased data complexity. Questionnaires and interviews can provide more complex data than numeric tests.

CONCLUSION

The results of this study offer valuable insights for navigating the future of research in music education. In 1988, the digital age was in its infancy. By 2009, improvements in personal computers and the Internet brought profound changes to the collection and processing of information. Research in music education has benefited from these changes. Benefits include the increased accessibility of articles and the development of sophisticated analytical tools. Researchers are now able to collect larger data sets and examine them with increased levels of complexity. In many ways, digital processing has facilitated the escalation of research activities.

Research in music education has reached new levels of prominence. The findings of this study have demonstrated that eminent journals in the field have increased their publication of research articles. This shift indicates that research has become more highly valued by others in the profession and considered an important contributor to improvements in music education. Along with these journals, new technology-based venues are being developed to provide even greater access to research information. These new venues include online journals, websites, and social media. Music education is making progress toward becoming a research-based profession.

Although there has been progress, traditional investigative processes dominated the research examined in this study. More quantitative studies were published than qualitative. This finding may not have negative repercussions for the field, but it is worthy of closer scrutiny. Questions may arise such as (a) Do we conduct more quantitative research simply because that is what we were trained to do?, or (b) Are more quantitative studies being conducted because more quantitative studies are being published? In either question, the tail is wagging the dog (cliché). I recommend that future researchers dig deeper and closely examine the questions being asked in research studies. The driving force behind research must be the questions and not the methodologies. Methodologies are tools to answer questions. We should be asking ourselves, are we asking the right questions? In the 322 articles reviewed for this study, no researcher investigated research questions. Future research must begin examining research questions and the relationship between those questions and the needs of the profession.

The significant change in data collection methodologies signifies trends on two levels. On one level, it suggests that researchers investigated different topics in 2009 than in 1988. Topics such as music achievement and aptitude can be collected with tests using numeric responses. Thoughts and opinions, however, are most authentically represented through the language of the individuals. Consequently, researchers must use questionnaires or interviews to collect the data. The shift away from tests and toward questionnaires found in this study provided evidence that researchers investigated topics in which data collection methods such as tests were not appropriate. The data consisted of language that could only be collected using other means. On a second level, I would speculate that researchers have become more adept at analyzing language. Coding responses from questionnaires is difficult and time-consuming work. The increased use of questionnaires may suggest that researchers are using new technologies to make their work faster and less burdensome. Future research on methodologies should examine the impact of software tools on researchers' methodological choices.

This investigation has raised questions not only about research methodologies, but also about the context of research in a field such as music education. For example, the increase in non-probability sampling may not necessarily indicate a lack of interest among researchers in probability sampling, but rather reflect the increasing difficulties researchers encounter as they attempt to include K–12 students as participants in their studies. In most cases, researchers have little choice but to accept convenience samples as participants. Most schools' reaction to violence in society has been to limit outsiders' access to students. Researchers would benefit from increasing their knowledge of convenience samples and understanding effective means to incorporate them into their studies. Probability sampling may not be an option.

In closing, I would like to acknowledge the overall improvement in quality of the research articles over time. More articles followed strict publication guidelines resulting in greater organizational consistency and clarity. Recent articles included information such as effect sizes and confidence intervals to assist in the interpretation of results. To better navigate the future, researchers can learn from the past. Cronbach and Meehl (1955) recommended constructing nomological networks that interrelate hypotheses based on theory. Although rigorous studies have been conducted in music education, the topics have been divergent. Researchers should consider connecting these topics by filling the knowledge gaps. This process may involve measuring and analyzing multiple constructs concurrently. The development of multivariate analyses and the availability of high quality software programs make this challenge a realistic goal. Finally, the lesson learned in this study may not be in what is observed, but in what is missing. There is much work left to be done. My hope is that this study will provide an impetus for future investigations into research methodologies.

REFERENCES

Abeles, H. F., & Conway, C. (2010). The inquiring music teacher. In H. F. Abeles & L. A. Custodero (Eds.), *Critical issues in music education: Contemporary theory and practice* (pp. 276–302). New York, NY: Oxford University Press.

Bartel, L. R., & Radocy, R. E. (2002). Trends in data acquisition and knowledge development. In R. Colwell & C. Richardson (Eds.), *The new handbook of research on music teaching and learning* (pp. 1108–27). New York, NY: Oxford University Press.

Choate, R. A. (1965). Research in music education. *Journal of Research in Music Education, 13*(2), 67–86.

Cronbach, L. J., & Meehl, P. E. (1955). Construct validity in psychological tests. *Psychological Bulletin, 52,* 281–302.

Draves, T. J., Cruse, C. S., Mills, M. M., & Sweet, B. M. (2008). Subjects in music education research 1991–2005. *Bulletin of the Council for Research in Music Education, 176,* 19–30.

Ebie, B. D. (2002). Characteristics of 50 years of research samples found in the "Journal of Research in Music Education," 1953–2002. *Journal of Research in Music Education, 50*(4), 280–91.

Flinders, D. J., & Richardson, C. P. (2002). Contemporary issues in qualitative research and music education. In R. Colwell & C. Richardson (Eds.), *The new handbook of research on music teaching and learning* (pp. 1159–76). New York, NY: Oxford University Press.

Gall, M. D., Gall, J. P., & Borg, W. R. (2007). *Educational research: An introduction.* New York, NY: Pearson Education.

Glass, G. V., & Hopkins, K. D. (1996). *Statistical methods in education and psychology.* Boston, MA: Allyn and Bacon.

Hamann, D. L., & Lucas, K. V. (1998). Establishing journal eminence in music education research. *Journal of Research in Music Education, 46*(3), 405–13.

Heller, G. N. (1985). On the meaning and value of historical research in music education. *Journal of Research in Music Education, 33*(1), 4–6.

Humphreys, J. T. (2006). 2006 senior researcher award acceptance address: Observations about music education. *Journal of Research in Music Education, 54*(3), 183–202.

Internet World Stats. (2013). Retrieved June 13, 2013, from www.internetworldstats.com/stats.htm

Jones, R. S. (1957). Current trends and new directions in educational research. *Journal of Research in Music Education, 5*(1), 16–22.

Kratus, J. (1993). Eminence in music education research as measured in the Handbook of Research on Music Teaching and Learning. *Bulletin of the Council for Research in Music Education, 118,* 21–32.

Krueger, P. J. (1987). Ethnographic research methodology in music education. *Journal of Research in Music Education, 35*(2), 69–77.

Landis, J. R., & Koch, G. G. (1977). The measurement of observer agreement for categorical data. *Biometrics, 33,* 159–74.

Mark, M. L. (1992). A history of music education research. In R. Colwell (Ed.), *Handbook of research on music teaching and learning* (pp. 48–59). New York, NY: Macmillan.

Patton, M. Q. (2002). *Qualitative research & evaluation methods.* Thousand Oaks, CA: Sage Publications.

Randles, C., Hagen, J., Gottlieb, B., & Salvador, K. (2010). Eminence in music education research as measured in the New Handbook of Research on Music Teaching and Learning. *Bulletin of the Council for Research in Music Education, 183,* 165–76.

Sample, D. (1992). Frequently cited studies as indicators of music education research interests, 1963–1989. *Journal of Research in Music Education, 40*(2), 153–7.

Schmidt, C. P., & Zdzinski, S. F. (1993). Cited quantitative research articles in music education research journals, 1975–1990: A content analysis of selected studies. *Journal of Research in Music Education, 41*(1), 5–18.

Yarbrough, C. (1984). A content analysis of the "Journal of Research in Music Education," 1953–1983. *Journal of Research in Music Education, 32*(4), 213–22.

Yarbrough, C. (2002). The first 50 years of the "Journal of Research in Music Education": A content analysis. *Journal of Research in Music Education, 50*(4), 276–9.

16 Critical Ethnography as/for Praxis

A Pathway for Music Education

Marissa Silverman

Deena: "I make my music. I got it goin' on!"
Cristina: "That's my song! That's my jam!"
Carlos: "I wanna be a producer and DJ. I love mixin' it up."

INTRODUCTION

As part of my university work, and for my professional development and personal enjoyment, I make regular visits to urban schools in New York City and New Jersey. My visits not only bring back memories of my previous work as a secondary music and English literature teacher in Long Island City (an extraordinarily diverse section of Queens, New York), they provide me with exceptionally important opportunities to engage in stimulating and transformative dialogues with today's students. I learn a great deal about/from these students—their school music experiences, their views on the strengths and weaknesses of their music programs, and their personal and musical activities and dreams.

For example, Deena said: "I make my music. I got it goin' on." Deena meant that she engaged in what I'll call "homemade music"; she drew from R&B and hip-hop to create her own beats, samples, melodies, and lyrics. In contrast, Rebekah was involved in a Baptist church Gospel choir: "I sing in my church. Me and my sister. I feel free when I'm singing my Gospel music." Rebekah asked me what kinds of music I made, listened to, and liked most. I said: "It depends on my mood. But lately I've been listening to 'Locked out in Heaven,' by Bruno Mars, because one of my university students asked me to listen to it to see if I liked it." Cristina joined in: "That's my song! That's my jam!" Carlos said: "I wanna be a producer and DJ. I love mixin' it up." When he said "mixin' it up," Carlos moved his hands back and forth in the air, as if he was "scratching" a record on a turntable.

In my locales, urban secondary school students have a very wide range of musical interests and involvements, including traditional school ensembles, community music programs, and homemade music making. For me, two major questions follow from dialogues with today's youth. What kinds of understandings do students bring to music classes, and how can teachers build on students' interests toward igniting and sustaining their motivations to experiment with musics beyond their immediate environments? Implicit in the latter question is another: How can students work with their teachers as co-teachers and co-agents of music curriculum development and change?

excellent question

PROBLEM

Many researchers (e.g., Jaffurs, 2004; Jones, 2007; Randles, 2012; Veblen, Messenger, Silverman, & Elliott, 2013) have alerted us to various types of disconnection between school, community, and homemade music making around the world. Reasons for this pattern of disconnection include the vast and growing expansion of community-based alternatives to school music and the ever-expanding range of accessible music technologies that facilitate young people's high quality home-based music production (Bell, 2012). Indeed, research suggests that, on average, traditional school music ensembles serve approximately 20% of most school populations (Elpus & Abril, 2011; Kuzmich & Dammers, 2013). Furthermore, school music ensembles tend to exclude members of marginalized groups (DeLorenzo, 2012a; DeLorenzo, 2012b; Elpus & Abril, 2011).

To alleviate school-community disconnections, some researchers suggest that students, especially minority students, need broader exposure to music mentors and role models, who have backgrounds similar to students (Lucas & Robinson, 2003; Quiocho & Rios, 2000). Others have suggested and/or operationalized various programs and pedagogical strategies that emphasize different ways of knowing (see the U.K. "Musical Futures Project"[1]; Green 2002, 2006; Myers, 2007). Other researchers focus on culturally relevant pedagogies that assist in making music classrooms more diverse in content and curriculum (Ladson-Billings, 1995; Volk, 2004; Prier, 2012).

While these solutions may be effective to various degrees (further research is necessary), I believe there are other possibilities for reconnecting today's youth with the musical and educational potentials of reconstructed *public school* music programs. Indeed, we should not be too quick to give up the fight to make public school music more relevant and effective (in every respect) for today's and tomorrow's youth. As the educational philosopher Chris Higgins (2011b) emphasizes: "Schools should be central to public life: key locations for the regeneration of values, the cultivation of judgment, and the creation of the conditions for positive freedom" (p. 451). He continues: "Schools can only revitalize public life if they return to . . . something very close to the heart of their mission: to provide a model of how to be together" (p. 466).

Indeed, and as other researchers note, unless students and teachers transform what *is* to what *can be*, and until we "challenge institutions, regimes of knowledge, and social practices that limit choices, constrain meaning, and denigrate identities and communities" (Madison, 2012, p. 6), we will not and cannot create pathways for more meaningful musical, interpersonal, and intersubjective transactions and transformations among students, teachers, and classrooms. How can we challenge educational practices and create new pathways? This chapter offers one suggestion in the form of a research praxis that allows us to get inside and under the skin of the problems and potentials of schools as sites of personal and musical empowerment and transformation.

PURPOSE

The purpose of this chapter is to explain the nature and strategies of critical ethnography as these apply to "intersections between theory, fieldwork methods, performance, critical practice, and social justice" (Madison, 2012, p. ix). Critical ethnography examines the interdependence between theory and practice and how, when united with an ethical stance, it creates spaces for ethical praxis (as explained by Marx, Freire, Arendt, and others—see below). At the conclusion of this chapter, I will explain the implications that this type of research holds for music education by focusing on teaching and learning in music-listening classes (e.g., secondary school "music appreciation" classes). I choose to focus on music-listening classes because, in my experience as an observer and evaluator of secondary school music programs, general music situations are especially prone to "banking-method" procedures (Freire, 1970).

By way of background, critical ethnographies utilize qualitative data collection methods for sociopolitical and ethical purposes. That is, critical ethnographies are "critical" in two senses: (a) they are framed and carried out with a social-ethical sense of responsibility to critique, and, if necessary, to change the specific contexts they investigate; and (b) they are grounded in "a self-referential form of reflexivity that aims to criticize the ethnographer's own production of an account" (Schwandt, 2007, p. 51).

From a philosophical perspective, critical ethnography exemplifies the central themes of praxis while highlighting the priorities of critical theory and critical pedagogy (e.g., McLaren, 1995; Freire, 1970). D. Soyini Madison (2012) explains that critical ethnography is "the 'doing'—or better the 'performance'—of critical theory" (p. 14). Joe L. Kinchloe and Peter McLaren (2002) describe critical ethnography as critical theory in action. According to Madison (2012) and others (Denzin, 2003; Noblit, Flores, & Murillo, 2004; Thomas, 1993; Carspecken, 1996), the critical ethnographer "disrupts the *status quo,* and unsettles both neutrality and taken-for-granted assumptions by bringing to light underlying and obscure operations of power and control. Therefore, the critical ethnographer . . . moves from 'what is' to 'what could be'" (Madison, 2012, p. 5). S/he aims to break through unjust social barriers "in defense of . . . the voices and experiences of subjects whose stories are otherwise restrained and out of reach" (p. 6) and to contribute to emancipatory knowledge and social justice.

CRITICAL ETHNOGRAPHY: A WAY OF BEING

Although there are overlaps among descriptive, interpretive, and critical approaches to ethnographic research, "critical" ethnographies are conventional ethnographies that rise to another level in virtue of their sociopolitical and ethical aims (Thomas, 1993). That is, critical ethnographers, like descriptive and interpretive ethnographers, gather qualitative data that provide "thick descriptions" (Geertz, 1973) and analyses of how knowledge develops from the discourses, actions, interactions, and gestures in a specific social context. However, critical ethnographers ground their research in a social-ethical sense of responsibility to contribute to changing the status quo of, for example, a specific school or classroom situation under investigation to empower students and teachers to achieve the dispositions required to take concrete actions for hope, greater freedom, and equity.

Why a social-ethical sense of responsibility? To understand this we need a clearer sense of "ethics" as connected to critical ethnography. Very often, people use the words "morality" and "ethics" interchangeably. However, some scholars make a careful distinction between these concepts (e.g., Williams, 1985; Foucault, 2000; Appiah, 2005; Higgins, 2011a). Accordingly, morality is one's sense of obligation and the decision-making processes (usually in deference to rules and regulations) that one undertakes to achieve the "right" action (i.e., "What should I do in x situation?"). Ethics, on the other hand, concerns the system of beliefs that underscore the kind of person one wishes to be ("Who do I want to be?"). Because of this, one of the distinguishing differences between morality and ethics is that ethics is contextually dependent. As Wayne Bowman (2012) states: "To act ethically, then, involves acting rightly in a situation where rightness cannot be stipulated in advance or fully determined aside from the particulars of the situation at hand" (p. 10). In other words, and in some ways, ethics is a way of "rightly" being and experiencing the world. How does this connect to critical ethnography? Madison (2012) answers by pointing out Foucault's sense of critique-as-virtue. She writes:

> . . . because critique is always an investigation of regimes of truth, critique is the transformation of individual subjects as well as the social life, territories, and structures they inhabit and that inhabit them. If critique is a practice of virtue, it constitutes ethics.
>
> (pp. 96–97)

As stated above, the doing (or "ethical action") of critical ethnography is aimed at transforming the "what is" to "what can be." Critical ethnographers feel a responsibility to "make a difference." This ethical action is transformative because it highlights and addresses the assumptions of a given paradigm and questions the legitimacy of the status quo. But how is this accomplished?

Before detailing critical ethnography further, we need to make a distinction between the terms methods, methodology, and epistemology. Scholars in various disciplines take different views of research methods. Researchers who embrace qualitative research tend to view "method," on the one hand, as concrete fieldwork that includes subjective and cultural interpretations; researchers embracing quantitative investigations tend to view fieldwork as validation and evidence-directed (Madison, 2012, p. 20). Regardless of the domain(s) in which researchers work, a "method" is often conceived in relation to the tools used for gathering data (i.e., participant observation, experimentation, interviews, statistical analyses, story-telling, journaling, etc.). "Methodology," on the other hand, relates to the research paradigm or principles detailing how to conduct research (e.g., ethnography, narrative inquiry, oral history).

As Harry F. Wolcott (2002) writes: "*ethnography is more than method*" (emphasis in original, p. 41). How so? This question brings us to a consideration of epistemology. One's epistemological stance is a key element of the philosophical foundation used to decide what does or does not count as "knowledge," and this is intimately connected to method in research. Judy Radigan (2002) explains that epistemology is "the nature of knowledge and the justification of knowledge claims" (p. 258). As such, one's view of knowledge and its generation inform the research process. The positionality of critical ethnography is such that knowledge generation is a contextually based, active process that is embedded in and infused with the values, histories, and practices of both the researcher and the community in which the research occurs.

Indeed, critical ethnography has a unique history and positionality. As noted earlier, critical ethnography integrates theory and practice; it rejects the notion of ethnographers as "detached, neutral participant observers" (Schwandt, 2007, p. 51); and it combines description and interpretation with sociopolitical and ethical aims. As Kay E. Cook (2008) writes, critical ethnography

> grew out of dissatisfaction with both the atheoretical stance of traditional ethnography, which ignored social structures such as class, patriarchy, and racism, and what some regarded as the overly deterministic and theoretical approaches of critical theory, which ignored the lived experience and agency of human actors.
>
> (p. 148)

As such, critical ethnography is a marriage of critical theory and ethnography. This marriage was crucial and timely. The ethnography that grew from the anthropological traditions of the 1960s–1970s was viewed as possessing hegemonic practices (e.g., Anderson, 1989), and critical theory was thought overly dense, idealistic, and lacking empirical method (e.g., Noblit, 2004). At the University of Chicago, ethnography (as part of sociology) began to transform how researchers examined issues and social worlds that were, more often than not, neglected (e.g., Park, 1932; Mead, 1934).

In England and other areas of the United Kingdom, the work of A. R. Radcliffe-Brown (1952) and Bronislaw Malinowski (1947) sought to define "social structures." This, in turn, led future social anthropologists to seek a more "dialectical representation of structure and agency" (Cox, 2002). This early work in England paved the way for the contributions of the British sociologist Paul Willis. In *Learning to Labour*, Willis (1977) builds on Marxist sentiments which argue that: "Universally developed individuals whose social relations, as their own communal [*gemeinschaftlich*] relations, are hence also subordinated to their own communal control, are no product of nature, but of history" (Marx, 1857/1973, p. 162). Willis offers a critical ethnographic account of the culture and conditioning of 12 working class boys (or "lads," he calls them) in industrial England. These students resisted and rejected school impositions. Rather than go along with "school culture," they created their own "counter-culture." Willis's breakthrough work in sociology is based upon this perspective.

Reading, Writing, and Resistance, Robert Everhart's (1983) account of junior high school students' acts of resistance, follows Paul Willis and *Learning to Labour*. However, Everhart's narrative seamlessly weaves theory and research together without any attempts at separation. Hence, in important ways, this book epitomizes the essence of critical ethnography. *Reading, Writing, and Resistance*, while Marxian in focus, is theoretically driven by Jürgen Habermas (1974, 1996). *Reading, Writing, and Resistance* illustrates the technical, practical, and emancipatory ways of learning (i.e., "cognitive interests") embodied in junior high school boys' behaviors (Habermas, 1971).

When critical ethnography became more "at home" in educational research, especially in studies of urban education, it became further politicized. This was a natural consequence of critical ethnography's concern for exposing, critiquing, problematizing, and transforming unjust social structures and practices. The more injustices and inequalities this research paradigm revealed, the more its dimensions deepened and broadened. In other words, critical ethnography became appropriately critical of "itself," a practice that has continued during the past 20 years with the help of the "critical traditions" of feminist theories of difference, critical race theory, postmodernism, and poststructuralism. All of these forces have contributed to the maturation of this transformative research practice.

Although there is no unified theory of critical ethnography, most critical ethnographies share four principles:

1. Education and research are culturally situated and political. Culture is viewed as "a complex circuit of production that includes a myriad of dialectically reinitiating and mutually informing sets of activities such as routines, rituals, action conditions, systems of intelligibility and meaning-making, conventions of interpretation, systems relations and conditions both external and internal to the social actor" (Kinchloe & McLaren, 2002, p. 122).
2. Education and research should strive to transform injustices (Freire, 1970; Anyon, 1997; Cochran-Smith, 2004).
3. Critical ethnographies highlight each researcher's ethical responsibilities to the people, context, and phenomena being researched (Thomas, 1993; Carspecken, 1996; Radigan, 2002; Noblit, 2004).
4. Critical ethnographies must be advocates for the oppressed by identifying and documenting oppressions and finding ways to assist the oppressed in empowering themselves and transforming their oppressive situations of injustice and inequality[3] (Thomas, 1993; Radigan, 2002; Noblit, 2004; Madison, 2012).

Again, and because the "critical" in critical ethnography is "a self-referential form of reflexivity that aims to criticize the ethnographer's own production of an account" (Schwandt, 2007, p. 51), it is explicit about essential concerns detailed by Francis Phil Carspecken (1996):

1. How claims to valid findings are acts of power in themselves and thus whose interests are being served by the research;
2. How values influence what is seen in facts; and
3. How we choose to represent reality is also an act of power and alters the interpretation of reality (quoted in Noblit, 2004, p. 185).

In other words, a self-reflexive understanding underscores a researcher's positionality, interpretation, and authority. It is not enough to identify these aspects. Madison (2012) asks us to take this further by considering questions such as, What good will this research do? Who will benefit and who won't?

And, as a reminder, critical ethnography should not be thought as a method, methodology, or epistemology, but as an integrative process:

Critical ethnography is one form of an empirical project associated with critical discourse, a form in which a researcher utilizing field methods . . . on-site attempts to re-present the "culture," the "consciousness," or the "lived experiences" of people living in asymmetrical power relations. As a "project," critical ethnography is recognized as having conscious political intentions that are oriented toward emancipatory and democratic goals. What is key to this approach is that for ethnography to be considered "critical" it should participate in a larger "critical" dialogue rather than follow any particular set of methods or research techniques.)

(Quantz, 1992, quoted in Noblit, 2004, pp. 185–6)

BUT THAT'S JUST GOOD PRAXIS

As mentioned above, because critical ethnography joins theory and practice with a foundation of ethics, critical ethnography is a form of "praxis." What do I mean by "praxis"? Unlike simplistic definitions of "praxis" or "praxial" as nothing more than "doing" or "action," praxis is much more complex and involves several interdependent dimensions.

Like critical ethnography, "praxis" has a long history of its own. Praxis has been conceptualized in slightly different ways by Aristotle, Hegel, Marx, Freire, and many others. For example, Aristotle conceived praxis as that which brings together critical reflection and ethical action. For Aristotle, theory (*episteme*), and three forms of practical knowledge (*techne, poeisis,* and *phronesis*), yield ethical activity (*praxis*) and virtues. As such, praxis is inclusive of critical thinking and action, emotions, techniques, motivations, aims, values, ethics, and all their interactions. In this conception, praxis "does its work" in social, political, and emotional space. Thus, Aristotle's praxis does not separate outcomes and processes. For Aristotle, praxis—as we see in the decisions and actions of an *educative* teacher and an ethical musician, lawyer, or doctor—is enacted and embodied in the doing of the activity (Elliott & Silverman, 2014).

Karl Marx, on the other hand, viewed praxis as action having revolutionary potential toward creating situations where people were not divided by class, nor were they alienated from one another by capitalist structures of wealth and status. As Madison (2012) writes, Marx "envisioned an unalienated world through the idea of *praxis.* Praxis is the creation of alternative ways of being and courageous engagement with the world in order to change it" (p. 67). Marx continues: "The philosophers have only *interpreted* the world, in various ways; the point, however, is to *change it*" (Marx & Engels, 1978, p. 145).

In a somewhat similar vein, Paulo Freire (1970) defines praxis as "the action and reflection of men and women upon their world in order to transform it" (p. 79). One of the major spaces for the implementation of Freire's concept of praxis is in "problem-posing" education. Problem-posing education (or "problematizing") is a liberatory process where teachers help students critique their specific social-cultural circumstances. This process, as Antonia Dardar (2002) explains, provides ways for students to develop "their critical abilities . . . to unveil ideological beliefs and practices that function to inhibit their democratic voice and participation" (p. 102). In such instances, Freire (1970) states, "education is thus constantly remade. . . . In order to *be*, it must *become*" (p. 86). For Freire, "good" education "is found in the interplay" of permanence and change. The banking method emphasizes permanence and becomes reactionary; problem-posing education—which accepts neither a "well-behaved" present nor a predetermined future—roots itself in the dynamic present and becomes revolutionary.

(p. 84)

It is in problem-posing education that people can find the self-actualization needed to promote personal and social change. Problem-posing education pivots on empathetic "communion" or "dialogue." In order to engage in dialogue, says Freire (1998), one needs a "capacity to love." As Dardar (2002) writes, "Throughout his life, Paulo Freire affirmed the revolutionary power of *teaching as an act of love*" (p. 91). Freire (1970) asks teachers and students to take notice of those around us, for "in the absence of a profound love for the world and for people . . . no matter where the oppressed are found, the act of love is commitment to their cause—the cause of liberation" (p. 89). Indeed, the liberatory potential for praxis is found in the care, consideration, and concern for the critical development of a collective consciousness.

Further explorations of the concept of praxis appear in Hannah Arendt's work. For Arendt (1958/1998), praxis is linked to what she calls the differentiation between the *vita contemplativa* (life of the mind) and *vita activa* (life of practical pursuits). Both, she believes, are essential, though distinctive (both within and between) and needs to be united in human relationships. As Arendt (1958/1998) notes, action can never be understood in "isolation": "to be isolated is to be deprived of the capacity to act" (p. 188). Once we understand how we are connected to one another through action, we can achieve mutual understanding and participatory democracy. Additionally, Arendt's understanding of praxis yields a humanistic dimension that the aforementioned scholars do not focus upon sufficiently. That is, Arendt (1958/1998) favors praxis over poeisis because for her, praxis maintains unpredictability and uncertainty, while poeisis tends towards "reliability" (p. 195). Why would praxis, as detailed by Arendt, be considered humanistic? Because part of the "human condition" is the understanding and negotiating of human subjects in relation with/for other human subjects. In other words, human action as praxis is plural, constantly evolving, and interactive. As Richard Bernstein (2011) writes: "[Arendt] warns us about the current danger of forgetting what action or *praxis* really is—the highest form of human activity, manifested in speech and deed and rooted in the human condition of plurality" (p. 44).

Other scholars have contributed their own views of praxis (e.g., Gadamer, Habermas, and Bernstein). But taken together, variations on praxis share key aspects in common. Stated briefly, praxis involves (1) active reflection and critically reflective action, (2) a concern for human flourishing, wellbeing, and (3) an "ethic of care" (e.g. Noddings, 2002, 2005), all of which seek (4) the positive transformation of people's everyday lives (Elliott & Silverman, 2014).[4]

Critical ethnography is rooted in contemporary concepts of praxis that integrate the works of numerous thinkers past and present (e.g., Aristotle, 1985; Freire, 1970; Habermas, 1974). As Stephen Gilbert Brown and Sidney I. Dobrin (2004) write, critical ethnography moves

> beyond the issues of the postmodern critique that gave birth to it . . . beyond its engagement with this theoretical critique to reimmersion in critical praxis: a praxis that is theoretically informed, methodologically dialectical, and politically and ethically oriented given its concerns for transformative cultural action. It is critiquing its critics, liberating itself from the reductive, contradictory chains of postmodern signification, opening up new critical spaces for itself, evolving a critical praxis that is at once emergent and immersed.
>
> (p. 3)

MUSIC LISTENING BEYOND APPRECIATION

How does the above relate to music education? First, I want to discuss music history/music theory courses taught primarily as music-listening courses. On too many occasions, I have observed secondary school classrooms where actual music making and creating are entirely absent. By way of comparison, other classes were focused on action. I observed physical education classes where students were actively moving, running, and jumping, depending on the context of the sport being explored. I spent time in art history classes where students were using Picasso paintings as models for their own "cubist" works. In every other discipline, students were engaged in the hands-on actions at the heart of the subject's "knowledge" base. However, more often than not, music history classes/music theory classes devolved into music-listening classes where students were passive recipients of auditory patterns. When I asked a music teacher of a music-listening class if his students would ever engage in actual music making, he said: "These students aren't interested in making music. If they were, they'd join the band or choir." But when I talked with three students after their class, I found out quickly that they were deeply interested in making music (recall the epigraphs to this chapter).

Indeed, the music "listening" classes I just referred to fell into the "music appreciation" trap. Why trap? As conceived and practiced in North America, teaching and learning music education as "music appreciation" assumes that student listeners should be prepared to become passive consumers. Students in music appreciation classrooms are most often expected to "sit and listen" quietly to pieces, and learn to identify the formal elements (i.e., melody, harmony, rhythm, timbre, texture, and form) of musical sound structures. Another assumption of this approach is that musical-structural acuity and verbal information about music prepares students for deep "aesthetic

Silverman disagrees

experiences" and greater/respect for masterpieces. Regelski (2006) articulates the reasons I reject this concept of music-listening instruction:

> Music appreciation, as a paradigm, assigns . . . reverent, informed, disciplined seriousness of connoisseurship established in connection with the aesthetic paradigm of "appreciating" classical music—namely, studying history and theory and other information "about" the music that . . . teachers have come to believe is the prerequisite "training" for "understanding" and thereby properly "appreciating" any music.
>
> (p. 285)

Aside from the passive, "data-banking" concept of education (Freire, 1970) that underpins music appreciation, it is highly arguable that the more one accumulates verbal information about and aural acuity for musical elements, the more deeply one will respond emotionally to music. For one thing, copious contemporary scholarship on the complex relationships between music and emotions (e.g., Juslin & Sloboda, 2001; Elliott & Silverman, 2012) does not support this claim. For another thing, billions of people worldwide respond deeply to music without any formal knowledge of musical elements and/or musical form and structure. Moreover, musical emotions are aroused by numerous variables that are not restricted to intramusical relationships (Elliott & Silverman, 2012). This does *not* mean that listening for musical elements is → *good point* unimportant; it means that there is a great deal more to understanding, valuing, responding to, and engaging emotionally in music than verbal information about and aural acuity for elements in sonic-musical structures can ever provide. Also, music appreciation methods often seek students' consensus about the "the truth" or "true meaning" of musical examples, which music appreciation teachers attribute to musical elements. As Regelski (2006) writes:

> "Music appreciation as connoisseurship" (MAAC) has become, then, a major curricular paradigm of music educators (Regelski, 2003). In classroom music, students are often subjected to watered-down music history and theory on the uncritical assumption that such "background information" is necessary for understanding and thus appreciating "good" music. However, this paradigm is regularly extended to studying jazz, rock, folk, and certain other exoteric musics, as well—e.g. so-called world musics.
>
> (p. 291)

A major reason for the continuing survival of the music appreciation paradigm is the availability of music appreciation textbooks that eliminate options for music making (Forney and Machlis's *The Enjoyment of Music* is an example of a textbook designed to encourage students' "passive consumption" of musical works). Other standard music appreciation textbooks provide students with "maps" or "perception charts" for selected works that they follow as they listen, as well as bits of historical and theoretical information about each piece. Equally important in our current "age of testing," music appreciation textbooks often include summative "evaluation charts" that test students' listening abilities in relation to pieces they have not studied during their courses. I recently talked with a colleague to query this very issue. She said: "Music history courses must be taught sequentially. And, they must focus on the objective qualities found in the music 'itself.' That is the way the textbooks work and that is what schools and parents expect."

I insist that we can and must do much better. As Phil Ford (2006) writes: "The 'appreciation' mode of pedagogy appears to imply values of transcendence and universality, and . . . these values are deeply out-of-fashion" (p. 31). This applies to all styles of music under consideration. Instead, music education ought to teach listening (a) in the context of all forms of music making (or "musicing": performing, composing, improvising, arranging, and conducting as related to specific musical practices) and (b) with selected recordings related to and that expand students' experiences outward. Music education without musicing is not music education at all. It is an abstract, commodified, cookie-cutter notion of the natures and values of music   *Big statement*

> whereby people who have greater authority, cultural capital or rhetorical skills (teachers, critics) tell others (students, fans) what they ought to be listening to (classical music, authentic rock) according to a single scale value. The presumption is that what they should be hearing is somehow better for them, although it is rare to find anyone attempting to explain just how or why this improvement will take place
> (Ford, 2006, p. 32).

This is where critical ethnography can help pave the way for improved pedagogies of music history and music theory classes that are transformative. I have written elsewhere about how critical ethnography can be utilized to transform music classrooms for praxis (Silverman, 2013). I explored how teachers and students can marshal strategies to create a space that contributes to personal/group empowerment and positive transformation. Indeed, music students tend to be marginalized and/or "silenced" (if not oppressed) during their schooling by (a) the large school bureaucracies that characterize contemporary American public education and (b) the exclusionary, "top-down" teaching methods driven by the priorities of American "marketplace education" and its corollaries, namely high-stakes testing and business-accounting procedures. Further marginalization can be found in urban schools located in low socioeconomic areas, because students in these contexts often experience inequitable conditions of all kinds (see Noguera, Ginwright, & Cammarota, 2006). These characteristics of American education and their deleterious effects on students and teachers have been thoroughly studied and supported by leading American educational scholars (e.g. Anyon, 1997; Apple, 2001, 2003; Bell, Joshi, & Zuniga, 2007; Cochran-Smith, 2004, 2005; Darling-Hammond, 2004).

Strong Quote

A music classroom, regardless of its title or orientation (whether, say, music history, music theory, or music appreciation; band, choir, or orchestra; laptop ensemble, or chamber ensemble) and location (rural, suburban, urban) should be a space that functions as *communitas*—a space in which students and teachers are free to clarify their individual and collective powers of sharing, each gaining a greater sense of their own and other's personhood in a context of social equality, solidarity, and togetherness. Critical ethnographies of music classrooms can help to create places where teachers and students can activate their music learning activities as social acts of becoming; where, through music, teachers and students can go beyond what *is* to what *can be*. This must happen with and for students *and* teachers together. As a community, students and teachers can decide ways of musically experiencing the world.

Critical ethnographies can support the above aims and activities because critical ethnographies do not "act on" teachers and students. Critical ethnography is a participatory pedagogy for transformative action. McLaren (1995) explains: "Critical ethnography must be *organic to* and not *administered upon* the plight of struggling peoples" (italics in original, p. 291). Critical ethnography breaks from traditional qualitative research traditions where the researcher engages in research "on" something or someone (banking concepts of teacher-student relationships function this way, too). Instead, critical ethnography is an emancipatory stance; it is research "with," as in a reflexive engagement where researcher and researched are part of the dialogical process together (recall Freire's "problem-posing" concept of education mentioned earlier). The researcher is as much a "subject" of the research as are the participants of the study; the participants of the study are afforded opportunities to help conceive the aims, focus, and purpose of the research, including the questions and design. Through the research process, the boundaries between researcher and researched are blurred. Both the researcher and the researched consider the problematics that need to be challenged. Critical ethnography empowers teachers and students to problematize the assumptions that often constitute what students and teachers conceive as music, personhood, and research (Madison, 2012).

CONSIDERATIONS

Scholars in music education ask teachers and teacher educators to value excellence *and* equity (Bradley, 2007). This is a just cause. However, the issues facing teachers in settings of disenfranchised learners are worrisome in scope and complexity. Because critical ethnography is a means of exposing, unpacking, and attacking inequities, we can utilize its tools for the benefits of many: "We must ask ourselves, To what end are we employing certain regimes of knowledge, and who or what is being heard or silenced?" (Madison, 2012, p. 111). Again, Madison (2012) asks us to consider questions such as, What good will this research do? Who will benefit and who won't? I would argue that by engaging in critical ethnographies, we all benefit. As music educators and researchers, we must invite students and colleagues to join conversations about serious questions and ask ourselves collectively:

1. How do music educators and music education students "reflect upon and evaluate our own purpose, intentions, and frames of analysis"?
2. How do music educators and music education students "predict consequences or evaluate our own potential to do harm"?
3. How do music educators and music education students "create and maintain a dialogue of collaboration in our projects between ourselves and Others"?
4. "How is the specificity of the local ["musical"] narrative relevant to the broader meanings and operations of the human condition"?
5. "How—in what location or through what intervention—will [music educators' and music education students'] work make the greatest contribution to equity, freedom, and justice"? (adapted from Madison, 2012, pp. 4–5).

All these questions, I suggest, are open to, and opened by, the deep analyses and the personally and socially transformative powers of critical ethnography.

NOTES

1. See www.musicalfutures.org
2. For those unfamiliar with Freire's (1970) banking concept of education, it maintains that some educators "turn [students] into 'containers,' into 'receptacles' to be 'filled' by the teacher. The more completely she fills the receptacles, the better a teacher she is. The more meekly the receptacles permit themselves to be filled, the better the students they are. Education like this becomes an act of depositing, in which the students are depositories and the teacher is the depositor" (p. 72).
3. While one could claim that many teachers are advocates for the oppressed, we must be careful to note distinctions between taking action, doing research, and engaging in "action research" projects that utilize critical ethnography as a tool for investigation.
4. Discussions of praxis in music education are found in the following: Elliott, 1995, 2012; Bowman, 2000; Allsup, 2003; Regelski, 2005; Jorgensen, 2005; Silverman, 2013; Elliott & Silverman, 2014..

REFERENCES

Allsup, R. (2003). Praxis and the possible: Thoughts in the writings of Maxine Greene and Paulo Freire. *Philosophy of Music Education Review, 11*(2), 157–69.
Anderson, G. (1989). Critical ethnography in education: Origins, current status, and new directions. *Review of Educational Research, 59*(3), 249–70.
Anyon, J. (1997). *Ghetto schooling: A political economy of urban educational reform.* New York, NY: Teachers College Press.

Appiah, K. A. (2005). *The ethics of identity.* Princeton, NJ: Princeton University Press.

Apple, M. (2001). *Educating the right way: Markets, standards, god, and inequality.* New York, NY: Routledge/Falmer.

Apple, M. (2003, Spring). Competition, knowledge, and the loss of educational vision. *Philosophy of Music Education Review,* 3–22.

Arendt, H. (1998). *The human condition.* Chicago, IL: University of Chicago Press. (Original work published 1958)

Aristotle. (1985). *Nichomachean ethics* (T. Irwin, Trans.). Indianapolis, IN: Hackett.

Bell, A. (2012). *Homemade records: A multiple case study of the role of recording technology in the music-making processes of informally trained musicians.* (Unpublished dissertation) New York University.

Bell, L. A., Joshi, K. Y., & Zuniga, X. (2007). Racism, immigration, and globalization curriculum design. In M. Adams, L. A. Bell, & P. Griffin (Eds.), *Teaching for diversity and social justice* (pp. 145–66). New York, NY: Routledge.

Bernstein, R. (2011). *Beyond objectivism and relativism: Science, hermeneutics, and praxis.* Philadelphia, PA: University of Pennsylvania Press.

Bowman, W. (2000). Discernment, respons/ability, and the goods of philosophical praxis. *Action, Criticism and Theory for Music Education, 1*(1). Retrieved from http://act.maydaygroup.org/articles/Bowman1_1a.pdf

Bowman, W. (2012). Practices, virtue ethics, and music education. *Action, Criticism, and Theory for Music Education, 11*(2). Retrieved from http://act.maydaygroup. org/articles/Bowman11_2.pdf

Bradley, D. (2007). The sounds of silence: Talking race in music education. *Action, Criticism, and Theory for Music Education, 6*(4), 132–62. Retrieved from http:// act.maydaygroup.org/articles/Bradley6_4.pdf

Brown, S. G. & Dobrin, S. I. (2004). Introduction. New writers of the cultural sage: From postmodern theory shock to critical praxis. In S. G. Brown & S. I. Dobrin (Eds.), *Ethnography unbound* (pp. 1–12). Albany, NY: State University of New York Press.

Carspecken, P. F. (1996). *Critical ethnography in educational research: A theoretical and practical guide.* New York, NY: Routledge.

Cochran-Smith, M. (2004). *Walking the road: Race, diversity, and social justice in teacher education.* New York, NY: Teachers College Press.

Cochran-Smith, M. (2005). The new teacher education: For better or worse? *Educational Researcher, 34*(7), 3–17.

Cook, K. (2008). Critical ethnography. In *The SAGE encyclopedia of qualitative research methods.* Retrieved from www.credoreference.com/entry/sagequalrm/critical_ethnography

Cox, R. (2002). *The political economy of a plural world: Critical reflection on power, morals, and civilization.* New York, NY: Routledge.

Dardar, A. (2002). *Reinventing Paolo Freire: A pedagogy of love.* Boulder, CO: Westview Press.

Darling-Hammond, L. (2004). From "separate but equal" to "No Child Left Behind": The collision of new standards and old inequalities. In D. Meier & G. Wood (Eds.), *Many children left behind* (pp. 3–32). Boston, MA: Beacon Press.

DeLorenzo, L. (2012a). *Sketches in democracy: Notes from an urban classroom.* New York, NY: Rowman & Littlefield Publishing.

DeLorenzo, L. (2012b). Missing faces from the orchestra: An issue of social justice? *Music Educators Journal, 98*(4), 39–46.

Denzin, N. K. (2003). *Performance ethnography: Critical pedagogy and the politics of culture.* Thousand Oaks, CA: Sage.

Elliott, D. J. (1995). *Music matters: A new philosophy of music education.* New York, NY: Oxford University Press.

Elliott, D.J. (2012). Music education as/for artistic citizenship. *Music Educators Journal, 99*(1), 21–7.

Elliott, D.J., & Silverman, M. (2012). Rethinking philosophy, re-viewing musical-emotional experiences. In W. Bowman & A.L. Frega (Eds.), *The Oxford handbook of philosophy in music education* (pp. 37–62). New York, NY: Oxford University Press.

Elliott, D. J., & Silverman, M. (2014). *Music matters: A philosophy of music education.* New York, NY: Oxford University Press.

Elpus, K., & Abril, C. (2011). High school music ensemble students in the United States: A demographic profile. *Journal of Research in Music Education, 59*(2), 128–45.

Everhart, R. (1983). *Reading, writing, and resistance: Adolescence and labor in a junior high school.* New York, NY: Routledge.

Ford, P. (2006). Appreciation without apologies. *College Music Symposium, 46,* 31–44.

Foucault, M. (2000). *Essential works, Vol. 1: Ethics.* London, UK: Penguin Books.

Freire, P. (1970). *Pedagogy of the oppressed* [Pedagogía del oprimido.]. New York, NY: Herder and Herder.

Freire, P. (1998). *Teachers as cultural workers: Letters to those who dare to teach.* Boulder, CO: Westview.

Geertz, C. (1973). *The interpretation of culture.* New York, NY: Basic Books.

Green, L. (2002). *How popular musicians learn: A way ahead for music education.* London, United Kingdom: Ashgate.

Green, L. (2006). Popular music education in and for itself, and for "other" music: Current research in the classroom. *International Journal of Music Education, 24*(2), 101–18.

Habermas, J. (1971). *Knowledge and human interests* (J. Shapiro, Trans.). Boston, MA: Beacon Press.

Habermas, J. (1974). *Theory and practice* [Theorie und Praxis]. London, United Kingdom: Heinemann.

Habermas, J. (1996). *Between facts and norms: Contributions to a discourse theory of law and democracy.* Cambridge, MA: MIT Press.

Higgins, C. (2011a). *The good life of teaching: An ethics of professional practice.* Hoboken, NJ: Wiley-Blackwell.

Higgins, C. (2011b). The possibility of public education in an instrumental age. *Educational Theory, 61*(4), 451–66.

Jaffurs, S. (2004). The impact of informal music learning practices in the classroom, or how I learned how to teach from a garage band. *International Journal of Music Education, 22*(3), 189–200.

Jones, P. (2007). Returning music education to the mainstream: Reconnecting with the community. *Visions of Research in Music Education. 7*(1). Retrieved from www.usr.rider.edu/~vrme/v7n1/visions/Jones%20Returning%20Music%20Education%20to%20the%20Mainstream.pdf

Jorgensen, E. (2005). Four philosophical models of the relation between theory and practice. *Philosophy of Music Education Review, 13*(1), 21–6.

Juslin, P.N., & Sloboda, J. (2001). *Music and emotion: Theory and research.* New York, NY: Oxford University Press.

Kinchloe, J., & McLaren, P. (2002). Rethinking critical theory and qualitative research. In Y. Zou & E.T. Trueba (Eds.), *Ethnography and schools: Qualitative approaches to the study of education* (pp. 87–138). New York, NY: Rowman & Littlefield Publishing.

Kuzmich, J., & Dammers, R. (2013). Alternative music. *SBO: School Band and Orchestra.* Retrieved from www.sbomagazine.com/431228/technology/alternative-music/

Ladson-Billings, G. (1995). But that's just good teaching! The case for culturally relevant pedagogy. *Theory Into Practice, 34*(3), 159–65.

Lucas, T., & Robinson, J. (2003). Reaching them early: Identifying and supporting prospective teachers. *Journal of Education for Teaching, 29*(2), 159–75.

Madison, D. S. (2012). *Critical ethnography: Method, ethics, and performance.* Thousand Oaks, CA: Sage.

Malinowski, B. (1947). *Dynamics of culture change: An inquiry into race relations in Africa.* New Haven, CT: Yale University Press.

Marx, K. (1857/1973). *Grundrisse* (M. Nicolaus, Trans.). London, United Kingdom: Penguin. (Original work published 1857)

Marx, K., & Engels, F. (1978). *The Marx-Engels reader* (2nd edition; R. Tucker, Ed.). New York, NY: W. W. Norton.

McLaren, P. (1995). Collisions with otherness: "Traveling" theory, postcolonial criticism, and the politics of ethnographic practice—the missions of the wounded ethnographer. In P. McLaren and J. Giarelli (Eds.), *Critical theory and educational research* (pp. 271–300). Albany, NY: SUNY Press.

Mead, G. H. (1934). *Mind, self, society.* Chicago, IL: Chicago University Press.

Myers, D. (2007). Freeing music education from schooling: Toward a lifespan perspective on music learning and teaching. *International Journal of Community Music, 1*(1), 49–61.

Noblit, G. W. (2004). Reinscribing critique in educational ethnography: Critical and postcritical ethnography. In K. DeMarrais & S. D. Lapan (Eds.), *Foundations for research: Method of inquiry in education and the social sciences.* Mahwah, NJ: Lawrence Erlbaum.

Noblit, G. W., Flores, S. Y., & Murillo, E. G. (2004). *Postcritical ethnography: Reinscribing critique.* Cresskill, NJ: Hampton Press.

Noddings, N. (2002). *Starting at home: Caring and social policy.* Berkeley: University of California Press.

Noddings, N. (2005). *The challenge to care in schools: An alternative approach to education.* New York, NY: Teachers College Press.

Noguera, P., Ginwright, S. A., & Cammarota, J. (2006). *Beyond resistance! Youth activism and community change: New democratic possibilities for practice and policy for America's youth.* New York, NY: Routledge.

Park, R. (1932). *The university and the community of races.* Honolulu, HA: University of Hawaii Press.

Prier, P. (2012). *Culturally relevant teaching.* New York, NY: Peter Lang.

Quantz, R A (1992). On Critical Ethnography with some Postmodern Considerations. In M.D. LeCompte, W.L. Millroy, & J. Preissle, *The Handbook of Qualitative Research in Education* (pp. 447–505). San Diego: Academic Press, Incorporated.

Quiocho, A., & Rios, F. (2000). The power of their presence: Minority group teachers and schooling. *Review of Educational Research, 70*(4), 485–528.

Radcliff-Brown, A. R. (1952). *Structure and function in primitive society, essays and addresses.* London, United Kingdom: Cohen & West.

Radigan, J. (2002). The class clown: A school laminar. In Y. Zou & E. T. Trueba (Eds.), *Ethnography and schools: Qualitative approaches to the study of education* (pp. 257–80). New York, NY: Rowman & Littlefield Publishing.

Randles, C. (2012). Music teacher as writer and producer. *Journal of Aesthetic Education, 46*(3), 36–52.

Regelski, T. (2005). Music and music education: Theory and praxis for "making a difference." *Educational Philosophy and Theory, 37*(1), 7–27.

Regelski, T. (2006). Music appreciation as praxis. *Music Education Research, 8*(2), 281–310.

Schwandt, T. A. (2007). *The Sage dictionary of qualitative inquiry.* Los Angeles, CA: Sage.

Silverman, M. (2013). A critical ethnography of democratic music listening. *British Journal of Music Education, 30*(1), 7–25.

Thomas, J. (1993). *Doing critical ethnography.* Newbury Park, CA: Sage.

Veblen, K., Messenger, S., Silverman, M., & Elliott, D. J. (2013). *Community music today.* Lanham, MD: Rowman & Littlefield.

Volk, T. (2004). *Music, education, and multiculturalism: Foundations and principles.* New York, NY: Oxford University Press.

Williams, B. (1985). *Ethics and the limits of philosophy.* Cambridge, MA: Harvard University Press.

Willis, P. E. (1977). *Learning to labour: How working class kids get working class jobs.* Farnborough, United Kingdom: Saxon House.

Wolcott, H. F. (2002). Ethnography? Or educational travel writing? In Y. Zou & E. T. Trueba (Eds.), *Ethnography and schools: Qualitative approaches to the study of education* (pp. 27–48). New York, NY: Rowman & Littlefield Publishing.

17 Application of Sound Studies to Qualitative Research in Music Education

Joseph Michael Abramo

Sounds matter. Think of the din of the music classroom and an array of sounds may come of mind:

- A teacher's voice as she lectures on triads;
- A recording of *Rite of Spring*;
- A rehearsal of Holst's *Second Suite*, complete with incorrect rhythms and pitches, followed by the teacher's verbal directions on how to fix those errors;
- The cacophonous sound of students working in groups on original compositions, including musical experimentation and students' disagreements and laughter;
- The buzz of florescent lights, coughs, and stirring in an otherwise silent room during an examination.

What can sounds reveal about how students and teachers communicate, gather meaning, and learn? How can researchers incorporate sound into the frameworks, fieldworks, and presentations of empirical research?

These questions may be answered by looking to the growing field commonly referred to as "sound studies." As Sterne (2012) notes, "*Sound studies* is a name for the interdisciplinary ferment in the human sciences that takes sound as its analytical point of departure or arrival" (p. 2). Sometimes known as "aurality" (Erlmann, 2010) or "auditory culture" (Bull & Back, 2004), sound studies:

> can begin from obviously sonic phenomena like speech, hearing, sound technologies, architecture, art, or music. But it does not have to. It may think sonically as it moves underwater, through the laboratory or into the halls of government; considers religion or nationalisms old and new; explores cities; tarries with the history of philosophy, literature or ideas; or critiques relations of power, property or intersubjectivity.
>
> (Sterne, 2012, p. 2)

The field of sound studies encompasses more than merely studying sound; it is to "think sonically." Sound studies "challenge us to think across sounds, to consider sonic phenomena in relationship to one another—*as types of sonic phenomena rather than as things-in-themselves*—whether they be music, voices, listening, media, buildings, performances, or another path into sonic life" (Sterne, 2012, p. 3, italics in original).

Investigating some of these themes and questions addressed in sound studies provides music education researchers new avenues of inquiry. In this paper, I explore how the epistemology, nature, and history of sound and listening's conception may provide new theoretical frameworks, including what I am calling here "individual" and "critical-historical" phenomenologies. Second, I suggest how these frameworks of sound and listening may provide new ways for researchers to conceive fieldwork, including considering ethnographic sites as found *soundscapes* (Schafer, 1994; Thompson, 2002) and what sound and listening may reveal about the collection and interpretation of "data," including the dilemmas of verbal and musical transcription. Third, I explore how researchers may incorporate sounds and listening into their presentations of research through researcher-created compositional soundscapes (Drever, 2002; Samuels et al., 2010; Truax, 2000). Throughout this paper, I hold the individual and critical-historical phenomenologies in tension with one another, exploring what each of them says about the stages of the research process I outline here. Because each of these topics are complicated, producing many articles and books on each facet, this paper serves as a starting point of dialogue on the role of sound in qualitative empirical research in music education.

THE PHENOMENOLOGY OF SOUND

Traditionally, inquiry into sound has focused on sound as a phenomenon separate from listeners, and has categorized it as an object or event. As O'Callaghan and Nudds (2009) note, "According to common sense tutored by science, sounds just are traveling waves" (p. 7), or what O'Callaghan (2009) calls the "*Wave View*" (p. 27). These waves are created by a physical body and, therefore, can be construed as secondary properties of that physical body, or what is called the "*Property View*" (O'Callaghan, 2009, p. 27). In other words, though sounds are a direct result of the vibration of this physical object, they are still distinct from those vibrations. But, because the vibrating objects take time to travel to their listeners, the "*event view*" (O'Callaghan, 2009, p. 36) suggests that sounds are not properties but *events,* because sound is necessarily temporal, happening over a time. Sounds are "events in which a moving object disturbs a surrounding medium and sets it moving. The striking and crashings are not the sounds, but are the causes of sounds. The waves in the medium are not the sounds themselves, but are the effects of sounds" (O'Callaghan, 2009, p. 28).

These definitions are limited because they fail to account for the listener. The study of sound not from the perspective of its source, but from its perceiver and the focus on perception is commonly referred to as "phenomenology." There are two areas of phenomenology as related to sound and listening that I would like to outline here. The first is an "individual" (Chion, 1994, p. 81) phenomenology of listening, which holds that "sounds are subjective and private and that they mediate auditory perceptual access to the world" (O'Callaghan & Nudds, 2009, p. 5). This view looks at the essence of the listening experience, what is unique to it and what epistemology is revealed through the act of listening. Contrary to this view is, what I am calling here, a "critical-historical phenomenology," which does not hold that sounds are subjective and personal. Instead, this theory suggests that the nature of listening, how one listens, and even what one hears is constituted by larger historical and material conditions. Though these two views have some aspects in common, and some academics sometimes encompass both views in their writings, I intend to highlight the critical-historical and individual phenomenologies' differences in order to establish two broad and differing ways of situating the experience of listening.

Individual Phenomenology of Sound

According to legend, the Pre-Socratic philosopher Pythagoras required his students to sit in silence while he lectured from behind a screen for the first years of their instruction. It was supposed that this process, which was termed *akousmatikoi*, focused on students' listening, allowing them to concentrate on the meaning of Pythagoras's words without visual distraction. In the twentieth century, proponents of *musique concrète* took this ethos to create what they called *acousmatic* music, electronic music in which there is no visual stimuli (Schaeffer, 2012). Like Pythagoras, composers of acousmatic music believed that visual stimuli distracted audiences, not allowing audience access to "pure" listening. Underlying these practices is the assumption that music is, or should be, solely a sonic art, the senses can be separated, and visual stimuli taint the listening experience.

Along similar lines, some scholars have suggested that Western thought traditionally is "ocularcentric," or "'dominated' by vision" (Jay, 1993, p. 3). As historian of philosophy Jay (1993) suggests, metaphors like Plato's allegory of the cave, the enlightenment, Descartes' "steadfast mental gaze," and Foucault's panopticon and medical gaze, suggest that Western philosophy has favored vision over the other senses. Philosophy, he continues, "has tended to accept without question the traditional sensual hierarchy" (p. 187). But while Western thought has privileged sight over the other senses, there are limits to ocularcentrism. As Janus (2011) notes, ocularcentrism has at least three limitations. First, it creates a subject-object dichotomy where phenomena around the individual are considered as "separate" from the subject who views those phenomena. Second, it creates signification as the final perspective, meaning that vision creates the need for language to represent the objects that are visually "at hand." Third, this denies the corporal in the senses, reducing ontology to a disembodied eye that observes the world around it objectively and disinterestedly.

From an anti-ocular standpoint, then, experiencing the world through differing senses provides differing accesses and conceptions of phenomena. Aural perception reveals the world in ways significantly different than sight. As Idhe (1976) notes, "An inquiry into the auditory is also an inquiry into the invisible. Listening makes the invisible *present* in a way similar to the presence of the mute in vision" (p. 51). Listening allows individuals to access ways of knowing and perceiving unavailable through sight. "This deliberate change of emphasis from the visual to the auditory dimension at first symbolizes a hope to find material for a recovery of the richness of primary experience which is now forgotten or covered over in the too tightly interpreted visualist traditions" (Idhe, 1976, p. 14).

Goodman (2010) extends this study of the "invisible" to include all things. He suggests that the study of sound allows access to the larger phenomenon of vibrations, of which sound is a subset. "If we subtract human perception, everything moves. Anything static is so only at the level of perceptibility. At the molecular or quantum level, everything is in motion, is vibrating" (p. 83). These vibrational forces allow access to vibration and how phenomena interact with one another. Thus, "ontology of vibrational force delves below a philosophy of sound and the physics of acoustics toward the basic processes of entities affecting other entities" (p. 81).

French phenomenological philosopher Nancy (2006) also suggests that sound is a way of examining how entities affect one another. Nancy argues that while truth is construed through ocularcentric terms, epistemology is better conceived of as sound. Nancy takes an "event view" because sound arrives in an envelope; it has a beginning and an end, unlike the visual, which, even when one turns her eye from it, continues to exist. For Nancy, though, sound is phenomenological because it must also pass from subject to subject. As an instrument sounds, sympathetic objects, (like sympathetic strings, drums, even people) vibrate in accordance with that instrument. But in the process of taking up those sounds, the body changes them, just as the sympathetic strings of a sitar changes the timbre of the originally vibrating string. Nancy argues that this has implications for epistemology. Like individual bodies taking up and then changing sound, these bodies do the same with knowledge and information. Individuals make "sense" of truths through their subjectivity, interpret it, and in the process, change that information, and finally send it out again. At risk of over simplifying, then, truth is socially constructed; each individual contributes to that truth through their sense and understanding and then letting that truth be known to others.

The ideas of Idhe (1976), Goodman (2010), and Nancy (2006) suggest that sound has a unique way of apprehending and rendering phenomena and conceiving of epistemology. Their philosophies have the potential to add to the well-established strain of music education philosophy and advocacy, which seeks to discover the unique qualities of music and its education. If sound and listening are a unique way of knowing the world, then music education holds a unique place in the curriculum. But further, music education is not limited to sound itself. If, as Goodman (2010) suggests, sound and music provide access to the larger field of vibration, of which everything is made up, music education has the potential to be a holistic, transdisciplinary education. For Nancy (2006), sound is a conduit for constructivist theories of learning and education better than any other medium. Thus, investigating theories of the nature of sound allows music educators new ways to philosophize and advocate for the uniqueness of music education.

Critical-Historical Phenomenology of Sound

Before music educators can claim a victory for their discipline, as critics note, this individual phenomenology has limitations. For example, the notion of vision as "objective" and sound as "subjective" and Western society's prevailing "ocularcentrism" (Janus, 2011; Jay, 1993; Nancy, 2006) have come under scrutiny. Sterne (2003) suggests that listening has been used for so-called objective purposes. Auscultation—the procedure that involves physicians using stethoscopes—is the process of listening to the body to objectively diagnose ailments. He notes that Foucault's "medical gaze"—the objective, clinical, disinterested diagnosis of bodies—was just as aural as it was visual. Erlmann (2010), similarly, tracks the use of sound in the enlightenment. *Reasonance,* as he calls it—which is a "joining together of reason and resonance in a new conception of personhood" (p. 31)—can be found in ostensibly ocularcentric philosophers like Descartes. As a result, he claims that such anti-ocularcentric positions are false, and it "does not bear out the tenet that modernity is, at root, a period dominated by vision, images and distanced observation" (p. 341). The anti-visualist claims that sight is privileged over listening only succeed in "*re*-re-establishing the visual/auditory dichotomy" (Rice, 2005, p. 201).

As a result, instead of positing inherent essential qualities of listening—like sight is objective and listening is subjective—some sound studies scholars have investigated the historical and material conditions that give rise to certain values and ways of listening. Historical investigations of sound and listening differ from an individual phenomenology because they do not conceive of listening as a simple "auditory perceptual access to the world" (O'Callaghan & Nudds, 2009, p. 5), or an uncomplicated, unaffected reception of the outside sonic world. Sterne argues that "human ears aren't natural reflectors of sound in the world. They are themselves transducers that make reality—the perception of sound is not a mirror of nature. Therefore, perception in a way *makes* sounds, and it makes sounds differently from a microphone and a computer detecting vibrations out in the world" (quoted in Gopnick, 2013, p. 38). Instead, one's listening is shaped by others' ideas and meanings. As Chion (1994) suggests, "Perception is not a purely individual phenomenon, since it partakes in a particular kind of objectivity, that of shared perceptions" (p. 29).

Listening, rather than a mere apprehension of the sonic world, is an intricate process where the brain highlights certain sounds, and deemphasizes others. "The ears don't have eyelids" (Nancy, 2006, p. 14), laying it susceptible to the assault of sound at all times. So, unlike the eyelid, which shuts the sensation of sight from the eye via physical means, "the ear's only protection is an elaborate psychological mechanism for filtering out undesirable sound in order to concentrate on what is desirable" (Schafer, 1994, p. 11). What is rendered as desirable and undesirable and what one chooses to concentrate on are not inherent in their properties or idiosyncratic psychology, but are based on cultural norms and sociological factors.

A personal anecdote may illustrate this critical-historical theory that "shared perception" creates what and how individuals hear. When attending graduate school, the instructor of a course I enrolled in asked the students to "do an analysis" of Bach's "C Major Prelude" of the *Well Tempered Clavier* as an out-of-class assignment. Despite the lack of specificity, everyone performed a Roman numeral analysis, dutifully labeling each chord in the composition. My study of Schenkerian analysis led me to question this uniform response from the class. A sketch of this composition completed by Schenker (1933/1969) suggests that the prelude is a group of compound melodies, rather than simply a progression of arpeggiated chords. In other words, the sketch invites listeners to listen vertically, rather than horizontally, to use a visual metaphor. When I pointed out in class that despite other conceptions of hearing this piece all the students chose to attend to it chordally, one student, in a manner that struck me as agitated, blurted out, "But this piece *is* about chords!"

Here, then, is an example of how Roman numerals dictated what the agitated student, her classmates, and perhaps many schooled musicians heard in Bach's "C Major Prelude." Roman numerals are not a "subjective" experience, but are instead a shared, socially agreed-upon—some might say forced and enforced—way of listening to music. The act of continually performing Roman numeral analyses throughout the students' musical training influenced their hearing. It is possible to argue that Roman numerals encouraged the students to hear the music differently, rendering the melodic lines inaudible. In poststructuralist terms, Roman numerals serve as what Foucault (1972) called *discourses*. Roman numeral analysis serves as a hermeneutic that shapes how one understands the world around him- or herself. In this sense, Roman numeral analysis, like all music theory, is not only descriptive, but also *proscriptive* (Boretz, 1992). Music theory doesn't merely describe; it shapes and creates how and what one hears (Moreno, 2004).

This anecdote illustrates that listening is not purely "individual"; we do not hear and *then* meaning is attached to it, based on individual traits. Rather, historical conditions and discourses literally make people "tune out" some sounds and highlight others. This approach may be called a "critical-historical phenomenology." "Such an orientation," that acknowledges the influence of discourses and history upon people's ears, Goodman (2010) notes, "should be differentiated from a phenomenology of sonic effects centered on the perceptions of a human subject, as a ready-made, interiorized human center of being and feeling" (p. 81).

One area that a historical-critical approach to phenomenology has been particularly fruitful is in the area of sound reproduction technology. In the 20th century, inventors and scientists shifted their study of sound from conceiving of it as an *object* and the producers of sound to receivers of sound and *perception*, or effect. This ushered in advances in sound reproduction technologies. As Sterne (2003) notes, in the 19th century, before the advent of the telephone and phonograph, inventors and scientists created technology that copied the sources of sounds, like player pianos, and astronomer Johannes Faber's *euphon*, an automaton which was a reproduction of the human lungs and mouth to mimic speech. Following these unsuccessful attempts, sound reproduction became realized in its modern conception when inventors simulated the receiver of sounds—the tympanum, or eardrum. Inventor of the telephone Alexander Graham Bell, and the phonograph's inventor Thomas Edison, both copied the ear, using tympanums as ways to capture and then re-realized sound waves emitted in the air. As a result, tympanums are used in sound reproduction: the diaphragm of a microphone and phone receivers to "capture" the sound, and speakers to vibrate the re-realizing of the vibrations captured by the microphone and receivers. Sterne (2003) uses the body to conceptualize this shift from object to perception and from source to effect as a shift from the "mouth to ear." The conception of sound as listening—in other words, as perception rather than production—precipitated the advent of sound technology.

Similarly, in sound technology, *acousmatic* listening in the 20th century, the attempt to eliminate visual stimuli from musical performances, was aided, in part, by the creation of sound reproduction. Schafer (1994) calls this "splitting of sounds from their original contexts . . . *schizophonia*" (p. 88). But technology alone does not explain this impulse to divorce sound from vision. Instead, it was also a modernist desire towards aesthetic "abstractionism" or the "absence of representation" (Albright, 2004, p. 11). And, as Pythagoras's acousmatic lectures suggest, this desire to divorce listening from vision was not created by sound reproduction technology. Thus, advancement alone cannot account for acousmatic music and the privileging of sound and the elimination of vision from the musical experience, as such a view would be described as "technologically determinist" (e.g., Borgmann, 2006). Instead, acousmatic music is a product of the interaction of technological advances with certain privileged discourses.

Inquiries of a similar nature can be of interest to music education researchers. Critical-historical avenues of inquiry might include questions like the following: How do advances in technology influence the ways music educators understand the phenomenology of sound? How do advances in technology influence the ways music educators engage with this phenomenology? The opposite is also a viable question: In what ways do historical trends of the phenomenology of sound in music education affect the use of technology? Questions broader than the application of technology might include: What historical conditions contribute to teacher and students' actions and beliefs? And, why and how are certain forms of listening and performance valued over another at any particular time in the history of music education?

COLLECTING, GENERATING, AND INTERPRETING DATA: FOUND SOUNDSCAPES AND NOISE

While sound studies provides varying conceptions of the epistemology and nature of sound and listening, it also affords music education researchers new ways of conducting fieldwork, particularly attending to sounds of an environment. Because of the increased accessibility to portable audio equipment, fieldwork has evolved to include the documentation of sounds. And although, as I will discuss below, a critical-historical position suggests that audio recordings are not a direct "capture" and then "reproduction" of these sounds, but, instead, requires socially learned sonic imagination, field recordings can serve new ways of presenting and analyzing the sounds found in the field.

Approaching fieldwork from a sound studies paradigm immediately brings into question the main way researchers describe fieldwork: as becoming a "participant *observer*." Traditionally, ethnographers have privileged seeing over listening (Samuels et al., 2010). But, as anthropologist Forsey (2010) suggests, "listening is at least as significant as observation to ethnographers. Ethnography is arguably more aural than ocular, the ethnographer more participant listener than observer" (p. 561). "Often what is reported [in ethnographies] as the 'seen' are in fact observations of people conversing, singing, listening, speechmaking—noise-making" (p. 563). In this sense, a researcher has to enter the field not as simply an eyewitness, but also as an "earwitness" (Schafer, 1994, p. 4); not as an observer, but, to use a neologism, as an *otoservers*.

Therefore, researchers might consider fieldwork as entering a sonic environment or what Schafer (1994) calls a *soundscape,* so they may turn their attention to an environment's "keynote sounds, signals, and soundmarks" (Schafer, 1994, p. 9). Thompson (2002) elaborates further. For her, a soundscape is:

> an auditory or aural landscape. Like a landscape, a soundscape is simultaneously a physical environment and a way of perceiving that environment; it is both a world and a culture constructed to make sense of that world. The physical aspects of a soundscape consist not only of the sounds themselves, the waves of acoustical energy permeating

the atmosphere in which people live, but also the material objects that create, and sometimes destroy, those sounds. A soundscape's cultural aspects incorporate scientific and aesthetic ways of listening, a listener's relationship to their environment, and the social circumstances that dictate who gets to hear what. A soundscape, like a landscape, ultimately has more to do with civilization than with nature, and as such, it is constantly under construction and always undergoing change.

(Thompson, 2002, pp. 1–2)

Soundscapes are political spaces rendered through sound: "The general acoustic environment of a society can be read as an indicator of social conditions which produce it and may tell us much about the trending and evolution of that society" (Schafer, 1994, p. 7).

Approaching classrooms and other places of learning as soundscapes allows researchers to attend to the sounds produced in that environment and to generate sociological explanations. The sounds of bells to signal the beginnings and ends of class periods, teacher- and student-talk, even the timbres of the instrument used, all arise because of economic, historical, and political influences. The bells are a vestige of progressive education's aim to train future factory workers. How often teachers talk compared to how often their students talk, in addition to what they say, can reveal not only the power dynamics in a classroom, but also how students are enculturated into society. Which instruments are used, how instruments are played, as well as the tone quality of the students' and teacher's singing voices can signal what genres, playing techniques, and aesthetics are privileged over others. Listening to and for the soundscape reveals an acoustical environment in new ways and can enrich fieldwork.

Noise

Perhaps the best way of finding the political and sociological aspects of a soundscape is by attending to noise. Although there are a variety of definitions of noise (Thompson, 2002)—as a neutral synonym with sound, as unintelligible or unimportant sounds, or as irritating sounds—Schafer's definitions serve as a starting point: "Noise is any undesired . . . [or] undesirable sound" (1986, p. 110) and "Noises are the sounds we have learned to ignore" (1994, p. 4). But these definitions leave the question, how does a sound become undesirable? The line between noise and music and other desirable sounds is thin and porous, and its placement is political. As Attali (1986) notes, "Any theory of power today must include a theory of the localization of noise and its endowment with form. . . . Noise is inscribed from the start within the panoply of power" (p. 6).

Prima facie, noises are unavoidable intrusions in fieldwork. They distract the researcher, making it difficult to concentrate. They interrupt and mask important sounds, rendering them inaudible and unintelligible. But attending to noise as artifacts of politics, rather than as commonsensical annoyances, reveals research sites in new ways. As Attali (1986) notes, "Our science has always desired to monitor, measure, abstract, and castrate meaning, forgetting that life is full of noise. . . . [But] nothing essential happens in the absence of noise" (p. 3). Noise is not senseless; it is data. "Noise may well interrupt or disturb; but we do not see that this need be a problem for the qualitative researcher—it may even be an opportunity" (Hall, Lashua, & Coffey, 2008, p. 1036). Thus, listening to the noise that one either consciously or unconsciously filters out of her aural experiences is valuable.

From this viewpoint, music classrooms are spaces of noise. And if, as Schafer (1994) notes, "the ear demands that insouciant and distracting sounds would be stopped in order that it may concentrate on those which truly matter" (p. 12), then attention to the processes people go through to learn what to attune to and what to ignore in classrooms could provide interesting avenues of research. Practicing teachers are required to ignore many sounds they hear. This includes extraneous sounds in performance, like the clicking of keys, string sounds on guitars, and exhalation during singing. But noisealso resides in classroom management including which sounds from students are ignored or addressed either positively or negatively. Teachers are required to distinguish students' "distracting" talk and sounds from positive contributions to class. This ability to distinguish amongst and to control the sounds in the classroom is one of authority: "Eavesdropping, censorship, recording, and surveillance are weapons of power" (Attali, 1986, p. 7). And "power reduces the noise made by others and adds sound prevention to its arsenal" (Attali, 1986, p. 122). Thus, what teachers label as noise is not a trivial, commonsensical decision; it is an act of authority and its use is a question of ethics. These ethics are a concern for researchers, too. I will return to this at the end of the chapter.

As an example, elsewhere (Abramo, 2011) I have suggested that in popular music settings boys often choose to rehearse in a constant wash of sound. Educators unfamiliar with the practices of rock musicians and their rehearsal techniques might find this "distracting"—as noise. But for the boys, this dizzying sonic environment was integral to their musical thought processes as well as how they communicated. What is noise to the teacher is the residue of musical learning and communication for the students. A teacher's well-intentioned attempt to silence this communication because it does not reflect the order typically found in classrooms, and because she deems it distracting, would be a disservice to her students and is a reflection of her power in the classroom.

While teachers are required to ignore or accept sounds and this is a political act, music teacher education has no formalized or theoretical way of addressing what teachers should "tune out." NASM accreditation requires preservice music education curricula to include courses in music theory, history, sight singing, ear training, and conducting in order to "sharpen the ear." They guide and focus the ear for what to listen to: to hear chord progressions, melodies, formal structures, stylistic nuances, and detection of errors. But this specificity is not lent to the ways educators ignore sounds. Asking students to reflect on what and how they define and then filter out noise and its political and sociological causes and effects can be another avenue towards informed practice.

Attention to noise, then, serves at least two purposes: it allows teacher educators ways of conceptualizing how to guide music education students through the noisy terrain of classrooms, allowing them not only to be conscious of what and how they attune their ears, but also to be cognizant to what they label as "noise" and choose to ignore or correct. With this, however, is the acknowledgement that noise is not objective, but is, instead, a political act that is based on historical and material conditions. Thus, what teachers label as "noise"—students' "excessive" talking, "playing out of turn," and "extraneous" and "irksome" sounds—may be a mechanism for control and silencing of students. Second, it allows those who do participant "observation" a more comprehensive way of attending to soundscapes. "Noise," rather than being intrusions upon hearing important information, is data in itself, and perhaps as an irony, by attending to noises in this way, they cease to be noise; they become wanted sounds.

A Critique of Soundscapes and Noise

Despite the advantages of conceiving fieldwork as entering soundscapes and attending to all its sounds, including noise, there is a danger of only reordering, not eliminating, the ocularcentric hierarchy. Instead, Pink (2009) argues for a conscious effort to include all the senses in ethnography. It would be impossible, if not foolish, to ignore other senses. In fieldwork, what researchers see, smell, and taste is as important as what they hear (Pink, 2009). Therefore, researchers might aim to create a "democracy of the senses" (Bull & Back, 2004, p. 2), and perhaps attention towards the listening in the research process simply allows the ear "an unromanticized place alongside the eye" (Erlmann, 2004, p. 5) in qualitative research. This may require a multimodal approach (see Chapter 7, this volume). People communicate simultaneously through several modes: visual, written language, physical movement, aural, verbal language including inflection, musical, and tactile. Research should not dismiss the ways these differing communication strategies intersect.

While it is reasonable and valuable for researchers to rely on all their senses, this critique opens up the question of priorities in music education. It can be argued that, more than any other discipline found in schooling, music education is the study of sound. And because of this, music education researchers must take sound and listening seriously, and perhaps privilege it above the other senses. If a goal of music educators is to help students listen more intently, to provide avenues for people to gleam meaning from sound, and in particular music, then music education practitioners and researchers ostensibly privilege sound and listening above the other phenomena and senses, or at least logically they *should*. So, while there are good arguments to include all the senses, the question remains open of whether researchers should privilege music education's *raison d'état*—namely, sound—to all facets of scholarship.

Transcription and Analysis

After researchers have entered soundscapes, attended to noise and other sounds, and taken field recordings and notes, they usually begin the process of transcription and analysis. But how should researchers attend to the act of transcription, which translates sound into silent and visual notation? As Oliver, Serovich, and Mason (2005) note, there are two ways to approach transcription: "naturalism, in which every utterance is captured in as much detail as possible, and . . . denaturalism, in which grammar is corrected, interview noise (e.g., stutters, pauses, etc.) is removed and non-standard accents (i.e., non-majority) are standardized" (p. 1273). In denaturalized transcription, transcribers clearly "edit" the material. But, even with a naturalist approach, transcription is an interpretive act because everything cannot be notated. The researcher may not attune to certain aspects of participants' speech, and this, therefore, makes transcription, too, a political act. For example, should transcriptions notate participants' diction, accent, pronunciation, nonverbal gestures, profanity, or involuntary noises like sneezing and coughing (Oliver, et al., 2005)? This process becomes more confounding when music is part of field recordings and notes. Should researchers transcribe the music that transpires in the classroom? To what degree should the transcriber be naturalistic and accurate in musical transcription? Should they then notate discrepancies in intonation, imperfections in tempo, or edit them to be a seemingly perfect performance?

The transcription of sound—whether it be verbal, musical, or other—into a notation in some sense "flattens" the sound, eliminating some of the information out of it. But sound is integral to verbal and musical communication, where inflection and other sonic clues change the meaning of the words or music. Ultimately, then, researchers should be aware that written speech and spoken speech are not equal in their communicative qualities and attention to *how* people vocalize is important data as well. Researchers may want to pay attention not only to what sound means in a linguistic sense, but also listen to data sonically and musically. This would be a shift away from "verbocentric" (Pink, 2009) renderings, and instead focus on how sound contributes to the meaning of verbal communication and other sounds.

Ultimately, the answer to "what to include in transcription" is to decide whether or not a particular aspect of sound is useful for a particular research inquiry. If it is important, then that aspect should be notated. For example, as Nettl (2005) notes, there are at least three types of transcriptions that reveal different aspects of music: "One gives us the events of one performance, and another attempts to give essence of a song or piece; perhaps a third provides what the culture might consider an ideal performance" (p. 81). Differing transcriptions of the same sounds render that sound differently and for varying purposes. There is no sense in transcribing students' "incorrect" performance if it is not part of the usefulness to the study or how the researcher hopes to frame the music or speech in his or her study. But, deciding what is "useful," of course, is deceptively difficult in qualitative research because, often, a researcher enters a field without a complete idea of what will be of interest. Transcribers might seek a "balance of thoroughness and elegance" (Nettl, 2005, p. 82), weighing their options of transcription. If researchers choose to transcribe spoken text and music, then they might not only consult the transcriptions when analyzing data. Instead, the inflection of talk, and the musical sounds and noise, which are "captured" in the audio field recordings, should be part of the analysis. Researchers might include transcribed text and audio and video recordings together as a multimodal way of presenting the research. Such attention to the sound of data will allow researchers to avoid strict verbocentrism and include sound in their analysis. But as I will discuss below, a critical-historical position suggests that referring to the audio recording, and to sounds in the field in general, are not a reference to "the real" communication in an attempt to circumvent interpretation, but rather to present social and political aspects.

(RE)PRESENTATION

As the issues surrounding transcription suggest, representation of research is important. If attention to sound is significant when gathering, generating, and interpreting data, then the representation of that data should attend equally to sound. How may researchers (re)create and represent the found soundscapes they researched sonically and musically?

Arts-based Research

Traditionally, research is exclusively represented in prose. Written as reports, research is rendered in concise unambiguous language, on paper, or the simulation of paper on computers and other media. But, starting in the 1990s, some researchers questioned this positivistic and prosaic representation of research and turned their attention to arts-based research. As Eisner (2003) notes, research in general has moved from the assumptions of quantification, experimental paradigms, research as the discovery of "true" knowledge, objectivity, statistical generalization, scientific inquiry, and simplistic and proscriptive application of research results to practice (pp. 210–15). Instead, arts-based researchers borrow from the arts to proliferate new and artistic forms of research; "Narratives, films, video, theater, even poems and collages can be used to deepen one's understanding of aspects of educational practice and its consequence" (Eisner, 2003, p. 210). Researchers can even add plays (Denzin, 2013; Saldaña, 2008) and cartoons (Bartlett, 2013) to this list.

How researchers present data is important because, as Eisner (2003) comments:

> form and meaning interact because the form in which ideas *appear* affects the kind of experience people will have. Hence, the use of forms of representation that previously had little or no place in research have been recognized as providing new meanings, something needed if understanding is to be enlarged.
>
> (p. 211, italics added)

Because of this, researchers need not make a false distinction between scientific research—which renders a "truth"—and the arts—which are merely aesthetic without truth claims. Instead, researcher can consider research methodologies on a continuum—a point I will return to shortly.

But we can extend Eisner's ideas by asking, "Why does research need to 'appear'"? If sound never appears, perhaps its research should not be visible as well. The form of audio recordings—ranging from raw field recordings, to soundscapes, to even musical compositions—enrich and change the ways researchers represent and gain meaning from data. These renderings are intended to display the ambiguity and polysemy of interpreting data and to make the material accessible to audiences beyond academics.

Some arts-education researchers have applied arts-based methodologies to their work. The *International Journal of Education and the Arts* has presented some of the visual arts data pictorially (Mans, 2000) and embedded audio into research reports (Bell, 2008). Gould (2010) has presented music and sound in new and interesting ways at conferences. How can music education researchers implement methodologies like these and others that implement sound? How can music educators present data so that it will stop *appearing* and start *resonating* with their audiences?

Researcher-Created Soundscapes

Again, *soundscapes* may provide avenues to reconceptualize representation of research and incorporate sound and music. Differing from Schafer (1994) and Thompson's (2002) description of soundscape as a found and studied auditory landscape, composers also use "soundscapes" to denote audio created from audio-recorded source material derived from environments to produce musical works. For purposes of clarity, I will refer to these as "researcher-created soundscapes" or "soundscape compositions" to distinguish them from "found soundscapes." As ethnomusicologist Feld (1994) notes, "Soundscape research really should be presented in the form of a musical composition. That is the one way to bend the loop back so that

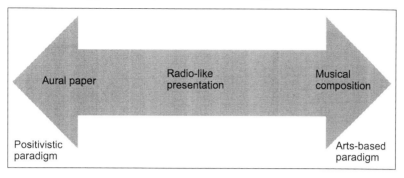

Figure 17.1   A continuum of implementing sound into research.

research and the artistry come together and we can auditorally cross those rivers and those creeks and climb those trees and walk those paths without the academic literalism, the print mediation" (p. 328). While soundscape compositions are intended as extracting sounds from an (usually natural) environment to create a musical composition, with some modifications, soundscapes can be useful to music education researchers (Drever, 2002).

As the figure displays, conceptualizing sound in research in continuum serves as a starting place to situate sounds and soundscapes. Researchers can vary their incorporation of sounds from embedding audio into traditional reports to musical compositions.

On one side, one closer to traditional and positivistic reports of research, a researcher could read a paper, perhaps inserting audio clips of field recordings and interviews, rather than transcribing them into text. On the other arts-based side, there could be strictly musical compositions, used to (re)present the environment without making explicit, language-based statements or theories about that environment. Somewhere in the middle could be something more akin to radio broadcasts like *Radiolab* and *This American Life,* which mix explanation and analysis with field and interview recordings.

The positivistic, radio-like, and artistic examples sit on a continuum and should not be conceived of as separate. Instead, researchers may blend and use them in the same study. There could be a study that is somewhere in between the radio-like and musical composition that combines field recordings, interview data, explanation, and interpretation of that data in prose as well as a researcher-generated musical composition comprised of data. Further, researchers may begin to think past the continuum by combining the poles. It may be possible to represent both a traditional aural report and an artistic composition of the same study side by side, using both sides of the continuum to polysemically (re)present the same phenomenon.

Rigor and Sound in Research

Whatever approaches researchers choose, ultimately, they have to answer to questions of academic rigor when producing these soundscapes. As Drever (2002) notes, "The challenge to soundscape composition artists is whether they can balance musical with representational concerns" (p. 26). To address this, Truax (2000) suggests four qualities of compositional soundscapes that may facilitate this rigor:

(a) listener recognizability of the source material is maintained, even if it subsequently undergoes transformation;
(b) the listener's knowledge of the environmental and psychological context of the soundscape material is invoked and encouraged to complete the network of meanings ascribed to the music;
(c) the composer's knowledge of the environmental and psychological context of the soundscape material is allowed to influence the shape of the composition at every level, and ultimately the composition is inseparable from some or all of those aspects of reality; and ideally,
(d) the work enhances our understanding of the world, and its influence carries over into everyday perceptual habits (Section IV. Conclusions).

These qualities are in accordance with general rules of rigor in qualitative research. Like quality *a*, researchers must attribute data to its source, whether it be the person or location that the researcher heard or observed that data. This remains true as the material "undergoes transformation," via transcription of text, or written description of what is observed. Like quality *b*, readers use prior knowledge when reading and interpreting a work, and researchers draw upon that knowledge. Like quality *c*, qualitative researchers acknowledge that their (re)presentation of data is not objective, but is filtered through their subjectivity and interpretation. And finally, like quality *d*, researchers hope that the research is useful and sharpens the audience's perception of the world. Truax's qualities of soundscape compositions resonate with some of the main tenets of qualitative research. From this perspective, researcher-created soundscapes allow two important functions. First, they allow the found soundscapes that were researched to "come alive" to the consumer, more than reading about them. Rather than describing the sound of a classroom, for example, the sounds are presented to the consumer. Second, they provide music educators—who, it would be assumed, are inclined towards aesthetics—to attend and present their studies artistically.

Critiques and Considerations

There are theoretical, logistical, and ethical considerations that may question the implementation of sound into research. First, a critical-historical investigation of research-created soundscapes reveals some assumptions.

Recordings are not a completely faithful rendering of sounds. Microphone placement, the medium (analogue—phonograph, audiotape; digital—wav and mp3), and processing of the audio necessarily "capture" and then render sounds differently. As Sterne (2003) notes, listening to recorded, "reproduced" sounds is not an access to "the real," but requires "audile technique" or sonic imagination to fill in the gaps of context and sounds that are literally not heard on the recording. Like listening in general, how a listener fills in these gaps is learned and constituted by social relations and material conditions. Thus, "'face-to-face' or 'live' sound events are a social practice fundamentally different from technological sound reproduction and its attendant forms of sound reproduction. It [is] not possible to sample the acoustic world, to audit an event, without participating in it" (Sterne, 2003, p. 284). Researcher-created soundscapes can never be an uncomplicated access to a found soundscape as suggested by Feld's (1994) belief that it allows the listener to "auditorally cross those rivers and those creeks and climb those trees and walk those paths without the academic literalism, the print mediation" (p. 328). Recordings do not relieve the researcher of the responsibilities of representation.

Recordings' limitations and assumptions are surmountable weaknesses. Researchers might exploit the assumed differences and relations between field recordings and what they "capture" by asking audiences to question the social relations of sound, technology, and verisimilitude. Their studies might be a space where the researcher draws attention to the social reaction between the listener, the recording, and the imagined found soundscapes they ostensibly represent. This might include recording sounds in multiple ways, like different media—mp3, wav, analog, even through the telephone—with different microphone placements, and with different processing—compression, equalizing, reverb—in order to draw attention to the artificiality of sound reproduction and the role recording medium plays in the interpretation. This may include playing the same recording several times, recontextualizing it to show the interpretation, imagination, and audio technique involved in listening to field recordings. In this way, soundscapes may be reflexive; they may call attention to the social transaction that takes place during the researchers' conveyance of the field to the audience.

Second, there are logistical barriers. Producing soundscapes requires different skills than research and writing. They require compositional experience, knowledge of recording software and hardware, and a way of crafting stories that is often found in radio. While some music education researchers may have these skills, they are not part of the traditional education of researchers and many may feel they lack the necessary skills and knowledge to compose soundscapes and incorporate sounds into their studies. But researchers must continually learn new skills, and there are resources to aid this process. Sites like Transom.org provide resources on how to create effective radio-like narratives and simple audio editing. Journals like *International Journal of Education & the Arts, Qualitative Research,* and

Qualitative Inquiry publish articles that implement cutting-edge methodologies that may inform research with sound.

Finally, field recordings' direct use reveals ethical considerations. Recordings may make it difficult to secure anonymity. Places where participants' names are revealed will have to be eliminated or edited. Even when identifiers are not spoken, the sound of person's voices may also reveal their identity. Therefore, researchers should be forthright with their participants and Institutional Review Boards (IRBs) about the use of audio recordings and the security of anonymity.

Also, as mentioned earlier, "eavesdropping, censorship, recording, and surveillance are weapons of power" (Attali, 1986, p. 7). Researchers hold the power of representation and can use recordings to surveil, censor, and control their subjects. While this is not an issue unique to sound in research (Miller et al., 2012), it adds another way researchers could unwittingly act unethically. Researchers may use commonly employed methodologies like gaining participants' approval of their representation, or what is called participant or member check-ins or co-constructing the study with the participants (Heron & Reason, 2006).

CONCLUSION

The interdisciplinary field of "sound studies" provides some avenues for research in music education. Phenomenological interpretations of sound allows for an investigation of the phenomena of sound and listening. An individual phenomenology can theorize the nature of perception, allowing music educators to philosophize and advocate for the unique qualities of music education. Conversely, a critical-historical account of listening provides ways of situating and explaining movements in music education as well as participants' beliefs of the listening and musical experience. Sound studies also invites researchers to attend to the sense of hearing in the collection of data. Approaching "the field" as a soundscape—its sounds, including noises, and the people and objects that make those sounds— attune ears to previously ignored or unheard sounds. Finally, sound studies may provide new ways of presenting data. Soundscapes need not be rendered into silent prose. Technology provides opportunities to capture, then interpret and recontextualize those sounds in the reports of studies. These aural renderings of research retain the sounds of the environment, including the inflection of what participants say, and the musical and environmental sounds that are integral to the education of music. Such a view, however, is not a mere objective documentation of sound, but is instead an interpretive, artistic act. These new ways of presenting research, however, require a shift in the rules of acceptable research "reporting" and of current structures of peer review reward in university settings. The emergence of quality venues for the dissemination of this sort of work can be viewed as the biggest hurdle to the implementation of soundscape renderings of research.

The "individual" and "critical-historical" phenomenologies of sound and listening that I have identified here are in dissonance with one another, perhaps irreconcilably so. An individual phenomenological position is relatively sanguine on finding *the* nature of listening and sound, the power of recordings to capture the experience of sounds. Conversely, a critical-historical phenomenological position is dubious of a universal listening experience, and questions access to "the real" that a recording can ever offer. Instead, critical-historical investigations reveal how fluid and historically and socially conditioned listening is. But while these two positions are probably not reconcilable, it is not self-evident that a researcher must exclusively choose one of these frameworks. Whether researchers use an individual phenomenology to determine and articulate the uniqueness of music education for the purposes of advocacy and philosophy, or critical-historical phenomenology to attend to the historical and material conditions that give rise to certain listening and educative practices, both frameworks serve valuable ways of conceptualizing music education. Researchers must ultimately navigate these differing ways of theorizing sound and listening in thorough and nuanced ways that best suit the aims of their scholarship. This is not easy to do and a course of action is not certain. But while this leaves more questions than answers, it opens up new possibilities, and how music education researchers produce these new areas remains to be seen. But treating sound as carefully in research as when it is performed, composed, or studied is a way for music education researchers to merge their artistic and scholarly identities.

REFERENCES

Abramo, J. M. (2011). Gender differences of popular music production in secondary schools. *Journal of Research in Music Education, 59*(1), 21–43. doi: 10.1177/0022429410396095

Albright, D. (2004). Introduction. In D. Albright (Ed.), *Modernism and music: An anthology of sources* (pp. 1–15). Chicago, IL: University of Chicago Press.

Attali, J. (1986). *Noise: The political economy of music* (B. Massumi, Trans.). Minneapolis: University of Minnesota Press.

Bartlett, R. (2013). Playing with meaning: Using cartoons to disseminate research findings. *Qualitative Research, 13*, 214–27. doi: 10.1177/1468794112451037

Bell, A. P. (2008). The heart of the matter: Composing music with an adolescent with special needs. *International Journal of Education & the Arts, 9*(9). Retrieved July 1, 2013, from www.ijea.org/v9n9/

Boretz, B. (1992). Experiences with no names. *Perspectives of New Music, 30*, 272–83.

Borgmann, A. (2006). Technology as a cultural force. *Canadian Journal of Sociology, 31*, 351–60.

Bull, M., & Back, L. (2004). Introduction: Into sound. In M. Bull & L. Back (Eds.) *Auditory culture reader.* New York, NY: Berg.

Chion, M. (1994). *Audio-vision* (C. Gorbman, Trans.). New York, NY: Columbia University Press.

Denzin, N. K. (2013). The traveling Indian gallery, Part two. *Qualitative Research.* Advanced online publication. doi: 10.1177/1468794112468477

Drever, J. L. (2002). Soundscape composition: The convergence of ethnography and acousmatic music. *Organised Sound, 7,* 21–7. doi:10.1017/S1355771802001048

Eisner, E. W. (2003). *The arts and the creation of mind.* New Haven, CT: Yale University Press.

Erlmann, V. (2004). *Hearing cultures: Essays on sound, listening and modernity.* New York, NY: Berg.

Erlmann, V. (2010). *Reason and resonance: A history of modern aurality.* New York, NY: Zone Books.

Feld, S. (1994, June). From ethnomusicology to echo-muse-ecology: Reading R. Murray Schafer in the Papua New Guinea rainforest. *The Soundscape Newsletter,* 8.

Forsey, M. G. (2010). Ethnography as participant listening. *Ethnography, 11,* 558–72. doi: 10.1177/1466138110372587

Foucault, M. (1972). *The archeology of knowledge and the discourse on language* (A. Sheridan, Trans.). New York, NY: Pantheon.

Goodman, S. (2010). *Sonic warfare: Sound, affect and the ecology of fear.* Cambridge, MA: MIT Press.

Gopnick, A. (2013, January 28). Music to your ears: The quest for 3-D recording and other mysteries of sound. *New Yorker Magazine,* 32–9.

Gould, E. (2010, October 23). Stories silences gasp: Stuttering stories stuttered story. Paper presented at the Race, Erasure, and Equity in Music Education Conference, Madison, WI.

Hall, T., Lashua, B., & Coffey, A. (2008). Sound and the everyday in qualitative research. *Qualitative Inquiry, 14,* 1019–40. doi: 10.1177/1077800407312054

Heron, J., & Reason, P. (2006). The practice of co-operative inquiry: Research "with" rather than "on" people. In P. Reason & H. Bradbury (Eds.), *Handbook of action research* (pp. 144–54). Thousand Oaks, CA: Sage.

Idhe, D. (1976). *Listening and voice: A phenomenology of sound.* Athens: Ohio University Press.

Janus, A. (2011). Listening: Jean-Luc Nancy and the "anti-ocular" turn in continental philosophy and critical theory. *Comparative Literature, 63,* 188–202. doi:10.1215/00104124–1265474

Jay, M. (1993). *Downcast eyes: The denigration of vision in twentieth-century French thought.* Los Angeles: University of California Press.

Mans, M. (2000). Using Namibian music/dance traditions as a basis for reforming arts education. *International Journal of Educations and the Arts, 1*(3). Retrieved from www.ijea.org/v1n3/index.htm

Miller, T., Birch, M., Mauthner, M., & Jessop, J. (Eds.) (2012). *Ethics in qualitative research* (2nd Ed.). London, United Kingdom: Sage.

Moreno, J. (2004). *Musical representations, subjects, and objects: The construction of musical thought in Zarlino, Descartes, Rameau, and Weber.* Bloomington: Indiana University Press.

Nancy, J.-L. (2006). *Listening* (Charlotte Mandell, Trans.). New York, NY: Fordham University.

Nettl, B. (2005). *The study of ethnomusicology: Thirty-one issues and concepts* (New Edition). Urbana: University of Illinois Press.

O'Callaghan, C. (2009). Sounds and events. In M. Nudds & C. O'Callaghan (Eds.), *Sounds and perception: New philosophical essays* (pp. 26–49). New York, NY: Oxford University Press.

O'Callaghan, C., & Nudds, M. (2009). Introduction: The philosophy of sounds and auditory perception. In M. Nudds & C. O'Callaghan (Eds.), *Sounds and perception: New philosophical essays* (pp. 1–25). New York, NY: Oxford University Press.

Oliver, D. G., Serovich, J. M., & Mason, T. L. (2005). Constraints and opportunities with interview transcription: Towards reflection in qualitative research. *Social Forces, 84,* 1273–89.

Pink, S. (2009). *Doing sensory ethnography.* Los Angeles, CA: Sage.

Rice, T. (2005). Getting a sense of listening. *Critique of Anthropology, 25,* 199–206.

Saldaña, J. (2008). Second chair: An autoethnodrama. *Research Studies in Music Education, 30,* 177–91. doi: 10.1177/1321103X08097506

Samuels, D. W., Meintjes, L., Ochoa, A. M., & Porcello T. (2010). Soundscapes: Toward a sounded anthropology. *Annual. Review of Anthropology, 39,* 329–45. doi: 10.1146/annurev-anthro-022510–132230

Schaeffer, P. (2012). *In search of concrete music* (J. Dack & C. North, Trans.). Los Angeles: University of California Press.

Schafer R. M. (1986). *The thinking ear.* Toronto, Canada: Arcana.

Schafer, R. M. (1994). *The soundscape: Our sonic environment and the turning of the world* (2nd Ed.). Rochester, VT: Destiny.

Schenker, H. (1969). *Five graphic music analyses.* New York, NY: Dover Publications. (Original work published 1933)

Sterne, J. (2003). *The audible past: Cultural origins of sound reproduction.* Durham, NC: Duke University Press.

Sterne, J. (2012). Sonic imaginations. In J. Sterne (Ed.), *The sound studies reader* (pp. 1–18). New York, NY: Routledge.

Thompson, E. (2002). *The soundscape of modernity: Architectural acoustics and the culture of listening in America 1900–1930.* Cambridge, MA: MIT Press.

Truax, B. (2000). *Soundscape composition as global music.* Retrieved from www.sfu.ca⁄truax/soundscape.html

18 Commentary on *Research Snapshot* and *Qualitative Approaches*

Richard Colwell

METHODOLOGICAL TRENDS

The chapter on methodological trends in music education clearly belongs in the research section and the description of methodology as provided by Borg and Gall is excellent. The guidelines are clear as to the conduct of the analysis. The author indicates that music education tends to follow research in education but there is no comparison as to whether the trends in music education during the three periods under consideration are parallel.

My impression is that in summarizing this pedestrian work the author found that he had failed to ask all of the questions pertinent to his study. The author knows that methodologies do not identify topics of interest: that issues determine research and that methodologies are only tools; and that methodologies are not informative about future research. We simply remain uninformed whether research topics have changed or whether any trend is evident.

I don't mean to second-guess the problem statement but had the author also looked at dissertations and funded research, a different trend might have emerged. It is possible that the study is most informative about the editors of the three journals. I regret that essays were not included as the other two research chapters are essentially essays. The omission of studies that used mixed methods (often referred to as mixed materials) was also unfortunate as these types of articles would be included in most any trend study (Mertens & Hesse-Biber, 2013). With mixed methods studies one conducts a type of experimental study and then employs various qualitative strategies to garner additional meanings from any findings.

I also missed the category of philosophical studies. Further, the writer does not discuss observation, which is a strategy used in many of the studies cited. I agree that computer searches represent a trend, most noticeable in related research. However, the author does not comment on changes in related research and/or interpretation of data. Further, he suggests that digital processing has facilitated the escalation of research activities; this seems to me to be an unsupported conclusion.

I fail to see the purpose of conducting a chi-square analysis and the Bonferroni p value at $p <.005$ when the percentages (not the raw numbers) over time demonstrated little difference. The change into the qualitative area, and the use of fewer tests (there are not many available), were an obvious difference.

There are always minor items in any chapter. In portraying the Borg and Gall definition of qualitative research, the writer suggests subjecting the resulting data to analytic induction. When he suggests that reliability could be enhanced by introducing a second coder, the concern is for employing both inductive *and* deductive analysis as Borg and Gall suggest, element: data analysis. It is arguable that the results of questionnaire and interview protocols provide a more complex data set—the answers are often tabulated.

The conclusions seem appropriate except for his opinion that the quality of research studies has improved and his idea that the reporting of effect sizes and confidence intervals has aided in the interpretation of results reported. Interpretation of related research continues to be a weakness in music education research.

CRITICAL ETHNOGRAPHY AS/FOR PRAXIS

Professor Silverman offers us a philosophical essay that is critical of one approach to music education found in some secondary schools. She asks two research questions: (1) What kinds of understandings do students bring to music classes and (2) how can teachers build on students' interests to motivate them to experiment with musics beyond their immediate environments that might have implications for curriculum development and change. She conducted no research to answer these questions; rather she provides an ideology that may be applicable to a required or an elective nonperformance secondary music course. Three student comments introduce the chapter; these comments fail to make clear whether the ideology being presented is applicable to both music as entertainment and music as education.

There is no quibble about the author's description of music appreciation classes that were historically prevalent. Few such remain today. The data offered that 20% of secondary students currently participate in music ensembles does not inform the reader of the population under consideration. An additional 20% of secondary school students are enrolled in music for at least one semester with these "non-ensemble" students in group piano, guitar, composition, music technology, and even AP theory. Further in the chapter, the author recognizes that listening is taught by all curricular forms. The scope of any research for "musics beyond their immediate environments" is unclear; one can assume that the music used in the research is not the music students listen to for hours on end on iPods and similar devices.

The author states her purpose as an explanation of the nature and strategies of critical ethnography as these strategies apply to intersections between theory, fieldwork methods, performance, critical practice, and social justice. She suggests that critical ethnographies utilize qualitative data collection methods for sociopolitical and ethical purposes. The chapter ranges from theory to practice; I here focus only on what appears to be her central argument: the importance of critical theory and social justice for a change in the music education curriculum.

Jorgensen and Yob (2013) warn against group think ideology, holding that Deleuze, an exponent of critical theory, would dismantle the State and its apparatus with no new plan. Deleuze's alternative, although somewhat unclear and abstruse, is a theory of everything in the world with its own axioms, principles, propositions, and theorems, and its own order, identity, and negation (Jorgensen & Yob, 2013, p. 39). Jorgensen and Yob (2013) would avoid an ideology and keep the somewhat messy and resulting tensions, conflicts, and exclusions that energize rather than the dualities, binaries, and polarities (p. 51). Such views should be subject to careful criticism.

Silverman emphasizes the sociopolitical and ethical aims of education and wants more "meaningful" music. She suggests that *praxis* is critical thinking, values, aims, motivation, techniques, and more, and that *methodology* is a research paradigm. To determine whether these claims can be justified is complex, involving the politicization of education and the priority to transform education to advocate for the oppressed. One element of Silverman's argument, supposedly from Juslin and Sloboda (2010), is that emotions in music are not dependent upon human emotions. Juslin and Sloboda (2010), in my reading, are making a different point from that of Silverman. She suggests that methodology (critical ethnography) is the way to conduct research; a concern might be the match between education and social justice.

In the *Journal of Teacher Education*, we learn that when special education is underpinned by cognitive perspectives, there is a sharp contrast with the sociocultural theories of learning that inform teachers working from a social justice perspective. Cochran-Smith and Dudley-Marling (2012) argue that social justice is non-contestable as a fundamental part of teaching, more important than content.

The question is raised whether what it means to be human has changed. The goal of education is not simply the personal good of each but the public good of all with which the personal good is intertwined.

Elizabeth Campbell (2013) argues that social justice is a distraction in ethical teaching. The moral and ethical dimensions of teaching and social justice differ (p. 216); the latter distracts teachers from examining their moral role as accountable professionals (p. 217). Agreeing with Jorgensen and Yob, Campbell believes that when there is no agent to whom social justice can be imputed, social justice itself is incoherent. Most of the theories of social justice focus on how power should be distributed in society and what the basic structure of society should be, not the central question of what is right and wrong. It is one thing to recognize that the curriculum is inherently political, and another to encourage the advocacy of one perspective to the exclusion of all others; arguments for social justice begin to resemble indoctrination (Campbell, 2013, p. 229). Social justice education conflates the moral and ethical aspects of teaching with the political, and represents moral and ethical values as entirely political. What should be foremost are the moral principles where the teacher is central, including fairness, truthfulness, integrity, empathy, and diligence, whereas social justice is concerned with power, privilege, identity, and diversity.

The author's interest is in better music education if researchers would ask better and/or different questions. Usually music education research is most effective when the focus remains on the music, change is gradual, and the resource requirements feasible.

SOUND STUDIES

Commenting on a chapter as wide ranging as the offering of Professor Abramo is a complex task. It is an olla podrida. One can easily focus on arguments that are not central to the chapter. One is left after reading the entire essay with the impression that the application of sound studies is justified music education research as a form of arts-based research. To grasp the content of the chapter one must consider phenomenology, perception, meaning, and even educational concerns of power and politics in the classroom, in addition to soundscapes. The research component is elusive. The paper might be an offering in physics with a few examples from music. As the chapter is placed in the research section of the text, traditional research comments are justified. The purpose of the chapter is revealed by the title and the two problems. These problems are (1) what can sounds reveal about how students and teachers communicate, gather (?) meaning, and learn? And (2) how can researchers incorporate sound into the frameworks, fieldworks, and presentations of empirical research? These problems are only loosely related to the material in the chapter, which addresses the communication issue by dividing perception into *individual* and *collective*. The author suggests that the presentation is primarily applicable to qualitative research and the presentations derived from empirical research. Empirical research is not limited to qualitative studies; quantitative research would work just as well. Empirical research is guided by practice, often observation or experience, rather than theory. Empirical research could, however, verify theory.

Sound is, of course, a critical element in all research in music education. Abramo encourages us to consider all classroom sounds, not only those traditionally defined as music. I agree that "private" student talk while a teacher is presenting could be considered disruptive. The students could be probing deeper into ideas or sounds just presented, which would be important to know. With the best recording equipment, however, considering all sounds would be difficult for any teacher to prioritize as classroom sounds for analysis related to communicating, meaning, or learning. Abramo has alerted us to be *qui vive* for all sounds. He divides these "sounds" into individual and historical phenomenologies and suggests that evidence from sounds will reduce the error of presenting data through verbal and musical transcriptions. One cannot disagree with the importance of using sound-scapes to more accurately present findings; the idea is not new to music education. Yes, individual perception, which he defines as phenomenology, may differ from cultural memes. Resolving these differences is the essence of all education.

Phenomenology, as I understand it, is concerned with the structure of experience or consciousness from the individual's point of view about some event or object. How one perceives the object (or sound) is a critical component but perception is not a simple skill. Perception ranges from simple to complex and is subject to both education and native talent. The depth of meaning derived from sounds depends upon this perceptual competence and although "gathering" meaning is central to the chapter, little is said about meaning or the theoretical constructs that are to be verified by the suggested observations. (One can be sure that Abramo knows how unreliable observations can be—see the research from MET [2013] on observing teachers.) There is intentionality in phenomenology and Abramo's intention in improving music education is unclear. His argument need not be limited to music. The connection between meaning and learning, an objective of the chapter, is not explained—aural learning is certainly the focus. My concern is that sounds must be expressive for them to be musical. Robert Schumann has said that notes in themselves cannot really paint what the emotions have not already portrayed. The history of all musics is a history of converting sounds to express moods, ideas, and events, resulting in a synthesis of music and poetry, inventive schemes to bring out and heighten the emotional content of verse, a match between solo and accompaniment; such sounds can move drama forward, and can convey celebrations, passions, moods, and even political stances—think of the songs of Bob Marley. Evelyn Glennie, the deaf concert artist, also uses the terms sound and listening with her definitions focused on expressive sounds. She not only responds to sound with her entire body but claims to view her audiences to produce the most expressive sounds.

The meaning of sounds in music (aural learning) is often enhanced by visual effects and also by kinesthesia. Teachers use Dalcroze movements to enhance musical meaning; a considerable body of research exists concerning the visual impact in music performances, festivals, and contests. I list a few quality studies in the references. The visual separates live performances (an important type of sound) from recordings and from the motions of performers, conductors, and audiences that affect perception. There is a reason why auditions for positions in symphony orchestras are conducted with the performer hidden from view by a screen.

It is difficult to ascertain what the author believes is new for research. He suggests that if sound and listening are a unique way of knowing the world then music education in the curriculum can be justified; but, of course, there are no references to sound as music. Composers and performers have long experimented with changing sounds to music. Stockhausen in the late 1960s worked on a series of pieces exploring different degrees of indeterminacy and performer involvement using his Plus Minus notation. The Beatles with *Sgt. Pepper* created artificial spaces by using reverb and echo units, sounds played backwards, filtered, changed speeds, and more. Ansuman Biswas (2011) argues that the basic ingredient of music is not so much sound as movement (p. 106). The reader should be alerted to a history of the use of sound in presenting results of research in music education. Edwin Knuth used sound in the mid-1930s, and one can imagine that Frances Clark was using RCA recordings to promote learning shortly after the turn of the 20th century. Folk music that could not be transcribed using traditional notation was incorporated into research presentations by Ruth Crawford at MENC meetings in the early 1960s. Recording musical sounds has always been a research tool for musicologists. The author cannot be expected to list all of the sound sources. A few contemporary composers have used spectrograms as an intermediate step in changing the intensity of different frequencies and judging how these changes can be used in new compositions. Computer music classes are popular when students are allowed to mix. Had he suggested present research projects, they would range from the MIT media lab, International Aural Literacy, to the Deep Listening Institute of Pauline Oliveros that recently hosted its first international conference.

I find no research evidence in the chapter of student meaning being enhanced by any of the suggestions. The author has provided an interesting thought-piece intended to connect sound and meaning. Focus within a soundscape would be critical for education. One learns through maturation and education to screen out visual and aural stimuli—a child sees and hears more than an adult. The author hints at a focus with his description of listening for melody or harmony but the idea is not developed. Meaning depends upon focus and is a topic in language as well as in music. "I never said she stole my money" is a classic example of seven different meanings depending upon which word is stressed. Language also uses punctuation for meaning. "Slow, children" is different from "Slow children."

Music uses silences, ornaments, and unexpected harmonies (or sounds) to convey expressive meaning. Expressive music can convey the emotional or even pictorial meaning of stories through the use of themes, harmonies, leitmotivs, timbres, and more. To recognize the expressive meaning of music, knowledge is not unimportant. Knowing the intention of a composer and/ or the historical/cultural setting facilitates understanding and sensitivity to musical meaning. The consciousness of phenomenology that is suggested requires reflection, analysis, and considerable additional musical experiences, passive and active—we listen to music holistically with no mental separation of mind and body. The author's suggestion that epistemology is sound may be a point I have overlooked; and I agree with him that we are in a visual culture. We do agree that music theory is not only descriptive but that it shapes and creates how and what one hears. In studying the interval of a 13th that is common in jazz, music theory assists in understanding how the ear fills in the missing notes of the chord.

REFERENCES

Biswas, A. (2011). The music of what happens: Mind, meditation, and music as movement. In D. Clark & E. Clarke (Eds.), *Music and consciousness: Philosophical, psychological, and cultural perspectives* (pp. 95–110). New York, NY: Oxford University Press.

Campbell, E. (2013). A moral critique of contemporary education. In H. Sockett & R. Boostrom (Eds.), *NSSE Yearbook, 112*(1) (pp. 216–37). New York, NY: Teachers College Press.

Chochran-Smith, M., & Dudley-Marling, C. (2012). Diversity in teacher education and special education: The issues that divide. *Journal of Teacher Education, 63*(4), 237–244.

Jorgensen, E., & Yob, I. (2013). Deconstructing Deleuze and Guattari's A Thousand Plateaus for music education. *Journal of Aesthetic Education, 47*(3), 36–55.

Juslin, P., & Sloboda, J. (2010). *Handbook of music and emotion: Theory, research, applications*. Oxford, United Kingdom: Oxford University Press.

Mertens, M., & Hesse-Biber, S. (2013). Mixed methods and credibility of evidence in evaluation. *New Directions for Evaluation, 138*, 5–13.

MET. (2013). *Ensuring fair and reliable measures of effective teaching*. Seattle, WA: The Bill & Melinda Gates Foundation.

19 Structural Equation Modeling and Multilevel Modeling in Music Education
Advancing Quantitative Research Data Analysis

Nicholas Stefanic

The primary and eventual goal of all research is to better inform our actions, which we do by gathering information, considering the information, and making decisions based on the information we have. We can gather information that describes (questions of who, what, where, when, to what degree) or information that explains (questions of why or how). The most crucial component of any type of research is asking critical, substantive questions of great consequence (Fung, 2008; Kemp, 1992). Research questions should be *critical* in that they are skeptical about assumptions and seek to illuminate rival arguments. Additionally, a good research question should be *substantive* in that it seeks an abundance of relevant information regarding an issue or phenomena, thus seeking well-supported answers, even if that involves contradictory information. Lastly, a research question is *of great consequence* if it has substantial value to one or more fields. Because research requires much time and resources, research questions of great consequence also represent a responsible use of those resources.

In quantitative research, and possibly in qualitative research as well, there is sometimes a tendency to develop research questions in relation to the techniques and tools one has at one's disposal for collecting relevant data, and more importantly, analyzing those data. In particular, there is a set of statistical procedures that most researchers learn, often in their graduate studies, all of which are essentially variations on a theme of linear regression (e.g., t-test, ANOVA, multiple regression). Because these statistical techniques require data to be structured in certain ways, research questions may be formed to match these structures. For example, if a researcher wishes to investigate how a group of individuals changes over time (e.g., change in a student's musical self-efficacy over four years), he/she is likely familiar with repeated-measures ANOVA as a means for dealing with time series data. In repeated-measures ANOVA, the categorical grouping variable is time (e.g., year 1, year 2, year 3, year 4) and there is a continuous dependent variable (e.g., musical self-efficacy). The research question that can be asked with this data structure is something like the following: Do these students (as a group) differ in their self-efficacy over four years? However, other questions that might be considered include the following: To what extent do individuals vary in their individual growth; how much is growth related to other predictor variables (e.g., IQ, musical aptitude, hours of practice); or how much is an individual's initial self-efficacy related to his/her change in self-efficacy? Each of these questions seek a deeper, more substantive picture of the change in a student's self-efficacy over time in comparison to the initial research question stated with the repeated-measures ANOVA framework. Unfortunately, some of these questions (and others like them, to be discussed later) either cannot be asked in a traditional ANOVA repeated-measures framework or cannot be handled in a very straightforward manner. These questions can be considered with other, possibly less well-known, data analysis techniques such as Structural Equation Modeling and Multi-level Modeling.

STRUCTURAL EQUATION MODELING

Structural Equation Modeling (SEM) is not a new technique, but it has gained popularity over the past few decades with the advent of personal computers with sufficient computing capabilities to handle the complex and tedious calculations and with the development of special-purpose SEM software. Interestingly, almost all univariate and multivariate General Linear Model (GLM) techniques are subsumed by SEM in a hierarchical manner and can be accomplished with SEM programs (Bagozzi & Yi, 2012; Graham, 2008).

Logic of SEM

For someone unfamiliar with SEM, it is perhaps beneficial to conceive of it as a combination of path analysis and Confirmatory Factor Analysis (CFA). With path analysis, a researcher hypothesizes a series of causal relationships (often mediating and moderating relationships) between a set of measured variables. Those relationships are displayed as a path diagram with single-headed arrows indicating direction of causality. Using a series of multiple regression equations the researcher then calculates coefficients (β), which are interpreted as the amount of change in an outcome variable with a given change in the predictor variable.

In CFA, a researcher hypothesizes a factor structure for a set of measured variables *a priori*. The latent variables (not actually directly measured) are believed to cause the responses seen on the respective items (the actual measured variables). The measured variables are called manifest variables because they are believed to be manifestations of the underlying, unobservable latent variable. CFA is different than Exploratory Factor Analysis (often referred to simply as factor analysis) in that CFA attempts to determine if the hypothesized factor structure *fits* the observed data, whereas

EFA attempts to *discover* the factor structure for the observed data. Conceptually, a structural equation model combines the structural aspect (causal relationships) of path analysis with the measurement aspect (hypothesized factor structure of latent variables) of CFA. SEM simultaneously evaluates a structural and a measurement model in relation to the observed data.

There is also another important distinction between SEM procedures and traditional GLM procedures. Typically, with inferential statistics we attempt to estimate the population parameter(s) from our sample data, and then use a statistical significance test to determine the probability of observing a parameter of that size (or greater) if in fact the parameter was something else (e.g., the mean is zero; there is no relationship between two variables). The observed sample data is treated as a known, and the parameter is treated as an unknown. With MLE (Maximum Likelihood Estimation), the logic is flipped, and we treat the parameter as a known, and the observed sample data as an unknown. Using an iterative process (i.e., an algorithm), MLE finds the parameter estimate(s) that would make the sample data the most likely to have been observed.

There is also another important distinction between SEM procedures and traditional GLM procedures. Since we rarely can study every individual in a population, we conduct research on samples of populations. The goal of inferential statistics is to estimate the parameters of these populations (e.g., mean, variance, covariance) from the sample statistics. There are many ways to go about estimating these parameters. Traditional GLM procedures often utilize the Ordinary Least Squares (OLS) method to estimate the population parameters. Most SEM software offer a wide variety of estimation methods, of which MLE is the most common. A full explanation of MLE is beyond the scope of this chapter, but an explanation can be found in virtually any SEM textbook.

Example of SEM

The following example will help to illustrate the potential uses of SEM by relating to an actual study in the music education literature (although this study did not use SEM). Brand (1986) investigated the relationship between the home musical environments of second graders and musical attributes (tonal perception, rhythmic perception, and musical achievement). Using EFA, Brand developed a 15-item Home Musical Environment Scale (HOMES), which measures four dimensions (factors): "(a) parents' attitude toward music and musical involvement with child; (b) parental concert attendance; (c) parent-child ownership and use of record/tape player, records, tapes; and (d) parent plays a musical instrument" (p. 115). Brand used setwise[2] multiple regression analysis to explore relationships between the four dimensions of HOMES and the musical attributes. With multiple regression analysis all items for a given factor have to be summed or averaged to produce a single number to use as the independent variable. So while a measurement instrument might be developed in a reflective latent variable framework (e.g., using EFA), it is actually analyzed as a composite variable (assumed to be measured without error), not as a true reflective latent variable, in traditional regression analyses. In essence, all item variance is treated as common factor variance and each variable contributes equally to the composite variable (i.e., has the same factor loading). In a SEM framework, the hypothesized factor structure can remain intact for any variable that assumes a latent variable measurement model, which means all information from each item is included in the model, and subsequently in the hypothesis testing and model evaluation.

To return to the Brand (1986) example, musical achievement was measured with a 12-item Musical Achievement Assessment Form (MAAF), which measures four areas: "musical knowledge (e.g., music symbols, terms, and instruments), skill in (instrumental and vocal) performance, music reading, and musical initiative (e.g., degree of interest and motivation" (p. 115). Gordon's Primary Measure of Music Audiation was used to measure tonal and rhythmic aptitude, an oft-used measure in music education. There are several options for how to handle this particular measure in a SEM framework. A latent musical aptitude variable could be modeled as being indicated by two items,[3] the rhythmic and tonal sub-scores. Another option would be to construct two latent variables, one for rhythmic and one for tonal, with their respective test items as effect indicators of the latent variable.

For didactic purposes, one potential (hypothetical) model for addressing questions about the relationships between home environment and musical attributes is shown in Figure 19.1. This particular model also illustrates the strength of SEM to test mediation in a straightforward manner. In this model, tonal and rhythmic aptitude mediates the relationship between home environment and musical achievement. This model also illustrates how SEM allows the researcher to make explicit the structure of the errors (random and measurement). All endogenous latent variables (variables with arrows pointing *toward* them) also have a disturbance pointed toward them, which represents the remaining variance not explainable by the variables that point to them. In addition, each manifest/measured variable also has a symbol similar to the disturbance, which represents unique variance for each item (variance that is not part of the common factor). This is but one potential model for investigating the relationships between these variables. Once the model has been specified, the parameters for the model would be estimated using the iterative procedure described above. Assuming convergence is reached (i.e., a solution is found), the model is then evaluated for overall fit. In addition to calculating various fit statistics, a chi-square test provides a formal inferential test of model fit. All of the various evaluation techniques (see Hu & Bentler, 1998, for a discussion of fit indices) are different ways of testing how well the data fit the specified model. If the model appears to have acceptable fit, then the model can be interpreted by examining the parameter estimates and R^2 values (i.e., explained variance). Hypothesis tests can be conducted on the various path coefficients and/or on the variance/covariance estimates.

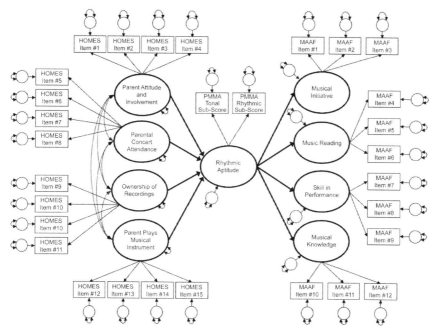

Figure 19.1 Hypothetical SEM model for Brand (1986). Item numbers are also hypothetical and do not relate to actual MAAF and HOMES measures. Circles are latent variables, rectangles are manifest/measured variables, straight arrows represent causal relationships, and curved arrows show covariance/correlation of exogenous variables.

Advantages of SEM

There are several advantages of SEM in comparison to other traditional GLM procedures, as explained by Bagozzi and Yi (2012) and Lei and Wu (2007), and described below. First, SEM allows the investigation of the relationships between latent variables. In path analysis, causal relationships can only be modeled with measured (observed) variables. With CFA, latent variables can only be modeled to affect measured (observed) variables. SEM overcomes these two limitations because latent variables can be modeled to impact other latent variables. CFA is actually a special case of SEM.

Second, from a measurement perspective, using latent variables in modeling causal relationships between constructs is ideal because latent variables have no measurement error. Multiple regression and ANOVA techniques, all of which use single indicators for each variable (often an average of multiple items), do not take measurement error into account when testing hypotheses because they have the assumption that variables were measured without error, which is rarely the case in social sciences. With SEM, the reliability of individual measures is taken into account in hypothesis tests.

Third, the specification process involved with SEM can help research-ers to be more particular in how they operationalize constructs and how they specify their hypotheses. Fourth, from a practical standpoint, the visual nature of SEM path diagrams not only helps the researcher think more glob-ally or holistically, but also can help to convey theories more easily through visual depiction of variable relationships. Fifth, the SEM framework works equally well for exploratory research, which involves model building, as for confirmatory research, which involves model testing. When done appropri-ately and with good reason, the combination of exploratory and confirma-tory research can advance theory development quite substantially.

While the SEM framework is most often used to examine covariances, it can also be used to examine means. Therefore, the sixth advantage of SEM is that it is possible to compare the means of groups on latent variables (e.g., using multiple group CFA). A traditional ANOVA can only compare means of observed/measured variables. Therefore, in addition to examining covari-ance structure, mean differences between groups can also be incorporated into a SEM analysis.

There are several caveats that should also be mentioned in regards to SEM. First and foremost, SEM is undoubtedly a large-sample technique. Although "rule-of-thumb" statements about sample size are difficult to make with SEM because models can vary in complexity, Jackson (2003) has provided some evidence for considering the ratio of sample size to the num-ber of parameters being estimated, suggesting 20:1 is ideal but certainly not less than 10:1. Second, SEM research tends to place less emphasis on indi-vidual tests of statistical significance and more emphasis on evaluation of entire models. Kline (2011) explains that this is because "there is a sense in SEM that the view of the entire landscape (the whole model) has precedence over that of specific details (individual effects)" (p. 13). In addition, because SEM is a large-sample technique, and because hypothesis tests are sensitive to sample size, it becomes more likely that null hypotheses are rejected sim-ply because of a large N. Kline (2004, 2011) is also a staunch advocate of focusing more on magnitudes of effect sizes, and thus practical significance, as opposed to primarily focusing on statistical significance.

MULTILEVEL MODELING

As previously mentioned, SEM is not a new technique, and subsumes all other traditional GLM procedures. More recently (within the last 30 years), an extension of the GLM has been developed to handle hierarchically orga-nized or nested data. Hierarchical linear modeling (HLM), also known as multilevel modeling, was developed in the 1980s, with some preliminary work accomplished in the 1970s, and has continued to develop since then, with the list of applications ever-expanding. The term multilevel modeling (MLM) will be used for the remainder of the chapter because it is a more general term that characterizes a range of analysis techniques that utilize a nested data structure. The need for MLM arose out of the recognition that using aggregates of data that are nested or hierarchical in nature leads to severe bias in estimates used in common statistical techniques.

Need for MLM

A fundamental assumption of virtually all traditional GLM statistical analysis techniques is that the residuals must be independent. This means that the reason why one particular observation deviates from the mean does not also affect the deviation of any other observation. This is done to simplify the statistical model, but it also limits the situations in which the assumption is appropriate. If our model seeks to explain the variance in our measurements in a certain way, and if we do not account for other sources of variance that are shared by two or more observations, then these other sources of variance can cloud the conclusions we draw from our data. In most situations where observations are organized hierarchically (nested in groups), there is likely some amount of variance explained by being in one group or another, and thus all the observations are not independent of each other, but rather are dependent on group membership. A hypothetical example of this problem in a music education research context will be helpful.

Imagine a researcher is interested in comparing the differences between two teaching styles (TS), an informal vs. a formal approach to teaching, in a general music context as they relate to students' musical creative self-efficacy (MCSE), that is, one's perceived ability to be creative in music. The research question might be the following: Are their differences in students' musical creative self-efficacy (MCSE) that result from different teaching styles (TS)? The researcher recruits 30 music teachers to participate in the study, 15 of which use an informal approach and 15 of which use a formal approach. For our purposes, I will avoid a discussion on the distinctions between and the merits of these two approaches and simply treat them as two different teaching approaches for experimental purposes. In addition to MCSE, the researcher would like to control for some other variables (covariates) that have been demonstrated in the literature to impact MCSE, such as students' private lessons experience (PLE), creative music-making experience (CMME), and musical aptitude (MA). In a traditional multiple regression analysis, the researcher collects measurements for each variable, regresses self-efficacy on teaching style (formal/informal) after controlling for the three covariates, and tests for statistically significant differences in MCSE. If student MCSE scores from all of these different classrooms are simply combined/aggregated, we fail to account for the impact of the specific classroom each student works in. This could include effects related to the specific teacher, the interactions between specific students in that classroom, or a number of other classroom-specific variables. These differences attributable to the between-classroom differences would be ignored so we could not tell if differences in MCSE are actually a result of teaching style or classroom-specific effects. MLM provides the appropriate framework for this situation.

Moreover, hierarchical or multilevel structure is much more prevalent in music education research contexts than one might expect. The following situations all represent contexts where a nested data structure is present, and therefore a MLM analysis framework would be beneficial: any time students are working in groups; comparing students from classrooms at different schools; comparing schools across a state when schools are nested within different school districts; and almost any repeated-measures design (each measurement occasion is nested within each individual student).

Advantages of MLM

There are several reasons for using MLM, both statistical and practical. From a statistics standpoint, MLM provides better estimates of fixed effects. For example, if traditional techniques were used to estimate the cross-level interaction of creative music-making experience and teaching experience, the assumption of independence would be violated because CMME is a level-one variable (student-level) and students are nested within classrooms, and therefore not independent. The issue of the independence assumption for traditional regression analyses is quite serious because violations result in severely biased estimates, which in turn leads to untrustworthy inferences (Kenny & Judd, 1986; Scariano & Davenport, 1987). While many analysis techniques are robust to violations of some of the other assumptions (e.g., normality), failure to account for non-independence in one's data is actually harmful to the research field because of the untrustworthiness of any conclusions drawn from such an analysis. In addition to the ability to ask questions about cross-level variability in the data, MLM also provides better level-one estimates. If separate regression analyses were done for each classroom in the MCSE example, the sample size for each classroom would be relatively small, which results in more error in the estimates.

From a practical standpoint, MLM offers an alternative to the loss of information that occurs when dependent (non-independent) data are aggregated. Information regarding differences between groups can be just as important as the information from all of the individuals within the groups. An MLM framework allows for all useful data to be incorporated. Finally, MLM provides a statistical framework by which cross-institution collaboration can be accomplished. Larger samples can be achieved when multiple institutions are involved and the nested nature of cross-institutional data can be accounted for with MLM.

A few additional comments should be made regarding the advantages of MLM specific to repeated-measures data. Repeated-measures data can also be conceived as being nested (in addition to being non-independent). Consider the previous example with musical creative self-efficacy, but this time as a repeated-measures design, and the researcher is interested in students' change in self-efficacy over the course of the year. The researcher has students complete a measure of self-efficacy once a month for the entire school year, which results in nine measurement occasions. In this example, level one is within-individual, the nine measurements over time per individual. We could refer to this as the occasion level. This means that level two is actually the individual, which we would refer to as the individual level. From this perspective, measurement occasions are nested within individuals, so a multilevel/hierarchical analysis is logical.

In traditional repeated-measures ANOVA analysis, the amount of time between measurements must be equal (equal intervals) and the number of observations per individual must be equal. MLM is capable of handling observations collected at different time points and different numbers of observations per individual. The reason for this is that MLM models time as a continuous variable as opposed to a categorical variable like in repeated-measures ANOVA or MANOVA. This is particularly helpful because it is fairly common in an educational setting for a student to be absent on the day a measurement is taken. If that observation needs to be made a week later, MLM can incorporate this difference in measurement interval. If that particular measurement is missed altogether and the student has only eight measurements instead of nine, MLM can handle the missing data much better than ANOVA. Most statistical programs will simply eliminate that individual from the analysis, which can result in a large amount of information loss.

While the flexible nature of MLM analysis is helpful from a data collection standpoint, it also offers several additional flexibilities from an analysis standpoint. The term hierarchical linear modeling implies an exclusiveness to linear growth, but MLM can also model nonlinear and even more complex growth curves. Another advantage of MLM is the ability to incorporate covariates (predictors) that vary over time (occasion-level) as well as covariates (predictors) that are constant (individual-level). For example, in addition to measuring MCSE, the researcher could also take a measure of motivation at each time point, thus representing an occasion-level predictor. Similarly, the same previously discussed covariates (e.g., musical aptitude) could be included as level two (individual-level) predictors. Lastly, in traditional repeated-measures analysis, there is an assumption that all individuals have the same growth curve. With MLM, it is possible to have different growth curves for each individual, something that is more likely the case in real life for many situations.

What is hopefully clear at this point is that both SEM and MLM are extremely powerful analytic techniques, with several advantages over traditional analysis techniques in many circumstances. We now consider the different types of questions that can be asked with these analysis techniques in comparison to traditional techniques.

BROADENING AND DEEPENING RESEARCH QUESTIONS

To begin, remember that SEM can be thought of as the overarching framework for all traditional GLM procedures. The biggest difference with SEM and more traditional approaches is that the emphasis is on more global or holistic aspects of theory building. The notion of generating and confirming theory can also be thought of as being hierarchical in nature. While SEM can be used for all traditional analysis techniques, the beauty of SEM is in its ability to handle huge amounts of complexity in a rather intuitive manner, with great flexibility. As such, SEM affords analysis of the types of research questions described in Table 1. In addition to providing general research questions, Table 1 also provides examples specific to the Brand (1986) hypothetical examples discussed in the SEM portion of this chapter. What is evident from the example questions is the focus on model fit and model comparison, which emphasizes larger-scale theory development.

Both of the approaches discussed in this chapter (SEM and MLM) can be used to address the questions in Table 19.1, but a multilevel framework affords different types of research questions, those that focus on between-level

Table 19.1   Example General Research Questions with Corresponding Examples in Music Education for SEM Approach

	General Examples	Music Education Examples
Confirmatory Approach	How well does this model fit the observed data?	How well does the model explaining the relationships of home musical environment, musical aptitude, and musical achievement fit the data?
	Can other models, mathematically equivalent but with different specified relationships and assumptions, better explain the observed data?	Same question (see Lee & Hershberger, 1990 for a discussion of equivalent models)
	Which of these rival models best fits the observed data?	Which of these models, one with musical aptitude as a mediator or one with musical aptitude as a separate effect of home musical environment, best fits the observed data?
Exploratory Approach	How much variance is explained by each individual component of the model?	How much variance is explained by rhythmic and tonal aptitude as mediators in this model?
	Given the results of the SEM analysis, what modifications to the model can be made to better fit the observed data? Are those modifications plausible and rational?	Same question. Many SEM programs generate suggestions for altering paths that might fit the data better. Are these alterations plausible and rational?
	Does one model fit the observed data better for one level of a categorical variable compared to other levels? Should two or more complimentary models be considered?	Is musical aptitude a mediator of home musical environment and musical achievement only for students from high SES families?

differences. Those questions are slightly different depending on whether the multilevel data is organizational (i.e., observations of individuals nested within groups) or longitudinal (i.e., measurement occasions nested within individuals). Table 19.2 identifies examples of general research questions for organizational data as well as specific examples as they would relate to the hypothetical study discussed in the MLM section of this chapter. As for longitudinal data, Table 19.3 displays the corresponding questions for a longitudinal multilevel design and examples specific to the hypothetical music education study discussed in the repeated-measures MLM section of this chapter.

These techniques can also be expanded beyond what has been discussed in this chapter. In short, it is possible to have multilevel SEM and there are also latent variable MLM approaches. Each have situations in which they are the better choice (for further discussion, see Stoel & Garre, 2011). It is also possible to create three-level models. For example, in a

Table 19.2 Example General Research Questions with Corresponding Examples in Music Education for an MLM Approach with Organizational Data (observations of individuals nested within groups)

General Research Questions	Music Education Examples
What is the proportion of variance within- and between- groups for the outcome variable?	What proportion of variance in musical creative self-efficacy is attributable to differences between classrooms and within classrooms?
Does the relationship between a given level-one predictor and the outcome vary across level-two units?	Does the relationship between musical aptitude and MCSE vary between classrooms?
When a level-one predictor is added, how much is the proportion of within-level variance reduced?	When musical aptitude is added as an individual-level (level one) predictor, how much is the proportion of within-classroom variance in MCSE reduced?
When a level-two predictor is added, how much is the proportion of between-level variance reduced?	When teaching experience is added as a classroom-level (level two) predictor, how much is the proportion of between-classroom variance in MCSE reduced?
What is the relationship between a given level-one predictor and the outcome variable?	What is the relationship between musical aptitude and MCSE?
What is the relationship between a given level-two predictor and the outcome variable?	What is the relationship between teaching experience and MCSE?
To what extent is the relationship between a given within-level variable and the outcome variable moderated by a given between-level variable?	To what extent is the relationship between musical aptitude and MCSE moderated by teaching experience?

Table 19.3 Example General Research Questions with Corresponding Examples in Music Education for an MLM Approach with Longitudinal Data (observations of measurement occasions nested within individuals)

General Research Questions	Music Education Examples
What is the form of the growth curve (nature of the change) between individuals (linear, quadratic, cubic, etc.)?	What is the form of the growth curve (nature of the change) for students' MCSE over nine months?
To what extent do individuals vary (between each other) in their initial status (intercept) on an outcome variable?	To what extent do individual students vary (between each other) in their initial MCSE score (intercept)?
To what extent do individuals vary (between each other) in their rate (slope) of change on an outcome variable?	To what extent do individual students vary (between each other) in their rate (slope) of change in MCSE?
What is the relationship between a given time-varying variable and individuals' intial status on an outcome variable?	What is the relationship between motivation and students' initial MCSE?
What is the relationship between a given time-varying variable and individuals' rate of change in an outcome variable?	What is the relationship between motivation and students' rate of change in MCSE?
What is the relationship between individuals' intial status on an outcome variable and their rate of change?	What is the relationship between students' intial MCSE and their rate of change in MCSE?
When a time-varying (level-one) covariate/predictor is added, how much is the proportion of within-individuals variance reduced?	When motivation is added as an occasion-level (level one) predictor, how much is the proportion of within-individual variance in MCSE reduced?
When an individual-level (level-two) predictor is added, how much is the proportion of between-individuals variance reduced?	When musical aptitude is added as an individual-level (level two) covariate/predictor, how much is the proportion of between-individuals variance in MCSE reduced?

longitudinal design where participants were sampled from different classrooms or schools, the first level is still within-individual, the second level is between-individuals, and the third level would correspond to the between-classroom differences. The MLM framework has also been extended to include nonlinear data, dichotomous outcomes, multivariate outcomes, latent variables, factor analysis, and situations where participants are cross-classified or have multiple group membership. From a measurement perspective, several authors have described how MLM can be extended to Item Response Theory (IRT) models as well (cf. Kamata & Cheong, 2007; Kamata & Vaughn, 2011), which incorporates a very different approach to measurement.

CONCLUSIONS

There have been many advances in statistical analysis techniques, many of which are not being incorporated with any regularity into the field of music education research. SEM and MLM offer opportunities to analyze complex and hierarchically structured data in a flexible manner. To be clear, complexity is not a goal in and of itself. Simply adding variables to a model to make it more complex does not make it better. The intent of this chapter is to emphasize that there are indeed techniques available to more effectively model the complexity of our world than traditional GLM approaches.

As many advanced statistics textbooks begin: the world is multivariate. As such, many researchers and statisticians alike have long argued for the need to approach research problems from a multivariate standpoint. That is, any effect of one thing on another is likely to be multifaceted and produce multiple effects, especially when the unit of analysis is the human being. I hope to further this argument by claiming that the world is also multilevel. Individuals live, work, learn, grow, and change within various social settings and geographical locations. Multilevel approaches are particularly important because they allow for the analysis of contextual effects. In an era when context is recognized as a necessary part of any explanation, MLM can provide a means for considering context in a quantitative manner.

The techniques discussed in this chapter are decidedly large sample techniques, a notion for which I have two comments. First, large samples should always be the goal in quantitative research. Small samples are particularly susceptible to capitalization on chance, which can lead to seemingly well-founded conclusions that are erroneous simply because of the characteristics of the specific small sample examined in the research.

Second, we must begin to think bigger with quantitative research, both in terms of sample sizes and in terms of large-scale theory development, both of which require collaboration in music education research. Collaboration can support and improve the cross-pollination of ideas, which can enrich the process of research. Along with collaboration, particularly between-institution collaboration, comes access to potentially larger sample sizes. A between-institution sample is problematic from a traditional GLM analysis standpoint (non-independence of observations), but can be easily managed with MLM techniques. As such, larger samples resulting from collaborative efforts can actually allow us to ask deeper research questions because of the affordances of these large-sample techniques, which have already been discussed. Such collaboration is easier than ever, logistically speaking, due to the global connectivity of the Internet.

It is not my intent to suggest that these approaches are necessary or even appropriate for all research situations. Every statistical analysis approach has its advantages and disadvantages and it is still the responsibility of the researcher to determine the most appropriate method. If ANOVA will work for answering the research question, then use ANOVA. However, if a broader research question can and should be developed, then the researcher should strongly consider these techniques for analyzing the data. It is my hope that by providing a brief overview of these very powerful approaches to data analysis, the statistical toolbox for music education research may be expanded. In addition, if we conceive our research questions in relation to our knowledge of techniques for analyzing the data, then I also hope this chapter will help to broaden and deepen the types of research questions that we ask in the general quantitative research context. In combination with high-quality qualitative research and mixed/multiple-methods approaches, this can in turn lead to more valuable, useful, and trustworthy research in the field of music education.

NOTES

1. This is the most common type of latent variable, often referred to as a reflective latent variable. Other specifications are possible, including composite and formative latent variables (cf. Bollen & Bauldry, 2011; Cadogan & Lee, 2013)
2. Setwise regression is a type of stepwise regression, but variables are entered into the model in sets of variables.
3. This is possible as long as (1) there is at least one more reflective latent variable in the model, which also has at least two effect indicator manifest variables; (2) the factors are properly scaled; (3) each item loads on only one factor; and (4) the errors are not correlated. Otherwise, the model is underidentified.

REFERENCES

Bagozzi, R. P., & Yi, Y. (2012). Specification, evaluation, and interpretation of structural equation models. *Journal of the Academy of Marketing Science, 40,* 8–34.

Bollen, K. A., & Bauldry, S. (2011). Three Cs in measurement models: Causal indicators, composite indicators, and covariates. *Psychological Methods, 16*(3), 265–84.

Brand, M. (1986). Relationship between home musical environment and selected musical attributes of second-grade children. *Journal of Research in Music Education, 34*(2), 111–20.

Cadogan, J. W., & Lee, N. (2013). Improper use of endogenous formative variables. *Journal of Business Research, 66,* 233–41.

Fung, C. V. (2008). In search of important research questions in music education: The case of the United States. *Bulletin of the Council for Research in Music Education, 176,* 31–43.

Graham, J. M. (2008). The general linear model as structural equation modeling. *Journal of Educational and Behavioral Statistics, 33*(4), 485–506.

Hu, L.-T., & Bentler, P. M. (1998). Fit indices in covariance structure modeling: Sensitivity to underparameterized model misspecification. *Psychological Methods, 3*(4), 424–53.

Jackson, D. L. (2003). Revisiting sample size and number of parameter estimates: Some support for the N:q hypothesis. *Structural Equation Modeling, 10*(1), 128–41.

Kamata, A., & Cheong, Y. F. (2007). Multilevel Rasch models. In M. Von Davier & C. H. Carstensen (Eds.), *Multivariate and mixture distribution Rasch models: Extensions and applications* (pp. 217–32). New York, NY: Springer.

Kamata, A., & Vaughn, B.K. (2011). Multilevel IRT modeling. In J. Hox & J.K. Roberts (Eds.), *Handbook of advanced multilevel analysis* (pp. 41–57). New York, NY: Routledge.

Kemp, A.E. (1992). Approaching research. In A.E. Kemp (Ed.), *Some approaches to research in music education* (pp. 7–18). Reading, United Kingdom: International Society for Music Education.

Kenny, D.A., & Judd, C.M. (1986). Consequences of violating the independence assumption in analysis of variance. *Psychological Bulletin, 99*(3), 422–31.

Kline, R.B. (2004). What's wrong with statistical tests—And where we go from here. In R. B. Kline, *Beyond significance testing: Reforming data analysis methods in behavioral research* (pp. 61–91). Washington, DC: American Psychological Association.

Kline, R.B. (2011). *Principles and practice of structural equation modeling* (3rd Ed.). New York, NY: The Guilford Press.

Lee, S., & Hershberger, S. (1990). A simple rule for generating equivalent models in structural equation modeling. *Multivariate Behavioral Research, 25*, 313–34.

Lei, P.W., & Wu, Q. (2007). Introduction to structural equation modeling: Issues and practical considerations. *Educational Measurement: Issues and Practice, 26*(3), 33–43.

Scariano, S.M., & Davenport, J.M. (1987). The effects of violations of independence assumptions in the one-way ANOVA. *The American Statistician, 41*(2), 123–9.

Stoel, R.D., & Garre, F.G. (2011). Growth curve analysis using multilevel regression and structural equation modeling. In J. Hox & J.K. Roberts (Eds.), *Handbook of advanced multilevel analysis* (pp. 97–111). New York, NY: Routledge.

20 Reflecting on *Guiding Researchers*

Peter R. Webster

Taken as a whole, the four chapters in this portion of *Music Education: Navigating the Future* provide both the practitioner and the researcher with a number of compelling ideas for improving the profession. But perhaps more importantly, they also reveal a need to recalibrate our approach as teacher educators to the way research is traditionally taught in both undergraduate and graduate programs. I begin noting some highlights of these chapters and end with some thoughts on research teaching.

METHODOLOGICAL TRENDS IN MUSIC EDUCATION RESEARCH

Zelenak's chapter on methodological trends is a fine way to begin this section on "Guiding Researchers." It reminds us of the tradition of research in our field, how new it is, and—in some ways—how far we need to go in years ahead. I enjoyed the reminder of the context of our research efforts, the historical roots that got us to where we are. I look forward to an expansion of this work to include perhaps more representative time periods and perhaps a few other journals, but I appreciate the restrictions.

The notion of taking a "snapshot" of studies across the different time frames was confirmatory and revealing. The increase in the actual numbers of published articles is encouraging and, when added to the rising number of national and international journals both printed and online, this is a most healthy sign for our profession. I was surprised that the proportion of qualitative versus quantitative studies remained constant; this was perhaps an artifact of the journals and the years studied. My sense is that a more even balance of methodologies is evident in recent times and, if true, represents another positive sign. The trend toward more social and cultural context studies is expected; the existence of fewer standardized test instruments used as measurement tools in deference to more questionnaires was revealing and well reasoned in the chapter. It was concerning to note the increase in convenience sampling, a trend that was also well explained by the author. Zelenak's conclusions about different topics studied and the ability of researchers to deal with questionnaire data more effectively in recent times are points well taken. Finally, the author touches on a critical point in the final pages of the chapter relating to the issue of the questions posed by researchers. He notes that no research to date has been done on the matter of questions chosen for study—an excellent and meaningful observation. Further, his concern for nomological networks and the need for connected studies, built upon each other for the intent of studying theories and models, is perhaps the most salient point to consider. Each of the chapters in this section speaks to this in different ways, some more directly than others.

APPLICATION OF SOUND STUDIES TO QUALITATIVE RESEARCH IN MUSIC EDUCATION

Abramo's chapter on the field of sound studies and its implications for both teaching and research represents a topic of major importance for a small but very talented group of music education researchers and theorists. As a compliment to his chapter, I recommend the work of Matthew Thibeault, Evan Tobias, and Alex Ruthmann, among others. New teachers and researchers, especially those interested in media and technology and their role in the emerging social structures of youth and music consumption today, will find this and other writings to be foundational.

For years, I have said in my classes and when giving talks to other audiences that music educators are "sound educators," with the pun intended. My motivation for this comes from passion about thinking in sound and its role in moving the agenda ahead for creative experiences to accompany more teacher-centered approaches that do not give time for the student voice. Embedded in this excellent chapter, and also in Silverman's to come, is this same disposition. Abramo touches on the importance of sound and its consideration both in terms of teaching practice but also in the ways we do and present research. His notion of "individual phenomenology" with respect to the sonic experiences of individuals is powerful. I feel this has major importance for the way to teach listening, something that we do not do well in my opinion. His example of the differing perceptions surrounding Bach's "C Major Prelude" of the *Well Tempered Clavier* is a brilliant example of how patterns of tradition in our institutions have effected personal construction of meaning. The more open consideration of the sonic experience of music is an important notion for music listening. I have in mind too the questions of recorded music today. For example, as teachers of music within the context of today's media, we need to be aware of the issues of sound production and reproduction. This chapter and the references therein welcome the music teachers to be sensitive to how the live sounds of artists of all types are processed for consumption. Yet another interesting facet of this discussion is the matter of visual experiences of music in performance as a factor in music listening.

But Abramo gives us more. His speculation and observations about its role in research might be an even more important question. His idea of more soundscapes in our conception of data sets is worth major consideration and invites us to be more thoughtful about the implications of sound. The advancements now in some research publications (both online and more traditional) that allow multiple forms of media as part of the evidence presented welcome this affordance. The use of sound in our presentations of research too are noted, opening up a way to think more creatively about making the findings more meaningful for audiences interested in the sonic experience. I found the examples offered about sounds betraying the sociological and historical record of schooling to be intriguing and potentially very useful for researchers interested in deconstructing the educational experience. His explanation of "noise" in this context is important.

The section on arts-based research, inspired in part by Eisner's writing, is also of importance, especially for those that frame the requirements for advanced degrees. Newer forms of "research" in our field that might include less discursive prose and more artistic products such as narratives, plays, and musical compositions place more attention on the arts experience as part of the research record. Perhaps it is time for us to welcome more creative approaches to terminal degree requirements and to the acceptance of research reports with more "musical" evidence.

CRITICAL ETHNOGRAPHY AS/FOR PRAXIS:
A PATHWAY FOR MUSIC EDUCATION

Silverman's chapter on critical ethnography resonated deeply for me. She frames her explanation of this kind of ethnography in the context of one of the most pressing problems facing music education today: the disconnect between the musical worlds of the vast majority of today's youth and the traditional ways we teach music in schools. In the opening pages of this chapter, she sets the groundwork for this problem. In so doing, she makes the purpose (and, I would argue, importance) of critical ethnography so much more meaningful. I share her passion for finding new "pathways" for school music programs that respect the past but also recognize the present. Her reinforcement of Madison's notion of a "more meaningful musical, interpersonal, and intersubjective transactions and transformations among students, teachers, and classrooms" serves as an excellent foundation for understanding critical ethnography research and its implications for practice.

Her description of critical ethnography as a study of the interdependence of theory and practice in the context of an ethical stance is revealing. For some, the idea of using qualitative data for supporting the study of social, political, and ethical questions might appear to be too prescriptive. Yet to adopt this view is to dismiss years of work in critical theory and critical pedagogy. Such work lays bear for all to see certain inequities and injustices that require our attention. Silverman's treatment of the historical background of critical ethnography and the fine distinctions between "method" and "methodology" in the context of epistemology is important reading for any researcher who intends to do any kind of ethnography or any type of research for that matter. She proceeds to explain the common principles that critical ethnographic studies contain and, in so doing, lays solid ground for how such work is done and how it relates to good teaching.

I really enjoyed the case she makes for critical ethnography helping the teaching process. It is generally believed that, in years to come, we must do a much better job of linking research to practice and her arguments bolster this view. She makes a more nuanced approach to the word "praxis," something that is badly needed. She reminds us of Freire in this context and earlier in the chapter when noting his notion of the "banking-method" of teaching. His "problem-posing" approach is also a very important concept in imagining change in the way teaching is done and I can understand how being sensitive to these notions can be the focus of critical ethnology and the change of teaching practices.

Silverman ends her chapter by focusing on music listening as a context for critical ethnography and teacher reform. Clearly, focus on music listening instruction that takes a "non-active" approach and privileges the Western art canon to the exclusion of other styles and nationalities of music are troublesome problems to be sure. However, I do want to caution about over compensation. I would personally maintain that adopting a posture of excluding Western art music from reform in music listening education is itself a kind of ethical problem, worthy also of carefully crafted critical ethnographic study. I am guessing that Silverman might agree with this and my reading of the section that follows about *communitas* reinforces this guess. Finally, the list of questions that serves as a conclusion to her excellent chapter deserves careful study and should be added to other research questions raised in other chapters in this section.

STRUCTURAL EQUATION MODELING AND MULTILEVEL MODELING IN MUSIC EDUCATION: ADVANCING QUANTITATIVE RESEARCH DATA ANALYSIS

From quite a different research perspective, Stefanic welcomes us into a level of sophisticated thinking about quantitative inquiry. Silverman and Abramo present cases for expanding and deepening our views of more qualitative work, and Stefanic does the same on the quantitative side. His work represents a growing interest among quantitative scholars in such fields as psychology, sociology, and learning science to try to account more completely for the complexities of human behavior variables and their interrelation in complex social and cultural settings. He begins his excellent chapter on structural equation and multilevel modeling by reminding us that research questions are at times chosen with statistical tools and classic research designs in mind rather than on carefully conceived wonderments about music teaching and learning. It is tempting for teachers of research at beginning levels to encourage this in an attempt to get musicians thinking quantitatively. Of course to deepen our thinking about problems that really matter, more advanced knowledge of more complicated multivariate procedures such as the ones advocated in this chapter is needed and must be embedded earlier in our teaching.

Stefanic's passion for modeling of complex behavior is evident and represents an important way to foster better research in our field. He sees this as existing at the very core of quantitative inquiry and I cannot agree more. By "model," Stefanic is not talking about a statistical model as much as a conception of how variables of importance relate to each other in our world—conceptual hypotheses that provide a rich view of our lives. For example, he has in mind a theory or model about motivation to study music, or a model that conceptualizes how creative thinking in music works, or a theory about the role of home environment on music learning. Such modeling of important questions often does not find its way into the conceptual foundation of quantitative empirical work. This has taken its toll on a fair amount of quantitative study in music teaching and learning over the years. The shortcomings of some quantitative studies that use limited designs, poor sampling, and questionable statistical applications has lead to the legitimate criticism by many who view quantitatively-driven work as shallow, false, and unrepresentative of meaning for music teaching and learning. He makes a solid case for more advanced multivariates addressing these concerns.

An important part of understanding this chapter is to already have a solid knowledge of basic statistics and research design, particularly those that are based on what might be categorized as belonging to the General Linear Model (GLM). These include the often taught procedures of ANOVA, ANCOVA, MANOVA, MANCOVA, ordinary linear regression, t-tests and F-tests. Stefanic explains how these are less effective in providing evidence of complex interaction of variables. The reader probably also needs to be somewhat familiar with different approaches to factor analysis and regression.

All that said, he provides a fine introduction to the application of structural equation and multilevel modeling in music. His use of the Brand study as an example of how the research questions might be viewed as structural equation modeling is useful, as is his example of teaching style effectiveness in his description of multilevel modeling.

Among the greatest strengths of this chapter are his clear descriptions of the advantages of using these procedures and also the limitations. It might be possible to get lost in some of the technical aspects of the descriptions, but it is much more important to see the larger picture of why these procedures can address the questions of a multivariate and multilevel world in which we live. By describing these techniques in hopes of increasing the quality of work, Stefanic opens the door for more nuanced understanding.

Tables 19.1, 19.2, and 19.3 offer a number of fascinating research questions that will help the new researcher broaden and deepen research agendas. He is quick to point out that not all research questions will require structural equation or multilevel modeling and that other approaches may well be worth employing. But at some point along the way, tapping into these more sophisticated multivariate procedures is more likely as we improve our research record.

CONCLUDING THOUGHTS

In all four of these chapters, one senses the importance of good research questions. This is sometimes implied in the writing and at other times is actually highlighted as a section. It is likely that our practice of teaching and research will only improve in coming years if professionals have a better understanding of research itself and the tools for doing it.

In each of these chapters, too, the clear role of interdisciplinary sensibility is present. A review of the reference lists of each chapter will demonstrate that each author is well-read in other disciplines and they apply this knowledge to their scholarship. The development of this kind of cross-disciplinary understanding does not happen by accident and probably needs to be instilled as a core value in our research education efforts. Related to this is a need for more collaboration between researchers in other fields of music and with those outside our field. The disposition toward research teams and a continuing agenda of research activity continues to evade most of our professional efforts.

Finally, a clear implication for me in reading these chapters and in considering all that they have in common (and how they are different) is that we need to upgrade our efforts to integrate research content into our professional education programs. Each of these chapters contain advanced thinking about research and powerful implications for practice. To lay groundwork for this, we simply need to do better at both our undergraduate and graduate levels in preparing our music teachers professionally. In undergraduate education, evidence-based practice should be at the forefront of "methods" classes (if we must continue to call them that). There is nothing inherently complicated about the basics of good research and to include some level of understanding in undergraduate programs is not asking too much if we are clever at what we do. Graduate school offerings in research need to build on this and lead readers to be better able to consume and apply the content of chapters by Abramo, Silverman, and Stefanic particularly. If we have any hope of really effecting reform in the way music is taught, better research questions, interdisciplinary and collaborative efforts, and advanced understanding of the context and techniques of research are all necessary for the future that we all want.

Part V

Plotting a Course of Action

.

21 A Theory of Change in Music Education

Clint Randles

The purpose of this chapter is to propose a theory of change that might be useful to the music education profession—theorists, researchers, and practitioners alike.[1] My experience as a school music teacher and as a music teacher educator has helped inform these ideas. The theory takes action in a conceptual model that I believe might serve as a frame of reference for individuals who are thinking of implementing some sort of change in practice, or to help frame the work of researchers in music education who wish to study change. It is based on (1) the notion that as we occupy a specific place, we seek to navigate the space that surrounds us, to the benefit of the students or communities that we find ourselves in, and (2) that this navigation is in and of itself a creative process. The development of this theory has helped me in my early career as a music teacher educator to conceive of change that is possible at my university, change with the potential to impact the way that future generations of students are educated in music. So, this theory is intended for all those who are interested in the transformation of music education practice at all levels, and the conceptual model is an attempt to account for many of the factors that influence change.

Understanding the ideas put forth in this chapter requires a cognitive leap, in that I speak of music education as if it were a specific person, able to think about, act on, and react to the environment that surrounds her. It is a bit tricky to make this leap, since when I speak about the "individual" in this case I am actually talking about many individuals and complex relationships among individuals that form schools or communities, with specific histories and sometimes deeply seated traditions. Just as every individual is unique, every school music culture is unique. And, of course, this analogy works on multiple levels, and one could think of the "individual" as a particular school or as music education in the United States. My hope is that you, the reader, can take these ideas and apply them to the specific area of change that you wish to implement in your specific setting.

CHANGE?

If you are reading this chapter, there is a good chance that you are someone with an interest in seeing music education be a valuable part of your community. It is likely that some of you are music teacher educators who would like to see the future teachers with whom you are working be well equipped to be successful in this the first part of the 21st century. I would like to suggest here that change, in both variety and in degree, is a product of the specific culture that you find yourself working within. It is possible that you are teaching in a setting that enjoys a 60 percent student participation rate, well above the national average in the United States (21 percent) and Florida (8 percent), and that the scope and quality of the music making that your students are engaged in is excellent. In your case, there might not be a need at the moment to change much of anything in the organization of what you do. However, there may be some who are reading this who are struggling in their specific setting to recruit students for and sustain meaningful interest in music. This theory might be a useful tool to assist both your thinking and action.

IDENTITY OF THE "INDIVIDUAL"

If one thinks of the term "individual" as applying to a specific culture of music education, then one can think of that individual as possessing an identity. However, thinking this way is not without its challenges. These ideas are situated within a foundationalist epistemological perspective, one that supposes that the self can be explained by categorizing it into smaller units for analysis. This has been the primary way that research in music education has been approached since the days of Carl Seashore. This perspective has been disputed over the past several decades (Siegel, 2006, p. 7). Poststructuralists argue that the traditional conception of the self, as something that can be conceptually reduced, scientifically studied, and then understood, is amiss. Similarly, Anderson (1997) asserted that "all human societies are built upon a lie, the lie of self" (p. xi), and suggested that instead of thinking of the self as a single entity that can be studied as such, the academic community should instead think of two different alternative perspectives—the "multiple-self" and the "no-self." The primary tenant of the "multiple-self" concept is that the self is, "decentered, multi-dimensional, [and] changeable," while the "no-self" concept suggests that we drop the idea of self completely and try to connect the notion of being human to our wider surroundings, including the earth (Anderson, 1997, p. xv).

I appreciate these other perspectives, as the impetus for proposing these alternatives is to strengthen the overall integrity of the metanarrative. While I do not abandon the traditional conception of the self as something that can be better understood through scientific and theoretical inquiry, I believe as Anderson does, that the self IS multidimensional and changeable. Furthermore, I believe that parts of the self change without us giving the matter much thought, and that some parts are more easily changeable than others. I devote more space to these ideas later in this essay.

I find it imperative at this time, keeping in line with my more foundationalist perspective, to provide a working definition of identity for this work. I define identity here as it has been popularly defined in the music education literature, well articulated by McCall and Simmons (1978):

> The character and the role that an individual devises for himself as an occupant of a particular social position. More intuitively, such a role-identity is his imaginative view of himself as he likes to think of himself being and acting as an occupant of that position.
>
> (p. 65)

I like to organize concepts as a way of envisioning relationships among what I perceive to be the various parts. This desire almost always leads me to construct models. Keeping with this tendency, I have constructed the *Model of Psychological Dimensions* as a way of accounting for the various components of the previous definition of identity (see Figure 21.1). The model visually depicts identity as an *individual*'s "imaginative view of himself" (the center of the figure, the heart of my conception of the self) that comes about as he interprets his "character" and "role" as part of a *collective* (the individual influences the collective and is influenced by the collective), that over time produces *culture* (a collective's legacy), that comes out of a particular *society* (defined broadly or loosely, depending on how one

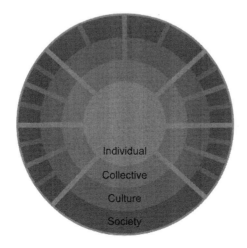

Figure 21.1   Model of psychological dimensions.

wants to apply this theory). This model complements the *Conceptual Model of Change in Music Education* that I will present later in this essay, and depicts another way that the individual, the place in this theory where cultural creativity is enacted, relates to the environment.

The individual for purposes of this theory can be considered a specific music education entity, school, or higher education institution. The model illustrates that where the *individual* and *society* meet, there are pockets of individuals who share a *collective* mind, or common "imaginative universe" (Geertz, 1973, p. 18). Music education certainly has numerous examples of this phenomenon. Various higher education institutions in the United States share similar "imaginative" universes. Prospective doctoral students will apply to numerous institutions that have come to stand for particular ideals. Groups of people, who form some sort of *collective*, over time produce *culture*, that includes: material culture (objects), social culture (institutions), and subjective culture (shared ideas and knowledge). Again, various music education institutions will host symposia on topics that represent "what they stand for." And, publications from these various symposia help spread the word to the academic world at large.

The model visually suggests that the *individual* (focal point) is manifest in the *collective* mind, produces *culture*, while being a part of *society*; that the *collective* mind is manifest in both *culture* and *society*; and that *culture* is manifest in *society*. The *individual* is not a lesser contributor to an understanding of the influence of *culture* and *society*. Rather, it is foundational to making sense of these relationships. The *individual* and *society* (also *culture* and the *collective* mind) are mutually constituted—"individuals and groups not only shape the contexts and settings in which they live and work, they are in time shaped by them" (Barrett, 2011, p. 3). In the model, *society* is the backdrop to all of the workings of the *individual,* the *collective,* and the *culture* that is produced over time.

PERCEPTUAL AND CULTURAL WORLDS

Cultural psychologists tell us that selfhood is comprised of *perceptual worlds* that help us locate ourselves and orientate ourselves among others, and *cultural worlds* that hold the keys to our sense of meaning (Benson, 2001, p. 4). The constructs most associated with *perceptual worlds* are self-esteem, self-efficacy, and self-concept, and the construct most associated with *cultural worlds* is identity. Both perceptual constructs and cultural constructs contribute to our understanding of the self. So, self in the broadest sense might be thought of as an individual's negotiation of the meaning of who she is (cultural worlds), based in part by her self-perceptions of herself (perceptual worlds) as a member of the social networks that she contributes to or functions within. The individual oftentimes desires to be like everyone else, and yet different in some way. These seemingly contrary desires can

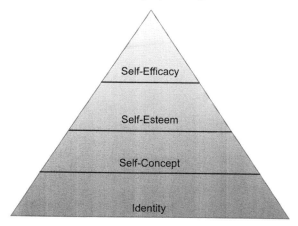

Figure 21.2   Model of identity as the foundation upon which "self" constructs rest.

Note: Identity is the most stable of the constructs, as it is the root of all of the other constructs.

interact daily, even moment-by-moment, at the perceptual level, and when considered over time, at the cultural level; cultural psychology is understood by way of history (Castro-Tejerina & Rosa, 2007; Seeger, 2001; Triandis, 2007).

Taking into account the connection of identity to history, one might think of it as the foundation upon which the other constructs most closely associated with the study of the self—self-esteem, self-efficacy, and self-concept—rest (see Figure 21.2). After all, with time often comes a sense of stability or permanence, as ways of thinking are reinforced. The historical component of identity, as a *cultural world,* is interwoven with meaning that has been built-up over time. Geertz (1973) referred to the individual in relation to culture when he stated that "man is an animal suspended in webs of significance he himself has spun" (p. 5). As time passes, the "webs of significance"—our beliefs about ourselves in relation to the world—contribute to what is our identity. While the perceptual worlds of individuals change continually, identity functions as the tried and true component of self that provides a root system or foundation, or like the anchor to a large ship. The time component in the formation of identity also makes it difficult to change quickly or easily.

I would like to suggest here that the music education profession, considered as a meta-collective of sorts, is made up of individuals who are who they are based in large part on how they got where they are now, their history. Identity, formed over time, has an inherent stability. For example, the way of preparing music teachers in North America has changed very little over the past 150 years. Each individual is, however, capable of perceiving

OTHER information and circumstances that might cause her to examine her identity, information assimilated from the perceptual world of selfhood. This information can chip away at the foundational relationship of the identity component of the self.

IDENTITY AS THE FOUNDATION FOR PERCEPTIONS OF SELF

Some scholars have argued that questions of identity are at the foundation of a person's belief system (Buss, 2001; Green, 2003; Roberts, 1991), that identity beliefs mark who a person is. Perceptual worlds, on the other hand, help to orientate a person to her surroundings, thus helping her to know *where*-she-is. Cultural worlds—with a connection to history—help a person to know *who*-she-is, thus helping shape her identity (Benson, 2001). Table 21.1 shows some of the common differences between self-esteem (a perceptual component of the self) and identity (a cultural component of the self). Notice that both areas are generally quite stable, however, identity is perhaps the most stable. Since identity deals with the portion of self that is concerned with meaning, it might be viewed as essentially one's philosophy of self as a function of time.

The self-systems located higher in the model, being more perceptually bound, that help answer the "where am I" locative questions, are more easily malleable. By completing a difficult task successfully, an individual can add to her self-efficacy (perception of her ability to complete a task in the future) of any number of musical or teacher-orientated tasks. That, in turn, can help in the self-esteem area (her evaluation of how worthwhile she is), and in turn, the self-concept area (the component of the self that sorts all of the incoming information related to self enhancement). Over an extended period of time, identity can also be affected.

One application for music education at the higher education level is that by locating particular efficacies in music that might lead future music

Table 21.1   The Difference Between Self-Esteem Questions and Identity Questions

Self-Esteem	Identity
How worthwhile am I?	Who am I?
Positive: adds pride in self	Positive: lends meaning to life
Lacking: self-effacement	Weak: rootlessness
Amnesia has little effect	Amnesia obliterates it
Romantic love adds to it	Marriage adds to it
How well a role is played	Commitment to a role
Group: vicarious self-esteem	Group: a feeling of belonging

Note: The table is borrowed from *Psychological Dimensions of the Self* (Buss, 2001, p. 89).

teachers to approach their jobs as music teachers in ways that could stretch currently immovable curricular offerings, music teacher educators will be able to feed, in a way, the future local cultural creative processes of music teachers. Efficacies in vernacular musicianship, composition, free improvisation, and others, could be infused in teacher education programs as "tools" of sorts for local change. Again, the model of cultural creativity presented later in this essay will illustrate how this might work in practice.

MAKING SENSE OF THE SELF-SYSTEM: SATURATION AS A MECHANISM FOR CHANGE

One might consider thinking about the relationship of these components as if they were levels of soil being subjected to a rainstorm (see Figure 21.3). The rainstorm might be thought of as the events, circumstances, and encounters with music, music making, and music education that an individual experiences. When these events occur, the perceptual worlds of individuals are the first levels to come in contact with the rain's bombardment. The locative mechanisms that give the self a sense of place with regard to a particular music-making phenomenon are engaged and sometimes challenged. These experiences then soak through the soil, and eventually can make it to the level of identity. Just as it takes a heavy rain to saturate soil, it will take a heavy rain to affect the "who am I" area of identity.

Each of the models serves a distinct function with regard to the presentation of ideas. Figure 21.2 is about the organizational structure of the

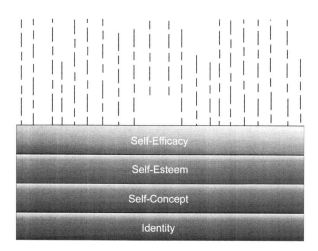

Figure 21.3   Model of the analogy of the self-system to soil in a rain storm.

Note: Identity as a cultural world is located the deepest, as it is the most stable, and the least directly affected by the bombardment of experience.

self-system, while Figure 21.3 is about the idea of the structure as it relates to the notion of change. (Saturation is what it will take to effectually "change" an individual at the "who am I" level (keep in mind the definition of individual presented earlier). Various efficacies are the first practical component of the self that should be addressed in this theory of change in music education. The idea of efficacies are explained in more detail as they relate to the *Conceptual Model of Change in Music Education,* presented later in this essay.

SPACE AND PLACE

Another way to think about the relationship between perceptual worlds and cultural worlds is to think of the two constructs not as one combined whole, such as in the previous model, but rather as separate members involved in a dynamic relationship characterized by interaction. Tuan (1977) wrote in his thought provoking book *Space and Place* that "place is security," something that we are attached to, while "space is for freedom," something we long for (p. 6). Space is where elements that are both novel and appropriate are searched out. These elements serve as food for the cultural creative processes that are engaged in at the individual level. Place is where these elements are checked and tested. Place can be thought of as the location of the cultural creative process.

Place can further represent the cultural worlds that we seek to nurture in our lives, our sense of who we are. Tuan (1977) stated that "what begins as undifferentiated space becomes place as we get to know it better and endow it with value" (p. 6). So, for Tuan, we constantly are aware of place, while we more comfortably explore the area of space. This exploration can be likened unto a personal quest for fulfillment or a hero's journey (Campbell, 1949/2008), where identity is maintained and over time extended. The hero's journey in the Campbellian sense is characterized by separation-initiation-return. Tuan (1997) suggested that once we conquer areas of space, they have the potential to become place to us (p. 6).

I shall now shift the focus of this essay to situating this theory within the history of the study of identity, before unpacking my conceptual model of change in music education.

SITUATING CHANGE

Work in the sociology of music education has been somewhat ongoing since the late 1950s (Mueller, 1958) and the mid-1960s (Kaplan, 1966), and continues to be a topic today (Froehlich, 2006; Green, 2011; Wright, 2010). Music education scholars and researchers have grappled with the realization/belief that social/historical/political forces have and probably always will impact music education practice on multiple levels (Campbell, 1997, 1998; Green, 2002; MacDonald et al., 2002). The complex interactions caused by these forces mean that teachers and students must work within systems that are sometimes predetermined, sometimes out of their control, while at the same time trying to do what they feel is best for their students. Doing what is best for students and working within existing social structures is not always easy, particularly when the social structures are rigid.

However, I do not want to suggest here that the situation is without hope, for music education is alive and well in many cases at the local level. Teachers who recognize that curriculum might best be conceptualized as a creative process are finding ways to enhance the musical experiences of their students by working within sometimes rigid social structures. In the United States, there is band, choir, and orchestra at the secondary level. These ensembles have been around since the beginning of the 1900s in the United States (Mark & Gary, 2007). These ensembles are promoted at the state and national level by NAfME, and are a part of nearly every college music program across the country. To be accepted into any of these programs, one must audition for a spot on one of the instruments or voices currently being represented in these standardized ensembles. Students who audition to get into the school have had at least thirteen years of enculturation into the world of that way of making music—performing from notation masterworks in a large ensemble under the direction of a conductor. This is the cultural world that music education theorists/practitioners in their specific cultures must work within and through. This is part of the reason why identity, in this essay, is conceptualized as a somewhat rigid construct. The "who we are" part of self has a legacy. This legacy is what we have to acknowledge and work with and around.

Identity is not impossible to change, though. Lucy Green (2011) describes the formation of musical identities this way:

> Musical identities are forged from a combination of personal, individual musical experiences on one hand, and membership in various social groups—from the family to the nation-state and beyond—on the other hand. They encompass musical tastes, values, practices (including reception activities such as listening or dancing), skills, and knowledge; and they are wrapped up with how, where, when, and why those tastes, values, practices, skills, and knowledge were acquired or transmitted.
>
> (p. 1)

So, going back to the *Model of the Analogy of the Self-System to Soil in a Rain Storm* (Figure 21.3), new experiences bombard our perceptual worlds, in this case the perceptual worlds of music education collectively, that cause the profession to become aware of things that it has not been aware of, and cause it to reevaluate its place. Over time (this is key) the profession searches the space containing all possible ways to expand first its perceptual world, then its own cultural world. For example, the notion of being multi-musical, being able to function as a reader of notation and as a vernacular music maker, or being multi-creative (Burnard, 2011, 2012), might capture the collective imagination of the profession. Members of the higher education community could search out ways of engaging their respective schools of music in the actualization of various plans to prepare the next generation of teachers to occupy a new and improved place (stemming from the collective mind of the profession). All the while, new experiences bombard the profession, as this dynamic interaction prompts change in new and exciting ways. It was formed over time, and so therefore, out of necessity, it must change over time. Music education scholars and curriculum reformers must take into consideration the rootedness of identity in terms of the individual preservice music teacher.

Music education faculty members often desire to assist students in forming a teacher identity through various observations and practicum experiences, sometimes seeking to encourage new ways of thinking and doing regarding music education theory and practice, with full knowledge that each preservice teacher has had at least 13 years of enculturation into the world of music learning and teaching as a student. This point complicates the work of music education faculty who have a mind for change in the profession. Identity is stable; it might be considered the root of our human self-systems. By the time music education majors reach the college level, the "who am I as a music maker" questions have been answered in the minds of students to a large extent. These questions can certainly still be approached by music teacher education faculty; however, given that they were developed over time, resulting beliefs regarding these important questions must morph over time.

A LOOK TO THE FUTURE

Cultural change at the everyday level always involves creativity, a combination of novelty and appropriateness. Novelty can be viewed as the transformation of cultural practice, and appropriateness can be viewed as the value to a community. However, with everyday cultural creativity we deal with the creation of practices, not the creation of products. The working out of cultural transmission on a day-to-day level always involves both *imitation* and *invention.* In order to function in the world around us, we as humans seek out ways of living and doing that have worked for those around us and *imitate* those ways. When those ways do not work, when they seem mundane, no longer necessary, or deficient in some compelling way, we invent new ways of accomplishing our goals. This kind of everyday creativity, at the micro-level, will continue to occur, without any intervention from music teachers or leaders in music education, indeed, without even giving it much thought. This type of cultural creativity allows societies to continue, reproducing themselves from generation to generation. There is surely an inherent stability in social structures, norms, and cultures. Some have argued that the main function of social systems is to maintain the status quo (Merton, 1968). Cultural creativity at the macro-level, however, must be more deliberately operationalized.

In order for this process to be initiated, the perceptual worlds of the collective mind must be made aware that things might not be where they should be or look how they should look. Technological innovations, particularly compelling philosophies, and examples of other ways of doing music education in both adaptive and innovative ways, must engage the perceptual worlds of the profession. If the imagination of the collective music education "self" is engaged, or saturated as the *Model of the Analogy of the Self-System to Soil in a Rain Storm* (Figure 21.3) suggests, the motivation to look outside of school music education and to music efficacies that occur in the real world might prompt cultural creative processes at the macro-level. As was mentioned previously, music education as a meta-individual, like many social structures that have existed over an extended period of time, have an inherent stability. Understanding this point is key to engaging the collective imagination of the profession.

Conceptual Model of Change in Music Education

The *Conceptual Model of Change in Music Education* (see Figure 21.4) is based on existing models that have been developed by Webster (2006) in creative thinking, the author (Randles, 2013) in music making, and the author in collaboration with Webster (Randles & Webster, 2013) in creative music making. It takes into consideration the compelling utility of Engestrom's (1987, 2001) model of the structure of a human activity system, which has been used by other researchers and scholars in music education (Burnard & Younker, 2008; Welch, 2011). "Community," "rules," "tools and signs," and "division of labor" were adapted from the Engestrom model and are used here as part of "context."

One of the strengths of the Engestrom model is that it provides a visual representation of the relationship of the various components of an activity system. *Community* accounts for the multiple points of view, traditions, and interests expressed by all those who associate themselves with a particular culture. One might think of *community* as comprising the various members of the "individual" as it has been described here. *Division of labor* accounts for the various positions that exist within and without the culture. *Rules* are the conventions and guidelines that regulate activity within the system. *Tools and signs* are the artifacts or concepts that regulate activity within the system. The change model presented here recognizes these components of the Engestrom model as being essential to understanding how change is actuated. One of the weaknesses of the model is that it does not adequately account for what takes place during the cultural creative process—the place

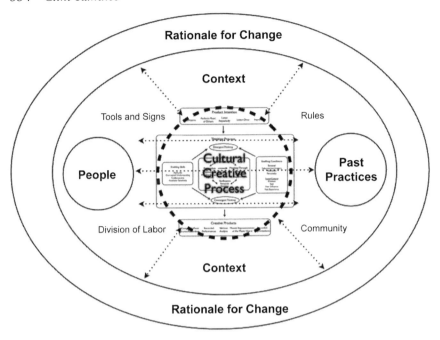

Figure 21.4 Conceptual model of change in music education.

of action—of the activity system. The *Conceptual Model of Change in Music Education* is a more action sensitive representation of how change is articulated in the real world of music education practice.

In order to understand how the *Conceptual Model of Change in Music Education* might be helpful, it is necessary to enlarge the "cultural creative process" component of the model (see Figure 21.5). Both *innovation* and *adaption* are seen as possible practice intentions in the "cultural creative process" (Kirton, 1976). *Innovation* occurs when the focus is on doing something differently. *Adaptation* is the goal when the focus is on doing something better. Music education could stand to gain from both doing things differently and from doing things better. Practices that could emerge from the cultural creative process include, but are not limited to, the creativities that Burnard details in her latest work (2011, 2012): individual, collaborative (or group), communal, empathic, intercultural, performance, symbolic, computational, and collective. Innovative practice intentions could include starting an iPad group in a school, a songwriting class, or a computer-music class. Adaptive practice intentions could include turning the high school drumline into a new music ensemble, turning the show choir into a songwriting lab, or introducing composition or improvisation into the band, choir, or orchestra. Examples of innovation and adaptation need

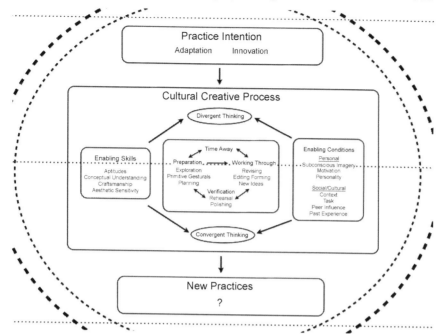

Figure 21.5 Cultural creative process.

Note: This is an enlarged version of the *Cultural Creative Process* portion of the *Conceptual Model of Change in Music Education.*

not be this prescriptive, although they might be. The creativity of the teacher is an essential ingredient to creating new practices that meet our "product intention" expectations.

An understanding of the components of the *Cultural Creative Process* provides a point of entry for how to use this model to enact change. *Enabling skills* might be a teacher's musical or teaching skills that have been developed as a result of his or her primary or secondary socialization. Teacher education is key to expanding these enabling skills for future generations of teachers and their students. Opportunities to arrange music by utilizing vernacular musicianship, composing and improvising in a variety of contexts, and using a variety of technological tools in the performance of digital music, are all examples of enabling skills that can have an impact on cultural creative processes. *Enabling conditions*, that include both personal and social/cultural factors, are the specific components of the larger model (context, people, past practices, etc.) that require immediate attention during the cultural creative process. Not all knowledge of people, context, and past practices (among other large conceptual areas) is useful during a particular

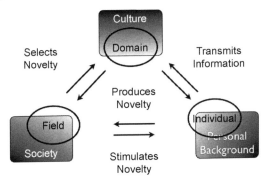

Figure 21.6   Csikszentmihalyi's systems view of creativity.

Note: This model was taken from a book chapter written by Csikszentmihalyi in Sternberg's (1999) *Handbook of Creativity.*

cultural creative process. This is the primary reason that the *Conceptual Model of Change in Music Education* accounts for the various components of change at both the macro and micro levels.

Specific practices are the end and the beginning of every cultural creative process. So how do we gauge the success or failure of the process? What makes a particular created practice more or less appropriate than another? Csikszentmihalyi's (1999) "Systems View of Creativity" (see Figure 21.6) might provide a useful way of conceptualizing how new experiences, new ideas, the work of practitioners, individual music education scholars, academic institutions, and even research centers might be able to engage the imagination of the profession. These are the outputs, the "new practices" of the "cultural creative process," what is created. These "new practices" then can be tested for appropriateness, first at the local level, and then, potentially, at the regional, state, and even national level. In Csikszentmihalyi's (1999) model, the individual, domain, and field work together to determine what is "novel" and "appropriate" (p. 315). In order for new ideas and practices to be accepted, they need to be introduced and promoted by individuals who possess a good feel for what is acceptable to the society and the consequent culture that he or she is working within. If the social groups and the culture that make up the "webs of significance," to quote Geertz (1973, p. 5) once again, that make up those cultures are not taken into consideration, then change might not be possible. I would like to argue, with much optimism, that change is possible.

A PLACE TO START

In this chapter, I introduced a *Model of Psychological Dimensions,* and suggested how it might help the profession conceptualize the nexus between the individual and society. Then, I defined identity as a manifestation of cultural psychology, and outlined the role and characteristics of both perceptual and cultural worlds. I then merged the idea of the selfhood of individuals to the idea of the selfhood of music education, and used the metaphor of a rainstorm to explain how the components of self, an understanding of "place" and "space," and knowledge of cultural creativity might help us understand the structure of change. I then concluded the chapter by presenting a *Conceptual Model of Change in Music Education*.

Just like all good research, curricular change must start with a good theory. I hope that the conceptual work in this chapter helps all those who have a mind for change in the profession. The center of the *Conceptual Model of Change in Music Education* is the Cultural Creative Process. This process consists of working with existing materials in a process that requires both divergent and convergent thinking. As the model suggests, preparation, working through, exploration, and verification are aspects of the creative process. Divergent thinking can be thought of as the imagination that it takes to get the process started. Convergent thinking can be thought of as the selection of the best, most appropriate solution.

Navigating the future of music education requires the connected processes of problem finding and problem solving. These processes are articulated in the *Conceptual Model of Change in Music Education* presented in this essay. As stated at the onset of this chapter, I hope that this theory of change in music education will be helpful to the profession—theorists, researchers, and practitioners alike. The future can be bright if we recognize that (1) change is articulated locally, (2) change is the product of imagination in conjunction with a lot of hard work, and (3) change is the result of the work of people whose histories and culture impact the community, divisions of labor, rules, tools, and signs as they relate to the process. Change in identity begins with changes in particular self-efficacies. Music education can change. Let us think about the process, and then take action.

NOTE

1. An earlier version of this paper exists in published form as:

   Randles, C. (2013). A theory of change in music education. *Music Education Research*, *15*(4), 471–85. Reprinted with permission by Taylor & Francis Group, London, UK.

REFERENCES

Anderson, W. T. (1997). *The future of the self: Inventing the postmodern person*. New York, NY: J. P. Tarcher.

Barrett, M. (2011). Towards a cultural psychology of music education. In M. Barrett (Ed.), *A cultural psychology of music education* (pp. 1–16). New York, NY: Oxford University Press.

Benson, C. (2001). *The cultural psychology of self: Place, morality, and art in human worlds*. New York, NY: Routledge.

Burnard, P. (2011). Rethinking "musical creativity" and the notion of multiple creativities in music. In O. Odena (Ed.), *Musical creativity: Insights from music education research* (pp. 5–28). Burlington, VT: Ashgate Publishing.

Burnard, P. (2012). *Musical creativities in practice*. New York, NY: Oxford University Press.

Burnard, P., & Younker, B. (2008). Investigating children's musical interactions within the activities systems of group composing and arranging: An application of Engestrom's activity theory. *International Journal of Educational Research, 47,* 60–74.

Buss, A. (2001). *Psychological dimensions of the self*. Thousand Oaks, CA: Sage Publishing.

Campbell, J. (2008). *The hero with a thousand faces* (3rd Ed.). Novato, CA: New World Library. (Original work published 1949)

Campbell, P. S. (1998). *Songs in their heads: Music and its meaning in children's lives*. New York, NY: Oxford University Press.

Campbell, P. S. (2007). Adolescents' expressed meanings of music in and out of school. *Journal of Research in Music Education, 55*(3), 220–36.

Casey, E. (1997). *The fate of place: A philosophical history*. Berkeley: University of California Press.

Castro-Tejerina, J., & Rosa, A. (2007). Psychology within time: Theorizing about the making of socio-cultural psychology. In J. Valsiner & A. Rosa (Eds.), *The Cambridge handbook of sociocultural psychology* (pp. 62–81). New York, NY: Cambridge University Press.

Csikszentmihalyi, M. (1999). Implications of a systems perspective for the study of creativity. In R. J. Sternberg (Ed.), *Handbook of creativity* (pp. 313–35). New York, NY: Cambridge University Press.

Engestrom, Y. (1987). *Learning by expanding: An activity-theoretical approach to developmental research*. Helsinki, Finland: Orienta-Konsultit.

Engestrom, Y. (2001). Expansive learning at work: Toward an activity theoretical reconceptualization. *Journal of Education and Work, 14*(1), 133–56.

Froehlich, H. (2006). *Sociology for music teachers: Perspectives for practice*. Upper Saddle River, NJ: Pearson Prentice Hall.

Geertz, C. (1973). *The interpretation of cultures*. New York, NY: Basic Books.

Green, L. (2002). *How popular musicians learn: A way ahead for music education*. Hampshire, England: Ashgate Publishing.

Green, L. (2003). Music education, cultural capital, and social group identity. In M. Clayton, T. Herbert, & R. Middleton (Eds.), *The cultural study of music: A critical introduction* (pp. 263–73). London, United Kingdom: Psychology Press.

Green, L., (Ed.) (2011). *Learning, teaching and musical identity*. Bloomington: Indiana University Press.

Kaplan, M. (1966). *Foundations and frontiers of music education*. New York, NY: Holt, Rinehart and Winston.

Kirton, M. J. (1976). Adaptors and innovators: A description and measure. *Journal of Applied Psychology, 61,* 622–98.

MacDonald, R., Hargreaves, D., & Miell, D. (2002). *Musical identities*. New York, NY: Oxford University Press.

Mark, M., & Gary, C. (2007). *A history of American music education* (3rd Ed.). Lanham, MD: Rowman & Littlefield Publishing.

McCall, G. J., & Simmons, J. L. (1978). *Identities and interactions: An examination of human associations in everyday life*. New York: Free Press.

Merton, R. K. (1968). *Social theory and social structure*. New York, NY: Free Press.

Mueller, J. H. (1958). Music and education: A sociological approach. In N. B. Henry (Ed.), *Basic concepts in music education: The fifty-seventh yearbook of the national society for the study of education* (pp. 88–122). Chicago, IL: University of Chicago Press.

Randles, C. (2013). Why composition in band and orchestra? In C. Randles & D. Stringham (Eds.), *Musicianship: Composing in band and orchestra* (pp. 5–14). Chicago, IL: GIA Publishing.

Randles, C., & Webster, P. (2013). Creativity in music teaching and learning. In G. Cariyannis (Ed.), *Encyclopedia of creativity, innovation, invention, and entrepreneurship* (pp. 420–9). New York, NY: Springer Publishing.

Roberts, B. (1991). Music teacher education as identity construction. *International Journal of Music Education, 18,* 30–9.

Seeger, F. (2001). The complementarity of theory and praxis in the cultural-historical approach: From self-application to self-regulation. In S. Chaiklin (Ed.), *The theory and practice of cultural-historical psychology* (pp. 35–55). Oakville, CT: Aarhus University Press.

Siegel, H. (2006). Epistemological diversity and education research: Much ado about nothing much? *Educational Researcher, 35*(3), 3–12.

Sternberg, R. J. (Ed.) (1999). *Handbook of creativity.* New York, NY: Cambridge University Press.

Triandis, H. C. (2007). Culture and psychology: A history of the study of their relationships. In S. Kitayama & D. Cohen (Eds.), *Handbook of cultural psychology* (pp. 59–76). New York, NY: Guilford Press.

Tuan, Y. (1977). *Space and place: The perspective of experience.* Minneapolis: University of Minnesota Press.

Webster, P. R. (2006, April). Refining a model of creative thinking in music: A basis for encouraging students to make aesthetic decisions. Paper presented at the National Convention, Music Educators National Conference, Salt Lake City, UT.

Welch, G. (2011). Culture and gender in a cathedral music context: An activity theory exploration. In M. Barrett, *A cultural psychology of music education* (pp. 225–58). New York, NY: Oxford University Press.

Wright, R. (Ed.) (2010). *Sociology and music education.* Burlington, VT: Ashgate Publishing.

22 The Role of Subversion in Changing Music Education

John Kratus

There is an apocryphal curse of dubious Chinese origin that threatens, "May you live in interesting times." Probably such a curse actually originated in a 20th-century fortune cookie rather than in an antediluvian tome authored by an ancient philosopher. Yet one authentic Chinese proverb does convey a similar sentiment: "It's better to be a dog in a peaceful time than to be a man in a chaotic period." The fear expressed in both sayings is the fear of change, that harbinger of an unknown and uncertain future, that menace to a comfortable and familiar status quo. Change does bring with it a certain justifiable fear. All change, regardless of how well-intentioned and well-conceived, carries with it the possibility of inadvertent disaster, and change does not come with a money-back guarantee.

But as Heraclitus reminded us, "Nothing is permanent but change." The one constant element in life-spans, in species, in institutions, in animate and inanimate objects, and, yes, even in music education, is change. When something ceases to change and adapt to shifting circumstances, it ceases to exist. The contexts in which we live and teach continue to change, and so must we in order to survive. And in our changing we act upon our contexts and necessitate further changes in them, and the cycles repeat. Change in all things is not an option; it is mandatory and inevitable.

When change comes to an institution, it can be viewed as a positive or negative occurrence. Some changes are readily accepted by stakeholders in meeting needs and addressing problems, whereas other institutional changes can be perceived by stakeholders as existential threats. When that is the case, initiating change can be a messy business, beset with institutional impediments, and opposed by those with a vested interest in stasis and who subscribe to the Chinese proverbs cited above. I do not raise the issues of fear and resistance to discourage change, but rather to acknowledge the difficulty of bringing about change, regardless of how necessary or well-intentioned.

THE LIMITS OF THEORY

When one seeks to initiate change in an institution like music education, it is helpful to understand the various currents that may oppose or support that change. This brings us to Clint Randles's theory of change in music education. According to Edwards (1992), models or theories have two main functions. The first function is to represent and focus on the essential attributes of a phenomenon to make understandable complex processes and relations. A street map is a good example of this, showing streets and their relation to each other while leaving out the location of trees. The second function of a model or theory is "dynamic and generative," proposing a method of action to accomplish a goal. A model used by the National Weather Service for forecasting storms is an example of this.

Randles makes use of both functions. His model of the analogy of the self-system to soil in a rainstorm serves the first function, as a map showing the direct exposure of self-efficacy to various experiences and the relative stability of identity. The application of Webster's (2006) model of creative thinking in music in Randles's theory of change in music education serves the second function, because it suggests that instituting change is essentially a creative process. The Randles theory serves as both a map to illustrate relations and an instruction manual to designate a means.

Randles writes that those persons who wish to initiate change in music education "seek to navigate the space around us," and that a theory may be useful in understanding the factors that influence such change. But all theories have their limits. I would like to consider an analogy regarding the limitations of theory, any theory, to guide practice. Imagine that the application of a theory to actual practice is like using a flashlight to navigate across a darkened living room. Without a flashlight we may eventually cross the room but it would take a long time, and we would probably stumble into the barely visible coffee table and sofa. A flashlight could offer some assistance in helping us to understand the layout of the room. Some flashlights cast a narrow but bright beam, illuminating a small space clearly, and other flashlights shine more dimly over a wider area. Each type has its own advantages. In music education the Kodaly approach of teaching so-mi before so-mi-la is like a narrow, bright beam, providing clear guidance over a very small space. The axiom "sound before symbol" is like a wide, dim beam, offering broader guidance but more diffusely. Flashlights, like theories, help us to make sense of unrevealed shapes and the dimly perceived terrain of our surroundings.

But it is important to note that no flashlight, no matter how powerful and practical, can light up an entire room. When we shine a light on one part of the room, the rest of the room reverts to darkness. Similarly no theory can reveal all the workings of a complex phenomenon or process. This is

John Kratus

not an imperfection of flashlights or theories; it is the nature of how they work. Theories can be improved but never perfected, and part of our rooms will always remain in the dark. Even Einstein failed in his quest to find the Grand Unified Theory that would have explained how all the forces in the universe interact.

In the early 1990s I created a multi-leveled theory to explain how people learn to improvise over time in developmentally different ways (Kratus, 1991, 1995). According to the theory, certain changes in the characteristics of a student's improvisation signal that the student is passing from one level of improvisation to another, and the teacher's role then changes. Teachers have told me that they have heard the changes I describe in their students' improvisations, and that this theory has helped them to plan and implement instruction more appropriately. But the theory does not address why or how students would be motivated to develop their approach to improvisation. The factor of joy is missing from the theory. Accordingly no teacher has ever told me whether her students took pleasure in improvising. Their flashlights were pointed elsewhere.

No theory can explain all of the factors affecting a particular process or phenomenon. Randles's theory views change in music education from the perspective of the change agent, that is, of the teacher or policy maker or institution desiring to try something new. I would like to suggest that there are also powerful forces aligned against change, and that these forces should not be left in the darkened part of the living room.

RESISTANCE TO CHANGE

Change in American music education has usually come very slowly. Randles pointed out that the formal education of music teachers in the United States has changed little over a long period of time. In 2009 I gave a presentation on collegiate curricular change in music for the Society for Music Teacher Education in Greensboro, North Carolina. One of the first slides in my presentation was an outline of Michigan State University's degree requirements for the Bachelor of Music in Music Education. The outline included certain numbers of semesters for applied lessons, large ensembles, theory and ear training, and history and literature, as well as music education requirements including three tracks (instrumental, string, choral/general), introduction to music education, conducting, instrument and voice classes dependent on track, methods classes dependent on track, college of education courses, and student teaching. I asked the audience members how many of them taught in a college program similar to that. Nearly every hand went up. Then I revealed that the program I described was taken from the Michigan State University Academic Programs book from 1959. The course descriptions, the performance repertoire, even the delivery of instruction were, for all practical purposes, nearly unchanged in 50 years. This inertia is dangerous, because institutions that do not change to accommodate their changing contexts ultimately cease to exist.

The stagnation in our music teacher education programs goes back much further than 50 years. It is not an exaggeration to say that the type of music education provided to contemporary collegiate music majors has deep roots in the conservatories of European capitals of the 19th century. In fact, more than its roots are located there—21st-century collegiate music has retained the stems, branches, leaves, flowers, seeds, and pollen of its 200-year-old predecessors.

A little history lesson is in order to uncover how we find ourselves today in such an intractable, anachronistic curriculum for music teacher education. Beginning in the early 1800s, the classical music business experienced a boom across Europe, especially in the urban centers. Prior to this time, this form of music was primarily available only to the secular and religious aristocracy. With the creation and increase of a European middle class, orchestral music and opera became accessible to a much broader audience. Orchestras and opera companies were formed in all the larger European cities and in many smaller ones as well. Opera companies and orchestras spread through the United States in the late 19th century and early 20th century. Classical music was a growth industry, and the demand for musicians was high.

Up to this time professional classical musicians learned their craft through an apprentice system. With the dramatic increase in orchestras and opera companies, the one-on-one apprentice system was unable to produce a sufficient number of trained musicians to fill the available positions. As a means to supply additional qualified musicians, the first secular music conservatory in the world, the Conservatoire National de Musique et d'Art Dramatique, was founded in Paris in 1795. Across Europe secular conservatories soon sprung up in Milan (1807), Naples (1808), Prague (1811), Vienna (1817), London (1822), Leipzig (1843), and elsewhere. The conservatory boom hit the United States later in the 19th century, with schools like Oberlin (1866), New England (1867), Boston (1867), and Peabody (1868).

> These conservatories are largely a 19th-century invention, designed in an era obsessed with the child protege, whose principal *raison d'etre* was the fostering of solo as well as rank-and-file talent for the burgeoning orchestras and opera houses at the mainstay of European musical life a century ago.
>
> (Bruno, 2006)

Conservatories offered a particular kind of vocational training for the growth industry of classical music performance. The course of study for 19th-century conservatory students should look familiar to 21st-century collegiate music educators: extensive private instruction focusing on a single instrument or voice in the classic tradition, extensive conductor-led large ensemble or opera experience with 19th-century repertoire, some piano study, multiple years of theory emphasizing written notation and solfege, and the historical study of European music literature.

This is, in fact, a near perfect description of the music core curriculum in contemporary schools of music. Even the repertoire and literature studied, with its emphasis on 19th-century European masterworks, is nearly identical. The question we should be asking ourselves is: Why is the musical training of 21st-century music educators nearly identical to that of 19th-century performers preparing to join orchestras and opera companies?

One might try to explain the static collegiate/conservatory music curriculum in terms of the classical music identity of a majority of the faculty stakeholders, many or most of whom may well oppose change that would undermine their hegemony and challenge their self-esteem. It is with pride that a violinist can claim that her teacher's teacher's teacher's teacher's teacher's teacher was Paganini. It is understandable that the performer's skill that has taken thousands of hours to develop and the performing experiences that accompanied that development have left an indelible mark that cannot be washed away with the introduction of iPad ensembles and vernacular musicianship.

But I think that the resistance to adapt to 21st-century musicianship cannot be completely explained by identity. Wind band and jazz faculty members, whose genres lack the centuries-old traditions of classical music, can also oppose curricular change. A factor that may trump identity is *responsibility*, a responsibility to the past.

Of all the performing arts in education, music is alone in its fealty to the past. It is not uncommon for a collegiate orchestra or opera company to perform most of its repertoire from the 19th century. Concert band and jazz ensembles lack such an extensive history, but they too typically perform more music from the past than the present. By contrast theater and dance pay homage to their past but tend to perform more contemporary works. Yes, Shakespeare is acted and 19th-century choreography is danced, but theater and dance education include more contemporary works in the education of their students than does music education.

Perhaps the reason for the disparity is that the music collegiate musicians perform in formal concert settings is notated in a more exacting way than are theatrical scripts and choreography. Conductors often speak of a responsibility to the composer, a responsibility to the past, in performing these works. Improvising and arranging is frowned upon in performing the standard music repertoire. The will of the individual performer becomes subservient to the will of the composer and the will of the director. In a sense the institution of music education has metaphorically taken it upon itself to be responsible for upholding and maintaining performance practices that existed 100 and 200 years ago. What gets lost is a sense of responsibility to the students and their musical futures.

We can see examples of this misplaced responsibility all around us. Why do collegiate music departments often have a faculty line for "oboe professor" but not for "guitar professor"? The number of guitar players on a college campus is almost certainly 100 times greater than the number of oboe players. But an oboe is required to perform the orchestral music of 100 years ago, and a guitar is not. Maintaining the orchestra and its music takes precedent over the musical interests of students. Similarly the standard instrumentation for symphonic bands, and the performance demands set by the music that was commissioned for that standard instrumentation, have created a responsibility to maintaining the band as an entity over the music interests and needs of music students.

The form of music education that existed for professionals in the 19th century existed for a particular purpose in a particular time. The purpose and time no longer exist, but the perceived responsibility to the past has restrained efforts to change music education, not only at the collegiate level, but at the secondary and elementary levels as well.

K–12 music teachers can only teach what they know. Their own music education at the collegiate level has provided them with musical knowledge and skills that are mismatched for their own times. Twenty-first century music teachers learning to perform at a high level of proficiency in large, conductor-led ensembles from scores by century-old composers is a style that discourages individual initiative and encourages following an autocratic leader. Is there any wonder why K–12 music education emphasizes large ensemble performance and music literacy, while discouraging creativity and vernacular musicianship? As Randles points out, we are all products of our own histories.

SMALL ACTS OF SUBVERSION

In the environment I have described, systematic change in music education is very difficult. The desires of an individual or a small group of individuals to promote change are often opposed by others within institutions who see themselves as responsible for upholding revered standards of the past. Both the proponents of change and proponents of the status quo believe that they hold the moral high ground.

Change in music education is made even more problematic, because those who would promote change are in the minority. In K–12 education the study of music does not directly contribute to economic wellbeing. In a pragmatic, profit-driven country like the United States, music will never be as important in K–12 schools as math, science, and reading. In many parts of the United States the culture of festivals, contests, and ensemble ratings is such an integral part of music education that opposing this culture is arduous. In collegiate schools of music, music education faculty will always be vastly outnumbered and outvoted by performance faculty, most of whom have a vested interest in the conservatory model of education. The mechanisms of change in music education, therefore, cannot be confrontational, because music educators are not working from a position of strength at either the K–12 or collegiate levels.

How then can change in music education occur? My suggestion is that those who advocate change in music education should embrace *small acts of subversion, or SAS.* Subversion is an attempt or act to overthrow or undermine structures of authority. Small acts of subversion are modest but meaningful changes moving in the direction of a perceived ideal. SAS do not challenge the power of those in control of the institution. SAS require patience and a long time frame to be effective. Eventually SAS after SAS undermine the status quo and systematic change occurs.

Large-scale changes in a music education program (e.g., eliminating the collegiate orchestra) may well engage those in power who would oppose such a change. Small acts of subversion (e.g., starting a songwriting class) can slip under the radar, because they do not directly confront anyone in a position of power. My own personal experience is that the former approach has little chance of success, and the latter approach can readily be accepted and if successful destabilize the prevailing paradigm.

Clint Randles's model of change in music education describes change as local, imaginative, and mindful of identity. My own additions to that theory are to be conscious of the limitations of theory and to recognize the inertia of a system that has defied most efforts to change. Together these approaches may create the "interesting times" that the ancient Chinese supposedly so greatly feared.

REFERENCES

Bruno, M. (2006). A high-level option. *Choir & Organ, 1*(1), 27–30.

Edwards, R.H. (1992). Model building. In R. Colwell (Ed.), *Handbook of research in music teaching and learning* (pp. 38–47). New York, NY: Schirmer.

Kratus, J. (1991). Growing with improvisation. *Music Educators Journal, 78*(4), 35–40.

Kratus, J. (1995). A developmental approach to teaching music improvisation. *International Journal of Music Education, 26,* 27–38.

Webster, P. R. (2006, April). Refining a model of creative thinking in music: A basis for encouraging students to make aesthetic decisions. Paper presented at the National Convention, Music Educators National Conference, Salt Lake City, UT.

Names and Addresses

MUSIC EDUCATION: NAVIGATING THE FUTURE

Joseph Abramo
University of Connecticut
Neag School of Education
Department of Curriculum and Instruction
249 Glenbrook Road, Unit 3033
Storrs, CT 06269–3033

Wayne Bowman
Brandon University
School of Music
Queen Elizabeth II Music Building
270—18th Street
Brandon, Manitoba
Canada, R7A 6A9

Richard Colwell
University of Illinois at Urbana/Champaign
School of Music
1114 W. Nevada St.
Urbana, IL 61801

Frank Heuser
UCLA
Herb Alpert School of Music
2539 Schoenberg Hall
Los Angeles, CA 90095–7234

John Kratus
Michigan State University
College of Music
214 Music Practice Building
East Lansing, MI 48824

Roger Mantie
Arizona State University
Herberger Institute for Design and the Arts
PO Box 872102
Tempe, AZ 85287–2102

Michael L. Mark
Towson University
Department of Music
Center for the Arts, Room # 3095
8000 York Road
Towson, MD 21252

Clint Randles
University of South Florida
School of Music
4202 East Fowler Ave.
Tampa, FL 33620

Bennett Reimer
Northwestern University
Bienen School of Music
711 Elgin Rd
Evanston, IL 60208

Alison Reynolds, Kerry Renzoni, Pamela Turowski, and Heather Waters
Temple University
Boyer College of Music and Dance
Presser Hall
2001 North 13th Street
Philadelphia, PA 19122

Lauren Kapalka Richerme
Indiana University
Jacobs School of Music
1201 East Third Street
Bloomington, IN 47405

Alex Ruthmann
New York University
Department of Music and Performing Arts Professions
35 W. 4th Street, Suite 1077
New York, NY 10012

Karen Salvador
University of Michigan-Flint
Department of Music
126 French Hall
303 East Kearsley St.
Flint, MI 48052

Marissa Silverman
Montclair State University
College of the Arts
1 Normal Ave
Montclair, NJ 07043

Gareth Dylan Smith
Institute of Contemporary Music Performance
Foundation House 1A Dyne Road
London, UK
NW6 7XG

Nicholas Stefanic
University of South Florida
School of Music
4202 East Fowler Ave.
Tampa, FL 33620

Brent C. Talbot
Gettysburg College
Sunderman Conservatory of Music
Campus Box 403
300 North Washington Street
Gettysburg, PA 17325

Matthew Thibeault
University of Illinois at Urbana/Champaign
School of Music
1114 W. Nevada St.
Urbana, IL 61801

Evan Tobias
Arizona State University
Herberger Institute for Design and the Arts
PO Box 872102
Tempe, AZ 85287

Peter R. Webster
University of Southern California
Thornton School of Music
Los Angeles, CA 90089-0851

David B. Williams
Illinois State University
School of Music
College of Fine Arts
Campus Box 5660
Normal, IL 61790–5660

Michael Zelenak
Alabama State University
Department of Music
915 S. Jackson Street
Montgomery, AL 36104

Index

18 Songs 6

Abelton Live 142, 151
advocacy 11, 44, 45, 210, 211, 274,
    289, 295
aesthetic education 8, 170
affordances 103, 126, 127, 128, 143,
    147, 149, 159, 160, 311
Alliance for Childhood 208
Apple 16, 17, 18, 25, 27, 84, 90, 130,
    132, 134, 161, 210, 264, 330
Aristotle 17, 27, 55, 168, 260, 262
Arts-based Research 283, 295, 316
Association for Childhood Education
    International 208
Association for Technology in Music
    Instruction 122

Beethoven 155
Bergson's Time Cone 19, 20, 25
Billings, William 5, 254
Bloom, Benjamin 8
body without organs 16, 22, 23, 26, 27
Boston School Committee 5
Britton, Allen 8
Brown v. Topeka 10
Bruner, Jerome 8, 30, 35

Cage, John 23, 108, 109, 110, 111,
    117, 142
Caruso 63, 68, 69, 70, 86
change 5, 6, 8, 10, 13, 15, 16, 18, 19,
    20, 21, 25, 26, 27, 30, 31, 32,
    38, 39, 40, 44, 47, 59, 63–87,
    94, 95, 97, 115–16, 123–4, 127,
    129, 131–6, 139, 143, 145,
    147, 149–51, 155, 156, 160–2,
    167–8, 170, 179, 186, 189, 193,
    196–7, 201, 212, 216–17, 219,
    226–7, 229, 235, 237, 243–4,

248–50, 254–6, 260–1, 274,
    279, 282, 284, 292–7, 299–300,
    306, 310–11, 317, 323–7, 340–6
cohesive society 4–5
Cole, Michael 29, 36–8, 40, 70
collective 49, 70, 79, 109, 132, 159,
    208, 212, 261, 265–6, 295,
    325–7, 331–4
commercial prosperity 4, 8, 11
Common Core Curriculum 11
competition 9, 65, 86, 151, 171, 173–6,
    179, 191
Conceptual Model of Change in Music
    Education 326, 330, 333–7
constraints 29, 59, 110, 126, 128,
    130–1, 136, 143, 145, 147, 149,
    159–60, 223, 291
Convergence Culture 81, 88, 94–6,
    101, 110, 112–13, 118, 141,
    158, 199
cultural 337
Cultural Creative Process 129, 132,
    329–30, 333–7
cultural elevation 4–5, 11, 14–15
cultural psychology 29–30, 40–1, 213,
    327, 337–8
culture 4–6, 10–11, 13–15, 30, 34–7,
    41, 53, 60, 65–7, 71–2, 74,
    78–9, 81, 86–7, 93–102, 108,
    110, 112–13, 115, 133–4, 136,
    138, 141–2, 147, 151, 155, 158,
    180, 185, 193, 196–7, 199, 206,
    211, 214, 216, 238–9, 245–6,
    258–9, 267–9, 271, 278, 283,
    289–91, 298, 323–7, 331, 333,
    336–9, 345
creativity 5, 14, 33, 50, 78, 81, 83, 85,
    124, 129, 131–2, 134, 136–8,
    140–1, 146–7, 151, 154, 158,
    345

Critical Ethnography 253, 255–9
Csikszentmihalyi, Mihalyi 132, 336

data analysis 218, 238, 241–8, 293,
    299–300, 312, 317
data collection 218, 238, 240–1, 243–50,
    255, 294, 307
Deleuze, Gilles 16, 18–28
Dewey, John 24, 28, 47, 63, 65, 88, 90
digital media 28, 90–105, 109–10,
    112–20, 126, 142–3, 146,
    156–8, 162
direct teaching 32
DJ Payne 78–80

Foucault, Michel 126, 167, 180, 256,
    268, 273, 275–6, 290
free will 124, 129–33, 143, 180

Gould, Glenn 19, 24, 28, 66, 73–88,
    133, 137, 139, 146, 284, 290
Guattari, Félix 16, 18–28, 111, 118, 298

Jobs, Steve 124, 129–34, 136–8, 143,
    162, 211, 270, 329
Joyce, James 66–79, 87–9, 156–7

Katz, Mark 71, 89, 135, 137
Kratus, John 92, 115, 119, 136, 138,
    186, 199, 236, 251, 340, 342

Leonhard, Charles 8, 169
leisure 167–82, 199
liminal 167, 169, 171, 173, 175, 177,
    179, 181, 199

Madlib 82–90
Mason, Lowell 4, 168, 282, 291
military bands 9, 86, 90, 151
Mixcraft 9, 151
multicultural 4, 10, 270
Multilevel Modeling 299, 300, 304,
    317–19
multimedia 93–4, 99–120, 124–9, 140,
    142, 145–6, 158, 163
music listening 156, 255, 262–3, 269,
    315, 317
Music Teacher Education 29, 40, 218,
    232, 280, 332, 339, 342–3

National Standards for Music
    Education 18
New Media 63–6

Participatory Culture 94–102, 108,
    110, 112, 115, 118–20
phenomenology 239, 272–8, 288–90,
    295–7, 315
philosophy 170, 180, 182, 186, 198,
    266–70
place 275, 279, 281, 284–5, 287–8,
    295, 304, 316, 323, 326,
    329–33, 336–9, 344
Plessy v. Ferguson 10, 12
Popular Music 15, 41, 86, 92, 98, 180,
    183–98
Progressive Education 169–170, 180,
    198, 279
prolepsis 20, 29, 36–8, 42

Qualitative Research 41, 197, 214, 232,
    239–40, 251, 257, 265, 267–71,
    273, 275, 277, 279–90, 293,
    295, 299, 312, 315

Randles, Clint 85, 89–90, 120, 122, 124,
    129, 139, 143, 161–2, 186, 199,
    216–17, 228, 232, 236, 251, 254,
    269, 323–4, 326, 333, 337, 341–6
Ruthmann, Alex 92–6, 119–20, 122,
    138, 315

sampling technique 238, 240, 242,
    244–8
self-concept 232, 242, 326–8
self-efficacy 219, 225–31, 299–300,
    305–6, 309, 326–8, 341
self-esteem 327–8, 341, 344
situated learning 26, 33, 41–2
soundscapes 272, 278–91, 295–6
social justice 4, 10–11, 15, 255–6, 267,
    294–5
sociocultural 29, 42, 130, 294, 338
Sound Studies 63, 87, 89–90, 135,
    137–8, 271–91, 295, 315
Soundation 151
Special Needs 289
St. Pierre 23, 28
streetcars 9
Structural Equation Modeling 242
Suncoast Music Education Research
    Symposium 183, 186
Systems View of Creativity 336

talent 189, 191, 198, 215, 219–29,
    236, 296, 315, 336, 343
Tanglewood Symposium 3–4, 189

technological determinism 66, 89, 120, 122, 124–5, 128–38
time cone 20, 25, 163
Tobias, Evan 85, 90–8, 109, 113–22, 139, 141–3, 147, 152, 157–9, 315
TPACK 149–50
transformation 5, 35, 40, 92, 132–3, 137, 215, 219, 226–31, 255–6, 261, 264, 286, 316, 323, 332

Transmedia 94, 99, 107–18, 142, 146, 152, 158

Webster, Peter 29, 42, 91, 94, 119, 121–2, 138–9, 143, 148, 154, 224, 314, 333, 339, 341

YouTube 64, 80–1, 95–100, 116, 120, 137, 141, 198